THE DECLINE AND FALL OF THE ROMAN EMPIRE

The most majestic work of history ever written, *The Decline and Fall of the Roman Empire* bridges the abyss between the ancient and modern worlds. A masterful narrative ranging over Europe, Asia, and North Africa, it spans thirteen hundred years, encompassing the rise of two world religions and the ebb and flow of major social and legal institutions.

The first great investigation of the remote past to retain its authority, Gibbon's masterpiece is remarkable both for its scholarly erudition and its contribution to the study of history itself. Focusing throughout on the interplay of political forces and the achievements of the sciences, it traces a unifying thread animating historical incidents and giving them purpose and meaning. Carefully and coherently structured, embellished with elegance of detail, flashes of wit, and that most famous of Gibbon's qualities, "grave and temperate irony," *The Decline and Fall of the Roman Empire* remains a monumental achievement of the Enlightenment.

This three-volume paperbound edition was originally published in one volume by Harcourt, Brace & World, Inc., at $8.00.

WASHINGTON SQUARE PRESS
POCKET BOOKS • NEW YORK

THE DECLINE AND FALL OF THE ROMAN EMPIRE

Volume Two

EDWARD GIBBON

ABRIDGMENT BY D. M. LOW

THE DECLINE AND FALL
OF THE ROMAN EMPIRE
VOLUME TWO

WASHINGTON SQUARE PRESS edition published May, 1962

4th printing......................August, 1975

L

Published by
POCKET BOOKS, a division of Simon & Schuster, Inc.,
630 Fifth Avenue, New York, N.Y.

WASHINGTON SQUARE PRESS editions are distrib-
uted in the U.S. by Simon & Schuster, Inc., 630 Fifth
Avenue, New York, N.Y. 10020, and in Canada by Simon
& Schuster of Canada, Ltd., Markham, Ontario, Canada.

Standard Book Number: 671-48764-7.

Contents

CONTENTS

THE
DECLINE AND FALL
OF THE
ROMAN EMPIRE
Volume II

The Pagan Counter-Reformation

22.

THE SUCCESSION OF JULIAN. HIS CHARACTER

Constantius after a tyrannical reign died in 361 on the eve of a civil war with Julian, who thus became sole emperor. Julian's brief reign was guided by two motives derived from his early studies. One was to realise the ideal of the philosopher-king. This he blended with practical reforms and economies and an attempt to exchange the orientalism of his predecessors' court for the simplicity of ancient manners. Secondly he had an ambition to emulate Alexander the Great in eastern conquests. Julian's special significance for posterity has been his rejection of Christianity and his attempt to reform as well as re-establish the pagan cults.

THE SUCCESSION OF JULIAN

IMPATIENT TO VISIT the place of his birth and the new capital of the empire, he advanced from Naissus through the mountains of Hæmus and the cities of Thrace. When he reached Heraclea, at the distance of sixty miles, all Constantinople was poured forth to receive him; and he made his triumphal entry amidst the dutiful acclamations of the soldiers, the people, and the senate. An innumerable multitude pressed around him with eager respect, and were perhaps disappointed when they beheld the small stature and simple garb of a hero, whose unexperienced youth had vanquished the barbarians of Germany, and who had now traversed, in a successful career, the whole continent of Europe from the shores of the Atlantic to those of the Bosphorus. A few days afterwards, when the remains of the deceased emperor were landed in the harbour, the subjects of Julian applauded the real or affected humanity of their sovereign. On foot, without his diadem, and clothed in a mourning habit, he

accompanied the funeral as far as the church of the Holy
Apostles, where the body was deposited: and if these marks
of respect may be interpreted as a selfish tribute to the birth
and dignity of his Imperial kinsman, the tears of Julian professed to the world that he had forgot the injuries, and
remembered only the obligations, which he had received
from Constantius. As soon as the legions of Aquileia were
assured of the death of the emperor, they opened the gates of
the city, and, by the sacrifice of their guilty leaders, obtained
an easy pardon from the prudence or lenity of Julian; who,
in the thirty-second year of his age, acquired the undisputed
possession of the Roman empire.

Philosophy had instructed Julian to compare the advantages
of action and retirement; but the elevation of his birth
and the accidents of his life never allowed him the freedom
of choice. He might perhaps sincerely have preferred the
groves of the Academy and the society of Athens; but he was
constrained, at first by the will, and afterwards by the injustice of Constantius, to expose his person and fame to the
dangers of Imperial greatness; and to make himself account-
able to the world and to posterity for the happiness of millions.
Julian recollected with terror the observation of his master
Plato, that the government of our flocks and herds is always
committed to beings of a superior species; and that the
conduct of nations requires and deserves the celestial powers
of the Gods or of the Genii. From this principle he justly
concluded that the man who presumes to reign should aspire
to the perfection of the divine nature; that he should purify
his soul from her mortal and terrestrial part; that he should
extinguish his appetites, enlighten his understanding, regulate
his passions, and subdue the wild beast which, according to
the lively metaphor of Aristotle, seldom fails to ascend the
throne of a despot. The throne of Julian, which the death of
Constantius fixed on an independent basis, was the seat of
reason, of virtue, and perhaps of vanity. He despised the
honours, renounced the pleasures, and discharged with incessant diligence the duties of his exalted station: and there
were few among his subjects who would have consented to
relieve him from the weight of the diadem, had they been
obliged to submit their time and their actions to the rigorous
laws which their philosophic emperor imposed on himself.
One of his most intimate friends, who had often shared the

frugal simplicity of his table, has remarked that his light and sparing diet (which was usually of the vegetable kind) left his mind and body always free and active for the various and important business of an author, a pontiff, a magistrate, a general, and a prince. In one and the same day he gave audience to several ambassadors, and wrote or dictated a great number of letters to his generals, his civil magistrates, his private friends, and the different cities of his dominions. He listened to the memorials which had been received, considered the subject of the petitions, and signified his intentions more rapidly than they could be taken in short-hand by the diligence of his secretaries. He possessed such flexibility of thought, and such firmness of attention, that he could employ his hand to write, his ear to listen, and his voice to dictate; and pursue at once three several trains of ideas without hesitation, and without error. While his ministers reposed, the prince flew with agility from one labour to another; and, after a hasty dinner, retired into his library till the public business which he had appointed for the evening summoned him to interrupt the prosecution of his studies. The supper of the emperor was still less substantial than the former meal; his sleep was never clouded by the fumes of indigestion; and, except in the short interval of a marriage which was the effect of policy rather than love, the chaste Julian never shared his bed with a female companion. He was soon awakened by the entrance of fresh secretaries, who had slept the preceding day; and his servants were obliged to wait alternately, while their indefatigable master allowed himself scarcely any other refreshment than the change of occupations. The predecessors of Julian, his uncle, his brother, and his cousin, indulged their puerile taste for the games of the Circus, under the specious pretence of complying with the inclinations of the people; and they frequently remained the greatest part of the day as idle spectators, and as a part of the splendid spectacle, till the ordinary round of twenty-four races was completely finished. On solemn festivals, Julian, who felt and professed an unfashionable dislike to these frivolous amusements, condescended to appear in the Circus; and, after bestowing a careless glance on five or six of the races, he hastily withdrew with the impatience of a philosopher, who considered every moment as lost that was not devoted to the advantage of the public or the improvement of his own mind. By this avarice of time he seemed to protract the short duration of his reign; and, if the dates were less securely ascertained, we should refuse to believe that only sixteen months elapsed between the death of Constantius and the departure of his successor for the Persian war. The actions of Julian can only be preserved by the care of the historian; but the portion of his voluminous writings which is still extant remains as a monument of the application, as well as of the genius, of the emperor. The Misopogon, the Cæsars, several of his orations, and his elaborate work against the Christian religion, were composed in the long nights of the two winters, the former of which he passed at Constantinople, and the latter at Antioch.

*   *   *   *   *

THE CHARACTER OF JULIAN

The laborious administration of military and civil affairs, which were multiplied in proportion to the extent of the empire, exercised the abilities of Julian; but he frequently assumed the two characters of Orator and of Judge, which are almost unknown to the modern sovereigns of Europe. The arts of persuasion, so diligently cultivated by the first Cæsars, were neglected by the military ignorance and Asiatic pride of their successors, and, if they condescended to harangue the soldiers, whom they feared, they treated with silent disdain the senators, whom they despised. The assemblies of the senate, which Constantius had avoided, were considered by Julian as the place where he could exhibit with the most propriety the maxims of a republican and the talents of a rhetorician. He alternately practised, as in a school of declamation, the several modes of praise, of censure, of exhortation; and his friend Libanius has remarked that the study of Homer taught him to imitate the simple, concise style of Menelaus, the copiousness of Nestor, whose words descended like the flakes of a winter's snow, or the pathetic and forcible eloquence of Ulysses. The functions of a judge, which are sometimes incompatible with those of a prince, were exercised by Julian not only as a duty, but as an amusement; and although he might have trusted the integrity and discernment of his Prætorian prefects, he often placed himself by their side on the seat of judgment. The acute penetration of his mind was agreeably occupied in detecting and defeating the chicanery of the advocates, who laboured to disguise the truth of facts and to pervert the sense of the laws. He sometimes forgot the gravity of his station, asked indiscreet or unseasonable questions, and betrayed, by the loudness of his voice and the agitation of his body, the earnest vehemence with which he maintained his opinion against the judges, the advocates, and their clients. But his knowledge of his own temper prompted him to encourage, and even to solicit, the reproof of his friends and ministers: and whenever they ventured to oppose the irregular sallies of his passions, the spectators could observe the shame as well as the gratitude of their monarch. The decrees of Julian were almost always founded on the principles of justice, and he had the firmness to resist the two most dangerous temptations which assault the tribunal of a sovereign under the specious forms of compassion and equity. He decided the merits of the cause without weighing the circumstances of the parties; and the poor, whom he wished to relieve, were condemned to satisfy the just demands of a noble and wealthy adversary. He carefully distinguished the judge from the legislator; and though he meditated a necessary reformation of the Roman jurisdiction, he pronounced sentence according to the strict and literal interpretation of those laws which the magistrates were bound to execute and the subjects to obey.

The generality of princes, if they were stripped of their purple and cast naked into the world, would immediately sink to the lowest rank of society, without a hope of emerging from their obscurity. But the personal merit of Julian was, in some measure, independent of his fortune. Whatever had been his choice of life, by the force of intrepid courage, lively wit, and intense application, he would have obtained, or at least he would have deserved, the highest honours of his profession, and Julian might have raised himself to the rank of minister or general of the state in which he was born a private citizen. If the jealous caprice of power had disappointed his expectations; if he had prudently declined the paths of greatness, the employment of the same talents in studious solitude would have placed beyond the reach of kings his present happiness and his immortal fame. When we inspect with minute, or perhaps malevolent, attention the portrait of Julian, something seems wanting to the grace and perfection of the whole figure.

His genius was less powerful and sublime than that of Cæsar, nor did he possess the consummate prudence of Augustus. The virtues of Trajan appear more steady and natural, and the philosophy of Marcus is more simple and consistent. Yet Julian sustained adversity with firmness, and prosperity with moderation. After an interval of one hundred and twenty years from the death of Alexander Severus, the Romans beheld an emperor who made no distinction between his duties and his pleasures, who laboured to relieve the distress and to revive the spirit of his subjects, and who endeavoured always to connect authority with merit, and happiness with virtue. Even faction, and religious faction, was constrained to acknowledge the superiority of his genius in peace as well as in war, and to confess, with a sigh, that the apostate Julian was a lover of his country, and that he deserved the empire of the world.

23.

THE RELIGION OF JULIAN. HIS FANATICISM. HIS
RESTORATION AND REFORM OF PAGANISM. HIS
CONDUCT TOWARDS THE JEWS. HIS OPPRESSION OF
THE CHRISTIANS. THE TEMPLE AND SACRED GROVE
OF DAPHNE. ST. GEORGE. JULIAN AND ATHANASIUS

THE CHARACTER of Apostate has injured the reputation of
Julian; and the enthusiasm which clouded his virtues has exaggerated the real and apparent magnitude of his faults. Our
partial ignorance may represent him as a philosophic monarch,
who studied to protect, with an equal hand, the religious factions of the empire, and to allay the theological fever which
had inflamed the minds of the people from the edicts of
Diocletian to the exile of Athanasius. A more accurate view
of the character and conduct of Julian will remove this favourable prepossession for a prince who did not escape the general
contagion of the times. We enjoy the singular advantage of
comparing the pictures which have been delineated by his
fondest admirers and his implacable enemies. The actions of
Julian are faithfully related by a judicious and candid historian, the impartial spectator of his life and death. The unanimous evidence of his contemporaries is confined by the public
and private declarations of the emperor himself; and his various writings express the uniform tenor of his religious sentiments, which policy would have prompted him to dissemble
rather than to affect. A devout and sincere attachment for the
gods of Athens and Rome constituted the ruling passion of
Julian; the powers of an enlightened understanding were betrayed and corrupted by the influence of superstitious prejudice; and the phantoms which existed only in the mind of the
emperor had a real and pernicious effect on the government
of the empire. The vehement zeal of the Christians, who despised the worship, and overturned the altars, of those fabulous
deities, engaged their votary in a state of irreconcilable hostil-

441

ity with a very numerous party of his subjects; and he was
sometimes tempted, by the desire of victory or the shame of
a repulse, to violate the laws of prudence, and even of justice.
The triumph of the party which he deserted and opposed has
fixed a stain of infamy on the name of Julian; and the unsuccessful apostate has been overwhelmed with a torrent of pious
invectives, of which the signal was given by the sonorous
trumpet of Gregory Nazianzen. The interesting nature of the
events which were crowded into the short reign of this active
emperor deserves a just and circumstantial narrative. His motives, his counsels, and his actions, as far as they are connected
with the history of religion, will be the subject of the present
chapter.

The cause of his strange and fatal apostasy may be derived
from the early period of his life when he was left an orphan
in the hands of the murderers of his family. The names of
Christ and of Constantius, the ideas of slavery and of religion,
were soon associated in a youthful imagination, which was
susceptible of the most lively impressions. The care of his
infancy was intrusted to Eusebius, bishop of Nicomedia, who
was related to him on the side of his mother; and till Julian
reached the twentieth year of his age, he received from his
Christian preceptors the education not of a hero but of a saint.
The emperor, less jealous of a heavenly than of an earthly
crown, contented himself with the imperfect character of a
catechumen, while he bestowed the advantages of baptism on
the nephews of Constantine. They were even admitted to the
inferior offices of the ecclesiastical order; and Julian publicly
read the Holy Scriptures in the church of Nicomedia. The
study of religion, which they assiduously cultivated, appeared
to produce the fairest fruits of faith and devotion. They
prayed, they fasted, they distributed alms to the poor, gifts
to the clergy, and oblations to the tombs of the martyrs; and
the splendid monument of St. Mamas, at Cæsarea, was erected, or at least was undertaken, by the joint labour of Gallus
and Julian. They respectfully conversed with the bishops who
were eminent for superior sanctity, and solicited the benediction of the monks and hermits who had introduced into Cappadocia the voluntary hardships of the ascetic life. As the
two princes advanced towards the years of manhood, they
discovered, in their religious sentiments, the difference of their
characters. The dull and obstinate understanding of Gallus

embraced, with implicit zeal, the doctrines of Christianity, which never influenced his conduct, or moderated his passions. The mild disposition of the younger brother was less repugnant to the precepts of the Gospel; and his active curiosity might have been gratified by a theological system which explains the mysterious essence of the Deity, and opens the boundless prospect of invisible and future worlds. But the independent spirit of Julian refused to yield the passive and unresisting obedience which was required, in the name of religion, by the haughty ministers of the church. Their speculative opinions were imposed as positive laws, and guarded by the terrors of eternal punishments; but while they prescribed the rigid formulary of the thoughts, the words, and the actions of the young prince; whilst they silenced his objections, and severely checked the freedom of his inquiries, they secretly provoked his impatient genius to disclaim the authority of his ecclesiastical guides. He was educated in the Lesser Asia, amidst the scandals of the Arian controversy. The fierce contests of the Eastern bishops, the incessant alterations of their creeds, and the profane motives which appeared to actuate their conduct, insensibly strengthened the prejudice of Julian that they neither understood nor believed the religion for which they so fiercely contended. Instead of listening to the proofs of Christianity with that favourable attention which adds weight to the most respectable evidence, he heard with suspicion, and disputed with obstinacy and acuteness, the doctrines for which he already entertained an invincible aversion. Whenever the young princes were directed to compose declamations on the subject of the prevailing controversies, Julian always declared himself the advocate of Paganism, under the specious excuse that, in the defence of the weaker cause, his learning and ingenuity might be more advantageously exercised and displayed.

As soon as Gallus was invested with the honours of the purple, Julian was permitted to breathe the air of freedom, of literature, and of Paganism. The crowd of sophists, who were attracted by the taste and liberality of their royal pupil, had formed a strict alliance between the learning and the religion of Greece; and the poems of Homer, instead of being admired as the original productions of human genius, were seriously ascribed to the heavenly inspiration of Apollo and the Muses.

The deities of Olympus, as they are painted by the immortal bard, imprint themselves on the minds which are the least addicted to superstitious credulity. Our familiar knowledge of their names and characters, their forms and attributes, *seems* to bestow on those airy beings a real and substantial existence; and the pleasing enchantment produces an imperfect and momentary assent of the imagination to those fables which are the most repugnant to our reason and experience. In the age of Julian every circumstance contributed to prolong and fortify the illusion—the magnificent temples of Greece and Asia; the works of those artists who had expressed, in painting or in sculpture, the divine conceptions of the poet; the pomp of festivals and sacrifices; the successful arts of divination; the popular traditions of oracles and prodigies; and the ancient practice of two thousand years. The weakness of polytheism was, in some measure, excused by the moderation of its claims; and the devotion of the Pagans was not incompatible with the most licentious scepticism. Instead of an indivisible and regular system, which occupies the whole extent of the believing mind, the mythology of the Greeks was composed of a thousand loose and flexible parts, and the servant of the gods was at liberty to define the degree and measure of his religious faith. The creed which Julian adopted for his own use was of the largest dimensions; and, by a strange contradiction, he disdained the salutary yoke of the Gospel, whilst he made a voluntary offering of his reason on the altars of Jupiter and Apollo. One of the orations of Julian is consecrated to the honour of Cybele, the mother of the gods, who required from her effeminate priests the bloody sacrifice so rashly performed by the madness of the Phrygian boy. The pious emperor condescends to relate, without a blush and without a smile, the voyage of the goddess from the shores of Pergamus to the mouth of the Tiber; and the stupendous miracle which convinced the senate and people of Rome that the lump of clay which their ambassadors had transported over the seas was endowed with life, and sentiment, and divine power. For the truth of this prodigy he appeals to the public monuments of the city; and censures, with some acrimony, the sickly and affected taste of those men who impertinently derided the sacred traditions of their ancestors.

But the devout philosopher, who sincerely embraced, and

warmly encouraged, the superstition of the people, reserved for himself the privilege of a liberal interpretation, and silently withdrew from the foot of the altars into the sanctuary of the temple. The extravagance of the Grecian mythology proclaimed, with a clear and audible voice, that the pious inquirer, instead of being scandalised or satisfied with the literal sense, should diligently explore the occult wisdom, which had been disguised, by the prudence of antiquity, under the mask of folly and of fable.[1] The philosophers of the Platonic school, Plotinus, Porphyry, and the divine Iamblichus, were admired as the most skilful masters of this allegorical science, which laboured to soften and harmonise the deformed features of Paganism. Julian himself, who was directed in the mysterious pursuit by Ædesius, the venerable successor of Iamblichus, aspired to the possession of a treasure which he esteemed, if we may credit his solemn asseverations, far above the empire of the world. It was indeed a treasure which derived its value only from opinion; and every artist who flattered himself that he had extracted the precious ore from the surrounding dross claimed an equal right of stamping the name and figure the most agreeable to his peculiar fancy. The fable of Atys and Cybele had been already explained by Porphyry; but his labours served only to animate the pious industry of Julian, who invented and published his own allegory of that ancient and mystic tale. This freedom of interpretation, which might gratify the pride of the Platonists, exposed the vanity of their art. Without a tedious detail the modern reader could not form a just idea of the strange allusions, the forced etymologies, the solemn trifling, and the impenetrable obscurity of these sages, who professed to reveal the system of the universe. As the traditions of Pagan mythology were variously related, the sacred interpreters were at liberty to select the most convenient circumstances; and as they translated an arbitrary cipher, they could extract from *any* fable *any* sense which was adapted to their favourite system of religion and philosophy. The lascivious form of a naked Venus was tortured into the discovery of some moral precept, or some physical truth; and the castration of Atys explained the revolution of the sun

---

[1] See the principles of allegory in Julian. His reasoning is less absurd than that of some modern theologians, who assert that an extravagant or contradictory doctrine *must* be divine, since no man alive could have thought of inventing it.

between the tropics, or the separation of the human soul from vice and error.[1]

The theological system of Julian appears to have contained the sublime and important principles of natural religion. But as the faith which is not founded on revelation must remain destitute of any firm assurance, the disciple of Plato imprudently relapsed into the habits of vulgar superstition; and the popular and philosophic notion of the Deity seems to have been confounded in the practice, the writings, and even in the mind of Julian. The pious emperor acknowledged and adored the Eternal Cause of the universe, to whom he ascribed all the perfections of an infinite nature, invisible to the eyes and inaccessible to the understanding of feeble mortals. The Supreme God had created, or rather, in the Platonic language, had generated, the gradual succession of dependent spirits, of gods, of dæmons, of heroes, and of men; and every being which derived its existence immediately from the First Cause received the inherent gift of immortality. That so precious an advantage might not be lavished upon unworthy objects, the Creator had intrusted to the skill and power of the inferior gods the office of forming the human body, and of arranging the beautiful harmony of the animal, the vegetable, and the mineral kingdoms. To the conduct of these divine ministers he delegated the temporal government of this lower world; but their imperfect administration is not exempt from discord or error. The earth and its inhabitants are divided among them, and the characters of Mars or Minerva, of Mercury or Venus, may be distinctly traced in the laws and manners of their peculiar votaries. As long as our immortal souls are confined in a mortal prison, it is our interest, as well as our duty, to solicit the favour, and to deprecate the wrath, of the powers of heaven; whose pride is gratified by the devotion of mankind, and whose grosser parts may be supposed to derive some nourishment from the fumes of sacrifice. The inferior gods might sometimes condescend to animate the statues, and to inhabit the temples, which were dedicated to their honour. They might occasionally visit the earth, but the heavens were the proper throne and symbol of their glory. The invariable

---

[1] See the fifth oration of Julian. But all the allegories which ever issued from the Platonic school are not worth the short poem of Catullus on the same extraordinary subject. The transition of Atys from the wildest enthusiasm to sober pathetic complaint for his irretrievable loss must inspire a man with pity, an eunuch with despair.

order of the sun, moon, and stars was hastily admitted by
Julian as a proof of their *eternal* duration; and their eternity
was a sufficient evidence that they were the workmanship,
not of an inferior deity, but of the Omnipotent King. In the
system of the Platonists the visible was a type of the invisible
world. The celestial bodies, as they were informed by a divine
spirit, might be considered as the objects the most worthy of
religious worship. The SUN, whose genial influence pervades
and sustains the universe, justly claimed the adoration of mankind, as the bright representative of the LOGOS, the lively, the
rational, the beneficent image of the intellectual Father.

THE FANATICISM OF JULIAN

In every age the absence of genuine inspiration is supplied
by the strong illusions of enthusiasm and the mimic arts of
imposture. If, in the time of Julian, these arts had been practised only by the Pagan priests, for the support of an expiring
cause, some indulgence might perhaps be allowed to the interest and habits of the sacerdotal character. But it may appear
a subject of surprise and scandal that the philosophers themselves should have contributed to abuse the superstitious
credulity of mankind,[1] and that the Grecian mysteries should
have been supported by the magic or theurgy of the modern
Platonists. They arrogantly pretended to control the order of
nature, to explore the secrets of futurity, to command the
service of the inferior dæmons, to enjoy the view and conversation of the superior gods, and, by disengaging the soul from
her material bands, to re-unite that immortal particle with the
Infinite and Divine Spirit.

The devout and fearless curiosity of Julian tempted the
philosophers with the hopes of an easy conquest, which, from
the situation of their young proselyte, might be productive of
the most important consequences. Julian imbibed the first rudiments of the Platonic doctrines from the mouth of Ædesius,
who had fixed at Pergamus his wandering and persecuted
school. But as the declining strength of that venerable sage was

---

[1] The sophists of Eunapius perform as many miracles as the saints of the
desert; and the only circumstance in their favour is that they are of a less
gloomy complexion. Instead of devils with horns and tails, Iamblichus evoked
the genii of love, Eros and Anteros, from two adjacent fountains. Two beautiful boys issued from the water, fondly embraced him as their father, and
retired at his command.

unequal to the ardour, the diligence, the rapid conception of his pupil, two of his most learned disciples, Chrysanthes and Eusebius, supplied, at his own desire, the place of their aged master. These philosophers seem to have prepared and distributed their respective parts; and they artfully contrived, by dark hints and affected disputes, to excite the impatient hopes of the *aspirant* till they delivered him into the hands of their associate, Maximus, the boldest and most skilful master of the Theurgic science. By his hands Julian was secretly initiated at Ephesus, in the twentieth year of his age. His residence at Athens confirmed this unnatural alliance of philosophy and superstition. He obtained the privilege of a solemn initiation into the mysteries of Eleusis, which, amidst the general decay of the Grecian worship, still retained some vestiges of their primæval sanctity; and such was the zeal of Julian that he afterwards invited the Eleusinian pontiff to the court of Gaul, for the sole purpose of consummating, by mystic rites and sacrifices, the great work of his sanctification. As these ceremonies were performed in the depth of caverns and in the silence of the night, and as the inviolable secret of the mysteries was preserved by the discretion of the initiated, I shall not presume to describe the horrid sounds and fiery apparitions which were presented to the senses or the imagination of the credulous aspirant,[1] till the visions of comfort and knowledge broke upon him in a blaze of celestial light. In the caverns of Ephesus and Eleusis the mind of Julian was penetrated with sincere, deep, and unalterable enthusiasm; though he might sometimes exhibit the vicissitudes of pious fraud and hypocrisy which may be observed, or at least suspected, in the characters of the most conscientious fanatics. From that moment he consecrated his life to the service of the gods; and while the occupations of war, of government, and of study seemed to claim the whole measure of his time, a stated portion of the hours of the night was invariably reserved for the exercise of private devotion. The temperance which adorned the severe manners of the soldier and the philosopher was connected with some strict and frivolous rules of religious abstinence; and it was in honour of Pan or Mercury, of Hecate or Isis, that Julian, on particular days, denied himself the

---

[1] When Julian, in a momentary panic, made the sign of the cross, the dæmons instantly disappeared. Gregory supposes that they were frightened, but the priests declared that they were indignant. The reader, according to the measure of his faith, will determine this profound question.

use of some particular food, which might have been offensive to his tutelar deities. By these voluntary fasts he prepared his senses and his understanding for the frequent and familiar visits with which he was honoured by the celestial powers. Notwithstanding the modest silence of Julian himself, we may learn from his faithful friend, the orator Libanius, that he lived in a perpetual intercourse with the gods and goddesses; that they descended upon earth to enjoy the conversation of their favourite hero; that they gently interrupted his slumbers by touching his hand or his hair; that they warned him of every impending danger, and conducted him, by their infallible wisdom, in every action of his life; and that he had acquired such an intimate knowledge of his heavenly guests, as readily to distinguish the voice of Jupiter from that of Minerva, and the form of Apollo from the figure of Hercules. These sleeping or waking visions, the ordinary effects of abstinence and fanaticism, would almost degrade the emperor to the level of an Egyptian monk. But the useless lives of Antony or Pachomius were consumed in these vain occupations. Julian could break from the dream of superstition to arm himself for battle; and after vanquishing in the field the enemies of Rome, he calmly retired into his tent, to dictate the wise and salutary laws of an empire, or to indulge his genius in the elegant pursuits of literature and philosophy.

The important secret of the apostasy of Julian was intrusted to the fidelity of the *initiated,* with whom he was united by the sacred ties of friendship and religion. The pleasing rumour was cautiously circulated among the adherents of the ancient worship; and his future greatness became the object of the hopes, the prayers, and the predictions of the Pagans in every province of the empire. From the zeal and virtues of their royal proselyte they fondly expected the cure of every evil and the restoration of every blessing; and instead of disapproving of the ardour of their pious wishes, Julian ingenuously confessed that he was ambitious to attain a situation in which he might be useful to his country and to his religion. But this religion was viewed with an hostile eye by the successor of Constantine, whose capricious passions alternately saved and threatened the life of Julian. The arts of magic and divination were strictly prohibited under a despotic government which condescended to fear them; and if the Pagans were reluctantly indulged in the exercise of their superstition, the rank of

Julian would have excepted him from the general toleration. The apostate soon became the presumptive heir of the monarchy, and his death could alone have appeased the just apprehensions of the Christians. But the young prince, who aspired to the glory of a hero rather than of a martyr, consulted his safety by dissembling his religion; and the easy temper of polytheism permitted him to join in the public worship of a sect which he inwardly despised. Libanius has considered the hypocrisy of his friend as a subject, not of censure, but of praise. "As the statues of the gods," says that orator, "which have been defiled with filth are again placed in a magnificent temple, so the beauty of truth was seated in the mind of Julian after it had been purified from the errors and follies of his education. His sentiments were changed; but as it would have been dangerous to have avowed his sentiments, his conduct still continued the same. Very different from the ass in Æsop, who disguised himself with a lion's hide, our lion was obliged to conceal himself under the skin of an ass; and, while he embraced the dictates of reason, to obey the laws of prudence and necessity." The dissimulation of Julian lasted above ten years, from his secret initiation at Ephesus to the beginning of the civil war; when he declared himself at once the implacable enemy of Christ and of Constantius. This state of constraint might contribute to strengthen his devotion; and as soon as he had satisfied the obligation of assisting, on solemn festivals, at the assemblies of the Christians, Julian returned, with the impatience of a lover, to burn his free and voluntary incense on the domestic chapels of Jupiter and Mercury. But as every act of dissimulation must be painful to an ingenuous spirit, the profession of Christianity increased the aversion of Julian for a religion which oppressed the freedom of his mind, and compelled him to hold a conduct repugnant to the noblest attributes of human nature—sincerity and courage.

The inclination of Julian might prefer the gods of Homer and of the Scipios to the new faith which his uncle had established in the Roman empire, and in which he himself had been sanctified by the sacrament of baptism. But, as a philosopher, it was incumbent on him to justify his dissent from Christianity, which was supported by the number of its converts, by the chain of prophecy, the splendour of miracles, and the weight of evidence. The elaborate work which he composed amidst the preparations of the Persian war contained the substance of those arguments which he had long revolved in his mind. Some fragments have been transcribed and preserved by his adversary, the vehement Cyril of Alexandria; and they exhibit a very singular mixture of wit and learning, of sophistry and fanaticism. The elegance of the style and the rank of the author recommended his writings to the public attention; and in the impious list of the enemies of Christianity the celebrated name of Porphyry was effaced by the superior merit or reputation of Julian. The minds of the faithful were either seduced, or scandalised, or alarmed; and the Pagans, who sometimes presumed to engage in the unequal dispute, derived, from the popular work of their Imperial missionary, an inexhaustible supply of fallacious objections. But in the assiduous prosecution of these theological studies the emperor of the Romans imbibed the illiberal prejudices and passions of a polemic divine. He contracted an irrevocable obligation to maintain and propagate his religious opinions; and whilst he secretly applauded the strength and dexterity with which he wielded the weapons of controversy, he was tempted to distrust the sincerity, or to despise the understandings, of his antagonists, who could obstinately resist the force of reason and eloquence.

The Christians, who beheld with horror and indignation the apostasy of Julian, had much more to fear from his power than from his arguments. The Pagans, who were conscious of his fervent zeal, expected, perhaps with impatience, that the flames of persecution should be immediately kindled against the enemies of the gods; and that the ingenious malice of Julian would invent some cruel refinements of death and torture which had been unknown to the rude and inexperienced fury of his predecessors. But the hopes, as well as the fears, of the religious factions were apparently disappointed by the prudent humanity of a prince who was careful of his own fame, of the public peace, and of the rights of mankind. Instructed by history and reflection, Julian was persuaded that, if the diseases of the body may sometimes be cured by salutary violence, neither steel nor fire can eradicate the erroneous opinions of the mind. The reluctant victim may be dragged to the foot of the altar; but the heart still abhors and disclaims the sacrilegious act of the hand. Religious obstinacy is hardened and exasperated by oppression; and, as soon as the persecution subsides, those who have yielded are restored as penitents, and those who have resisted are honoured as saints and martyrs. If Julian adopted the unsuccessful cruelty of Diocletian and his colleagues, he was sensible that he should stain his memory with the name of tyrant, and add new glories to the catholic church, which had derived strength and increase from the severity of the Pagan magistrates. Actuated by these motives, and apprehensive of disturbing the repose of an unsettled reign, Julian surprised the world by an edict which was not unworthy of a statesman or a philosopher. He extended to all the inhabitants of the Roman world the benefits of a free and equal toleration; and the only hardship which he inflicted on the Christians was to deprive them of the power of tormenting their fellow-subjects, whom they stigmatised with the odious titles of idolaters and heretics. The Pagans received a gracious permission, or rather an express order, to open ALL their temples; and they were at once delivered from the oppressive laws and arbitrary vexations which they had sustained under the reign of Constantine and of his sons. At the same time, the bishops and clergy who had been banished by the Arian monarch were recalled from exile, and restored to their respective churches; the Donatists, the Novatians, the Macedonians, the Eunomians, and those who, with a more prosperous fortune, adhered to the doctrine of the council of Nice. Julian, who understood and derided their theological disputes, invited to the palace the leaders of the hostile sects, that he might enjoy the agreeable spectacle of their furious encounters. The clamour of controversy sometimes provoked the emperor to exclaim, "Hear me! the Franks have heard me, and the Alemanni"; but he soon discovered that he was now engaged with more obstinate and implacable enemies; and though he exerted the powers of oratory to persuade them to live in concord, or at least in peace, he was perfectly satisfied, before he dismissed them from his presence, that he had nothing to dread from the union of the Christians. The impartial Ammianus has ascribed this affected clemency to the desire of fomenting the intestine divisions of the church; and the insidious design of undermining the foundations of Christianity was inseparably connected with the zeal which Julian professed to restore the ancient religion of the empire.

JULIAN'S RESTORATION AND REFORM OF PAGANISM

As soon as he ascended the throne, he assumed, according to the custom of his predecessors, the character of supreme pontiff; not only as the most honourable title of Imperial greatness, but as a sacred and important office, the duties of which he was resolved to execute with pious diligence. As the business of the state prevented the emperor from joining every day in the public devotion of his subjects, he dedicated a domestic chapel to his tutelar deity the Sun; his gardens were filled with statues and altars of the gods; and each apartment of the palace displayed the appearance of a magnificent temple. Every morning he saluted the parent of light with a sacrifice; the blood of another victim was shed at the moment when the Sun sunk below the horizon; and the Moon, the Stars, and the Genii of the night received their respective and seasonable honours from the indefatigable devotion of Julian. On solemn festivals he regularly visited the temple of the god or goddess to whom the day was peculiarly consecrated, and endeavoured to excite the religion of the magistrates and people by the example of his own zeal. Instead of maintaining the lofty state of a monarch, distinguished by the splendour of his purple, and encompassed by the golden shields of his guards, Julian solicited, with respectful eagerness, the meanest offices which contributed to the worship of the gods. Amidst the sacred but licentious crowd of priests, of inferior ministers, and of female dancers, who were dedicated to the service of the temple, it was the business of the emperor to bring the wood, to blow the fire, to handle the knife, to slaughter the victim, and, thrusting his bloody hands into the bowels of the expiring animal, to draw forth the heart or liver, and to read, with the consummate skill of an haruspex, the imaginary signs of future events. The wisest of the Pagans censured this extravagant superstition, which affected to despise the restraints of prudence and decency. Under the reign of a prince who practised the rigid maxims of economy, the expense of religious worship consumed a very large portion of the revenue; a constant supply of the scarcest and most beautiful birds was transported from distant climates, to bleed on the altars of the gods; an hundred oxen were frequently

sacrificed by Julian on one and the same day; and it soon became a popular jest, that, if he should return with conquest
from the Persian war, the breed of horned cattle must infalli-
bly be extinguished. Yet this expense may appear inconsiderable, when it is compared with the splendid presents which
were offered, either by the hand or by order of the emperor,
to all the celebrated places of devotion in the Roman world;
and with the sums allotted to repair and decorate the ancient
temples, which had suffered the silent decay of time, or the
recent injuries of Christian rapine. Encouraged by the example, the exhortations, the liberality of their pious sovereign,
the cities and families resumed the practice of their neglected
ceremonies. "Every part of the world," exclaims Libanius,
with devout transport, "displayed the triumph of religion, and
the grateful prospect of flaming altars, bleeding victims, the
smoke of incense, and a solemn train of priests and prophets,
without fear and without danger. The sound of prayer and
of music was heard on the tops of the highest mountains; and
the same ox afforded a sacrifice for the gods, and a supper
for their joyous votaries."

But the genius and power of Julian were unequal to the
enterprise of restoring a religion which was destitute of theological principles, of moral precepts, and of ecclesiastical discipline; which rapidly hastened to decay and dissolution, and
was not susceptible of any solid or consistent reformation. The
jurisdiction of the supreme pontiff, more especially after that
office had been united with the Imperial dignity, comprehended the whole extent of the Roman empire. Julian named
for his vicars, in the several provinces, the priests and philosophers, whom he esteemed the best qualified to co-operate in
the execution of his great design; and his pastoral letters, if
we may use that name, still represent a very curious sketch
of his wishes and intentions. He directs that in every city the
sacerdotal order should be composed, without any distinction
of birth or fortune, of those persons who were the most conspicuous for their love of the gods and of men. "If they are
guilty," continues he, "of any scandalous offence, they should
be censured or degraded by the superior pontiff; but as long
as they retain their rank, they are entitled to the respect of
the magistrates and people. Their humility may be shown in
the plainness of their domestic garb; their dignity, in the

pomp of holy vestments. When they are summoned in their turn to officiate before the altar, they ought not, during the appointed number of days, to depart from the precincts of the temple; nor should a single day be suffered to elapse without the prayers and the sacrifice which they are obliged to offer for the prosperity of the state and of individuals. The exercise of their sacred functions requires an immaculate purity both of mind and body; and even when they are dismissed from the temple to the occupations of common life, it is incumbent on them to excel in decency and virtue the rest of their fellow-citizens. The priest of the gods should never be seen in theatres or taverns. His conversation should be chaste, his diet temperate, his friends of honourable reputation; and if he sometimes visits the Forum or the Palace, he should appear only as the advocate of those who have vainly solicited either justice or mercy. His studies should be suited to the sanctity of his profession. Licentious tales, or comedies, or satires, must be banished from his library, which ought solely to consist of historical and philosophical writings; of history, which is founded in truth, and of philosophy, which is connected with religion. The impious opinions of the Epicureans and sceptics deserve his abhorrence and contempt;[1] but he should diligently study the systems of Pythagoras, of Plato, and of the Stoics, which unanimously teach that there *are* gods; that the world is governed by their providence; that their goodness is the source of every temporal blessing; and that they have prepared for the human soul a future state of reward or punishment." The Imperial pontiff inculcates, in the most persuasive language, the duties of benevolence and hospitality; exhorts his inferior clergy to recommend the universal practice of those virtues; promises to assist their indigence from the public treasury; and declares his resolution of establishing hospitals in every city, where the poor should be received without any invidious distinction of country or of religion. Julian beheld with envy the wise and humane regulations of the church; and he very frankly confesses his intention to deprive the Christians of the applause, as well as advantage,

---

[1] The exultation of Julian that these impious sects, and even their writings, are extinguished, may be consistent enough with the sacerdotal character; but it is unworthy of a philosopher to wish that any opinions and arguments the most repugnant to his own should be concealed from the knowledge of mankind.

which they had acquired by the exclusive practice of charity and beneficence.[1] The same spirit of imitation might dispose the emperor to adopt several ecclesiastical institutions, the use and importance of which were approved by the success of his enemies. But if these imaginary plans of reformation had been realised, the forced and imperfect copy would have been less beneficial to Paganism than honourable to Christianity. The Gentiles, who peaceably followed the customs of their ancestors, were rather surprised than pleased with the introduction of foreign manners; and, in the short period of his reign, Julian had frequent occasions to complain of the want of fervour of his own party.

The enthusiasm of Julian prompted him to embrace the friends of Jupiter as his personal friends and brethren; and though he partially overlooked the merit of Christian constancy, he admired and rewarded the noble perseverance of those Gentiles who had preferred the favour of the gods to that of the emperor. If they cultivated the literature as well as the religion of the Greeks, they acquired an additional claim to the friendship of Julian, who ranked the Muses in the number of his tutelar deities. In the religion which he had adopted, piety and learning were almost synonymous; and a crowd of poets, of rhetoricians, and of philosophers, hastened to the Imperial court to occupy the vacant places of the bishops who had seduced the credulity of Constantius. His successor esteemed the ties of common initiation as far more sacred than those of consanguinity; he chose his favourites among the sages who were deeply skilled in the occult sciences of magic and divination, and every impostor who pretended to reveal the secrets of futurity was assured of enjoying the present hour in honour and affluence. Among the philosophers, Maximus obtained the most eminent rank in the friendship of his royal disciple, who communicated, with unreserved confidence, his actions, his sentiments, and his religious designs, during the anxious suspense of the civil war. As soon as Julian had taken possession of the palace of Constantinople, he despatched an honourable and pressing

---

[1] Yet he insinuates that the Christians, under the pretence of charity, inveigled children from their religion and parents, conveyed them on shipboard, and devoted those victims to a life of poverty or servitude in a remote country. Had the charge been proved, it was his duty not to complain but to punish.

invitation to Maximus, who then resided at Sardes in Lydia, with Chrysanthius, the associate of his art and studies. The prudent and superstitious Chrysanthius refused to undertake a journey which showed itself, according to the rules of divination, with the most threatening and malignant aspect; but his companion, whose fanaticism was of a bolder cast, persisted in his interrogations till he had extorted from the gods a seeming consent to his own wishes and those of the emperor. The journey of Maximus through the cities of Asia displayed the triumph of philosophic vanity, and the magistrates vied with each other in the honourable reception which they prepared for the friend of their sovereign. Julian was pronouncing an oration before the senate, when he was informed of the arrival of Maximus. The emperor immediately interrupted his discourse, advanced to meet him, and, after a tender embrace, conducted him by the hand into the midst of the assembly, where he publicly acknowledged the benefits which he had derived from the instructions of the philosopher. Maximus, who soon acquired the confidence, and influenced the councils, of Julian, was insensibly corrupted by the temptations of a court. His dress became more splendid, his demeanour more lofty, and he was exposed, under a succeeding reign, to a disgraceful inquiry into the means by which the disciple of Plato had accumulated, in the short duration of his favour, a very scandalous proportion of wealth. Of the other philosophers and sophists who were invited to the Imperial residence by the choice of Julian, or by the success of Maximus, few were able to preserve their innocence or their reputation. The liberal gifts of money, lands, and houses were insufficient to satiate their rapacious avarice, and the indignation of the people was justly excited by the remembrance of their abject poverty and disinterested professions. The penetration of Julian could not always be deceived, but he was unwilling to despise the characters of those men whose talents deserved his esteem; he desired to escape the double reproach of imprudence and inconstancy, and he was apprehensive of degrading, in the eyes of the profane, the honour of letters and of religion.

The favour of Julian was almost equally divided between the Pagans who had firmly adhered to the worship of their ancestors, and the Christians who prudently embraced the religion of their sovereign. The acquisition of new proselytes [1] gratified the ruling passions of his soul, superstition and vanity; and he was heard to declare, with the enthusiasm of a missionary, that if he could render each individual richer than Midas, and every city greater than Babylon, he should not esteem himself the benefactor of mankind unless, at the same time, he could reclaim his subjects from their impious revolt against the immortal gods. A prince, who had studied human nature, and who possessed the treasures of the Roman empire, could adapt his arguments, his promises, and his rewards to every order of Christians; and the merit of a seasonable conversion was allowed to supply the defects of a candidate, or even to expiate the guilt of a criminal. As the army is the most forcible engine of absolute power, Julian applied himself, with peculiar diligence, to corrupt the religion of his troops, without whose hearty concurrence every measure must be dangerous and unsuccessful, and the natural temper of soldiers made this conquest as easy as it was important. The legions of Gaul devoted themselves to the faith, as well as to the fortunes, of their victorious leader; and even before the death of Constantius, he had the satisfaction of announcing to his friends that they assisted, with fervent devotion and voracious appetite, at the sacrifices, which were repeatedly offered in his camp, of whole hecatombs of fat oxen. The armies of the East, which had been trained under the standard of the cross and of Constantius, required a more artful and expensive mode of persuasion. On the days of solemn and public festivals the emperor received the homage, and rewarded the merit, of the troops. His throne of state was encircled with the military ensigns of Rome and the republic; the holy name of Christ was erased from the *Labarum;* and the symbols of war, of majesty, and of Pagan superstition were so dexterously blended that the faithful subject incurred the guilt of idolatry when he respectfully saluted the person or image of his sovereign. The soldiers passed successively in review, and each of them, before he received from the hand of Julian a liberal donative, proportioned to his rank and services, was required to cast a few grains of incense into the flame which burnt upon the altar. Some Christian confessors might resist, and others might

---

[1] Under the reign of Louis XIV, his subjects of every rank aspired to the glorious title of *Conve tisseu*, expressive of their zeal and success in making proselytes. The word and the idea are growing obsolete in France; may they never be introduced into England!

repent; but the far greater number, allured by the prospect of gold and awed by the presence of the emperor, contracted the criminal engagement, and their future perseverance in the worship of the gods was enforced by every consideration of duty and of interest. By the frequent repetition of these arts, and at the expense of sums which would have purchased the service of half the nations of Scythia, Julian gradually acquired for his troops the imaginary protection of the gods, and for himself the firm and effectual support of the Roman legions. It is indeed more than probable that the restoration and encouragement of Paganism revealed a multitude of pretended Christians, who, from motives of temporal advantage, had acquiesced in the religion of the former reign, and who afterwards returned, with the same flexibility of conscience, to the faith which was professed by the successors of Julian.

JULIAN AND THE JEWS

While the devout monarch incessantly laboured to restore and propagate the religion of his ancestors, he embraced the extraordinary design of rebuilding the temple of Jerusalem. In a public epistle to the nation of community of the Jews dispersed through the provinces, he pities their misfortunes, condemns their oppressors, praises their constancy, declares himself their gracious protector, and expresses a pious hope that, after his return from the Persian war, he may be permitted to pay his grateful vows to the Almighty in his holy city of Jerusalem. The blind superstition and abject slavery of those unfortunate exiles must excite the contempt of a philosophic emperor, but they deserved the friendship of Julian by their implacable hatred of the Christian name. The barren synagogue abhorred and envied the fecundity of the rebellious church; the power of the Jews was not equal to their malice, but their gravest rabbis approved the private murder of an apostate, and their seditious clamours had often awakened the indolence of the Pagan magistrates. Under the reign of Constantine, the Jews became the subjects of their revolted children, nor was it long before they experienced the bitterness of domestic tyranny. The civil immunities which had been granted or confirmed by Severus were gradually repealed by the Christian princes; and a rash tumult, excited by the Jews of Palestine, seemed to justify the lucrative modes of oppression which were invented by the bishops and eunuchs of the court of Constantius. The Jewish patriarch, who was still permitted to exercise a precarious jurisdiction, held his residence at Tiberias, and the neighbouring cities of Palestine were filled with the remains of a people who fondly adhered to the promised land. But the edict of Hadrian was renewed and enforced, and they viewed from afar the walls of the holy city, which were profaned in their eyes by the triumph of the cross and the devotion of the Christians.

In the midst of a rocky and barren country the walls of Jerusalem enclosed the two mountains of Sion and Acra within an oval figure of about three English miles. Towards the south, the upper town and the fortress of David were erected on the lofty ascent of Mount Sion; on the north side, the buildings of the lower town covered the spacious summit of Mount Acra; and a part of the hill, distinguished by the name of Moriah, and levelled by human industry, was crowned with the stately temple of the Jewish nation. After the final destruction of the temple by the arms of Titus and Hadrian a ploughshare was drawn over the consecrated ground, as a sign of perpetual interdiction. Sion was deserted, and the vacant space of the lower city was filled with the public and private edifices of the Ælian colony, which spread themselves over the adjacent hill of Calvary. The holy places were polluted with monuments of idolatry, and, either from design or accident, a chapel was dedicated to Venus on the spot which had been sanctified by the death and resurrection of Christ. Almost three hundred years after those stupendous events, the profane chapel of Venus was demolished by the order of Constantine, and the removal of the earth and stones revealed the holy sepulchre to the eyes of mankind. A magnificent church was erected on that mystic ground by the first Christian emperor, and the effects of his pious munificence were extended to every spot which had been consecrated by the footsteps of patriarchs, of prophets, and of the Son of God.

The passionate desire of contemplating the original monuments of their redemption attracted to Jerusalem a successive crowd of pilgrims from the shores of the Atlantic Ocean and the most distant countries of the East: and their piety was authorised by the example of the empress Helena, who appears to have united the credulity of age with the warm feelings of a recent conversion. Sages and heroes, who have visited the memorable scenes of ancient wisdom or glory, have confessed the inspiration of the genius of the place; and the Christian who knelt before the holy sepulchre ascribed his lively faith and his fervent devotion to the more immediate influence of the Divine Spirit. The zeal, perhaps the avarice, of the clergy of Jerusalem cherished and multiplied these beneficial visits. They fixed, by unquestionable tradition, the scene of each memorable event. They exhibited the instruments which had been used in the passion of Christ; the nails and the lance that had pierced his hands, his feet, and his side; the crown of thorns that was planted on his head; the pillar at which he was scourged; and, above all, they showed the cross on which he suffered, and which was dug out of the earth in the reign of those princes who inserted the symbol of Christianity in the banners of the Roman legions. Such miracles as seemed necessary to account for its extraordinary preservation and seasonable discovery were gradually propagated without opposition. The custody of the *true cross*, which on Easter Sunday was solemnly exposed to the people, was intrusted to the bishop of Jerusalem; and he alone might gratify the curious devotion of the pilgrims by the gift of small pieces, which they enchased in gold or gems, and carried away in triumph to their respective countries. But as this gainful branch of commerce must soon have been annihilated, it was found convenient to suppose that the marvellous wood possessed a secret power of vegetation, and that its substance, though continually diminished, still remained entire and unimpaired. It might perhaps have been expected that the influence of the place and the belief of a perpetual miracle should have produced some salutary effects on the morals, as well as on the faith, of the people. Yet the most respectable of the ecclesiastical writers have been obliged to confess, not only that the streets of Jerusalem were filled with the incessant tumult of business and pleasure, but that every species of vice—adultery, theft, idolatry, poisoning, murder—was familiar to the inhabitants of the holy city. The wealth and pre-eminence of the church of Jerusalem excited the ambition of Arian as well as orthodox candidates; and the virtues of Cyril, who since his death has been honoured with the title of Saint, were displayed in the exercise, rather than in the acquisition, of his episcopal dignity.[1]

The vain and ambitious mind of Julian might aspire to restore the ancient glory of the temple of Jerusalem. As the Christians were firmly persuaded that a sentence of everlasting destruction had been pronounced against the whole fabric of the Mosaic law, the Imperial sophist would have converted the success of his undertaking into a specious argument against the faith of prophecy and the truth of revelation.[2] He was displeased with the spiritual worship of the synagogue; but he approved the institutions of Moses, who had not disdained to adopt many of the rites and ceremonies of Egypt. The local and national deity of the Jews was sincerely adored by a polytheist who desired only to multiply the number of the gods; and such was the appetite of Julian for bloody sacrifice, that his emulation might be excited by the piety of Solomon, who had offered at the feast of the dedication twenty-two thousand oxen and one hundred and twenty thousand sheep. These considerations might influence his designs; but the prospect of an immediate and important advantage would not suffer the impatient monarch to expect the remote and uncertain event of the Persian war. He resolved to erect, without delay, on the commanding eminence of Moriah, a stately temple, which might eclipse the splendour of the church of the Resurrection on the adjacent hill of Calvary; to establish an order of priests, whose interested zeal would detect the arts and resist the ambition of their Christian rivals; and to invite a numerous colony of Jews, whose stern fanaticism would be always prepared to second, and even to anticipate, the hostile measures of the Pagan government. Among the friends of the emperor (if the names of emperor and of friend are not incompatible) the first place was assigned, by Julian himself, to the virtuous and learned Alypius. The humanity of Alypius was tempered by severe justice and manly fortitude; and while he exercised his abilities in the civil

---

[1] He renounced his orthodox ordination, officiated as a deacon, and was re-ordained by the hands of the Arians. But Cyril afterwards changed with the times, and prudently conformed to the Nicene faith. Tillemont, who treats his memory with tenderness and respect, has thrown his virtues into the text, and his faults into the notes, in decent obscurity, at the end of the volume.

[2] The secret intentions of Julian are revealed by the late bishop of Gloucester, the learned and dogmatic Warburton; who, with the authority of a theologian, prescribes the motives and conduct of the Supreme Being. The discourse entitled *Julian* is strongly marked with all the peculiarities which are imputed to the Warburtonian school.

administration of Britain, he imitated, in his poetical compositions, the harmony and softness of the odes of Sappho. This minister, to whom Julian communicated, without reserve, his most careless levities and his most serious counsels, received an extraordinary commission to restore, in its pristine beauty, the temple of Jerusalem; and the diligence of Alypius required and obtained the strenuous support of the governor of Palestine. At the call of their great deliverer, the Jews from all the provinces of the empire assembled on the holy mountain of their fathers; and their insolent triumph alarmed and exasperated the Christian inhabitants of Jerusalem. The desire of rebuilding the temple has in every age been the ruling passion of the children of Israel. In this propitious moment the men forgot their avarice, and the women their delicacy; spades and pickaxes of silver were provided by the vanity of the rich, and the rubbish was transported in mantles of silk and purple. Every purse was opened in liberal contributions, every hand claimed a share in the pious labour; and the command of a great monarch was executed by the enthusiasm of a whole people.

Yet, on this occasion, the joint efforts of power and enthusiasm were unsuccessful; and the ground of the Jewish temple, which is now covered by a Mahometan mosque, still continued to exhibit the same edifying spectacle of ruin and desolation. Perhaps the absence and death of the emperor, and the new maxims of a Christian reign, might explain the interruption of an arduous work, which was attempted only in the last six months of the life of Julian. But the Christians entertained a natural and pious expectation that in this memorable contest the honour of religion would be vindicated by some signal miracle. An earthquake, a whirlwind, and a fiery eruption, which overturned and scattered the new foundations of the temple, are attested, with some variations, by contemporary and respectable evidence. This public event is described by Ambrose, bishop of Milan, in an epistle to the emperor Theodosius, which must provoke the severe animadversion of the Jews; by the eloquent Chrysostom, who might appeal to the memory of the elder part of his congregation at Antioch; and by Gregory Nazianzen, who published his account of the miracle before the expiration of the same year. The last of these writers has boldly declared that this preternatural event was not disputed by the infidels; and his

assertion, strange as it may seem, is confirmed by the unexceptionable testimony of Ammianus Marcellinus. The
philosophic soldier, who loved the virtues without adopting
the prejudices of his master, has recorded, in his judicious and
candid history of his own times, the extraordinary obstacles
which interrupted the restoration of the temple of Jerusalem.
"Whilst Alypius, assisted by the governor of the province,
urged with vigour and diligence the execution of the work,
horrible balls of fire, breaking out near the foundations, with
frequent and reiterated attacks, rendered the place, from time
to time, inaccessible to the scorched and blasted workmen;
and, the victorious element continuing in this manner obstinately and resolutely bent, as it were, to drive them to a distance, the undertaking was abandoned." Such authority should
satisfy a believing, and must astonish an incredulous, mind.
Yet a philosopher may still require the original evidence of
impartial and intelligent spectators. At this important crisis
any singular accident of nature would assume the appearance,
and produce the effects, of a real prodigy. This glorious
deliverance would be speedily improved and magnified by the
pious art of the clergy of Jerusalem, and the active credulity
of the Christian world; and, at the distance of twenty years,
a Roman historian, careless of theological disputes, might
adorn his work with the specious and splendid miracle.

JULIAN'S OPPRESSION OF THE CHRISTIANS

The restoration of the Jewish temple was secretly connected
with the ruin of the Christian church. Julian still continued to
maintain the freedom of religious worship, without distinguishing whether this universal toleration proceeded from his justice
or his clemency. He affected to pity the unhappy Christians,
who were mistaken in the most important object of their
lives; but his pity was degraded by contempt, his contempt
was embittered by hatred; and the sentiments of Julian were
expressed in a style of sarcastic wit, which inflicts a deep and
deadly wound whenever it issues from the mouth of a sovereign. As he was sensible that the Christians gloried in the
name of their Redeemer, he countenanced, and perhaps enjoined, the use of the less honourable appellation of GALI-
LÆANS. He declared that, by the folly of the Galilæans, whom
he describes as a sect of fanatics, contemptible to men and

odious to the gods, the empire had been reduced to the brink of destruction; and he insinuates in a public edict that a frantic patient might sometimes be cured by salutary violence. An ungenerous distinction was admitted into the mind and counsels of Julian, that, according to the difference of their religious sentiments, one part of his subjects deserved his favour and friendship, while the other was entitled only to the common benefits that his justice could not refuse to an obedient people. According to a principle pregnant with mischief and oppression, the emperor transferred to the pontiffs of his own religion the management of the liberal allowances from the public revenue which had been granted to the church by the piety of Constantine and his sons. The proud system of clerical honours and immunities, which had been constructed with so much art and labour, was levelled to the ground; the hopes of testamentary donations were intercepted by the rigour of the laws; and the priests of the Christian sect were confounded with the last and most ignominious class of people. Such of these regulations as appeared necessary to check the ambition and avarice of the ecclesiastics were soon afterwards imitated by the wisdom of an orthodox prince. The peculiar distinctions which policy has bestowed, or superstition has lavished, on the sacerdotal order, *must* be confined to those priests who profess the religion of the state. But the will of the legislator was not exempt from prejudice and passion; and it was the object of the insidious policy of Julian to deprive the Christians of all the temporal honours and advantages which rendered them respectable in the eyes of the world.

A just and severe censure has been inflicted on the law which prohibited the Christians from teaching the arts of grammar and rhetoric. The motives alleged by the emperor to justify this partial and oppressive measure might command, during his lifetime, the silence of slaves and the applause of flatterers. Julian abuses the ambiguous meaning of a word which might be indifferently applied to the language and the religion of the GREEKS: he contemptuously observes that the men who exalt the merit of implicit faith are unfit to claim or to enjoy the advantages of science; and he vainly contends that, if they refuse to adore the gods of Homer and Demosthenes, they ought to content themselves with expounding Luke and Matthew in the churches of the Galilæans. In all the cities of the Roman world the education of the youth was intrusted to masters of grammar and rhetoric, who were elected by the magistrates, maintained at the public expense, and distinguished by many lucrative and honourable privileges. The edict of Julian appears to have included the physicians, and professors of all the liberal arts; and the emperor, who reserved to himself the approbation of the candidates, was authorized by the laws to corrupt, or to punish, the religious constancy of the most learned of the Christians. As soon as the resignation of the more obstinate teachers had established the unrivalled dominion of the Pagan sophists, Julian invited the rising generation to resort with freedom to the public schools, in a just confidence that their tender minds would receive the impressions of literature and idolatry. If the greatest part of the Christian youth should be deterred by their own scruples, or by those of their parents, from accepting this dangerous mode of instruction, they must, at the same time, relinquish the benefits of a liberal education. Julian had reason to expect that, in the space of a few years, the church would relapse into its primæval simplicity, and that the theologians, who possessed an adequate share of the learning and eloquence of the age, would be succeeded by a generation of blind and ignorant fanatics, incapable of defending the truth of their own principles, or of exposing the various follies of Polytheism.

It was undoubtedly the wish and the design of Julian to deprive the Christians of the advantages of wealth, of knowledge, and of power; but the injustice of excluding them from all offices of trust and profit seems to have been the result of his general policy, rather than the immediate consequence of any positive law. Superior merit might deserve and obtain some extraordinary exceptions; but the greater part of the Christian officers were gradually removed from their employments in the state, the army, and the provinces. The hopes of future candidates were extinguished by the declared partiality of a prince who maliciously reminded them that it was unlawful for a Christian to use the sword, either of justice or of war, and who studiously guarded the camp and the tribunals with the ensigns of idolatry. The powers of government were intrusted to the Pagans, who professed an ardent zeal for the religion of their ancestors; and as the choice of the emperor was often directed by the rules of divination, the favourites whom he preferred as the most agreeable to the gods did not always obtain the approbation of mankind. Under the administration of their enemies, the Christians had much to suffer, and more to apprehend. The temper of Julian was averse to cruelty; and the care of his reputation, which was exposed to the eyes of the universe, restrained the philosophic monarch from violating the laws of justice and toleration which he himself had so recently established. But the provincial ministers of his authority were placed in a less conspicuous station. In the exercise of arbitrary power, they consulted the wishes, rather than the commands, of their sovereign; and ventured to exercise a secret and vexatious tyranny against the sectaries on whom they were not permitted to confer the honours of martyrdom. The emperor, who dissembled as long as possible his knowledge of the injustice that was exercised in his name, expressed his real sense of the conduct of his officers by gentle reproofs and substantial rewards.

The most effectual instrument of oppression with which they were armed was the law that obliged the Christians to make full and ample satisfaction for the temples which they had destroyed under the preceding reign. The zeal of the triumphant church had not always expected the sanction of the public authority; and the bishops, who were secure of impunity, had often marched at the head of their congregations to attack and demolish the fortresses of the prince of darkness. The consecrated lands, which had increased the patrimony of the sovereign or of the clergy, were clearly defined, and easily restored. But on these lands, and on the ruins of Pagan superstition, the Christians had frequently erected their own religious edifices: and as it was necessary to remove the church before the temple could be rebuilt, the justice and piety of the emperor were applauded by one party, while the other deplored and execrated his sacrilegious violence. After the ground was cleared, the restitution of those stately structures which had been levelled with the dust, and of the precious ornaments which had been converted to Christian uses, swelled into a very large account of damages and debt. The authors of the injury had neither the ability nor the inclination to discharge this accumulated demand: and the impartial wisdom of a legislator would have been displayed in balancing the adverse claims and complaints by an equitable and temperate arbitration. But the whole empire, and particularly the

East, was thrown into confusion by the rash edicts of Julian; and the Pagan magistrates, inflamed by zeal and revenge, abused the rigorous privilege of the Roman law, which substitutes, in the place of his inadequate property, the person of the insolvent debtor. Under the preceding reign, Mark, bishop of Arethusa, had laboured in the conversion of his people with arms more effectual than those of persuasion. The magistrates required the full value of a temple which had been destroyed by his intolerant zeal; but as they were satisfied of his poverty, they desired only to bend his inflexible spirit to the promise of the slightest compensation. They apprehended the aged prelate, they inhumanly scourged him, they tore his beard; and his naked body, anointed with honey, was suspended, in a net, between heaven and earth, and exposed to the stings of insects and the rays of a Syrian sun. From this lofty station, Mark still persisted to glory in his crime, and to insult the impotent rage of his persecutors. He was at length rescued from their hands, and dismissed to enjoy the honour of his divine triumph. The Arians celebrated the virtue of their pious confessor; the catholics ambitiously claimed his alliance, and the Pagans, who might be susceptible of shame or remorse, were deterred from the repetition of such unavailing cruelty. Julian spared his life: but if the bishop of Arethusa had saved the infancy of Julian, posterity will condemn the ingratitude, instead of praising the clemency, of the emperor.

THE TEMPLE AND SACRED GROVE OF DAPHNE

At the distance of five miles from Antioch, the Macedonian kings of Syria had consecrated to Apollo one of the most elegant places of devotion in the Pagan world. A magnificent temple rose in honour of the god of light; and his colossal figure almost filled the capacious sanctuary, which was enriched with gold and gems, and adorned by the skill of the Grecian artists. The deity was represented in a bending attitude, with a golden cup in his hand, pouring out a libation on the earth; as if he supplicated the venerable mother to give to his arms the cold and beauteous DAPHNE: for the spot was ennobled by fiction; and the fancy of the Syrian poets had transported the amorous tale from the banks of the Peneus to those of the Orontes. The ancient rites of Greece were imitated by the royal colony of Antioch. A stream of prophecy, which rivalled the truth and reputation of the Delphic oracle, flowed from the *Castalian* fountain of Daphne. In the adjacent fields a stadium was built by a special privilege, which had been purchased from Elis; the Olympic games were celebrated at the expense of the city; and a revenue of thirty thousand pounds sterling was annually applied to the public pleasures. The perpetual resort of pilgrims and spectators insensibly formed, in the neighbourhood of the temple, the stately and populous village of Daphne, which emulated the splendour, without acquiring the title, of a provincial city. The temple and the village were deeply bosomed in a thick grove of laurels and cypresses, which reached as far as a circumference of ten miles, and formed in the most sultry summers a cool and impenetrable shade. A thousand streams of the purest water, issuing from every hill, preserved the verdure of the earth and the temperature of the air; the senses were gratified with harmonious sounds and aromatic odours; and the peaceful grove was consecrated to health and joy, to luxury and love. The vigorous youth pursued, like Apollo, the object of his desires; and the blushing maid was warned, by the fate of Daphne, to shun the folly of unseasonable coyness. The soldier and the philosopher wisely avoided the temptation of this sensual paradise; where pleasure, assuming the character of religion, imperceptibly dissolved the firmness of manly virtue. But the groves of Daphne continued for many ages to enjoy the veneration of natives and strangers; the privileges of the holy ground were enlarged by the munificence of succeeding emperors; and every generation added new ornaments to the splendour of the temple.

When Julian, on the day of the annual festival, hastened to adore the Apollo of Daphne, his devotion was raised to the highest pitch of eagerness and impatience. His lively imagination anticipated the grateful pomp of victims, of libations, and of incense; a long procession of youths and virgins, clothed in white robes, the symbol of their innocence; and the tumultuous concourse of an innumerable people. But the zeal of Antioch was diverted, since the reign of Christianity, into a different channel. Instead of hecatombs of fat oxen sacrificed by the tribes of a wealthy city to their tutelar deity, the emperor complains that he found only a single goose, provided at the expense of a priest, the pale and solitary inhabitant of this decayed temple.[1] The altar was deserted, the oracle had been reduced to silence, and the holy ground was profaned by the introduction of Christian and funereal rites. After Babylas (a bishop of Antioch, who died in prison in the persecution of Decius) had rested near a century in his grave, his body, by the order of the Cæsar Gallus, was transported into the midst of the grove of Daphne. A magnificent church was erected over his remains; a portion of the sacred lands was usurped for the maintenance of the clergy, and for the burial of the Christians of Antioch, who were ambitious of lying at the feet of their bishop; and the priests of Apollo retired, with their affrighted and indignant votaries. As soon as another revolution seemed to restore the fortune of Paganism, the church of St. Babylas was demolished, and new buildings were added to the mouldering edifice which had been raised by the piety of Syrian kings. But the first and most serious care of Julian was to deliver his oppressed deity from the odious presence of the dead and living Christians, who had so effectually suppressed the voice of fraud or enthusiasm. The scene of infection was purified, according to the forms of ancient rituals; the bodies were decently removed; and the ministers of the church were permitted to convey the remains of St. Babylas to their former habitation within the walls of Antioch. The modest behaviour, which might have assuaged the jealousy of an hostile government, was neglected on this occasion by the zeal of the Christians. The lofty car that transported the relics of Babylas was followed, and accompanied, and received, by an innumerable multitude, who chanted, with thundering acclamations, the Psalms of David the most expressive of their contempt for idols and idolaters. The return of the saint was a triumph; and the triumph was an insult on the religion of the emperor, who exerted his pride to dissemble his resentment. During the night which terminated this indiscreet procession the temple of Daphne was in flames; the statue of Apollo was consumed; and the walls of the edifice were left a naked and awful monument of ruin. The Christians of Antioch asserted, with religious confidence, that the powerful intercession of St. Babylas had pointed the lightnings of heaven against the devoted roof: but as Julian was reduced to the alternative of believing either a crime or

---

[1] Julian (*Misopogon*) discovers his own character with that *naïveté*, that unconscious simplicity, which always constitutes genuine humour.

a miracle, he chose, without hesitation, without evidence, but with some colour of probability, to impute the fire of Daphne to the revenge of the Galilæans. Their offence, had it been sufficiently proved, might have justified the retaliation, which was immediately executed by the order of Julian, of shutting the doors, and confiscating the wealth, of the cathedral of Antioch. To discover the criminals who were guilty of the tumult, of the fire, or of secreting the riches of the church, several ecclesiastics were tortured; and a presbyter, of the name of Theodoret, was beheaded by the sentence of the count of the East. But this hasty act was blamed by the emperor, who lamented, with real or affected concern, that the imprudent zeal of his ministers would tarnish his reign with the disgrace of persecution.

The zeal of the ministers of Julian was instantly checked by the frown of their sovereign; but when the father of his country declares himself the leader of a faction, the licence of popular fury cannot easily be restrained, nor consistently punished. Julian, in a public composition, applauds the devotion and loyalty of the holy cities of Syria, whose pious inhabitants had destroyed, at the first signal, the sepulchres of the Galilæans; and faintly complains that they had revenged the injuries of the gods with less moderation than he should have recommended. This imperfect and reluctant confession may appear to confirm the ecclesiastical narratives—that in the cities of Gaza, Ascalon, Cæsarea, Heliopolis, etc., the Pagans abused, without prudence or remorse, the moment of their prosperity; that the unhappy objects of their cruelty were released from torture only by death; that, as their mangled bodies were dragged through the streets, they were pierced (such was the universal rage) by the spits of cooks, and the distaffs of enraged women; and that the entrails of Christian priests and virgins, after they had been tasted by those bloody fanatics, were mixed with barley, and contemptuously thrown to the unclean animals of the city. Such scenes of religious madness exhibit the most contemptible and odious picture of human nature; but the massacre of Alexandria attracts still more attention, from the certainty of the fact, the rank of the victims, and the splendour of the capital of Egypt.

ST. GEORGE

George, from his parents or his education, surnamed the Cappadocian, was born at Epiphania in Cilicia, in a fuller's shop. From this obscure and servile origin he raised himself by the talents of a parasite; and the patrons whom he assiduously flattered procured for their worthless dependent a lucrative commission, or contract, to supply the army with bacon. His employment was mean; he rendered it infamous. He accumulated wealth by the basest arts of fraud and corruption; but his malversations were so notorious, that George was compelled to escape from the pursuits of justice. After this disgrace, in which he appears to have saved his fortune at the expense of his honour, he embraced, with real or affected zeal, the profession of Arianism. From the love, or the ostentation, of learning, he collected a valuable library of history, rhetoric, philosophy, and theology;[1] and the choice of the prevailing faction promoted George of Cappadocia to the throne of Athanasius. The entrance of the new archbishop was that of a barbarian conqueror; and each moment of his reign was polluted by cruelty and avarice. The catholics of Alexandria and Egypt were abandoned to a tyrant, qualified, by nature and education, to exercise the office of persecution; but he oppressed with an impartial hand the various inhabitants of his extensive diocese. The primate of Egypt assumed the pomp and insolence of his lofty station; but he still betrayed the vices of his base and servile extraction. The merchants of Alexandria were impoverished by the unjust and almost universal monopoly, which he acquired, of nitre, salt, paper, funerals, etc.: and the spiritual father of a great people condescended to practise the vile and pernicious arts of an informer. The Alexandrians could never forget, nor forgive, the tax which he suggested on all the houses of the city, under an obsolete claim that the royal founder had conveyed to his successors, the Ptolemies and the Cæsars, the perpetual prop-

---

[1] After the massacre of George, the emperor Julian repeatedly sent orders to preserve the library for his own use, and to torture the slaves who might be suspected of secreting any books. He praises the merit of the collection, from whence he had borrowed and transcribed several manuscripts while he pursued his studies in Cappadocia. He could wish indeed that the works of the Galilæans might perish; but he requires an exact account even of those theological volumes, lest other treatises more valuable should be confounded in their loss.

erty of the soil. The Pagans, who had been flattered with the hopes of freedom and toleration, excited his devout avarice; and the rich temples of Alexandria were either pillaged or insulted by the haughty prelate, who exclaimed in a loud and threatening tone, "How long will these sepulchres be permitted to stand?" Under the reign of Constantius he was expelled by the fury, or rather by the justice, of the people; and it was not without violent struggle that the civil and military powers of the state could restore his authority, and gratify his revenge. The messenger who proclaimed at Alexandria the accession of Julian announced the downfall of the archbishop. George, with two of his obsequious ministers, count Diodorus, and Dracontius, master of the mint, were ignominiously dragged in chains to the public prison. At the end of twenty-four days the prison was forced open by the rage of a superstitious multitude, impatient of the tedious forms of judicial proceedings. The enemies of gods and men expired under their cruel insults; the lifeless bodies of the archbishop and his associates were carried in triumph through the streets on the back of a camel; and the inactivity of the Athanasian party was esteemed a shining example of evangelical patience. The remains of these guilty wretches were thrown into the sea; and the popular leaders of the tumult declared their resolution to disappoint the devotion of the Christians, and to intercept the future honours of these *martyrs*, who had been punished, like their predecessors, by the enemies of their religion. The fears of the Pagans were just, and their precautions ineffectual. The meritorious death of the archbishop obliterated the memory of his life. The rival of Athanasius was dear and sacred to the Arians, and the seeming conversion of those sectaries introduced his worship into the bosom of the catholic church. The odious stranger, disguising every circumstance of time and place, assumed the mask of a martyr, a saint, and a Christian hero,[1] and the infamous George of Cappadocia has been transformed[2] into the renowned St. George of England, the patron of arms, of chivalry, and of the garter.[3]

---

[1] The saints of Cappadocia, Basil and the Gregories, were ignorant of their holy companion. Pope Gelasius (A.D. 494), the first catholic who acknowledges St. George, places him among the martyrs "qui Deo magis quam hominibus noti sunt." He rejects his Acts as the composition of heretics. Some, perhaps not the oldest, of the spurious Acts, are still extant; and, through a cloud of fiction, we may yet distinguish the combat which St. George of

About the same time that Julian was informed of the tumult of Alexandria he received intelligence from Edessa that the proud and wealthy faction of the Arians had insulted the weakness of the Valentinians, and committed such disorders as ought not to be suffered with impunity in a well-regulated state. Without expecting the slow forms of justice, the exasperated prince directed his mandate to the magistrates of Edessa, by which he confiscated the whole property of the church: the money was distributed among the soldiers; the lands were added to the domain; and this act of oppression was aggravated by the most ungenerous irony. "I show myself," says Julian, "the true friend of the Galilæans. Their *admirable* law has promised the kingdom of heaven to the poor; and they will advance with more diligence in the paths of virtue and salvation when they are relieved by my assistance from the load of temporal possessions. Take care," pursued the monarch, in a more serious tone, "take care how you provoke my patience and humanity. If these disorders continue, I will revenge on the magistrates the crimes of the people; and you will have reason to dread, not only confiscation and exile, but fire and the sword." The tumults of Alexandria were doubtless of a more bloody and dangerous nature; but a Christian bishop had fallen by the hands of the Pagans; and the public epistle of Julian affords a very lively proof of the partial spirit of his administration. His reproaches to the citizens of Alexandria are mingled with expressions of esteem and tenderness; and he laments that, on this occasion, they should have departed from the gentle and generous manners which attested their Grecian extraction. He gravely censures the offence which they had committed against the laws of justice and humanity; but he recapitulates, with visible complacency, the intolerable provocations which they had so long endured from the impious tyranny of George of Cappadocia. Julian admits the principle that a wise and vigorous government should chastise the insolence of the people; yet,

---

Cappadocia sustained, in the presence of Queen *Alexandra*, against the *magician Athanasius*.

² This transformation is not given as absolutely certain, but as *extremely* probable.

³ A curious history of the worship of St. George, from the sixth century (when he was already revered in Palestine, in Armenia, at Rome, and at Treves in Gaul), might be extracted from Dr. Heylin (History of St. George), and the Bollandists. His fame and popularity in Europe, and especially in England, proceeded from the Crusades.

in consideration of their founder Alexander, and of Serapis their tutelar deity, he grants a free and gracious pardon to the guilty city, for which he again feels the affection of a brother.

JULIAN AND ATHANASIUS

After the tumult of Alexandria had subsided, Athanasius, amidst the public acclamations, seated himself on the throne from whence his unworthy competitor had been precipitated: and as the zeal of the archbishop was tempered with discretion, the exercise of his authority tended not to inflame, but to reconcile, the minds of the people. His pastoral labours were not confined to the narrow limits of Egypt. The state of the Christian world was present to his active and capacious mind; and the age, the merit, the reputation of Athanasius, enabled him to assume, in a moment of danger, the office of Ecclesiastical Dictator. Three years were not yet elapsed since the majority of the bishops of the West had, ignorantly or reluctantly, subscribed the Confession of Rimini. They repented, they believed, but they dreaded the unseasonable rigour of their orthodox brethren; and if their pride was stronger than their faith, they might throw themselves into the arms of Arians, to escape the indignity of a public penance, which must degrade them to the condition of obscure laymen. At the same time the domestic differences concerning the union and distinction of the divine persons were agitated with some heat among the catholic doctors; and the progress of this metaphysical controversy seemed to threaten a public and lasting division of the Greek and Latin churches. By the wisdom of a select synod, to which the name and presence of Athanasius gave the authority of a general council, the bishops who had unwarily deviated into error were admitted to the communion of the church, on the easy condition of subscribing the Nicene Creed, without any formal acknowledgment of their past fault, or any minute definition of their scholastic opinions. The advice of the primate of Egypt had already prepared the clergy of Gaul and Spain, of Italy and Greece, for the reception of this salutary measure; and, notwithstanding the opposition of some ardent spirits, the fear of the common enemy promoted the peace and harmony of the Christians.

The skill and diligence of the primate of Egypt had improved the season of tranquillity before it was interrupted by the hostile edicts of the emperor. Julian, who despised the Christians, honoured Athanasius with his sincere and peculiar hatred. For his sake alone he introduced an arbitrary distinction, repugnant at least to the spirit of his former declarations. He maintained that the Galilæans whom he had recalled from exile were not restored, by that general indulgence, to the possession of their respective churches; and he expressed his astonishment that a criminal, who had been repeatedly condemned by the judgment of the emperors, should dare to insult the majesty of the laws, and insolently usurp the archiepiscopal throne of Alexandria, without expecting the orders of his sovereign. As a punishment for the imaginary offence, he again banished Athanasius from the city; and he was pleased to suppose that this act of justice would be highly agreeable to his pious subjects. The pressing solicitations of the people soon convinced him that the majority of the Alexandrians were Christians; and that the greatest part of the Christians were firmly attached to the cause of their oppressed primate. But the knowledge of their sentiments, instead of persuading him to recall his decree, provoked him to extend to all Egypt the term of the exile of Athanasius. The zeal of the multitude rendered Julian still more inexorable: he was alarmed by the danger of leaving at the head of a tumultuous city a daring and popular leader; and the language of his resentment discovers the opinion which he entertained of the courage and abilities of Athanasius. The execution of the sentence was still delayed, by the caution or negligence of Ecdicius, prefect of Egypt, who was at length awakened from his lethargy by a severe reprimand. "Though you neglect," says Julian, "to write to me on any other subject, at least it is your duty to inform me of your conduct towards Athanasius, the enemy of the gods. My intentions have been long since communicated to you. I swear by the great Serapis, that unless, on the calends of December, Athanasius has departed from Alexandria, nay from Egypt, the officers of your government shall pay a fine of one hundred pounds of gold. You know my temper: I am slow to condemn, but I am still slower to forgive." This epistle was enforced by a short postscript written with the emperor's own hand. "The contempt that is shown for all the gods fills me with grief and indignation. There is nothing that I shall see, nothing that I should hear, with more pleasure, than the expulsion of Athanasius from all Egypt. The abominable wretch! Under my reign, the baptism of several Grecian ladies of the highest rank has been the effect of his persecutions." The death of Athanasius was not *expressly* commanded; but the prefect of Egypt understood that it was safer for him to exceed than to neglect the orders of an irritated master. The archbishop prudently retired to the monasteries of the Desert; eluded, with his usual dexterity, the snares of the enemy; and lived to triumph over the ashes of a prince who, in words of formidable import, had declared his wish that the whole venom of the Galilæan school were contained in the single person of Athanasius.

I have endeavoured faithfully to represent the artful system by which Julian proposed to obtain the effects, without incurring the guilt or reproach, of persecution. But if the deadly spirit of fanaticism perverted the heart and understanding of a virtuous prince, it must, at the same time, be confessed, that the *real* sufferings of the Christians were inflamed and magnified by human passions and religious enthusiasm. The meekness and resignation which had distinguished the primitive disciples of the Gospel was the object of the applause, rather than of the imitation, of their successors. The Christians, who had now possessed above forty years the civil and ecclesiastical government of the empire, had contracted the insolent vices of prosperity, and the habit of believing that the saints alone were entitled to reign over the earth. As soon as the enmity of Julian deprived the clergy of the privileges which had been conferred by the favour of Constantine, they complained of the most cruel oppression; and the free toleration of idolaters and heretics was a subject of grief and scandal to the orthodox party. The acts of violence, which were no longer countenanced by the magistrates, were still committed by the zeal of the people. At Pessinus the altar of Cybele was overturned almost in the presence of the emperor; and in the city of Cæsarea, in Cappadocia, the temple of Fortune, the sole place of worship which had been left to the Pagans, was destroyed by the rage of a popular tumult. On these occasions, a prince who felt for the honour of the gods was not disposed to interrupt the course of justice; and his mind was still more deeply exasperated when he found that the fanatics, who had deserved and suffered the punishment of incendiaries, were rewarded

with the honours of martyrdom. The Christian subjects of
Julian were assured of the hostile designs of their sovereign;
and, to their jealous apprehension, every circumstance of his
government might afford some grounds of discontent and
suspicion. In the ordinary administration of the laws, the
Christians, who formed so large a part of the people, must
frequently be condemned; but their indulgent brethren, without examining the merits of the cause, presumed their innocence, allowed their claims, and imputed the severity of
their judge to the partial malice of religious persecution.
These present hardships, intolerable as they might appear,
were represented as a slight prelude of the impending calamities. The Christians considered Julian as a cruel and crafty
tyrant, who suspended the execution of his revenge till he
should return victorious from the Persian war. They expected that, as soon as he had triumphed over the foreign
enemies of Rome, he would lay aside the irksome mask of
dissimulation; that the amphitheatres would stream with the
blood of hermits and bishops; and that the Christians who
still persevered in the profession of the faith would be deprived of the common benefits of nature and society. Every
calumny that could wound the reputation of the Apostate
was credulously embraced by the fears and hatred of his
adversaries; and their indiscreet clamours provoked the temper
of a sovereign whom it was their duty to respect, and their
interest to flatter. They still protested that prayers and tears
were their only weapons against the impious tyrant, whose
head they devoted to the justice of offended Heaven. But
they insinuated, with sullen resolution, that their submission
was no longer the effect of weakness; and that, in the imperfect state of human virtue, the patience which is founded
on principle may be exhausted by persecution. It is impossible to determine how far the zeal of Julian would have
prevailed over his good sense and humanity; but, if we
seriously reflect on the strength and spirit of the church, we
shall be convinced that, before the emperor could have extinguished the religion of Christ, he must have involved
his country in the horrors of a civil war.

24.

ELECTION OF JOVIAN. REFLECTIONS ON THE DEATH OF JULIAN

Julian took the field with some success against the Persians. He was compelled however to withdraw and during a critical battle beyond the river Tigris he was mortally wounded. He died on June 26th, 363.

THE ELECTION OF JOVIAN

THE TRIUMPH of Christianity, and the calamities of the empire, may, in some measure, be ascribed to Julian himself, who had neglected to secure the future execution of his designs by the timely and judicious nomination of an associate and successor. But the royal race of Constantius Chlorus was reduced to his own person; and if he entertained any serious thoughts of investing with the purple the most worthy among the Romans, he was diverted from his resolution by the difficulty of the choice, the jealousy of power, the fear of ingratitude, and the natural presumption of health, of youth, and of prosperity. His unexpected death left the empire without a master, and without an heir, in a state of perplexity and danger which, in the space of fourscore years, had never been experienced, since the election of Diocletian. In a government which had almost forgotten the distinction of pure and noble blood, the superiority of birth was of little moment; the claims of official rank were accidental and precarious; and the candidates who might aspire to ascend the vacant throne could be supported only by the consciousness of personal merit, or by the hopes of popular favour. But the situation of a famished army, encompassed on all sides by an host of barbarians, shortened the moments of grief and deliberation. In these scenes of terror and distress, the body of the deceased prince, according to his own directions, was decently embalmed; and, at the dawn of day, the generals

convened a military senate, at which the commanders of the
legions, and the officers both of cavalry and infantry, were
invited to assist. Three or four hours of the night had not
passed away without some secret cabals; and when the election of an emperor was proposed, the spirit of faction began
to agitate the assembly. Victor and Arinthæus collected the
remains of the court of Constantius; the friends of Julian attached themselves to the Gallic chiefs Dagalaiphus and
Nevitta; and the most fatal consequences might be apprehended from the discord of two factions, so opposite in their
character and interest, in their maxims of government, and
perhaps in their religious principles. The superior virtues of
Sallust could alone reconcile their divisions and unite their
suffrages; and the venerable prefect would immediately have
been declared the successor of Julian, if he himself, with
sincere and modest firmness, had not alleged his age and infirmities, so unequal to the weight of the diadem. The generals, who were surprised and perplexed by his refusal,
showed some disposition to adopt the salutary advice of an
inferior officer, that they should act as they would have
acted in the absence of the emperor; that they should exert
their abilities to extricate the army from the present distress;
and, if they were fortunate enough to reach the confines of
Mesopotamia, they should proceed with united and deliberate
counsels in the election of a lawful sovereign. While they debated, a few voices saluted Jovian, who was no more than
first of the domestics, with the names of Emperor and
Augustus. The tumultuary acclamation was instantly repeated
by the guards who surrounded the tent, and passed, in a few
minutes, to the extremities of the line. The new prince,
astonished with his own fortune, was hastily invested with
the Imperial ornaments, and received an oath of fidelity from
the generals, whose favour and protection he so lately
solicited. The strongest recommendation of Jovian was the
merit of his father, Count Varronian, who enjoyed, in
honourable retirement, the fruit of his long services. In the
obscure freedom of a private station, the son indulged his
taste for wine and women; yet he supported, with credit,
the character of a Christian and a soldier. Without being conspicuous for any of the ambitious qualifications which excite
the admiration and envy of mankind, the comely person of
Jovian, his cheerful temper, and familiar wit, had gained the

affection of his fellow-soldiers; and the generals of both parties acquiesced in a popular election which had not been conducted by the arts of their enemies. The pride of this unexpected elevation was moderated by the just apprehension that the same day might terminate the life and reign of the new emperor. The pressing voice of necessity was obeyed without delay; and the first orders issued by Jovian, a few hours after his predecessor had expired, were to prosecute a march which could alone extricate the Romans from their actual distress.

The esteem of an enemy is most sincerely expressed by his fears; and the degree of fear may be accurately measured by the joy with which he celebrates his deliverance. The welcome news of the death of Julian, which a deserter revealed to the camp of Sapor, inspired the desponding monarch with a sudden confidence of victory. He immediately detached the royal cavalry, perhaps the ten thousand *Immortals,* to second and support the pursuit; and discharged the whole weight of his united forces on the rear-guard of the Romans. The rear-guard was thrown into disorder; the renowned legions, which derived their titles from Diocletian and his warlike colleague, were broke and trampled down by the elephants; and three tribunes lost their lives in attempting to stop the flight of their soldiers. The battle was at length restored by the persevering valour of the Romans; the Persians were repulsed with a great slaughter of men and elephants; and the army, after marching and fighting a long summer's day, arrived, in the evening, at Samara, on the banks of the Tigris, about one hundred miles above Ctesiphon. On the ensuing day the barbarians, instead of harassing the march, attacked the camp, of Jovian, which had been seated in a deep and sequestered valley. From the hills, the archers of Persia insulted and annoyed the wearied legionaries; and a body of cavalry, which had penetrated with desperate courage through the Prætorian gate, was cut in pieces, after a doubtful conflict, near the Imperial tent. In the succeeding night the camp of Carche was protected by the lofty dykes of the river; and the Roman army, though incessantly exposed to the vexatious pursuit of the Saracens, pitched their tents near the city of Dura four days after the death of Julian. The Tigris was still on their left; their hopes and provisions were almost consumed; and the impatient soldiers, who had fondly persuaded themselves that the frontiers of the empire were not far distant, requested their new sovereign that they might be permitted to hazard the passage of the river. With the assistance of his wisest officers, Jovian endeavoured to check their rashness, by representing that, if they possessed sufficient skill and vigour to stem the torrent of a deep and rapid stream, they would only deliver themselves naked and defenceless to the barbarians, who had occupied the opposite banks. Yielding at length to their clamorous importunities, he consented, with reluctance, that five hundred Gauls and Germans, accustomed from their infancy to the waters of the Rhine and Danube, should attempt the bold adventure, which might serve either as an encouragement or as a warning for the rest of the army. In the silence of the night they swam the Tigris, surprised an unguarded post of the enemy, and displayed at the dawn of day the signal of their resolution and fortune. The success of this trial disposed the emperor to listen to the promises of his architects, who proposed to construct a floating bridge of the inflated skins of sheep, oxen, and goats, covered with a floor of earth and fascines. Two important days were spent in the ineffectual labour; and the Romans, who already endured the miseries of famine, cast a look of despair on the Tigris, and upon the barbarians, whose numbers and obstinacy increased with the distress of the Imperial army.

In this hopeless situation, the fainting spirits of the Romans were revived by the sound of peace. The transient presumption of Sapor had vanished: he observed, with serious concern, that, in the repetition of doubtful combats, he had lost his most faithful and intrepid nobles, his bravest troops, and the greatest part of his train of elephants: and the experienced monarch feared to provoke the resistance of despair, the vicissitudes of fortune, and the exhausted powers of the Roman empire, which might soon advance to relieve, or to revenge, the successor of Julian. The Surenas himself, accompanied by another satrap, appeared in the camp of Jovian, and declared that the clemency of his sovereign was not averse to signify the conditions on which he would consent to spare and to dismiss the Cæsar with the relics of his captive army. The hopes of safety subdued the firmness of the Romans; the emperor was compelled, by the advice of his council and the cries of the soldiers, to embrace the offer of peace; and the prefect Sallust was immediately sent, with the

general Arinthæus, to understand the pleasure of the Great
King. The crafty Persian delayed, under various pretences,
the conclusion of the agreement; started difficulties, required
explanations, suggested expedients, receded from his concessions, increased his demands, and wasted four days in the
arts of negociation, till he had consumed the stock of provisions which yet remained in the camp of the Romans. Had
Jovian been capable of executing a bold and prudent measure,
he would have continued his march with unremitting diligence;
the progress of the treaty would have suspended the attacks of
the barbarians; and, before the expiration of the fourth day,
he might have safely reached the fruitful province of Cor-
duene, at the distance only of one hundred miles. The ir-
resolute emperor, instead of breaking through the toils of
the enemy, expected his fate with patient resignation; and accepted the humiliating conditions of peace which it was no
longer in his power to refuse. The five provinces beyond the
Tigris, which had been ceded by the grandfather of Sapor,
were restored to the Persian monarchy. He acquired, by a
single article, the impregnable city of Nisibis, which had
sustained, in three successive sieges, the effort of his arms.
Singara, and the castle of the Moors, one of the strongest
places of Mesopotamia, were likewise dismembered from the
empire. It was considered as an indulgence that the inhabitants of those fortresses were permitted to retire with their
effects; but the conqueror rigorously insisted that the Romans
should for ever abandon the king and kingdom of Armenia.
A peace, or rather a long truce, of thirty years, was stipulated
between the hostile nations; the faith of the treaty was ratified
by solemn oaths and religious ceremonies; and hostages of
distinguished rank were reciprocally delivered to secure the
performance of the conditions.

The sophist of Antioch, who saw with indignation the
sceptre of his hero in the feeble hand of a Christian successor,
professes to admire the moderation of Sapor in contenting
himself with so small a portion of the Roman empire. If
he had stretched as far as the Euphrates the claims of his
ambition, he might have been secure, says Libanius, of not
meeting with a refusal. If he had fixed, as the boundary of
Persia, the Orontes, the Cydnus, the Sangarius, or even the
Thracian Bosphorus, flatterers would not have been wanting
in the court of Jovian to convince the timid monarch that

his remaining provinces would still afford the most ample gratifications of power and luxury. Without adopting in its full force this malicious insinuation, we must acknowledge that the conclusion of so ignominious a treaty was facilitated by the private ambition of Jovian. The obscure domestic, exalted to the throne by fortune, rather than by merit, was impatient to escape from the hands of the Persians, that he might prevent the designs of Procopius, who commanded the army of Mesopotamia, and establish his doubtful reign over the legions and provinces which were still ignorant of the hasty and tumultuous choice of the camp beyond the Tigris. In the neighbourhood of the same river, at no very considerable distance from the fatal station of Dura, the ten thousand Greeks, without general, or guides, or provisions, were abandoned, above twelve hundred miles from their native country, to the resentment of a victorious monarch. The difference of *their* conduct and success depended much more on their character than on their situation. Instead of tamely resigning themselves to the secret deliberations and private views of a single person, the united councils of the Greeks were inspired by the generous enthusiasm of a popular assembly, wherein the mind of each citizen is filled with the love of glory, the pride of freedom, and the contempt of death. Conscious of their superiority over the barbarians in arms and discipline, they disdained to yield, they refused to capitulate: every obstacle was surmounted by the patience, courage, and military skill; and the memorable retreat of the ten thousand exposed and insulted the weakness of the Persian monarchy.

As the price of his disgraceful concessions, the emperor might perhaps have stipulated that the camp of the hungry Romans should be plentifully supplied, and that they should be permitted to pass the Tigris on the bridge which was constructed by the hands of the Persians. But if Jovian presumed to solicit those equitable terms, they were sternly refused by the haughty tyrant of the East, whose clemency had pardoned the invaders of his country. The Saracens sometimes intercepted the stragglers of the march; but the generals and troops of Sapor respected the cessation of arms, and Jovian was suffered to explore the most convenient place for the passage of the river. The small vessels which had been saved from the conflagration of the fleet performed the most essential service. They first conveyed the emperor and his favourites, and afterwards transported, in many successive voyages, a great part of the army. But, as every man was anxious for his personal safety and apprehensive of being left on the hostile shore, the soldiers, who were too impatient to wait the slow returns of the boats, boldly ventured themselves on light hurdles or inflated skins, and drawing after them their horses, attempted, with various success, to swim across the river. Many of these daring adventurers were swallowed by the waves; many others, who were carried along by the violence of the stream, fell an easy prey to the avarice or cruelty of the wild Arabs; and the loss which the army sustained in the passage of the Tigris was not inferior to the carnage of a day of battle. As soon as the Romans had landed on the western bank, they were delivered from the hostile pursuit of the barbarians; but in a laborious march of two hundred miles over the plains of Mesopotamia they endured the last extremities of thirst and hunger. They were obliged to traverse a sandy desert, which, in the extent of seventy miles, did not afford a single blade of sweet grass nor a single spring of fresh water, and the rest of the inhospitable waste was untrod by the footsteps either of friends or enemies. Whenever a small measure of flour could be discovered in the camp, twenty pounds weight were greedily purchased with ten pieces of gold, the beasts of burden were slaughtered and devoured, and the desert was strewed with the arms and baggage of the Roman soldiers, whose tattered garments and meagre countenances displayed their past sufferings and actual misery. A small convoy of provisions advanced to meet the army as far as the castle of Ur; and the supply was the more grateful, since it declared the fidelity of Sebastian and Procopius. At Thilsaphata the emperor most graciously received the generals of Mesopotamia, and the remains of a once flourishing army at length reposed themselves under the walls of Nisibis. The messengers of Jovian had already proclaimed, in the language of flattery, his election, his treaty, and his return, and the new prince had taken the most effectual measure to secure the allegiance of the armies and provinces of Europe by placing the military command in the hands of those officers who, from motives of interest or inclination, would firmly support the cause of their benefactor.

The friends of Julian had confidently announced the success of his expedition. They entertained a fond persuasion that the temples of the gods would be enriched with the spoils of the East; that Persia would be reduced to the humble state of a tributary province, governed by the laws and magistrates of Rome; that the barbarians would adopt the dress, and manners, and language of their conquerors; and that the youth of Ecbatana and Susa would study the art of rhetoric under Grecian masters. The progress of the arms of Julian interrupted his communication with the empire, and, from the moment that he passed the Tigris, his affectionate subjects were ignorant of the fate and fortunes of their prince. Their contemplation of fancied triumphs was disturbed by the melancholy rumour of his death, and they persisted to doubt, after they could no longer deny, the truth of that fatal event. The messengers of Jovian promulgated the specious tale of a prudent and necessary peace; the voice of fame, louder and more sincere, revealed the disgrace of the emperor and the conditions of the ignominious treaty. The minds of the people were filled with astonishment and grief, with indignation and terror, when they were informed that the unworthy successor of Julian relinquished the five provinces which had been acquired by the victory of Galerius, and that he shamefully surrendered to the barbarians the important city of Nisibis, the firmest bulwark of the provinces of the East. The deep and dangerous question, how far the public faith should be observed when it becomes incompatible with the public safety, was freely agitated in popular conversation, and some hopes were entertained that the emperor would redeem his pusillanimous behaviour by a splendid act of patriotic perfidy. The inflexible spirit of the Roman senate had always disclaimed the unequal conditions which were extorted from the distress of her captive armies; and, if it were necessary to satisfy the national honour by delivering the guilty general into the hands of the barbarians, the greatest part of the subjects of Jovian would have cheerfully acquiesced in the precedent of ancient times.

But the emperor, whatever might be the limits of his constitutional authority, was the absolute master of the laws and arms of the state; and the same motives which had forced him to subscribe, now pressed him to execute the treaty of peace. He was impatient to secure an empire at the expense of a few provinces, and the respectable names of religion and honour concealed the personal fears and the ambition of Jovian. Notwithstanding the dutiful solicitations of the inhabitants, decency, as well as prudence, forbade the emperor to lodge in the palace of Nisibis; but the next morning after his arrival, Bineses, the ambassador of Persia, entered the place, displayed from the citadel the standard of the Great King, and proclaimed, in his name, the cruel alternative of exile or servitude. The principal citizens of Nisibis, who, till that fatal moment, had confided in the protection of their sovereign, threw themselves at his feet. They conjured him not to abandon, or, at least, not to deliver, a faithful colony to the rage of a barbarian tyrant, exasperated by the three successive defeats which he had experienced under the walls of Nisibis. They still possessed arms and courage to repel the invaders of their country; they requested only the permission of using them in their own defence, and, as soon as they had asserted their independence, they should implore the favour of being again admitted into the rank of his subjects. Their arguments, their eloquence, their tears, were ineffectual. Jovian alleged, with some confusion, the sanctity of oaths; and as the reluctance with which he accepted the present of a crown of gold convinced the citizens of their hopeless condition, the advocate Sylvanus was provoked to exclaim, "O emperor! may you thus be crowned by all the cities of your dominions!" Jovian, who in a few weeks had assumed the habits of a prince,[1] was displeased with freedom, and offended with truth; and as he reasonably supposed that the discontent of the people might incline them to submit to the Persian government, he published an edict, under pain of death, that they should leave the city within the term of three days. Ammianus has delineated in lively colours the scene of universal despair, which he seems to have viewed with an eye of compassion. The martial youth deserted, with indignant grief, the walls which they had so gloriously defended; the disconsolate mourner dropped a last tear over the tomb of a son or husband, which must soon be profaned by the rude hand of a barbarian master; and the aged citizen kissed the threshold and clung to the doors of the house where he had passed the cheerful and careless hours of in-

---

[1] At Nisibis he performed a *royal* act. A brave officer, his namesake, who had been thought worthy of the purple, was dragged from supper, thrown into a well, and stoned to death without any form of trial or evidence of guilt.

fancy. The highways were crowded with a trembling multitude; the distinctions of rank, and sex, and age, were lost in the general calamity. Every one strove to bear away some fragment from the wreck of his fortunes; and as they could not command the immediate service of an adequate number of horses or waggons, they were obliged to leave behind them the greatest part of their valuable effects. The savage insensibility of Jovian appears to have aggravated the hardships of these unhappy fugitives. They were seated, however, in a new-built quarter of Amida; and that rising city, with the reinforcement of a very considerable colony, soon recovered its former splendour and became the capital of Mesopotamia. Similar orders were despatched by the emperor for the evacuation of Singara and the castle of the Moors, and for the restitution of the five provinces beyond the Tigris. Sapor enjoyed the glory and the fruits of his victory; and this ignominious peace has justly been considered as a memorable era in the decline and fall of the Roman empire. The predecessors of Jovian had sometimes relinquished the dominion of distant and unprofitable provinces; but, since the foundation of the city, the genius of Rome, the god Terminus, who guarded the boundaries of the republic, had never retired before the sword of a victorious enemy.

REFLECTIONS ON THE DEATH OF JULIAN

After Jovian had performed those engagements which the voice of his people might have tempted him to violate, he hastened away from the scene of his disgrace, and proceeded with his whole court to enjoy the luxury of Antioch. Without consulting the dictates of religious zeal, he was prompted, by humanity and gratitude, to bestow the last honours on the remains of his deceased sovereign; and Procopius, who sincerely bewailed the loss of his kinsman, was removed from the command of the army, under the decent pretence of conducting the funeral. The corpse of Julian was transported from Nisibis to Tarsus, in a slow march of fifteen days, and, as it passed through the cities of the East, was saluted by the hostile factions with mournful lamentations and clamorous insults. The Pagans already placed their beloved hero in the rank of those gods whose worship he had restored, while the invectives of the Christians pursued the soul of the apostate to hell, and his body to the grave. One party lamented the approaching ruin of their altars, the other celebrated the marvellous deliverance of the church. The Christians applauded, in lofty ambiguous strains, the stroke of divine vengeance which had been so long suspended over the guilty head of Julian. They acknowledged that the death of the tyrant, at the instant he expired beyond the Tigris, was *revealed* to the saints of Egypt, Syria, and Cappadocia; and instead of suffering him to fall by the Persian darts, their indiscretion ascribed the heroic deed to the obscure hand of some mortal or immortal champion of the faith. Such imprudent declarations were eagerly adopted by the malice or credulity of their adversaries, who darkly insinuated or confidently asserted that the governors of the church had instigated and directed the fanaticism of a domestic assassin. Above sixteen years after the death of Julian, the charge was solemnly and vehemently urged in a public oration addressed by Libanius to the emperor Theodosius. His suspicions are unsupported by fact or argument, and we can only esteem the generous zeal of the sophist of Antioch for the cold and neglected ashes of his friend.

It was an ancient custom in the funerals, as well as in the triumphs of the Romans, that the voice of praise should be corrected by that of satire and ridicule, and that, in the midst of the splendid pageants which displayed the glory of the living or of the dead, their imperfections should not be concealed from the eyes of the world. This custom was practised in the funeral of Julian. The comedians, who resented his contempt and aversion for the theatre, exhibited, with the applause of a Christian audience, the lively and exaggerated representation of the faults and follies of the deceased emperor. His various character and singular manners afforded an ample scope for pleasantry and ridicule. In the exercise of his uncommon talents he often descended below the majesty of his rank. Alexander was transformed into Diogenes,—the philosopher was degraded into a priest. The purity of his virtue was sullied by excessive vanity; his superstition disturbed the peace and endangered the safety of a mighty empire; and his irregular sallies were the less entitled to indulgence, as they appeared to be the laborious efforts of art, or even of affection. The remains of Julian were interred at Tarsus in Cilicia; but his stately tomb, which arose in that city on the banks of the cold and limpid Cydnus, was displeasing to the faithful friends who loved and revered the memory of that extraordinary man. The philosopher expressed a very reasonable wish that the disciple of Plato might have reposed amidst the groves of the Academy, while the soldier exclaimed, in bolder accents, that the ashes of Julian should have been mingled with those of Cæsar, in the field of Mars, and among the ancient monuments of Roman virtue. The history of princes does not very frequently renew the example of a similar competition.

The Return of Christianity
to Favour

25.

THE CHRISTIANS UNDER JOVIAN

THE DEATH of Julian had left the public affairs of the empire in a very doubtful and dangerous situation. The Roman army was saved by an inglorious, perhaps a necessary, treaty; [1] and the first moments of peace were consecrated by the pious Jovian to restore the domestic tranquillity of the church and state. The indiscretion of his predecessor, instead of reconciling, had artfully fomented the religious war; and the balance which he affected to preserve between the hostile factions served only to perpetuate the contest by the vicissitudes of hope and fear, by the rival claims of ancient possession and actual favour. The Christians had forgotten the spirit of the Gospel, and the Pagans had imbibed the spirit of the church. In private families the sentiments of nature were extinguished by the blind fury of zeal and revenge; the majesty of the laws was violated or abused; the cities of the East were stained with blood; and the most implacable enemies of the Romans were in the bosom of their country. Jovian was educated in the profession of Christianity; and as he marched from Nisibis to Antioch, the banner of the Cross, the LABARUM of Constantine, which was again displayed at the head of the legions, announced to the people the faith of their new emperor. As soon as he ascended the throne he transmitted a circular epistle to all the governors of provinces, in which he confessed the divine truth and secured the legal establishment of the Christian religion. The insidious edicts

---

[1] The medals of Jovian adorn him with victories, laurel crowns, and prostrate captives. Flattery is a foolish suicide; she destroys herself with her own hands.

of Julian were abolished, the ecclesiastical immunities were restored and enlarged, and Jovian condescended to lament that the distress of the times obliged him to diminish the measure of charitable distributions. The Christians were unanimous in the loud and sincere applause which they bestowed on the pious successor of Julian; but they were still ignorant what creed or what synod he would choose for the standard of orthodoxy, and the peace of the church immediately revived those eager disputes which had been suspended during the season of persecution. The episcopal leaders of the contending sects, convinced from experience how much their fate would depend on the earliest impressions that were made on the mind of an untutored soldier, hastened to the court of Edessa, or Antioch. The highways of the East were crowded with Homoousian, and Arian, and Semi-Arian, and Eunomian bishops, who struggled to outstrip each other in the holy race; the apartments of the palace resounded with their clamours, and the ears of the prince were assaulted, and perhaps astonished, by the singular mixture of metaphysical argument and passionate invective. The moderation of Jovian, who recommended concord and charity, and referred the disputants to the sentence of a future council, was interpreted as a symptom of indifference; but his attachment to the Nicene Creed was at length discovered and declared by the reverence which he expressed for the *celestial* virtues of the great Athanasius. The intrepid veteran of the faith, at the age of seventy, had issued from his retreat on the first intelligence of the tyrant's death. The acclamations of the people seated him once more on the archiepiscopal throne, and he wisely accepted or anticipated the invitation of Jovian. The venerable figure of Athanasius, his calm courage and insinuating eloquence, sustained the reputation which he had already acquired in the courts of four successive princes. As soon as he had gained the confidence and secured the faith of the Christian emperor, he returned in triumph to his diocese, and continued, with mature counsels and undiminished vigour, to direct, ten years longer, the ecclesiastical government of Alexandria, Egypt, and the catholic church. Before his departure from Antioch, he assured Jovian that his orthodox devotion would be rewarded with a long and peaceful reign. Athanasius had reason to hope that he should be allowed either the merit of a successful prediction, or the excuse of a grateful though ineffectual prayer.

Jovian died after a reign of only eight months. After Jovian Valentinian became emperor and associated his brother Valens. The western and eastern provinces were now formally divided. Valentinian maintained religious toleration in the West. Valens professed Arianism in the East.

Barbarian pressure was increasing on different frontiers, in Gaul from the Alemanni and Burgundians, in Britain from the Picts and Scots, on the Danube from the Goths and Sarmatians. These peoples were now being pushed forward by the Huns. As a result of this pressure the Visigoths were allowed to settle within the Danube. Here however they revolted and threatened Constantinople. Valens met them at Adrianople and was defeated and killed in a decisive battle which in tactics asserted the supremacy of cavalry over infantry which was to endure until the battle of Crécy and which inflicted losses in men and damage to the prestige of the Roman army from which it never recovered.

In the general calamities which followed, the investiture of Theodosius as emperor in the East marks a turning point in secular and ecclesiastical government. He defeated the Goths and made treaties with them which none the less involved further settlements within the empire. He earned the title of the Great by his enforcement of Catholic orthodoxy. After the deaths of Gratian, Valentinian II and a usurper, Eugenius, Theodosius was the last sole ruler of the empire in the West and the East. These events are narrated in the remainder of this chapter and in Chapter 26.[1]

----

[1] The origin of the Huns, discussed by Gibbon in Chapter 26, remains somewhat obscure. The best modern account is E. A. Thompson's *Attila and the Huns*, 1948.

27.

AMBROSE, ARCHBISHOP OF MILAN. VIRTUES AND
FAULTS OF THEODOSIUS. SEDITION OF ANTIOCH AND
MASSACRE OF THESSALONICA. PENANCE OF
THEODOSIUS. CHARACTER AND DEATH OF VALEN-
TINIAN. DEATH OF THEODOSIUS.

---

*Constantinople had been a stronghold of Arianism for forty
years. Theodosius was the first emperor to be baptised in the
orthodox faith of the Trinity. In 380 an orthodox bishop,
Gregory Nazianzen, was established in Constantinople and
Arianism was driven from the East. At the Council of Constantinople in 381 the theological system of the Trinity, which
had been established by the Council of Nicæa, was completed.
Between 380 and 394 Theodosius promulgated a number of
severe edicts against the heretics.*

*Meanwhile the lazy disposition of Gratian, emperor of the
West, had aroused discontent among the Roman troops.
Maximus, leading a revolt from Britain, defeated him near
Lyons before Theodosius could march to his relief. Gratian
was assassinated and Theodosius formed an alliance with
Maximus, by which Maximus reigned beyond the Alps and
Gratian's brother Valentinian was confirmed in the sovereign-
ty of Italy.*

AMBROSE, ARCHBISHOP OF MILAN

AMONG THE ECCLESIASTICS who illustrated the reign of Theodosius, Gregory Nazianzen was distinguished by the talents of
an eloquent preacher; the reputation of miraculous gifts
added weight and dignity to the monastic virtues of Martin
of Tours; but the palm of episcopal vigour and ability was
justly claimed by the intrepid Ambrose. He was descended
from a noble family of Romans; his father had exercised the
important office of Prætorian prefect of Gaul; and the son,

after passing through the studies of a liberal education, attained, in the regular gradation of civil honours, the station of consular of Liguria, a province which included the Imperial residence of Milan. At the age of thirty-four, and before he had received the sacrament of baptism, Ambrose, to his own surprise and to that of the world, was suddenly transformed from a governor to an archbishop. Without the least mixture, as it is said, of art or intrigue, the whole body of the people unanimously saluted him with the episcopal title; the concord and perseverance of their acclamations were ascribed to a preternatural impulse; and the reluctant magistrate was compelled to undertake a spiritual office for which he was not prepared by the habits and occupations of his former life. But the active force of his genius soon qualified him to exercise, with zeal and prudence, the duties of his ecclesiastical jurisdiction; and while he cheerfully renounced the vain and splendid trappings of temporal greatness, he condescended, for the good of the church, to direct the conscience of the emperors, and to control the administration of the empire. Gratian loved and revered him as a father; and the elaborate treatise on the faith of the Trinity was designed for the instruction of the young prince. After his tragic death, at a time when the empress Justina trembled for her own safety, and for that of her son Valentinian, the archbishop of Milan was despatched on two different embassies to the court of Trèves. He exercised, with equal firmness and dexterity, the powers of his spiritual and political characters; and perhaps contributed, by his authority and eloquence, to check the ambition of Maximus, and to protect the peace of Italy. Ambrose had devoted his life and his abilities to the service of the church. Wealth was the object of his contempt; he had renounced his private patrimony; and he sold, without hesitation, the consecrated plate for the redemption of captives. The clergy and people of Milan were attached to their archbishop; and he deserved the esteem, without soliciting the favour, or apprehending the displeasure, of his feeble sovereigns.

The government of Italy, and of the young emperor, naturally devolved to his mother Justina, a woman of beauty and spirit, but who, in the midst of an orthodox people, had the misfortune of professing the Arian heresy, which she endeavoured to instil into the mind of her son. Justina was persuaded that a Roman emperor might claim, in his own dominions, the public exercise of his religion; and she proposed to the archbishop, as a moderate and reasonable concession, that he should resign the use of a single church, either in the city or suburbs of Milan. But the conduct of Ambrose was governed by very different principles. The palaces of the earth might indeed belong to Cæsar, but the churches were the houses of God; and, within the limits of his diocese, he himself, as the lawful successor of the apostles, was the only minister of God. The privileges of Christianity, temporal as well as spiritual, were confined to the true believers; and the mind of Ambrose was satisfied that his own theological opinions were the standard of truth and orthodoxy. The archbishop, who refused to hold any conference or negociation with the instruments of Satan, declared, with modest firmness, his resolution to die a martyr, rather than to yield to the impious sacrilege; and Justina, who resented the refusal as an act of insolence and rebellion, hastily determined to exert the Imperial prerogative of her son. As she desired to perform her public devotions on the approaching festival of Easter, Ambrose was ordered to appear before the council. He obeyed the summons with the respect of a faithful subject, but he was followed, without his consent, by an innumerable people: they pressed, with impetuous zeal, against the gates of the palace; and the affrighted ministers of Valentinian, instead of pronouncing a sentence of exile on the archbishop of Milan, humbly requested that he would interpose his authority to protect the person of the emperor, and to restore the tranquillity of the capital. But the promises which Ambrose received and communicated were soon violated by a perfidious court; and, during six of the most solemn days which Christian piety has set apart for the exercise of religion, the city was agitated by the irregular convulsions of tumult and fanaticism. The officers of the household were directed to prepare, first the Portian, and afterwards the new, *Basilica,* for the immediate reception of the emperor and his mother. The splendid canopy and hangings of the royal seat were arranged in the customary manner; but it was found necessary to defend them, by a strong guard, from the insults of the populace. The Arian ecclesiastics who ventured to show themselves in the streets were exposed to the most imminent danger of their lives; and

Ambrose enjoyed the merit and reputation of rescuing his personal enemies from the hands of the enraged multitude.

But while he laboured to restrain the effects of their zeal, the pathetic vehemence of his sermons continually inflamed the angry and seditious temper of the people of Milan. The characters of Eve, of the wife of Job, of Jezebel, of Herodias, were indecently applied to the mother of the emperor; and her desire to obtain a church for the Arians was compared to the most cruel persecutions which Christianity had endured under the reign of Paganism. The measures of the court served only to expose the magnitude of the evil. A fine of two hundred pounds of gold was imposed on the corporate body of merchants and manufacturers: an order was signified, in the name of the emperor, to all the officers and inferior servants of the courts of justice, that, during the continuance of the public disorders, they should strictly confine themselves to their houses: and the ministers of Valentinian imprudently confessed that the most respectable part of the citizens of Milan was attached to the cause of their archbishop. He was again solicited to restore peace to his country, by a timely compliance with the will of his sovereign. The reply of Ambrose was couched in the most humble and respectful terms, which might, however, be interpreted as a serious declaration of civil war. "His life and fortune were in the hands of the emperor; but he would never betray the church of Christ, or degrade the dignity of the episcopal character. In such a cause he was prepared to suffer whatever the malice of the dæmon could inflict; and he only wished to die in the presence of his faithful flock, and at the foot of the altar; *he* had not contributed to excite, but it was in the power of God alone to appease, the rage of the people: he deprecated the scenes of blood and confusion which were likely to ensue; and it was his fervent prayer that he might not survive to behold the ruin of a flourishing city, and perhaps the desolation of all Italy." The obstinate bigotry of Justina would have endangered the empire of her son, if, in this contest with the church and people of Milan, she could have depended on the active obedience of the troops of the palace. A large body of Goths had marched to occupy the *Basilica,* which was the object of the dispute: and it might be expected from the Arian principles and barbarous manners of these foreign mercenaries, that they would not entertain any scruples in the execution of the most sanguinary orders. They were encountered on the sacred threshold by the archbishop, who, thundering against them a sentence of excommunication, asked them, in the tone of a father and a master, Whether it was to invade the house of God that they had implored the hospitable protection of the republic? The suspense of the barbarians allowed some hours for a more effectual negociation; and the empress was persuaded by the advice of her wisest counsellors to leave the catholics in possession of all the churches of Milan; and to dissemble, till a more convenient season, her intentions of revenge. The mother of Valentinian could never forgive the triumph of Ambrose: and the royal youth uttered a passionate exclamation, that his own servants were ready to betray him into the hands of an insolent priest.

The laws of the empire, some of which were inscribed with the name of Valentinian, still condemned the Arian heresy, and seemed to excuse the resistance of the catholics. By the influence of Justina, an edict of toleration was promulgated in all the provinces which were subject to the court of Milan; the free exercise of their religion was granted to those who professed the faith of Rimini; and the emperor declared that all persons who should infringe this sacred and salutary constitution should be capitally punished, as the enemies of the public peace. The character and language of the archbishop of Milan may justify the suspicion that his conduct soon afforded a reasonable ground, or at least a specious pretence, to the Arian ministers, who watched the opportunity of surprising him in some act of disobedience to a law which he strangely represents as a law of blood and tyranny. A sentence of easy and honourable banishment was pronounced, which enjoined Ambrose to depart from Milan without delay, whilst it permitted him to choose the place of his exile and the number of his companions. But the authority of the saints, who have preached and practised the maxims of passive loyalty, appeared to Ambrose of less moment than the extreme and pressing danger of the church. He boldly refused to obey; and his refusal was supported by the unanimous consent of his faithful people. They guarded by turns the person of their archbishop; the gates of the cathedral and the episcopal palace were strongly secured; and the Imperial troops, who had formed the blockade, were unwilling to risk the attack of that impregnable fortress. The numerous poor, who had been relieved by the liberality of Ambrose, embraced the fair occasion of signalising their zeal and gratitude; and as the patience of the multitude might have been exhausted by the length and uniformity of nocturnal vigils, he prudently introduced into the church of Milan the useful institution of a loud and regular psalmody. While he maintained this arduous contest, he was instructed, by a dream, to open the earth in a place where the remains of two martyrs, Gervasius and Protasius, had been deposited above three hundred years. Immediately under the pavement of the church two perfect skeletons were found, with the heads separated from their bodies, and a plentiful effusion of blood. The holy relics were presented, in solemn pomp, to the veneration of the people; and every circumstance of this fortunate discovery was admirably adapted to promote the designs of Ambrose. The bones of the martyrs, their blood, their garments, were supposed to contain a healing power; and the preternatural influence was communicated to the most distant objects, without losing any part of its original virtue. The extraordinary cure of a blind man, and the reluctant confessions of several dæmoniacs, appeared to justify the faith and sanctity of Ambrose; and the truth of those miracles is attested by Ambrose himself, by his secretary Paulinus, and by his proselyte, the celebrated Augustin, who, at that time, professed the art of rhetoric in Milan. The reason of the present age may possibly approve the incredulity of Justina and her Arian court, who derided the theatrical representations which were exhibited by the contrivance, and at the expense, of the archbishop. Their effect, however, on the minds of the people, was rapid and irresistible; and the feeble sovereign of Italy found himself unable to contend with the favourite of Heaven. The powers likewise of the earth interposed in the defence of Ambrose: the disinterested advice of Theodosius was the genuine result of piety and friendship; and the mask of religious zeal concealed the hostile and ambitious designs of the tyrant of Gaul.

Maximus invaded Italy in 387. Valentinian and his mother fled to Theodosius in Thessalonica. Theodosius married Valentinian's sister and ended the civil war by defeating and beheading Maximus.

THE VIRTUES AND FAULTS OF THEODOSIUS

The orator, who may be silent without danger, may praise without difficulty and without reluctance; and posterity will confess that the character of Theodosius might furnish the subject of a sincere and ample panegyric. The wisdom of his laws and the success of his arms rendered his administration respectable in the eyes both of his subjects and of his enemies. He loved and practised the virtues of domestic life, which seldom hold their residence in the palaces of kings. Theodosius was chaste and temperate; he enjoyed, without excess, the sensual and social pleasures of the table, and the warmth of his amorous passions was never diverted from their lawful objects. The proud titles of Imperial greatness were adorned by the tender names of a faithful husband, an indulgent father; his uncle was raised, by his affectionate esteem, to the rank of a second parent; Theodosius embraced, as his own, the children of his brother and sister, and the expressions of his regard were extended to the most distant and obscure branches of his numerous kindred. His familiar friends were judiciously selected from amongst those persons who, in the equal intercourse of private life, had appeared before his eyes without a mask; the consciousness of personal and superior merit enabled him to despise the accidental distinction of the purple, and he proved by his conduct that he had forgotten all the injuries, while he most gratefully remembered all the favours and services, which he had received before he ascended the throne of the Roman empire. The serious or lively tone of his conversation was adapted to the age, the rank, or the character of his subjects whom he admitted into his society; and the affability of his manners displayed the image of his mind. Theodosius respected the simplicity of the good and virtuous: every art, every talent, of an useful or even of an innocent nature, was rewarded by his judicious liberality; and, except the heretics, whom he persecuted with implacable hatred, the diffusive circle of his benevolence was circumscribed only by the limits of the human race. The government of a mighty empire may assuredly suffice to occupy the time and the abilities of a mortal; yet the diligent prince, without aspiring to the unsuitable reputation of profound learning, always reserved some moments of his leisure for the instructive amusement of reading. History, which enlarged his experience, was his favourite study. The annals of Rome, in the long period of eleven hundred years, presented him with a various and splendid picture of human life; and it has been particularly observed that, whenever he perused the cruel acts of Cinna, of Marius, or of Sylla, he warmly expressed his generous detestation of those enemies of humanity and freedom. His disinterested opinion of past events was usefully applied as the rule of his own actions, and Theodosius has deserved the singular commendation that his virtues always seemed to expand with his fortune; the season of his prosperity was that of his moderation, and his clemency appeared the most conspicuous after the danger and success of the civil war. The Moorish guards of the tyrant had been massacred in the first heat of the victory, and a small number of the most obnoxious criminals suffered the punishment of the law. But the emperor showed himself much more attentive to relieve the innocent than to chastise the guilty. The oppressed subjects of the West, who would have deemed themselves happy in the restoration of their lands, were astonished to receive a sum of money equivalent to their losses; and the liberality of the conqueror supported the aged mother and educated the orphan daughters of Maximus. A character thus accomplished might almost excuse the extravagant supposition of the orator Pacatus that, if the elder Brutus could be permitted to revisit the earth, the stern republican would abjure, at the feet of Theodosius, his hatred of kings; and ingenuously confess that such a monarch was the most faithful guardian of the happiness and dignity of the Roman people.

Yet the piercing eye of the founder of the republic must have discerned two essential imperfections, which might, perhaps, have abated his recent love of despotism. The virtuous mind of Theodosius was often relaxed by indolence, and it was sometimes inflamed by passion. In the pursuit of an important object his active courage was capable of the most vigorous exertions; but as soon as the design was accomplished, or the danger was surmounted, the hero sunk into inglorious repose, and, forgetful that the time of a prince is the property of his people, resigned himself to the enjoyment of the innocent but trifling pleasures of a luxurious court. The natural disposition of Theodosius was hasty and choleric; and, in a station where none could resist and few would dissuade the

fatal consequence of his resentment, the humane monarch
was justly alarmed by the consciousness of his infirmity and
of his power. It was the constant study of his life to suppress
or regulate the intemperate sallies of passion; and the success of his efforts enhanced the merit of his clemency. But
the painful virtue which claims the merit of victory is exposed to the danger of defeat; and the reign of a wise and
merciful prince was polluted by an act of cruelty which would
stain the annals of Nero or Domitian. Within the space of
three years the inconsistent historian of Theodosius must relate the generous pardon of the citizens of Antioch, and the
inhuman massacre of the people of Thessalonica.

THE SEDITION OF ANTIOCH

The lively impatience of the inhabitants of Antioch was
never satisfied with their own situation, or with the character
and conduct of their successive sovereigns. The Arian subjects
of Theodosius deplored the loss of their churches; and, as
three rival bishops disputed the throne of Antioch, the sentence
which decided their pretensions excited the murmurs of the
two unsuccessful congregations. The exigencies of the Gothic
war, and the inevitable expense that accompanied the conclusion of the peace, had constrained the emperor to aggra-
vate the weight of the public impositions; and the provinces
of Asia, as they had not been involved in the distress, were
the less inclined to contribute to the relief of Europe. The
auspicious period now approached of the tenth year of his
reign; a festival more grateful to the soldiers, who received
a liberal donative, than to the subjects, whose voluntary
offerings had been long since converted into an extraordinary
and oppressive burden. The edicts of taxation interrupted the
repose and pleasures of Antioch; and the tribunal of the
magistrate was besieged by a suppliant crowd, who, in
pathetic, but at first in respectful language, solicited the re-
dress of their grievances. They were gradually incensed by
the pride of their haughty rulers, who treated their complaints
as a criminal resistance; their satirical wit degenerated into
sharp and angry invectives; and, from the subordinate powers
of government, the invectives of the people insensibly rose
to attack the sacred character of the emperor himself. Their
fury, provoked by a feeble opposition, discharged itself on

the images of the Imperial family which were erected, as objects of public veneration, in the most conspicuous places of the city. The statues of Theodosius, of his father, of his wife Flaccilla, of his two sons Arcadius and Honorius, were insolently thrown down from their pedestals, broken in pieces, or dragged with contempt through the streets; and the indignities which were offered to the representations of Imperial majesty sufficiently declared the impious and treasonable wishes of the populace. The tumult was almost immediately suppressed by the arrival of a body of archers; and Antioch had leisure to reflect on the nature and consequences of her crime. According to the duty of his office, the governor of the province despatched a faithful narrative of the whole transaction, while the trembling citizens intrusted the confession of their crime and the assurances of their repentance to the zeal of Flavian their bishop, and to the eloquence of the senator Hilarius, the friend, and most probably the disciple, of Libanius, whose genius on the melancholy occasion was not useless to his country. But the two capitals, Antioch and Constantinople, were separated by the distance of eight hundred miles; and, notwithstanding the diligence of the Imperial posts, the guilty city was severely punished by a long and dreadful interval of suspense. Every rumour agitated the hopes and fears of the Antiochans, and they heard with terror that their sovereign, exasperated by the insult which had been offered to his own statues, and more especially to those of his beloved wife, had resolved to level with the ground the offending city, and to massacre, without distinction of age or sex, the criminal inhabitants, many of whom were actually driven, by their apprehensions, to seek a refuge in the mountains of Syria and the adjacent desert. At length, twenty-four days after the sedition, the general Hellebicus, and Cæsarius, master of the offices, declared the will of the emperor and the sentence of Antioch. That proud capital was degraded from the rank of a city; and the metropolis of the East, stripped of its lands, its privileges, and its revenues, was subjected, under the humiliating denomination of a village, to the jurisdiction of Laodicea. The baths, the circus, and the theatres were shut; and, that every source of plenty and pleasure might at the same time be intercepted, the distribution of corn was abolished by the severe instructions of Theodosius. His commissioners then proceeded to inquire into the guilt of individuals—of those who had perpetrated, and of those who had not prevented, the destruction of the sacred statues. The tribunal of Hellebicus and Cæsarius, encompassed with armed soldiers, was erected in the midst of the Forum. The noblest and most wealthy of the citizens of Antioch appeared before them in chains; the examination was assisted by the use of torture, and their sentence was pronounced or suspended, according to the judgment of these extraordinary magistrates. The houses of the criminals were exposed to sale, their wives and children were suddenly reduced from affluence and luxury to the most abject distress, and a bloody execution was expected to conclude the horrors of a day which the preacher of Antioch, the eloquent Chrysostom, has represented as a lively image of the last and universal judgment of the world. But the ministers of Theodosius performed with reluctance the cruel task which had been assigned them; they dropped a gentle tear over the calamities of the people, and they listened with reverence to the pressing solicitations of the monks and hermits, who descended in swarms from the mountains. Hellebicus and Cæsarius were persuaded to suspend the execution of their sentence; and it was agreed that the former should remain at Antioch, while the latter returned, with all possible speed, to Constantinople, and presumed once more to consult the will of his sovereign. The resentment of Theodosius had already subsided; the deputies of the people, both the bishop and the orator, had obtained a favourable audience; and the reproaches of the emperor were the complaints of injured friendship rather than the stern menaces of pride and power. A free and general pardon was granted to the city and citizens of Antioch; the prison-doors were thrown open; the senators, who despaired of their lives, recovered the possession of their houses and estates; and the capital of the East was restored to the enjoyment of her ancient dignity and splendour. Theodosius condescended to praise the senate of Constantinople, who had generously interceded for their distressed brethren; he rewarded the eloquence of Hilarius with the government of Palestine, and dismissed the bishop of Antioch with the warmest expressions of his respect and gratitude. A thousand new statues arose to the clemency of Theodosius; the applause of his subjects was ratified by the approbation of his own heart; and the emperor confessed that, if the exercise of justice is the most important duty, the indulgence of mercy is the most exquisite pleasure of a sovereign.

THE MASSACRE OF THESSALONICA

The sedition of Thessalonica is ascribed to a more shameful cause, and was productive of much more dreadful consequences. That great city, the metropolis of all the Illyrian provinces, had been protected from the dangers of the Gothic war by strong fortifications and a numerous garrison. Botheric, the general of those troops, and, as it should seem from his name, a barbarian, had amongst his slaves a beautiful boy, who excited the impure desires of one of the charioteers of the circus. The insolent and brutal lover was thrown into prison by the order of Botheric; and he sternly rejected the importunate clamours of the multitude, who, on the day of the public games, lamented the absence of their favourite, and considered the skill of a charioteer as an object of more importance than his virtue. The resentment of the people was embittered by some previous disputes; and, as the strength of the garrison had been drawn away for the service of the Italian war, the feeble remnant, whose numbers were reduced by desertion, could not save the unhappy general from their licentious fury. Botheric and several of his principal officers were inhumanly murdered; their mangled bodies were dragged about the streets; and the emperor, who then resided at Milan, was surprised by the intelligence of the audacious and wanton cruelty of the people of Thessalonica. The sentence of a dispassionate judge would have inflicted a severe punishment on the authors of the crime; and the merit of Botheric might contribute to exasperate the grief and indignation of his master. The fiery and choleric temper of Theodosius was impatient of the dilatory forms of a judicial inquiry; and he hastily resolved that the blood of his lieutenant should be expiated by the blood of the guilty people. Yet his mind still fluctuated between the counsels of clemency and of revenge; the zeal of the bishops had almost extorted from the reluctant emperor the promise of a general pardon; his passion was again inflamed by the flattering suggestions of his minister Rufinus; and, after Theodosius had despatched the messengers of death, he attempted, when it was too late, to prevent the execution of his orders. The punishment of a Roman city was blindly committed to the undistinguishing sword of the barbarians; and the hostile preparations were concerted with the dark and perfidious artifice of an illegal conspiracy. The people of Thessalonica were treacherously invited, in the name of their sovereign, to the games of the circus; and such was their insatiate avidity for those amusements that every consideration of fear or suspicion was disregarded by the numerous spectators. As soon as the assembly was complete, the soldiers, who had secretly been posted round the circus, received the signal, not of the races, but of a general massacre. The promiscuous carnage continued three hours, without discrimination of strangers or natives, of age or sex, of innocence or guilt; the most moderate accounts state the number of the slain at seven thousand; and it is affirmed by some writers that more than fifteen thousand victims were sacrificed to the manes of Botheric. A foreign merchant, who had probably no concern in his murder, offered his own life and all his wealth to supply the place of *one* of his two sons; but, while the father hesitated with equal tenderness, while he was doubtful to choose, and unwilling to condemn, the soldiers determined his suspense by plunging their daggers at the same moment into the breasts of the defenceless youths. The apology of the assassins, that they were obliged to produce the prescribed number of heads, serves only to increase, by an appearance of order and design, the horrors of the massacre, which was executed by the commands of Theodosius. The guilt of the emperor is aggravated by his long and frequent residence at Thessalonica. The situation of the unfortunate city, the aspect of the streets and buildings, the dress and faces of the inhabitants, were familiar, and even present, to his imagination; and Theodosius possessed a quick and lively sense of the existence of the people whom he destroyed.

The respectful attachment of the emperor for the orthodox clergy had disposed him to love and admire the character of Ambrose, who united all the episcopal virtues in the most eminent degree. The friends and ministers of Theodosius imitated the example of their sovereign; and he observed, with more surprise than displeasure, that all his secret counsels were immediately communicated to the archbishop, who acted from the laudable persuasion that every measure of civil government may have some connexion with the glory of God and the interest of the true religion. The monks and populace of Callinicum, an obscure town on the frontier of Persia, excited by their own fanaticism, and by that of their bishop, had tumultuously burnt a conventicle of the Valentinians and a synagogue of the Jews. The seditious prelate was condemned by the magistrate of the province either to rebuild the synagogue or to repay the damage; and this moderate sentence was confirmed by the emperor. But it was not confirmed by the archbishop of Milan. He dictated an epistle of censure and reproach, more suitable, perhaps, if the emperor had received the mark of circumcision and renounced the faith of his baptism. Ambrose considers the toleration of the Jewish as the persecution of the Christian religion; boldly declares that he himself and every true believer would eagerly dispute with the bishop of Callinicum the merit of the deed and the crown of martyrdom; and laments, in the most pathetic terms, that the execution of the sentence would be fatal to the fame and salvation of Theodosius. As this private admonition did not produce an immediate effect, the archbishop from his pulpit publicly addressed the emperor on his throne; nor would he consent to offer the oblation of the altar till he had obtained from Theodosius a solemn and positive declaration which secured the impunity of the bishop and monks of Callinicum. The recantation of Theodosius was sincere; and, during the term of his residence at Milan, his affection for Ambrose was continually increased by the habits of pious and familiar conversation.

THE PENANCE OF THEODOSIUS

When Ambrose was informed of the massacre of Thessalonica, his mind was filled with horror and anguish. He retired into the country to indulge his grief and to avoid the presence of Theodosius. But as the archbishop was satisfied that a timid silence would render him the accomplice of his guilt, he represented in a private letter the enormity of the crime, which could only be effaced by the tears of penitence. The episcopal vigour of Ambrose was tempered by prudence; and he contented himself with signifying an indirect sort of excommunication, by the assurance that he had been warned in a vision not to offer the oblation in the name or in the presence of Theodosius, and by the advice that he would confine himself to the use of prayer, without presuming to approach the altar of Christ, or to receive the holy eucharist with those hands that were still polluted with the blood of an innocent people. The emperor was deeply affected by his own reproaches and by those of his spiritual father; and after he had bewailed the mischievous and ir-reparable consequences of his rash fury, he proceeded in the accustomed manner to perform his devotions in the great church of Milan. He was stopped in the porch by the arch-bishop, who, in the tone and language of an ambassador of Heaven, declared to his sovereign that private contrition was not sufficient to atone for a public fault or to appease the justice of the offended Deity. Theodosius humbly represented that, if he had contracted the guilt of homicide, David, the man after God's own heart, had been guilty not only of murder but of adultery. "You have imitated David in his crime, imitate then his repentance," was the reply of the undaunted Ambrose. The rigorous conditions of peace and pardon were accepted; and the public penance of the emperor Theodosius has been recorded as one of the most honourable events in the annals of the church. According to the mildest rules of ecclesiastical discipline which were established in the fourth century, the crime of homicide was expiated by the penitence of twenty years: and as it was impossible in the period of human life to purge the accumulated guilt of the massacre of Thessalonica, the murderer should have been excluded from the holy communion till the hour of his death. But the archbishop, consulting the maxims of religious policy, granted some indulgence to the rank of his illustrious penitent, who humbled in the dust the pride of the diadem; and the public edification might be admitted as a weighty reason to abridge the duration of his punishment. It was sufficient that the emperor of the Romans, stripped of the ensigns of royalty, should appear in a mournful and suppliant posture; and that, in the midst of the church of Milan, he should humbly solicit, with sighs and tears, the pardon of his sins. In this spiritual cure Ambrose employed the various methods of mildness and severity. After a delay of about eight months Theodosius was restored to the communion of the faithful; and the edict, which interposes a salutary interval

of thirty days between the sentence and the execution, may
be accepted as the worthy fruits of his repentance. Posterity
has applauded the virtuous firmness of the archbishop; and
the example of Theodosius may prove the beneficial influence
of those principles which could force a monarch, exalted
above the apprehension of human punishment, to respect the
laws and ministers of an invisible Judge. "The prince," says
Montesquieu, "who is actuated by the hopes and fears of
religion, may be compared to a lion, docile only to the voice,
and tractable to the hand, of his keeper." The motions of
the royal animal will therefore depend on the inclination and
interest of the man who has acquired such dangerous authority
over him; and the priest who holds in his hand the conscience of a king may inflame or moderate his sanguinary
passions. The cause of humanity and that of persecution have
been asserted by the same Ambrose with equal energy and
with equal success.

After the defeat and death of the tyrant of Gaul, the Roman
world was in the possession of Theodosius. He derived from
the choice of Gratian his honourable title to the provinces of
the East; he had acquired the West by the right of conquest; and the three years which he spent in Italy were
usefully employed to restore the authority of the laws and to
correct the abuses which had prevailed with impunity under
the usurpation of Maximus and the minority of Valentinian.
The name of Valentinian was regularly inserted in the public
acts, but the tender age and doubtful faith of the son of
Justina appeared to require the prudent care of an orthodox
guardian, and his specious ambition might have excluded the
unfortunate youth, without a struggle and almost without
a murmur, from the administration and even from the inheritance of the empire. If Theodosius had consulted the
rigid maxims of interest and policy, his conduct would have
been justified by his friends, but the generosity of his behaviour on this memorable occasion has extorted the applause
of his most inveterate enemies. He seated Valentinian on the
throne of Milan, and without stipulating any present or
future advantages, restored him to the absolute dominion of all
the provinces from which he had been driven by the arms
of Maximus. To the restitution of his ample patrimony
Theodosius added the free and generous gift of the countries
beyond the Alps which his successful valour had recovered

from the assassin of Gratian. Satisfied with the glory which he had acquired by revenging the death of his benefactor and delivering the West from the yoke of tyranny, the emperor returned from Milan to Constantinople, and, in the peaceful possession of the East, insensibly relapsed into his former habits of luxury and indolence. Theodosius discharged his obligation to the brother, he indulged his conjugal tenderness to the sister, of Valentinian; and posterity, which admires the pure and singular glory of his elevation, must applaud his unrivalled generosity in the use of victory.

THE CHARACTER AND DEATH OF VALENTINIAN

The empress Justina did not long survive her return to Italy, and, though she beheld the triumph of Theodosius, she was not allowed to influence the government of her son. The pernicious attachment to the Arian sect which Valentinian had imbibed from her example and instructions was soon erased by the lessons of a more orthodox education. His growing zeal for the faith of Nice, and his filial reverence for the character and authority of Ambrose, disposed the catholics to entertain the most favourable opinion of the virtues of the young emperor of the West.[1] They applauded his chastity and temperance, his contempt of pleasure, his application to business, and his tender affection for his two sisters, which could not, however, seduce his impartial equity to pronounce an unjust sentence against the meanest of his subjects. But this amiable youth, before he had accomplished the twentieth year of his age, was oppressed by domestic treason, and the empire was again involved in the horrors of a civil war. Arbogastes, a gallant soldier of the nation of the Franks, held the second rank in the service of Gratian. On the death of his master he joined the standard of Theodosius, contributed, by his valour and military conduct, to the destruction of the tyrant, and was appointed, after the victory, master-general of the armies of Gaul. His real merit and apparent fidelity had gained the confidence both of the prince and people; his boundless liberality corrupted the allegiance of the troops; and, whilst he was universally esteemed as the pillar

---

[1] When the young emperor gave an entertainment, he fasted himself; he refused to see an handsome actress, etc. Since he ordered his wild beasts to be killed, it is ungenerous in Philostorgius to reproach him with the love of that amusement.

of the state, the bold and crafty barbarian was secretly determined either to rule or to ruin the empire of the West. The important commands of the army were distributed among the Franks; the creatures of Arbogastes were promoted to all the honours and offices of the civil government; the progress of the conspiracy removed every faithful servant from the presence of Valentinian; and the emperor, without power and without intelligence, insensibly sunk into the precarious and dependent condition of a captive. The indignation which he expressed, though it might arise only from the rash and impatient temper of youth, may be candidly ascribed to the generous spirit of a prince who felt that he was not unworthy to reign. He secretly invited the archbishop of Milan to undertake the office of a mediator, as the pledge of his sincerity and the guardian of his safety. He contrived to apprise the emperor of the East of his helpless situation, and he declared that, unless Theodosius could speedily march to his assistance, he must attempt to escape from the palace, or rather prison, of Vienne, in Gaul, where he had imprudently fixed his residence in the midst of the hostile faction. But the hopes of relief were distant and doubtful; and, as every day furnished some new provocation, the emperor, without strength or counsel, too hastily resolved to risk an immediate contest with his powerful general. He received Arbogastes on the throne, and, as the count approached with some appearance of respect, delivered to him a paper which dismissed him from all his employments. "My authority," replied Arbogastes, with insulting coolness, "does not depend on the smile or the frown of a monarch"; and he contemptuously threw the paper on the ground. The indignant monarch snatched at the sword of one of the guards, which he struggled to draw from its scabbard, and it was not without some degree of violence that he was prevented from using the deadly weapon against his enemy or against himself. A few days after this extraordinary quarrel, in which he had exposed his resentment and his weakness, the unfortunate Valentinian was found strangled in his apartment, and some pains were employed to disguise the manifest guilt of Arbogastes, and to persuade the world that the death of the young emperor had been the voluntary effect of his own despair. His body was conducted with decent pomp to the sepulchre of Milan, and the archbishop pronounced a funeral oration to commemorate his virtue and his misfortunes. On this occasion the humanity of Ambrose tempted him to make a singular breach in his theological system, and to comfort the weeping sisters of Valentinian by the firm assurance that their pious brother, though he had not received the sacrament of baptism, was introduced, without difficulty, into the mansions of eternal bliss.

The prudence of Arbogastes had prepared the success of his ambitious designs, and the provincials, in whose breasts every sentiment of patriotism or loyalty was extinguished, expected, with tame resignation, the unknown master whom the choice of a Frank might place on the Imperial throne. But some remains of pride and prejudice still opposed the elevation of Arbogastes himself, and the judicious barbarian thought it more advisable to reign under the name of some dependent Roman. He bestowed the purple on the rhetorician Eugenius, whom he had already raised from the place of his domestic secretary to the rank of master of the offices. In the course both of his private and public service the count had always approved the attachment and abilities of Eugenius; his learning and eloquence, supported by the gravity of his manners, recommended him to the esteem of the people, and the reluctance with which he seemed to ascend the throne may inspire a favourable prejudice of his virtue and moderation. The ambassadors of the new emperor were immediately despatched to the court of Theodosius, to communicate with affected grief, the unfortunate accident of the death of Valentinian, and, without mentioning the name of Arbogastes, to request that the monarch of the East would embrace as his lawful colleague the respectable citizen who had obtained the unanimous suffrage of the armies and provinces of the West. Theodosius was justly provoked that the perfidy of a barbarian should have destroyed in a moment the labours and the fruit of his former victory; and he was excited by the tears of his beloved wife to revenge the fate of her unhappy brother, and once more to assert by arms the violated majesty of the throne. But as the second conquest of the West was a task of difficulty and danger, he dismissed, with splendid presents and an ambiguous answer, the ambassadors of Eugenius, and almost two years were consumed in the preparations of the civil war. Before he formed any decisive resolution, the pious emperor was anxious to discover the will of Heaven; and as the progress of Christianity had silenced the oracles of Delphi and Dodona, he consulted an Egyptian monk, who possessed, in the opinion of the age, the gift of miracles and the knowledge of futurity. Eutropius, one of the favourite eunuchs of the palace of Constantinople, embarked for Alexandria, from whence he sailed up the Nile as far as the city of Lycopolis, or of Wolves, in the remote province of Thebais. In the neighbourhood of that city, and on the summit of a lofty mountain, the holy John had constructed with his own hands an humble cell, in which he had dwelt above fifty years, without opening his door, without seeing the face of a woman, and without tasting any food that had been prepared by fire or any human art. Five days of the week he spent in prayer and meditation, but on Saturdays and Sundays he regularly opened a small window, and gave audience to the crowd of suppliants who successively flowed from every part of the Christian world. The eunuch of Theodosius approached the window with respectful steps, proposed his questions concerning the event of the civil war, and soon returned with a favourable oracle, which animated the courage of the emperor by the assurance of a bloody but infallible victory. The accomplishment of the prediction was forwarded by all the means that human prudence could supply. The industry of the two master-generals, Stilicho and Timasius, was directed to recruit the numbers and to revive the discipline of the Roman legions. The formidable troops of barbarians marched under the ensigns of their national chieftains. The Iberian, the Arab, and the Goth, who gazed on each other with mutual astonishment, were enlisted in the service of the same prince; and the renowned Alaric acquired, in the school of Theodosius, the knowledge of the art of war which he afterwards so fatally exerted for the destruction of Rome.

The emperor of the West, or, to speak more properly, his general Arbogastes, was instructed by the misconduct and misfortune of Maximus how dangerous it might prove to extend the line of defence against a skilful antagonist, who was free to press or to suspend, to contract or to multiply, his various methods of attack. Arbogastes fixed his station on the confines of Italy; the troops of Theodosius were permitted to occupy, without resistance, the provinces of Pannonia, as far as the foot of the Julian Alps; and even the passes of the

mountains were negligently, or perhaps artfully, abandoned
to the bold invader. He descended from the hills, and beheld,
with some astonishment, the formidable camp of the Gauls
and Germans that covered with arms and tents the open
country which extends to the walls of Aquileia and the banks
of the Frigidus, or Cold River. This narrow theatre of the
war, circumscribed by the Alps and the Adriatic, did not
allow much room for the operations of military skill; the
spirit of Arbogastes would have disdained a pardon; his
guilt extinguished the hope of a negociation; and Theodosius
was impatient to satisfy his glory and revenge by the chastisement of the assassins of Valentinian. Without weighing the
natural and artificial obstacles that opposed his efforts, the
emperor of the East immediately attacked the fortifications
of his rivals, assigned the post of honourable danger to the
Goths, and cherished a secret wish that the bloody conflict
might diminish the pride and numbers of the conquerors.
Ten thousand of those auxiliaries, and Bacurius, general of
the Iberians, died bravely on the field of battle. But the
victory was not purchased by their blood; the Gauls maintained their advantage, and the approach of night protected
the disorderly flight, or retreat, of the troops of Theodosius.
The emperor retired to the adjacent hills, where he passed
a disconsolate night, without sleep, without provisions, and
without hopes,[1] except that strong assurance which, under
the most desperate circumstances, the independent mind may
derive from the contempt of fortune and of life. The triumph
of Eugenius was celebrated by the insolent and dissolute joy
of his camp, whilst the active and vigilant Arbogastes secretly
detached a considerable body of troops to occupy the passes
of the mountains and to encompass the rear of the Eastern
army. The dawn of day discovered to the eyes of Theodosius
the extent and the extremity of his danger, but his apprehensions were soon dispelled by a friendly message from the
leaders of those troops, who expressed their inclination to
desert the standard of the tyrant. The honourable and lucrative
rewards which they stipulated as the price of their perfidy
were granted without hesitation, and, as ink and paper could
not easily be procured, the emperor subscribed on his own

---

[1] Theodoret affirms that St. John and St. Philip appeared to the waking or
sleeping emperor, on horseback, etc. This is the first instance of apostolic
chivalry, which afterwards became so popular in Spain and in the Crusades.

tablets the ratification of the treaty. The spirit of his soldiers was revived by this seasonable reinforcement, and they again marched with confidence to surprise the camp of a tyrant whose principal officers appeared to distrust either the justice or the success of his arms. In the heat of the battle a violent tempest, such as is often felt among the Alps, suddenly arose from the East. The army of Theodosius was sheltered by their position from the impetuosity of the wind, which blew a cloud of dust in the faces of the enemy, disordered their ranks, wrested their weapons from their hands, and diverted or repelled their ineffectual javelins. This accidental advantage was skilfully improved: the violence of the storm was magnified by the superstitious terrors of the Gauls, and they yielded without shame to the invisible powers of heaven, who seemed to militate on the side of the pious emperor. His victory was decisive, and the deaths of his two rivals were distinguished only by the difference of their characters. The rhetorician Eugenius, who had almost acquired the dominion of the world, was reduced to implore the mercy of the conqueror, and the unrelenting soldiers separated his head from his body as he lay prostrate at the feet of Theodosius. Arbogastes, after the loss of a battle in which he had discharged the duties of a soldier and a general, wandered several days among the mountains. But when he was convinced that his cause was desperate, and his escape impracticable, the intrepid barbarian imitated the example of the ancient Romans, and turned his sword against his own breast. The fate of the empire was determined in a narrow corner of Italy; and the legitimate successor of the house of Valentinian embraced the archbishop of Milan, and graciously received the submission of the provinces of the West. Those provinces were involved in the guilt of rebellion; while the inflexible courage of Ambrose alone had resisted the claims of successful usurpation. With a manly freedom, which might have been fatal to any other subject, the archbishop rejected the gifts of Eugenius, declined his correspondence, and withdrew himself from Milan to avoid the odious presence of a tyrant whose downfall he predicted in discreet and ambiguous language. The merit of Ambrose was applauded by the conqueror, who secured the attachment of the people by his alliance with the church: and the clemency of Theodosius is ascribed to the humane intercession of the archbishop of Milan.

THE DEATH OF THEODOSIUS

After the defeat of Eugenius, the merit, as well as the authority, of Theodosius was cheerfully acknowledged by all the inhabitants of the Roman world. The experience of his past conduct encouraged the most pleasing expectations of his future reign; and the age of the emperor, which did not exceed fifty years, seemed to extend the prospect of the public felicity. His death, only four months after his victory, was considered by the people as an unforeseen and fatal event, which destroyed in a moment the hopes of the rising generation. But the indulgence of ease and luxury had secretly nourished the principles of disease. The strength of Theodosius was unable to support the sudden and violent transition from the palace to the camp; and the increasing symptoms of a dropsy announced the speedy dissolution of the emperor. The opinion, and perhaps the interest, of the public had confirmed the division of the Eastern and Western empires; and the two royal youths, Arcadius and Honorius, who had already obtained, from the tenderness of their father, the title of Augustus, were destined to fill the thrones of Constantinople and of Rome. Those princes were not permitted to share the danger and glory of the civil war; but as soon as Theodosius had triumphed over his unworthy rivals, he called his younger son, Honorius, to enjoy the fruits of the victory, and to receive the sceptre of the West from the hands of his dying father. The arrival of Honorius at Milan was welcomed by a splendid exhibition of the games of the circus; and the emperor, though he was oppressed by the weight of his disorder, contributed by his presence to the public joy. But the remains of his strength were exhausted by the painful effort which he made to assist at the spectacles of the morning. Honorius supplied, during the rest of the day, the place of his father; and the great Theodosius expired in the ensuing night. Notwithstanding the recent animosities of a civil war, his death was universally lamented. The barbarians, whom he had vanquished, and the churchmen, by whom he had been subdued, celebrated with loud and sincere applause the qualities of the deceased emperor which appeared the most valuable in their eyes. The Romans were terrified by the impending dangers of a feeble and divided administration; and every disgraceful moment of the unfortunate reigns of Arcadius and Honorius revived the memory of their irreparable loss.

In the faithful picture of the virtues of Theodosius, his imperfections have not been dissembled; the act of cruelty, and the habits of indolence, which tarnished the glory of one of the greatest of the Roman princes. An historian perpetually adverse to the fame of Theodosius has exaggerated his vices and their pernicious effects; he boldly asserts that every rank of subjects imitated the effeminate manners of their sovereign; that every species of corruption polluted the course of public and private life; and that the feeble restraints of order and decency were insufficient to resist the progress of that degenerate spirit which sacrifices, without a blush, the consideration of duty and interest to the base indulgence of sloth and appetite. The complaints of contemporary writers, who deplore the increase of luxury and depravation of manners, are commonly expressive of their peculiar temper and situation. There are few observers who possess a clear and comprehensive view of the revolutions of society, and who are capable of discovering the nice and secret springs of action which impel, in the same uniform direction, the blind and capricious passions of a multitude of individuals. If it can be affirmed, with any degree of truth, that the luxury of the Romans was more shameless and dissolute in the reign of Theodosius than in the age of Constantine, perhaps, or of Augustus, the alteration cannot be ascribed to any beneficial improvements which had gradually increased the stock of national riches. A long period of calamity or decay must have checked the industry and diminished the wealth of the people; and their profuse luxury must have been the result of that indolent despair which enjoys the present hour and declines the thoughts of futurity. The uncertain condition of their property discouraged the subjects of Theodosius from engaging in those useful and laborious undertakings which require an immediate expense, and promise a slow and distant advantage. The frequent examples of ruin and desolation tempted them not to spare the remains of a patrimony which might, every hour, become the prey of the rapacious Goth. And the mad prodigality which prevails in the confusion of a shipwreck or a siege may serve to explain the progress of luxury amidst the misfortunes and terrors of a sinking nation.

The effeminate luxury, which infected the manners of courts and cities, had instilled a secret and destructive poison into the camps of the legions; and their degeneracy has been marked by the pen of a military writer, who had accurately studied the genuine and ancient principles of Roman discipline. It is the just and important observation of Vegetius, that the infantry was invariably covered with defensive armour from the foundation of the city to the reign of the emperor Gratian. The relaxation of discipline and the disuse of exercise rendered the soldiers less able and less willing to support the fatigues of the service; they complained of the weight of the armour, which they seldom wore; and they successively obtained the permission of laying aside both their cuirasses and their helmets. The heavy weapons of their ancestors, the short sword and the formidable *pilum,* which had subdued the world, insensibly dropped from their feeble hands. As the use of the shield is incompatible with that of the bow, they reluctantly marched into the field, condemned to suffer either the pain of wounds or the ignominy of flight, and always disposed to prefer the more shameful alternative. The cavalry of the Goths, the Huns, and the Alani, had felt the benefits and adopted the use of defensive armour; and, as they excelled in the management of missile weapons, they easily overwhelmed the naked and trembling legions, whose heads and breasts were exposed, without defence, to the arrows of the barbarians. The loss of armies, the destruction of cities, and the dishonour of the Roman name, ineffectually solicited the successors of Gratian to restore the helmets and cuirasses of the infantry. The enervated soldiers abandoned their own and the public defence; and their pusillanimous indolence may be considered as the immediate cause of the downfall of the empire.

28.

THE END OF PAGANISM. DESTRUCTION OF THE
TEMPLE OF SERAPIS. PROHIBITION OF PAGAN RITES.
WORSHIP OF THE CHRISTIAN MARTYRS AND
REVIVAL OF POLYTHEISTIC PRACTICES

THE RUIN of Paganism, in the age of Theodosius, is perhaps
the only example of the total extirpation of any ancient and
popular superstition, and may therefore deserve to be considered as a singular event in the history of the human mind.
The Christians, more especially the clergy, had impatiently
supported the prudent delays of Constantine and the equal
toleration of the elder Valentinian; nor could they deem
their conquest perfect or secure as long as their adversaries
were permitted to exist. The influence which Ambrose and his
brethren had acquired over the youth of Gratian and the
piety of Theodosius was employed to infuse the maxims of
persecution into the breasts of their Imperial proselytes. Two
specious principles of religious jurisprudence were established,
from whence they deduced a direct and rigorous conclusion
against the subjects of the empire who still adhered to the
ceremonies of their ancestors: *that* the magistrate is, in some
measure, guilty of the crimes which he neglects to prohibit or
to punish; and *that* the idolatrous worship of fabulous deities
and real dæmons is the most abominable crime against the
supreme majesty of the Creator. The laws of Moses and the
examples of Jewish history were hastily, perhaps erroneously,
applied by the clergy to the mild and universal reign of
Christianity. The zeal of the emperors was excited to vindicate
their own honour and that of the Deity; and the temples of
the Roman world were subverted about sixty years after the
conversion of Constantine.

From the age of Numa to the reign of Gratian, the Romans
preserved succession of the several colleges of the sacerdotal
order. Fifteen PONTIFFS exercised their supreme jurisdiction

over all things and persons that were consecrated to the service of the gods; and the various questions which perpetually arose in a loose and traditionary system were submitted to the judgment of their holy tribunal. Fifteen grave and learned Augurs observed the face of the heavens, and prescribed the actions of heroes according to the flight of birds. Fifteen keepers of the Sibylline books (their name of Quindecemvirs was derived from their number) occasionally consulted the history of future, and, as it should seem, of contingent events. Six Vestals devoted their virginity to the guard of the sacred fire and of the unknown pledges of the duration of Rome, which no mortal had been suffered to behold with impunity. Seven Epulos prepared the table of the gods, conducted the solemn procession, and regulated the ceremonies of the annual festival. The three Flamens of Jupiter, of Mars, and of Quirinus, were considered as the peculiar ministers of the three most powerful deities, who watched over the fate of Rome and of the universe. The King of the Sacrifices represented the person of Numa and of his successors in the religious functions, which could be performed only by royal hands. The confraternities of the Salians, the Lupercals, etc., practised such rites as might extort a smile of contempt from every reasonable man, with a lively confidence of recommending themselves to the favour of the immortal gods. The authority which the Roman priests had formerly obtained in the counsels of the republic was gradually abolished by the establishment of monarchy and the removal of the seat of empire. But the dignity of their sacred character was still protected by the laws and manners of their country; and they still continued, more especially the college of pontiffs, to exercise in the capital, and sometimes in the provinces, the rights of their ecclesiastical and civil jurisdiction. Their robes of purple, chariots of state, and sumptuous entertainments, attracted the admiration of the people; and they received, from the consecrated lands and the public revenue, an ample stipend, which liberally supported the splendour of the priesthood and all the expenses of the religious worship of the state. As the service of the altar was not incompatible with the command of armies, the Romans, after their consulships and triumphs, aspired to the place of pontiff or of augur; the seats of Cicero and Pompey were filled, in the fourth century, by the most illustrious members of the senate; and the dignity of their birth reflected additional splendour on their sacerdotal character. The fifteen priests who composed the college of pontiffs enjoyed a more distinguished rank as the companions of their sovereign; and the Christian emperors condescended to accept the robe and ensigns which were appropriated to the office of supreme pontiff. But when Gratian ascended the throne, more scrupulous or more enlightened, he sternly rejected those profane symbols; applied to the service of the state or of the church the revenues of the priests and vestals; abolished their honours and immunities; and dissolved the ancient fabric of Roman superstition, which was supported by the opinions and habits of eleven hundred years. Paganism was still the constitutional religion of the senate. The hall or temple in which they assembled was adorned by the statue and altar of Victory; a majestic female standing on a globe, with flowing garments, expanded wings, and a crown of laurel in her outstretched hand. The senators were sworn on the altar of the goddess to observe the laws of the emperor and of the empire; and a solemn offering of wine and incense was the ordinary prelude of their public deliberations. The removal of this ancient monument was the only injury which Constantius had offered to the superstition of the Romans. The altar of Victory was again restored by Julian, tolerated by Valentinian, and once more banished from the senate by the zeal of Gratian. But the emperor yet spared the statues of the gods which were exposed to the public veneration: four hundred and twenty-four temples, or chapels, still remained to satisfy the devotion of the people, and in every quarter of Rome the delicacy of the Christians was offended by the fumes of idolatrous sacrifice.

But the Christians formed the least numerous party in the senate of Rome; and it was only by their absence that they could express their dissent from the legal, though profane, acts of a Pagan majority. In that assembly the dying embers of freedom were, for a moment, revived and inflamed by the breath of fanaticism. Four respectable deputations were successively voted to the Imperial court, to represent the grievances of the priesthood and the senate, and to solicit the restoration of the altar of Victory. The conduct of this important business was intrusted to the eloquent Symmachus, a wealthy and noble senator, who united the sacred characters of pontiff and augur with the civil dignities of proconsul of Africa and prefect of the city. The breast of Symmachus was animated by the warmest zeal for the cause of expiring Paganism; and his religious antagonists lamented the abuse of his genius and the inefficacy of his moral virtues. The orator, whose petition is extant to the emperor Valentinian, was conscious of the difficulty and danger of the office which he had assumed. He cautiously avoids every topic which might appear to reflect on the religion of his sovereign; humbly declares that prayers and entreaties are his only arms; and artfully draws his arguments from the schools of rhetoric rather than from those of philosophy. Symmachus endeavours to seduce the imagination of a young prince, by displaying the attributes of the goddess of Victory; he insinuates that the confiscation of the revenues which were consecrated to the service of the gods was a measure unworthy of his liberal and disinterested character; and he maintains that the Roman sacrifices would be deprived of their force and energy, if they were no longer celebrated at the expense as well as in the name of the republic. Even scepticism is made to supply an apology for superstition. The great and incomprehensible *secret* of the universe eludes the inquiry of man. Where reason cannot instruct, custom may be permitted to guide; and every nation seems to consult the dictates of prudence, by a faithful attachment to those rites and opinions which have received the sanction of ages. If those ages have been crowned with glory and prosperity; if the devout people has frequently obtained the blessings which they have solicited at the altars of the gods,—it must appear still more advisable to persist in the same salutary practice, and not to risk the unknown perils that may attend any rash innovations. The test of antiquity and success was applied with singular advantage to the religion of Numa; and ROME herself, the celestial genius that presided over the fates of the city, is introduced by the orator to plead her own cause before the tribunal of the emperors. "Most excellent princes," says the venerable matron, "fathers of your country! pity and respect my age, which has hitherto flowed in an uninterrupted course of piety. Since I do not repent, permit me to continue in the practice of my ancient rites. Since I am born free, allow me to enjoy my domestic institutions. This religion has reduced the world under my laws. These rites have repelled Hannibal from the city, and the Gauls from the Capitol. Were my grey hairs reserved for such intolerable disgrace? I am ignorant of the new system that I am required to adopt; but I am well assured that the correction of old age is always an ungrateful and ignominious office." The fears of the people supplied what the discretion of the orator had suppressed; and the calamities which afflicted or threatened the declining empire were unanimously imputed by the Pagans to the new religion of Christ and of Constantine.

But the hopes of Symmachus were repeatedly baffled by the firm and dexterous opposition of the archbishop of Milan, who fortified the emperors against the fallacious eloquence of the advocate of Rome. In this controversy Ambrose condescends to speak the language of a philosopher, and to ask, with some contempt, why it should be thought necessary to introduce an imaginary and invisible power as the cause of those victories, which were sufficiently explained by the valour and discipline of the legions. He justly derides the absurd reverence for antiquity, which could only tend to discourage the improvements of art and to replunge the human race into their original barbarism. From thence gradually rising to a more lofty and theological tone, he pronounces that Christianity alone is the doctrine of truth and salvation, and that every mode of Polytheism conducts its deluded votaries through the paths of error to the abyss of eternal perdition. Arguments like these, when they were suggested by a favourite bishop, had power to prevent the restoration of the altar of Victory; but the same arguments fell with much more energy and effect from the mouth of a conqueror, and the gods of antiquity were dragged in triumph at the chariot-wheels of Theodosius. In a full meeting of the senate the emperor proposed, according to the forms of the republic, the important question, whether the worship of Jupiter or that of Christ should be the religion of the Romans? The liberty of suffrages, which he affected to allow, was destroyed by the hopes and fears that his presence inspired; and the arbitrary exile of Symmachus was a recent admonition that it might be dangerous to oppose the wishes of the monarch. On a regular division of the senate, Jupiter was condemned and degraded by the sense of a very large majority; and it is rather surprising that any members should be found bold enough to declare, by their speeches and votes, that they were still attached to the interest of an abdicated deity. The hasty conversion of the senate must be attributed either to supernatural or to sordid motives; and many of these reluctant proselytes betrayed, on every favourable occasion, their secret disposition to throw aside the mask of odious dissimulation. But they were gradually fixed in the new religion, as the cause of the ancient became more hopeless; they yielded to the authority of the emperor, to the fashion of the times, and to the entreaties of their wives and children, who were instigated and governed by the clergy of Rome and the monks of the East. The edifying example of the Anician family was soon imitated by the rest of the nobility: the Bassi, the Paullini, the Gracchi, embraced the Christian religion; and "the luminaries of the world, the venerable assembly of Catos (such are the high-flown expressions of Prudentius), were impatient to strip themselves of their pontifical garment; to cast the skin of the old serpent; to assume the snowy robes of baptismal innocence; and to humble the pride of the consular fasces before the tombs of the martyrs." The citizens, who subsisted by their own industry, and the populace, who were supported by the public liberality, filled the churches of the Lateran and Vatican with an incessant throng of devout proselytes. The decrees of the senate, which proscribed the worship of idols, were ratified by the general consent of the Romans; the splendour of the Capitol was defaced, and the solitary temples were abandoned to ruin and contempt. Rome submitted to the yoke of the Gospel; and the vanquished provinces had not yet lost their reverence for the name and authority of Rome.

The filial piety of the emperors themselves engaged them to proceed with some caution and tenderness in the reformation of the eternal city. Those absolute monarchs acted with less regard to the prejudices of the provincials. The pious labour, which had been suspended near twenty years since the death of Constantius, was vigorously resumed, and finally accomplished, by the zeal of Theodosius. Whilst that warlike prince yet struggled with the Goths, not for the glory, but for the safety of the republic, he ventured to offend a considerable party of his subjects, by some acts which might perhaps secure the protection of Heaven, but which must seem rash and unseasonable in the eye of human prudence. The success of his first experiments against the Pagans encouraged the pious emperor to reiterate and enforce his edicts of proscription: the same laws which had been originally published in the provinces of the East were applied, after the defeat of Maximus, to the whole extent of the Western empire; and every victory of the orthodox Theodosius contributed to the triumph of the Christian and catholic faith. He attacked superstition in her most vital part, by prohibiting the use of sacrifices, which he declared to be criminal as well as infamous; and if the terms of his edicts more strictly condemned the impious curiosity which examined the entrails of the victims, every subsequent explanation tended to involve in the same guilt the general practice of *immolation,* which essentially constituted the religion of the Pagans. As the temples had been erected for the purpose of sacrifice, it was the duty of a benevolent prince to remove from his subjects the dangerous temptation of offending against the laws which he had enacted. A special commission was granted to Cynegius, the Prætorian prefect of the East, and afterwards to the counts Jovius and Gaudentius, two officers of distinguished rank in the West, by which they were directed to shut the temples, to seize or destroy the instruments of idolatry, to abolish the privileges of the priests, and to confiscate the consecrated property for the benefit of the emperor, of the church, or of the army. Here the desolation might have stopped: and the naked edifices, which were no longer employed in the service of idolatry, might have been protected from the destructive rage of fanaticism. Many of those temples were the most splendid and beautiful monuments of Grecian architecture: and the emperor himself was interested not to deface the splendour of his own cities, or to diminish the value of his own possessions. Those stately edifices might be suffered to remain, as so many lasting trophies of the victory of Christ. In the decline of the arts, they might be usefully converted into magazines, manufactures, or places of public assembly: and perhaps, when the walls of the temple had been sufficiently purified by holy rites, the worship of the true Deity might be allowed to expiate the ancient guilt of idolatry. But as long as they subsisted, the Pagans fondly cherished the secret hope that an auspicious revolution, a second Julian, might again restore the altars of the gods: and the earnestness with which they addressed their unavailing prayers to the throne increased the zeal of the Christian reformers to extirpate, without mercy, the root of superstition. The laws of the emperors exhibit some symptoms of a milder disposition: but their cold and languid efforts were insufficient to stem the torrent of enthusiasm and rapine, which was conducted, or rather impelled, by the spiritual rulers of the church. In Gaul, the holy Martin, bishop of Tours,[1] marched at the head of his faithful monks to destroy the idols, the temples, and the consecrated trees of his extensive diocese; and, in the execution of this arduous task, the prudent reader will judge whether Martin was supported by the aid of miraculous powers or of carnal weapons. In Syria, the divine and excellent Marcellus, as he is styled by Theodoret, a bishop animated with apostolic fervour, resolved to level with the ground the stately temples within the diocese of Apamea. His attack was resisted by the skill and solidity with which the temple of Jupiter had been constructed. The building was seated on an eminence: on each of the four sides the lofty roof was supported by fifteen massy columns, sixteen feet in circumference; and the large stones of which they were composed were firmly cemented with lead and iron. The force of the strongest and sharpest tools had been tried without effect. It was found necessary to undermine the foundations of the columns, which fell down as soon as the temporary wooden props had been consumed with fire; and the difficulties of the enterprise are described under the allegory of a black dæmon, who retarded, though he could not defeat, the operations of the Christian engineers. Elated with victory, Marcellus took the field in person against the powers of darkness; a numerous troop of soldiers and gladiators marched under the episcopal banner, and he successively attacked the villages and country temples of the diocese of Apamea. Whenever any resistance or danger was apprehended, the champion of the faith, whose lameness would not allow him either to fight or fly, placed himself at a convenient distance, beyond the reach of darts. But this prudence was the occasion of his death; he was surprised and slain by a body of exasperated rustics; and the synod of the province pronounced, without hesitation, that the holy Marcellus had sacrificed his life in the cause of God. In the support of this cause, the monks, who rushed

---

[1] See the Life of Martin by Sulpicius Severus. The saint once mistook (as Don Quixote might have done) an harmless funeral for an idolatrous procession, and imprudently committed a miracle.

with tumultuous fury from the desert, distinguished themselves by their zeal and diligence. They deserved the enmity of the Pagans; and some of them might deserve the reproaches of avarice and intemperance—of avarice, which they gratified with holy plunder; and of intemperance, which they indulged at the expense of the people, who foolishly admired their tattered garments, loud psalmody, and artificial paleness.[1] A small number of temples was protected by the fears, the venality, the taste, or the prudence of the civil and ecclesiastical governors. The temple of the Celestial Venus at Carthage, whose sacred precincts formed a circumference of two miles, was judiciously converted into a Christian church; and a similar consecration has preserved inviolate the majestic dome of the Pantheon at Rome. But in almost every province of the Roman world, an army of fanatics, without authority and without discipline, invaded the peaceful inhabitants; and the ruin of the fairest structures of antiquity still displays the ravages of *those* barbarians who alone had time and inclination to execute such laborious destruction.

THE DESTRUCTION OF THE TEMPLE OF SERAPIS

In this wide and various prospect of devastation, the spectator may distinguish the ruins of the temple of Serapis, at Alexandria. Serapis does not appear to have been one of the native gods, or monsters, who sprung from the fruitful soil of superstitious Egypt. The first of the Ptolemies had been commanded, by a dream, to import the mysterious stranger from the coast of Pontus, where he had been long adored by the inhabitants of Sinope; but his attributes and his reign were so imperfectly understood, that it became a subject of dispute whether he represented the bright orb of day, or the gloomy monarch of the subterraneous regions. The Egyptians, who were obstinately devoted to the religion of their fathers, refused to admit this foreign deity within the walls of their cities. But the obsequious priests, who were seduced by the liberality of the Ptolemies, submitted, without resistance, to the power of the god of Pontus: an honourable and domestic genealogy was provided; and this fortunate usurper was introduced into the throne and bed of Osiris,

---

[1] Libanius. He rails at these black-garbed men, the Christian monks, who eat more than elephants. Poor elephants! *they* are temperate animals.

the husband of Isis, and the celestial monarch of Egypt. Alexandria, which claimed his peculiar protection, gloried in the name of the city of Serapis. His temple, which rivalled the pride and magnificence of the Capitol, was erected on the spacious summit of an artificial mount, raised one hundred steps above the level of the adjacent parts of the city; and the interior cavity was strongly supported by arches, and distributed into vaults and subterraneous apartments. The consecrated buildings were surrounded by a quadrangular portico; the stately halls and exquisite statues displayed the triumph of the arts; and the treasures of ancient learning were preserved in the famous Alexandrian library, which had arisen with new splendour from its ashes. After the edicts of Theodosius had severely prohibited the sacrifices of the Pagans, they were still tolerated in the city and temple of Serapis; and this singular indulgence was imprudently ascribed to the superstitious terrors of the Christians themselves: as if they had feared to abolish those ancient rites which could alone secure the inundations of the Nile, the harvests of Egypt, and the subsistence of Constantinople.

At that time the archiepiscopal throne of Alexandria was filled by Theophilus, the perpetual enemy of peace and virtue; a bold, bad man, whose hands were alternately polluted with gold and with blood. His pious indignation was excited by the honours of Serapis; and the insults which he offered to an ancient chapel of Bacchus convinced the Pagans that he meditated a more important and dangerous enterprise. In the tumultuous capital of Egypt, the slightest provocation was sufficient to inflame a civil war. The votaries of Serapis, whose strength and numbers were much inferior to those of their antagonists, rose in arms at the instigation of the philosopher Olympius, who exhorted them to die in the defence of the altars of the gods. These Pagan fanatics fortified themselves in the temple, or rather fortress, of Serapis; repelled the besiegers by daring sallies and resolute defence; and, by the inhuman cruelties which they exercised on their Christian prisoners, obtained the last consolation of despair. The efforts of the prudent magistrate were usefully exerted for the establishment of a truce till the answer of Theodosius should determine the fate of Serapis. The two parties assembled, without arms, in the principal square; and the Imperial rescript was publicly read. But when a sentence of destruction against the idols of Alexandria was pronounced, the Christians sent up a shout of joy and exultation, whilst the unfortunate Pagans, whose fury had given way to consternation, retired with hasty and silent steps, and eluded, by their flight or obscurity, the resentment of their enemies. Theophilus proceeded to demolish the temple of Serapis, without any other difficulties than those which he found in the weight and solidity of the materials; but these obstacles proved so insuperable, that he was obliged to leave the foundations, and to content himself with reducing the edifice itself to a heap of rubbish, a part of which was soon afterwards cleared away, to make room for a church erected in honour of the Christian martyrs. The valuable library of Alexandria was pillaged or destroyed; and near twenty years afterwards, the appearance of the empty shelves excited the regret and indignation of every spectator whose mind was not totally darkened by religious prejudice. The compositions of ancient genius, so many of which have irretrievably perished, might surely have been excepted from the wreck of idolatry, for the amusement and instruction of succeeding ages; and either the zeal or the avarice of the archbishop might have been satiated with the rich spoils which were the reward of his victory. While the images and vases of gold and silver were carefully melted, and those of a less valuable metal were contemptuously broken and cast into the streets, Theophilus laboured to expose the frauds and vices of the ministers of the idols: their dexterity in the management of the loadstone; their secret methods of introducing an human actor into a hollow statue; and their scandalous abuse of the confidence of devout husbands and unsuspecting females.[1] Charges like these may seem to deserve some degree of credit, as they are not repugnant to the crafty and interested spirit of superstition. But the same spirit is equally prone to the base practice of insulting and calumniating a fallen enemy; and our belief is naturally checked by the reflection that it is much less difficult to invent a fictitious story than to support a practical fraud. The colossal statue of Serapis was involved in the ruin of his temple and religion. A great number of plates of

---

[1] Rufinus names the priest of Saturn who, in the character of the god, familiarly conversed with many pious ladies of quality; till he betrayed himself, in a moment of transport, when he could not disguise the tone of his voice. The authentic and impartial narrative of Æschines, and the adventure of Mundus, may prove that such amorous frauds have been practised with success.

different metals, artificially joined together, composed the majestic figure of the deity, who touched on either side the walls of the sanctuary. The aspect of Serapis, his sitting posture, and the sceptre which he bore in his left hand, were extremely similar to the ordinary representations of Jupiter. He was distinguished from Jupiter by the basket, or bushel, which was placed on his head; and by the emblematic monster which he held in his right hand; the head and body of a serpent branching into three tails, which were again terminated by the triple heads of a dog, a lion, and a wolf. It was confidently affirmed, that, if any impious hand should dare to violate the majesty of the god, the heavens and the earth would instantly return to their original chaos. An intrepid soldier, animated by zeal, and armed with a weighty battle-axe, ascended the ladder; and even the Christian multitude expected with some anxiety the event of the combat. He aimed a vigorous stroke against the cheek of Serapis; the cheek fell to the ground; the thunder was still silent, and both the heavens and the earth continued to preserve their accustomed order and tranquillity. The victorious soldier repeated his blows: the huge idol was overthrown and broken in pieces; and the limbs of Serapis were ignominiously dragged through the streets of Alexandria. His mangled carcase was burnt in the amphitheatre, amidst the shouts of the populace; and many persons attributed their conversion to this discovery of the impotence of their tutelar deity. The popular modes of religion, that propose any visible and material objects of worship, have the advantage of adapting and familiarising themselves to the senses of mankind; but this advantage is counterbalanced by the various and inevitable accidents to which the faith of the idolater is exposed. It is scarcely possible that, in every disposition of mind, he should preserve his implicit reverence for the idols, or the relics, which the naked eye and the profane hand are unable to distinguish from the most common productions of art or nature; and if, in the hour of danger, their secret and miraculous virtue does not operate for their own preservation, he scorns the vain apologies of his priests, and justly derides the object and the folly of his superstitious attachment. After the fall of Serapis, some hopes were still entertained by the Pagans that the Nile would refuse his annual supply to the impious masters of Egypt; and the extraordinary delay of the inundation seemed to announce the displeasure of the river-god. But this delay was soon compensated by the rapid swell of the waters. They suddenly rose to such an unusual height as to comfort the discontented party with the pleasing expectation of a deluge; till the peaceful river again subsided to the well-known and fertilising level of sixteen cubits, or about thirty English feet.

THE PROHIBITION OF PAGAN RITES

The temples of the Roman empire were deserted or destroyed; but the ingenious superstition of the Pagans still attempted to elude the laws of Theodosius, by which all sacrifices had been severely prohibited. The inhabitants of the country, whose conduct was less exposed to the eye of malicious curiosity, disguised their *religious* under the appearance of *convivial* meetings. On the days of solemn festivals they assembled in great numbers under the spreading shade of some consecrated trees; sheep and oxen were slaughtered and roasted; and this rural entertainment was sanctified by the use of incense and by the hymns which were sung in honour of the gods. But it was alleged that, as no part of the animal was made a burnt-offering, as no altar was provided to receive the blood, and as the previous oblation of salt cakes and the concluding ceremony of libations were carefully omitted, these festal meetings did not involve the guests in the guilt or penalty of an illegal sacrifice. Whatever might be the truth of the facts or the merit of the distinction, these vain pretences were swept away by the last edict of Theodosius, which inflicted a deadly wound on the superstition of the Pagans. This prohibitory law is expressed in the most absolute and comprehensive terms. "It is our will and pleasure," says the emperor, "that none of our subjects, whether magistrates or private citizens, however exalted or however humble may be their rank and condition, shall presume in any city or in any place to worship an inanimate idol by the sacrifice of a guiltless victim." The act of sacrificing and the practice of divination by the entrails of the victim are declared (without any regard to the object of the inquiry) a crime of high-treason against the state, which can be expiated only by the death of the guilty. The rites of Pagan superstition which might seem less bloody and atrocious are abolished as highly injurious to the truth and honour of religion; luminaries, garlands, frankincense, and libations of wine are specially enumerated and condemned; and the harmless claims of the domestic genius, of the household gods are included in this rigorous proscription. The use of any of these profane and illegal ceremonies subjects the offender to the forfeiture of the house or estate where they have been performed; and if he has artfully chosen the property of another for the scene of his impiety, he is compelled to discharge, without delay, a heavy fine of twenty-five pounds of gold, or more than one thousand pounds sterling. A fine not less considerable is imposed on the connivance of the secret enemies of religion who shall neglect the duty of their respective stations, either to reveal or to punish the guilt of idolatry. Such was the persecuting spirit of the laws of Theodosius, which were repeatedly enforced by his sons and grandsons, with the loud and unanimous applause of the Christian world.

In the cruel reigns of Decius and Diocletian Christianity had been proscribed, as a revolt from the ancient and hereditary religion of the empire; and the unjust suspicions which were entertained of a dark and dangerous faction were in some measure countenanced by the inseparable union and rapid conquests of the catholic church. But the same excuses of fear and ignorance cannot be applied to the Christian emperors, who violated the precepts of humanity and of the Gospel. The experience of ages had betrayed the weakness as well as folly of Paganism; the light of reason and of faith had already exposed to the greatest part of mankind the vanity of idols; and the declining sect, which still adhered to their worship, might have been permitted to enjoy in peace and obscurity the religious customs of their ancestors. Had the Pagans been animated by the undaunted zeal which possessed the minds of the primitive believers, the triumph of the church must have been stained with blood; and the martyrs of Jupiter and Apollo might have embraced the glorious opportunity of devoting their lives and fortunes at the foot of their altars. But such obstinate zeal was not congenial to the loose and careless temper of Polytheism. The violent and repeated strokes of the orthodox princes were broken by the soft and yielding substance against which they were directed; and the ready obedience of the Pagans protected them from the pains and penalties of the Theodosian Code. Instead of asserting that the authority of the gods was superior to that of the emperor, they desisted, with a plaintive murmur, from the use of those sacred rites which their sovereign had condemned. If they were sometimes tempted by a sally of passion, or by the hopes of concealment, to indulge their favourite superstition, their humble repentance disarmed the severity of the Christian magistrate, and they seldom refused to atone for their rashness by submitting, with some secret reluctance, to the yoke of the Gospel. The churches were filled with the increasing multitude of these unworthy proselytes, who had conformed, from temporal motives, to the reigning religion; and whilst they devoutly imitated the postures and recited the prayers of the faithful, they satisfied their conscience by the silent and sincere invocation of the gods of antiquity. If the Pagans wanted patience to suffer, they wanted spirit to resist; and the scattered myriads, who deplored the ruin of the temples, yielded, without a contest, to the fortune of their adversaries. The disorderly opposition of the peasants of Syria and the populace of Alexandria to the rage of private fanaticism was silenced by the name and authority of the emperor. The Pagans of the West, without contributing to the elevation of Eugenius, disgraced by their partial attachment the cause and character of the usurper. The clergy vehemently exclaimed that he aggravated the crime of rebellion by the guilt of apostasy; that, by his permission, the altar of Victory was again restored; and that the idolatrous symbols of Jupiter and Hercules were displayed in the field against the invincible standard of the cross. But the vain hopes of the Pagans were soon annihilated by the defeat of Eugenius; and they were left exposed to the resentment of the conqueror, who laboured to deserve the favour of Heaven by the extirpation of idolatry.

A nation of slaves is always prepared to applaud the clemency of their master who, in the abuse of absolute power, does not proceed to the last extremes of injustice and oppression. Theodosius might undoubtedly have proposed to his Pagan subjects the alternative of baptism or of death; and the eloquent Libanius has praised the moderation of a prince who never enacted, by any positive law, that all his subjects should immediately embrace and practise the religion of their sovereign. The profession of Christianity was not made an essential qualification for the enjoyment of the civil rights of society, nor were any peculiar hardships imposed on the sectaries who credulously received the fables of Ovid and obstinately rejected the miracles of the Gospel. The palace, the schools, the army, and the senate were filled with declared and devout Pagans; they obtained, without distinction, the civil and military honours of the empire. Theodosius distinguished his liberal regard for virtue and genius by the consular dignity which he bestowed on Symmachus, and by the personal friendship which he expressed to Libanius; and the two eloquent apologists of Paganism were never required either to change or to dissemble their religious opinions. The Pagans were indulged in the most licentious freedom of speech and writing; the historical and philosophic remains of Eunapius, Zosimus, and the fanatic teachers of the school of Plato, betray the most furious animosity, and contain the sharpest invectives, against the sentiments and conduct of their victorious adversaries. If these audacious libels were publicly known, we must applaud the good sense of the Christian princes, who viewed with a smile of contempt the last struggles of superstition and despair. But the Imperial laws which prohibited the sacrifices and ceremonies of Paganism were rigidly executed; and every hour contributed to destroy the influence of a religion which was supported by custom rather than by argument. The devotion of the poet or the philosopher may be secretly nourished by prayer, meditation, and study; but the exercise of public worship appears to be the only solid foundation of the religious sentiments of the people, which derive their force from imitation and habit. The interruption of that public exercise may consummate, in the period of a few years, the important work of a national revolution. The memory of theological opinions cannot long be preserved without the artificial helps of priests, of temples, and of books. The ignorant vulgar, whose minds are still agitated by the blind hopes and terrors of superstition, will be soon persuaded by their superiors to direct their vows to the reigning deities of the age; and will insensibly imbibe an ardent zeal for the support and propagation of the new doctrine, which spiritual hunger at first compelled them to accept. The generation that arose in the world after the promulgation of the Imperial laws was attracted within the pale of the catholic church: and so rapid, yet so gentle, was the fall of Paganism, that only twenty-eight years after the death of Theodosius the faint and minute vestiges were no longer visible to the eye of the legislator.

WORSHIP OF THE CHRISTIAN MARTYRS AND REVIVAL OF POLYTHEISTIC PRACTICES

The ruin of the Pagan religion is described by the sophists as a dreadful and amazing prodigy, which covered the earth with darkness and restored the ancient dominion of chaos and of night. They relate in solemn and pathetic strains that the temples were converted into sepulchres, and that the holy places, which had been adorned by the statues of the gods, were basely polluted by the relics of Christian martyrs. "The monks" (a race of filthy animals, to whom Eunapius is tempted to refuse the name of men) "are the authors of the new worship, which, in the place of those deities who are conceived by the understanding, has substituted the meanest and most contemptible slaves. The heads, salted and pickled, of those infamous malefactors, who for the multitude of their crimes have suffered a just and ignominious death; their bodies, still marked by the impression of the lash and the scars of those tortures which were inflicted by the sentence of the magistrate; such" (continues Eunapius) "are the gods which the earth produces in our days; such are the martyrs, the supreme arbitrators of our prayers and petitions to the Deity, whose tombs are now consecrated as the objects of the veneration of the people." Without approving the malice, it is natural enough to share the surprise of the sophist, the spectator of a revolution which raised those obscure victims of the laws of Rome to the rank of celestial and invisible protectors of the Roman empire. The grateful respect of the Christians for the martyrs of the faith was exalted, by time and victory, into religious adoration; and the most illustrious of the saints and prophets were deservedly associated to the honours of the martyrs. One hundred and fifty years after the glorious deaths of St. Peter and St. Paul, the Vatican and the Ostian road were distinguished by the tombs, or rather by the trophies, of those spiritual heroes. In the age which followed the conversion of Constantine, the emperors, the consuls, and the generals of armies devoutly visited the sepulchres of a tentmaker and a fisherman; and their venerable bones were deposited under the altars of Christ, on which the bishops of the royal city continually offered the unbloody sacrifice. The new capital of the Eastern world, unable to produce any ancient and domestic trophies, was enriched by the spoils of dependent provinces. The bodies of St. Andrew, St. Luke, and St. Timothy had reposed near three hundred years in the obscure graves from whence they were transported, in solemn pomp, to the church of the apostles, which the magnificence of Constantine had founded on the banks of the Thracian Bosphorus. About fifty years afterwards the same banks were honoured by the presence of Samuel, the judge and prophet of the people of Israel. His ashes, deposited in a golden vase, and covered with a silken veil, were delivered by the bishops into each other's hands. The relics of Samuel were received by the people with the same joy and reverence which they would have shown to the living prophet; the highways, from Palestine to the gates of Constantinople, were filled with an uninterrupted procession; and the emperor Arcadius himself, at the head of the most illustrious members of the clergy and senate, advanced to meet his extraordinary guest, who had always deserved and claimed the homage of kings. The example of Rome and Constantinople confirmed the faith and discipline of the catholic world. The honours of the saints and martyrs, after a feeble and ineffectual murmur of profane reason, were universally established; and in the age of Ambrose and Jerom something was still deemed wanting to the sanctity of a Christian church, till it had been consecrated by some portion of holy relics, which fixed and inflamed the devotion of the faithful. In the long period of twelve hundred years, which elapsed between the reign of Constantine and the reformation of Luther, the worship of saints and relics corrupted the pure and perfect simplicity of the Christian model: and some symptoms of degeneracy may be observed even in the first generations which adopted and cherished this pernicious innovation.

I. The satisfactory experience that the relics of saints were more valuable than gold or precious stones stimulated the clergy to multiply the treasures of the church. Without much regard for truth or probability, they invented names for skeletons, and actions for names. The fame of the apostles, and of the holy men who had imitated their virtues, was darkened by religious fiction. To the invincible band of genuine and primitive martyrs they added myriads of imaginary heroes, who had never existed, except in the fancy of crafty or credulous legendaries; and there is reason to suspect that Tours might not be the only diocese in which the bones of a malefactor were adored instead of those of a saint.[1] A superstitious practice, which tended to increase the temptations of fraud and credulity, insensibly extinguished the light of history and of reason in the Christian world.

II. But the progress of superstition would have been much less rapid and victorious if the faith of the people had not been assisted by the seasonable aid of visions and miracles to ascertain the authenticity and virtue of the most suspicious relics. In the reign of the younger Theodosius, Lucian, a presbyter of Jerusalem, and the ecclesiastical minister of the village of Caphargamala, about twenty miles from the city, related a very singular dream, which, to remove his doubts, had been repeated on three successive Saturdays. A venerable figure stood before him, in the silence of the night, with a long beard, a white robe, and a gold rod; announced himself by the name of Gamaliel; and revealed to the astonished presbyter, that his own corpse, with the bodies of his son Abibas, his friend Nicodemus, and the illustrious Stephen, the first martyr of the Christian faith, were secretly buried in the adjacent field. He added, with some impatience, that it was time to release himself and his companions from their obscure prison; that their appearance would be salutary to a distressed world; and that they had made choice of Lucian to inform the bishop of Jerusalem of their situation and their wishes. The doubts and difficulties which still retarded this important discovery were successively removed by new visions; and the ground was opened by the bishop, in the presence of an innumerable multitude. The coffins of Gamaliel, of his son, and of his friend, were found in regular order; but when the fourth coffin, which contained the remains of Stephen, was shown to the light, the earth trembled, and an odour such as that of Paradise was smelt, which instantly cured the various diseases of seventy-three of the assistants. The companions of Stephen were left in their peaceful residence of Caphargamala; but the relics of the first martyr were transported, in solemn procession, to a church constructed in their honour on Mount Sion;

---

[1] Martin of Tours extorted this confession from the mouth of the dead man. The error is allowed to be natural; the discovery is supposed to be miraculous. Which of the two was likely to happen most frequently?

and the minute particles of those relics, a drop of blood,[1] or
the scrapings of a bone, were acknowledged, in almost every
province of the Roman world, to possess a divine and miraculous virtue. The grave and learned Augustin,[2] whose understanding scarcely admits the excuse of credulity, has attested
the innumerable prodigies which were performed in Africa by
the relics of St. Stephen; and this marvellous narrative is inserted in the elaborate work of the City of God, which the
bishop of Hippo designed as a solid and immortal proof of
the truth of Christianity. Augustin solemnly declares that he
has selected those miracles only which were publicly certified
by the persons who were either the objects, or the spectators,
of the power of the martyr. Many prodigies were omitted or
forgotten; and Hippo had been less favourably treated than
the other cities of the province. And yet the bishop enumerates
above seventy miracles, of which three were resurrections
from the dead, in the space of two years, and within the
limits of his own diocese.[3] If we enlarge our view to all the
dioceses, and all the saints, of the Christian world, it will not
be easy to calculate the fables, and the errors, which issued
from this inexhaustible source. But we may surely be allowed
to observe that a miracle, in that age of superstition and
credulity, lost its name and its merit, since it could scarcely
be considered as a deviation from the ordinary and established
laws of nature.

III. The innumerable miracles, of which the tombs of the
martyrs were the perpetual theatre, revealed to the pious believer the actual state and constitution of the invisible world;
and his religious speculations appeared to be founded on the
firm basis of fact and experience. Whatever might be the
condition of vulgar souls in the long interval between the
dissolution and the resurrection of their bodies, it was evident
that the superior spirits of the saints and martyrs did not
consume that portion of their existence in silent and inglorious

---

[1] A phial of St. Stephen's blood was annually liquefied at Naples till he
was superseded by St. Januarius.

[2] Augustin composed the two-and-twenty books de Civitate Dei in the space
of thirteen years, A.D. 413-426. His learning is too often borrowed, and his
arguments are too often his own; but the whole work claims the merit of a
magnificent design, vigorously, and not unskilfully, executed.

[3] See Augustin de Civitate Dei, l. xxii. c. 22, and the Appendix, which
contains two books of St. Stephen's miracles, by Evodius, bishop of Uzalis.
Freculphus has preserved a Gallic or Spanish proverb, "Whoever pretends to
have read all the miracles of St. Stephen, he lies."

sleep. It was evident (without presuming to determine the place of their habitation, or the nature of their felicity) that they enjoyed the lively and active consciousness of their happiness, their virtue, and their powers; and that they had already secured the possession of their eternal reward. The enlargement of their intellectual faculties surpassed the measure of the human imagination; since it was proved by *experience* that they were capable of hearing and understanding the various petitions of their numerous votaries, who, in the same moment of time, but in the most distant parts of the world, invoked the name and assistance of Stephen or of Martin. The confidence of their petitioners was founded on the persuasion that the saints, who reigned with Christ, cast an eye of pity upon earth; that they were warmly interested in the prosperity of the catholic church; and that the individuals who imitated the example of their faith and piety were the peculiar and favourite objects of their most tender regard. Sometimes, indeed, their friendship might be influenced by considerations of a less exalted kind: they viewed with partial affection the places which had been consecrated by their birth, their residence, their death, their burial, or the possession of their relics. The meaner passions of pride, avarice, and revenge, may be deemed unworthy of a celestial breast; yet the saints themselves condescended to testify their grateful approbation of the liberality of their votaries; and the sharpest bolts of punishment were hurled against those impious wretches who violated their magnificent shrines, or disbelieved their supernatural power. Atrocious, indeed, must have been the guilt, and strange would have been the scepticism, of those men, if they had obstinately resisted the proofs of a divine agency, which the elements, the whole range of the animal creation, and even the subtle and invisible operations of the human mind, were compelled to obey. The immediate, and almost instantaneous, effects, that were supposed to follow the prayer, or the offence, satisfied the Christians of the ample measure of favour and authority which the saints enjoyed in the presence of the Supreme God; and it seemed almost superfluous to inquire whether they were continually obliged to intercede before the throne of grace, or whether they might not be permitted to exercise, according to the dictates of their benevolence and justice, the delegated powers of their subordinate ministry. The imagination, which had been raised by a painful effort to the contemplation and worship of the Universal Cause, eagerly embraced such inferior objects of adoration as were more proportioned to its gross conceptions and imperfect faculties. The sublime and simple theology of the primitive Christians was gradually corrupted: and the MONARCHY of heaven, already clouded by metaphysical subtleties, was degraded by the introduction of a popular mythology, which tended to restore the reign of polytheism.

IV. As the objects of religion were gradually reduced to the standard of the imagination, the rites and ceremonies were introduced that seemed most powerfully to affect the senses of the vulgar. If, in the beginning of the fifth century, Tertullian, or Lactantius, had been suddenly raised from the dead, to assist at the festival of some popular saint or martyr, they would have gazed with astonishment and indignation on the profane spectacle which had succeeded to the pure and spiritual worship of a Christian congregation. As soon as the doors of the church were thrown open, they must have been offended by the smoke of incense, the perfume of flowers, and the glare of lamps and tapers, which diffused, at noon-day, a gaudy, superfluous, and, in their opinion, a sacrilegious light. If they approached the balustrade of the altar, they made their way through the prostrate crowd, consisting, for the most part, of strangers and pilgrims, who resorted to the city on the vigil of the feast; and who already felt the strong intoxication of fanaticism, and, perhaps, of wine. Their devout kisses were imprinted on the walls and pavement of the sacred edifice; and their fervent prayers were directed, whatever might be the language of their church, to the bones, the blood, or the ashes of the saint, which were usually concealed, by a linen or silken veil, from the eyes of the vulgar. The Christians frequented the tombs of the martyrs, in the hope of obtaining, from their powerful intercession, every sort of spiritual, but more especially of temporal, blessings. They implored the preservation of their health, or the cure of their infirmities; the fruitfulness of their barren wives, or the safety and happiness of their children. Whenever they undertook any distant or dangerous journey, they requested that the holy martyrs would be their guides and protectors on the road; and if they returned without having experienced any misfortune, they again hastened to the tombs of the martyrs, to celebrate, with grateful thanksgivings, their obligations to the memory and relics of those heavenly patrons. The walls were hung round with symbols of the favours which they had received; eyes, and hands, and feet, of gold and silver: and edifying pictures, which could not long escape the abuse of indiscreet or idolatrous devotion, represented the image, the attributes, and the miracles of the tutelar saint. The same uniform original spirit of superstition might suggest, in the most distant ages and countries, the same methods of deceiving the credulity, and of affecting the senses of mankind: but it must ingenuously be confessed that the ministers of the catholic church imitated the profane model which they were impatient to destroy. The most respectable bishops had persuaded themselves that the ignorant rustics would more cheerfully renounce the superstitions of Paganism, if they found some resemblance, some compensation, in the bosom of Christianity. The religion of Constantine achieved, in less than a century, the final conquest of the Roman empire: but the victors themselves were insensibly subdued by the arts of their vanquished rivals.

After Theodosius the western and eastern halves of the empire were finally separated. His sons Arcadius and Honorius ruled respectively in the East and the West. Honorius was a feeble character and the dominant figures in the West were his administrator, Rufinus, and Stilicho, a Vandal, able both as a general and a negotiator. His part in the latter role is obscure, and in his campaigns he was thwarted by the growing antipathy between the East and West.

In the years from 395 to 398 the Goths under Alaric invaded Greece and were almost cut off in the Peloponnese. Alaric extricated himself with Stilicho's connivance, made a secret agreement with the eastern government, was made master general of the forces in eastern Illyria and was proclaimed King of the Visigoths. Alaric made a first incursion into Italy but was repulsed. Honorius celebrated a triumph in Rome and then fixed his residence at Ravenna. In 406 Radagaisus invaded Italy. His army was destroyed by Stilicho, who opened negotiations with Alaric but was overthrown by a palace intrigue and put to death.

These events are described by Gibbon in Chapters 29 and 30.

31.

INVASION OF ITALY BY ALARIC. CHARACTER OF
THE NOBLES AND PEOPLE OF ROME. THREE SIEGES
AND SACK OF ROME. RETREAT OF THE GOTHS AND
DEATH OF ALARIC

THE INCAPACITY of weak and distracted government may often
assume the appearance and produce the effects of a treasonable correspondence with the public enemy. If Alaric himself
had been introduced into the council of Ravenna, he would
probably have advised the same measures which were actually pursued by the ministers of Honorius. The king of the
Goths would have conspired, perhaps with some reluctance,
to destroy the formidable adversary by whose arms, in Italy
as well as in Greece, he had been twice overthrown. *Their*
active and interested hatred laboriously accomplished the disgrace and ruin of the great Stilicho. The valour of Sarus, his
fame in arms, and his personal or hereditary influence over
the confederate barbarians, could recommend him only to
the friends of their country who despised or detested the
worthless characters of Turpilio, Varanes, and Vigilantius.
By the pressing instances of the new favourites, these generals, unworthy as they had shown themselves of the name of
soldiers, were promoted to the command of the cavalry, of the
infantry, and of the domestic troops. The Gothic prince would
have subscribed with pleasure the edict which the fanaticism
of Olympius dictated to the simple and devout emperor.
Honorius excluded all persons who were adverse to the catholic church from holding any office in the state; obstinately
rejected the service of all those who dissented from his religion; and rashly disqualified many of his bravest and most

skilful officers who adhered to the Pagan worship or who had imbibed the opinions of Arianism. These measures, so advantageous to an enemy, Alaric would have approved, and might perhaps have suggested; but it may seem doubtful whether the barbarian would have promoted his interest at the expense of the inhuman and absurd cruelty which was perpetrated by the direction, or at least with the connivance, of the Imperial ministers. The foreign auxiliaries who had been attached to the person of Stilicho lamented his death; but the desire of revenge was checked by a natural apprehension for the safety of their wives and children, who were detained as hostages in the strong cities of Italy, where they had likewise deposited their most valuable effects. At the same hour, and as if by a common signal, the cities of Italy were polluted by the same horrid scenes of universal massacre and pillage, which involved in promiscuous destruction the families and fortunes of the barbarians. Exasperated by such an injury, which might have awakened the tamest and most servile spirit, they cast a look of indignation and hope towards the camp of Alaric, and unanimously swore to pursue with just and implacable war the perfidious nation that had so basely violated the laws of hospitality. By the imprudent conduct of the ministers of Honorius the republic lost the assistance, and deserved the enmity, of thirty thousand of her bravest soldiers; and the weight of that formidable army, which alone might have determined the event of the war, was transferred from the scale of the Romans into that of the Goths.

In the arts of negociation, as well as in those of war, the Gothic king maintained his superior ascendant over an enemy whose seeming changes proceeded from the total want of counsel and design. From his camp, on the confines of Italy, Alaric attentively observed the revolutions of the palace, watched the progress of faction and discontent, disguised the hostile aspect of a barbarian invader, and assumed the more popular appearance of the friend and ally of the great Stilicho; to whose virtues, when they were no longer formidable, he could pay a just tribute of sincere praise and regret. The pressing invitation of the malcontents, who urged the king of the Goths to invade Italy, was enforced by a lively sense of his personal injuries; and he might speciously complain that the Imperial ministers still delayed and eluded the payment of

the four thousand pounds of gold which had been granted by
the Roman senate either to reward his services or to appease
his fury. His decent firmness was supported by an artful
moderation, which contributed to the success of his designs.
He required a fair and reasonable satisfaction; but he gave the
strongest assurances that, as soon as he had obtained it, he
would immediately retire. He refused to trust the faith of the
Romans, unless Aëtius and Jason, the sons of two great officers
of state, were sent as hostages to his camp: but he offered to
deliver in exchange several of the noblest youths of the Gothic
nation. The modesty of Alaric was interpreted by the ministers of Ravenna as a sure evidence of his weakness and
fear. They disdained either to negociate a treaty or to assem-
ble an army; and with a rash confidence, derived only from
their ignorance of the extreme danger, irretrievably wasted
the decisive moments of peace and war. While they expected,
in sullen silence, that the barbarians should evacuate the
confines of Italy, Alaric, with bold and rapid marches, passed
the Alps and the Po; hastily pillaged the cities of Aquileia,
Altinum, Concordia, and Cremona, which yielded to his arms;
increased his forces by the accession of thirty thousand auxiliaries; and, without meeting a single enemy in the field, advanced as far as the edge of the morass which protected the
impregnable residence of the emperor of the West. Instead
of attempting the hopeless siege of Ravenna, the prudent
leader of the Goths proceeded to Rimini, stretched his ravages
along the sea-coast of the Adriatic, and meditated the conquest of the ancient mistress of the world. An Italian hermit,
whose zeal and sanctity were respected by the barbarians
themselves, encountered the victorious monarch, and boldly
denounced the indignation of Heaven against the oppressors
of the earth: but the saint himself was confounded by the
solemn asseveration of Alaric that he felt a secret and preternatural impulse, which directed, and even compelled, his
march to the gates of Rome. He felt that his genius and his
fortune were equal to the most arduous enterprises; and the
enthusiasm which he communicated to the Goths insensibly
removed the popular and almost superstitious reverence of
the nations for the majesty of the Roman name. His troops,
animated by the hopes of spoil, followed the course of the
Flaminian way, occupied the unguarded passes of the Apen-

nine,[1] descended into the rich plains of Umbria; and, as they lay encamped on the banks of the Clitumnus, might wantonly slaughter and devour the milk-white oxen which had been so long reserved for the use of Roman triumphs. A lofty situation and a seasonable tempest of thunder and lightning preserved the little city of Narni: but the king of the Goths, despising the ignoble prey, still advanced with unabated vigour; and after he had passed through the stately arches, adorned with the spoils of barbaric victories, he pitched his camp under the walls of Rome.

During a period of six hundred and nineteen years the seat of empire had never been violated by the presence of a foreign enemy. The unsuccessful expedition of Hannibal served only to display the character of the senate and people; of a senate degraded, rather than ennobled, by the comparison of an assembly of kings; and of a people to whom the ambassador of Pyrrhus ascribed the inexhaustible resources of the Hydra. Each of the senators in the time of the Punic war had accomplished his term of military service, either in a subordinate or a superior station; and the decree which invested with temporary command all those who had been consuls, or censors, or dictators, gave the republic the immediate assistance of many brave and experienced generals. In the beginning of the war the Roman people consisted of two hundred and fifty thousand citizens of an age to bear arms. Fifty thousand had already died in the defence of their country; and the twenty-three legions which were employed in the different camps of Italy, Greece, Sardinia, Sicily, and Spain, required about one hundred thousand men. But there still remained an equal number in Rome and the adjacent territory who were animated by the same intrepid courage; and every citizen was trained from his earliest youth in the discipline and exercises of a soldier. Hannibal was astonished by the constancy of the senate, who, without raising the siege of Capua or recalling their scattered forces, expected his approach. He encamped on the banks of the Anio, at the distance of three miles from the city: and he was soon informed that the ground on which he had pitched his tent was sold for an adequate price at a public auction; and that a body of troops was dismissed by an

---

[1] Addison has given a very picturesque description of the road through the Apennine. The Goths were not at leisure to observe the beauties of the prospect; but they were pleased to find that the Saxa Intercisa, a narrow passage which Vespasian had cut through the rock, was totally neglected.

opposite road to reinforce the legions of Spain. He led his
Africans to the gates of Rome, where he found three armies
in order of battle prepared to receive him; but Hannibal
dreaded the event of a combat from which he could not hope
to escape unless he destroyed the last of his enemies; and his
speedy retreat confessed the invincible courage of the Romans.

THE CHARACTER OF THE ROMAN NOBLES

From the time of the Punic war the uninterrupted succession of senators had preserved the name and image of the
republic; and the degenerate subjects of Honorius ambitiously
derived their descent from the heroes who had repulsed the
arms of Hannibal and subdued the nations of the earth.
The temporal honours which the devout Paula inherited and
despised are carefully recapitulated by Jerom, the guide of
her conscience and the historian of her life. The genealogy of
her father, Rogatus, which ascended as high as Agamemnon,
might seem to betray a Grecian origin; but her mother, Blæsil-
la, numbered the Scipios, Æmilius Paulus, and the Gracchi in
the list of her ancestors; and Toxotius, the husband of Paula,
deduced his royal lineage from Æneas, the father of the Julian
line. The vanity of the rich, who desired to be noble, was
gratified by these lofty pretensions. Encouraged by the applause of their parasites, they easily imposed on the credulity
of the vulgar; and were countenanced in some measure by
the custom of adopting the name of their patron, which had
always prevailed among the freedmen and clients of illustrious
families. Most of those families, however, attacked by so
many causes of external violence or internal decay, were
gradually extirpated: and it would be more reasonable to
seek for a lineal descent of twenty generations among the
mountains of the Alps or in the peaceful solitude of Apulia,
than on the theatre of Rome, the seat of fortune, of danger,
and of perpetual revolutions. Under each successive reign and
from every province of the empire a crowd of hardy adventurers, rising to eminence by their talents or their vices,
usurped the wealth, the honours, and the palaces of Rome;
and oppressed or protected the poor and humble remains of
consular families, who were ignorant, perhaps, of the glory
of their ancestors.

In the time of Jerom and Claudian the senators unanimously

yielded the pre-eminence to the Anician line; and a slight view of *their* history will serve to appreciate the rank and antiquity of the noble families which contended only for the second place. During the five first ages of the city the name of the Anicians was unknown; they appear to have derived their origin from Præneste; and the ambition of those new citizens was long satisfied with the plebeian honours of tribunes of the people. One hundred and sixty-eight years before the Christian era the family was ennobled by the prætorship of Anicius, who gloriously terminated the Illyrian war by the conquest of the nation and the captivity of their king. From the triumph of that general three consulships in distant periods mark the succession of the Anician name. From the reign of Diocletian to the final extinction of the Western empire that name shone with a lustre which was not eclipsed in the public estimation by the majesty of the Imperial purple. The several branches to whom it was communicated united, by marriage or inheritance, the wealth and titles of the Annian, the Petronian, and the Olybrian houses; and in each generation the number of consulships was multiplied by an hereditary claim. The Anician family excelled in faith and in riches: they were the first of the Roman senate who embraced Christianity; and it is probable that Anicius Julian, who was afterwards consul and prefect of the city, atoned for his attachment to the party of Maxentius by the readiness with which he accepted the religion of Constantine. Their ample patrimony was increased by the industry of Probus, the chief of the Anician family, who shared with Gratian the honours of the consulship, and exercised four times the high office of Prætorian prefect. His immense estates were scattered over the wide extent of the Roman world; and though the public might suspect or disapprove the methods by which they had been acquired, the generosity and magnificence of that fortunate statesman deserved the gratitude of his clients and the admiration of strangers. Such was the respect entertained for his memory, that the two sons of Probus, in their earliest youth and at the request of the senate, were associated in the consular dignity: a memorable distinction, without example in the annals of Rome.

"The marbles of the Anician palace" was used as a proverbial expression of opulence and splendour; but the nobles and senators of Rome aspired in due gradation to imitate that illustrious family. The accurate description of the city, which was composed in the Theodosian age, enumerates one thousand seven hundred and eighty *houses*, the residence of wealthy and honourable citizens. Many of these stately mansions might almost excuse the exaggeration of the poet—that Rome contained a multitude of palaces, and that each palace was equal to a city: since it included within its own precincts everything which could be subservient either to use or luxury; markets, hippodromes, temples, fountains, baths, porticos, shady groves, and artificial aviaries. The historian Olympiodorus, who represents the state of Rome when it was besieged by the Goths, continues to observe that several of the richest senators received from their estates an annual income of four thousand pounds of gold, above one hundred and sixty thousand pounds sterling; without computing the stated provision of corn and wine, which, had they been sold, might have equalled in value one-third of the money. Compared to this immoderate wealth, an ordinary revenue of a thousand or fifteen hundred pounds of gold might be considered as no more than adequate to the dignity of the senatorian rank, which required many expenses of a public and ostentatious kind. Several examples are recorded in the age of Honorius of vain and popular nobles who celebrated the year of their prætorship by a festival which lasted seven days and cost above one hundred thousand pounds sterling. The estates of the Roman senators, which so far exceed the proportion of modern wealth, were not confined to the limits of Italy. Their possessions extended far beyond the Ionian and Ægean seas to the most distant provinces: the city of Nicopolis, which Augustus had founded as an eternal monument of the Actian victory, was the property of the devout Paula; and it is observed by Seneca, that the rivers which had divided hostile nations now flowed through the lands of private citizens. According to their temper and circumstances, the estates of the Romans were either cultivated by the labour of their slaves, or granted, for a certain and stipulated rent, to the industrious farmer. The economical writers of antiquity strenuously recommend the former method wherever it may be practicable; but if the object should be removed by its distance or magnitude from the immediate eye of the master, they prefer the active care of an old hereditary tenant, attached to the soil and interested in the produce, to the mercenary administration of a negligent, perhaps an unfaithful, steward.

The opulent nobles of an immense capital, who were never excited by the pursuit of military glory, and seldom engaged in the occupations of civil government, naturally resigned their leisure to the business and amusements of private life. At Rome commerce was always held in contempt; but the senators, from the first age of the republic, increased their patrimony and multiplied their clients by the lucrative practice of usury, and the obsolete laws were eluded or violated by the mutual inclinations and interest of both parties. A considerable mass of treasure must always have existed at Rome, either in the current coin of the empire, or in the form of gold and silver plate; and there were many sideboards in the time of Pliny which contained more solid silver than had been transported by Scipio from vanquished Carthage. The greater part of the nobles, who dissipated their fortunes in profuse luxury, found themselves poor in the midst of wealth, and idle in a constant round of dissipation. Their desires were continually gratified by the labour of a thousand hands; of the numerous train of their domestic slaves, who were actuated by the fear of punishment; and of the various professions of artificers and merchants, who were more powerfully impelled by the hopes of gain. The ancients were destitute of many of the conveniences of life which have been invented or improved by the progress of industry; and the plenty of glass and linen has diffused more real comforts among the modern nations of Europe than the senators of Rome could derive from all the refinements of pompous or sensual luxury.[1] Their luxury and their manners have been the subject of minute and laborious disquisition; but as such inquiries would divert me too long from the design of the present work, I shall produce an authentic state of Rome and its inhabitants which is more peculiarly applicable to the period of the Gothic invasion. Ammianus Marcellinus, who prudently chose the capital of the empire as the residence best adapted to the historian of his own times, has mixed with the narrative of public events a lively representation of the scenes with which he was familiarly conversant. The judicious reader will not always approve the asperity of censure, the choice of circumstances, or the style of expression; he will perhaps detect the latent prejudices

---

[1] The learned Arbuthnot has observed with humour, and I believe with truth, that Augustus had neither glass to his windows nor a shirt to his back. Under the lower empire the use of linen and glass became somewhat more common.

and personal resentments which soured the temper of Ammianus himself; but he will surely observe, with philosophic curiosity, the interesting and original picture of the manners of Rome.[1]

"The greatness of Rome (such is the language of the historian) was founded on the rare and almost incredible alliance of virtue and of fortune. The long period of her infancy was employed in a laborious struggle against the tribes of Italy, the neighbours and enemies of the rising city. In the strength and ardour of youth she sustained the storms of war, carried her victorious arms beyond the seas and the mountains, and brought home triumphal laurels from every country of the globe. At length, verging towards old age, and sometimes conquering by the terror only of her name, she sought the blessings of ease and tranquillity. The VENERABLE CITY, which had trampled on the necks of the fiercest nations, and established a system of laws, the perpetual guardians of justice and freedom, was content, like a wise and wealthy parent, to devolve on the Cæsars, her favourite sons, the care of governing her ample patrimony. A secure and profound peace, such as had been once enjoyed in the reign of Numa, succeeded to the tumults of a republic; while Rome was still adored as the queen of the earth, and the subject nations still reverenced the name of her people and the majesty of the senate. But this native splendour (continues Ammianus) is degraded and sullied by the conduct of some nobles, who, unmindful of their own dignity and of that of their country, assume an unbounded licence of vice and folly. They contend with each other in the empty vanity of titles and surnames, and curiously select or invent the most lofty and sonorous appellations—Reburrus or Fabunius, Pagonius or Tarrasius—which may impress the ears of the vulgar with astonishment and respect. From a vain ambition of perpetuating their memory, they affect to multiply their likeness in statues of bronze and marble; nor are they satisfied unless those statues are covered with plates of gold; an honourable distinction, first granted to Acilius the

---

[1] It is incumbent on me to explain the liberties which I have taken with the text of Ammianus. 1. I have melted down into one piece the sixth chapter of the fourteenth and the fourth of the twenty-eighth book. 2. I have given order and connexion to the confused mass of materials. 3. I have softened *some* extravagant hyperboles and pared away some superfluities of the original. 4. I have developed some observations which were insinuated rather than expressed. With these allowances my version will be found, not literal indeed, but faithful and exact.

consul, after he had subdued by his arms and counsels the power of king Antiochus. The ostentation of displaying, of magnifying perhaps, the rent-roll of the estates which they possess in all the provinces, from the rising to the setting sun, provokes the just resentment of every man who recollects that their poor and invincible ancestors were not distinguished from the meanest of the soldiers by the delicacy of their food or the splendour of their apparel. But the modern nobles measure their rank and consequence according to the loftiness of their chariots,[1] and the weighty magnificence of their dress. Their long robes of silk and purple float in the wind; and as they are agitated, by art or accident, they occasionally discover the under garments, the rich tunics, embroidered with the figures of various animals.[2] Followed by a train of fifty servants, and tearing up the pavement, they move along the streets with the same impetuous speed as if they travelled with post-horses; and the example of the senators is boldly imitated by the matrons and ladies, whose covered carriages are continually driving round the immense space of the city and suburbs. Whenever these persons of high distinction condescend to visit the public baths, they assume, on their entrance, a tone of loud and insolent command, and appropriate to their own use the conveniences which were designed for the Roman people. If, in these places of mixed and general resort, they meet any of the infamous ministers of their pleasures, they express their affection by a tender embrace, while they proudly decline the salutations of their fellow-citizens, who are not permitted to aspire above the honour of kissing their hands or their knees. As soon as they have indulged themselves in the refreshment of the bath, they resume their rings and the other ensigns of their dignity, select from their private wardrobe of the finest linen, such as might suffice for a dozen persons, the garments the most agreeable

---

[1] The *carrucæ*, or coaches of the Romans, were often of solid silver curiously carved and engraved; and the trappings of the mules or horses were embossed with gold. This magnificence continued from the reign of Nero to that of Honorius; and the Appian way was covered with the splendid equipages of the nobles, who came out to meet St. Melania when she returned to Rome six years before the Gothic siege. Yet pomp is well exchanged for convenience; and a plain modern coach that is hung upon springs is much preferable to the silver or gold *carts* of antiquity, which rolled on the axletree, and were exposed, for the most part, to the inclemency of the weather.

[2] In a homily of Asterius, bishop of Amasia, M. de Valois has discovered that this was a new fashion; that bears, wolves, lions, and tigers, woods, hunting-matches, etc., were represented in embroidery; and that the more pious coxcombs substituted the figure or legend of some favourite saint.

to their fancy, and maintain till their departure the same haughty demeanour, which perhaps might have been excused in the great Marcellus after the conquest of Syracuse. Sometimes indeed these heroes undertake more arduous achievements: they visit their estates in Italy, and procure themselves, by the toil of servile hands, the amusements of the chase. If at any time, but more especially on a hot day, they have courage to sail in their painted galleys from the Lucrine lake to their elegant villas on the sea-coast of Puteoli and Caieta, they compare their own expeditions to the marches of Cæsar and Alexander. Yet should a fly presume to settle on the silken folds of their gilded umbrellas, should a sunbeam penetrate through some unguarded and imperceptible chink, they deplore their intolerable hardships, and lament in affected language that they were not born in the land of the Cimmerians, the regions of eternal darkness. In these journeys into the country the whole body of the household marches with their master. In the same manner as the cavalry and infantry, the heavy and the light armed troops, the advanced guard and the rear, are marshalled by the skill of their military leaders, so the domestic officers, who bear a rod as an ensign of authority, distribute and arrange the numerous train of slaves and attendants. The baggage and wardrobe move in the front, and are immediately followed by a multitude of cooks and inferior ministers employed in the service of the kitchens and of the table. The main body is composed of a promiscuous crowd of slaves, increased by the accidental concourse of idle or dependent plebeians. The rear is closed by the favourite band of eunuchs, distributed from age to youth, according to the order of seniority. Their numbers and their deformity excite the horror of the indignant spectators, who are ready to execrate the memory of Semiramis for the cruel art which she invented of frustrating the purposes of nature, and of blasting in the bud the hopes of future generations. In the exercise of domestic jurisdiction the nobles of Rome express an exquisite sensibility for any personal injury, and a contemptuous indifference for the rest of the human species. When they have called for warm water, if a slave has been tardy in his obedience, he is instantly chastised with three hundred lashes; but should the same slave commit a wilful murder, the master will mildly observe that he is a worthless fellow, but that if he repeats the offence he shall not escape punishment. Hospitality was formerly the virtue of the Romans; and every stranger who could plead either merit or misfortune was relieved or rewarded by their generosity. At present, if a foreigner, perhaps of no contemptible rank, is introduced to one of the proud and wealthy senators, he is welcomed indeed in the first audience with such warm professions and such kind inquiries, that he retires enchanted with the affability of his illustrious friend, and full of regret that he had so long delayed his journey to Rome, the native seat of manners as well as of empire. Secure of a favourable reception, he repeats his visit the ensuing day, and is mortified by the discovery that his person, his name, and his country are already forgotten. If he still has resolution to persevere, he is gradually numbered in the train of dependents, and obtains the permission to pay his assiduous and unprofitable court to a haughty patron, incapable of gratitude or friendship, who scarcely deigns to remark his presence, his departure, or his return. Whenever the rich prepare a solemn and popular entertainment, whenever they celebrate with profuse and pernicious luxury their private banquets, the choice of the guests is the subject of anxious deliberation. The modest, the sober, and the learned are seldom preferred; and the nomenclators, who are commonly swayed by interested motives, have the address to insert in the list of invitations the obscure names of the most worthless of mankind. But the frequent and familiar companions of the great are those parasites who practise the most useful of all arts, the art of flattery; who eagerly applaud each word and every action of their immortal patron; gaze with rapture on his marble columns and variegated pavements, and strenuously praise the pomp and elegance which he is taught to consider as a part of his personal merit. At the Roman tables the birds, the *squirrels*,[1] or the fish, which appear of an uncommon size, are contemplated with curious attention; a pair of scales is accurately applied to ascertain their real weight; and, while the more rational guests are disgusted by the vain and

---

[1] The want of an English name obliges me to refer to the common genus of squirrels, the Latis *glis*, the French *loir*; a little animal who inhabits the woods and remains torpid in cold weather. The art of rearing and fattening great numbers of *glires* was practised in Roman villas as a profitable article of rural economy. The excessive demand of them for luxurious tables was increased by the foolish prohibitions of the censors; and it is reported that they are still esteemed in modern Rome, and are frequently sent as presents by the Colonna princes.

tedious repetition, notaries are summoned to attest by an authentic record the truth of such a marvellous event. Another method of introduction into the houses and society of the great is derived from the profession of gaming; or, as it is more politely styled, of play. The confederates are united by a strict and indissoluble bond of friendship, or rather of conspiracy; a superior degree of skill in the *Tesserarian* art (which may be interpreted the game of dice and tables[1]) is a sure road to wealth and reputation. A master of that sublime science, who in a supper or assembly is placed below a magistrate, displays in his countenance the surprise and indignation which Cato might be supposed to feel when he was refused the prætorship by the votes of a capricious people. The acquisition of knowledge seldom engages the curiosity of the nobles, who abhor the fatigue and disdain the advantages of study; and the only books which they peruse are the Satires of Juvenal, and the verbose and fabulous histories of Marius Maximus. The libraries which they have inherited from their fathers are secluded, like dreary sepulchres, from the light of day. But the costly instruments of the theatre, flutes, and enormous lyres, and hydraulic organs, are constructed for their use; and the harmony of vocal and instrumental music is incessantly repeated in the palaces of Rome. In those palaces sound is preferred to sense, and the care of the body to that of the mind. It is allowed as a salutary maxim, that the light and frivolous suspicion of a contagious malady is of sufficient weight to excuse the visits of the most intimate friends; and even the servants who are despatched to make the decent inquiries are not suffered to return home till they have undergone the ceremony of a previous ablution. Yet this selfish and unmanly delicacy occasionally yields to the more imperious passion of avarice. The prospect of gain will urge a rich and gouty senator as far as Spoleto; every sentiment

---

[1] This game, which might be translated by the more familiar names of *trictrac*, or backgammon, was a favourite amusement of the gravest Romans; and old Mucius Scævola, the lawyer, had the reputation of a very skilful player. It was called *ludus duodecim scriptorum*, from the twelve *scripta* or lines which equally divided the *alveolus* or table. On these the two armies, the white and the black, each consisting of fifteen men, or *calculi*, were regularly placed and alternately moved according to the laws of the game, and the chances of the *tesseræ* or dice. Dr. Hyde, who diligently traces the history and various species of the *nerdiludium* (a name of Persic etymology) from Ireland to Japan, pours forth on this trifling subject a copious torrent of classic and Oriental learning.

of arrogance and dignity is subdued by the hopes of an inheritance, or even of a legacy; and a wealthy childless citizen is the most powerful of the Romans. The art of obtaining the signature of a favourable testament, and sometimes of hastening the moment of its execution, is perfectly understood; and it has happened that in the same house, though in different apartments, a husband and a wife, with the laudable design of overreaching each other, have summoned their respective lawyers, to declare at the same time their mutual but contradictory intentions. The distress which follows and chastises extravagant luxury often reduces the great to the use of the most humiliating expedients. When they desire to borrow, they employ the base and supplicating style of the slave in the comedy; but when they are called upon to pay, they assume the royal and tragic declamation of the grandsons of Hercules. If the demand is repeated, they readily procure some trusty sycophant, instructed to maintain a charge of poison, or magic, against the insolent creditor, who is seldom released from prison till he has signed a discharge of the whole debt. These vices, which degrade the moral character of the Romans, are mixed with a puerile superstition that disgraces their understanding. They listen with confidence to the predictions of haruspices, who pretend to read in the entrails of victims the signs of future greatness and prosperity; and there are many who do not presume either to bathe or to dine, or to appear in public, till they have diligently consulted, according to the rules of astrology, the situation of Mercury and the aspect of the moon. It is singular enough that this vain credulity may often be discovered among the profane sceptics who impiously doubt or deny the existence of a celestial power."

THE PEOPLE OF ROME

In populous cities, which are the seat of commerce and manufactures, the middle ranks of inhabitants, who derive their subsistence from the dexterity or labour of their hands, are commonly the most prolific, the most useful, and, in that sense, the most respectable part of the community. But the plebeians of Rome, who disdained such sedentary and servile arts, had been oppressed from the earliest times by the weight of debt and usury, and the husbandman, during the term of his military service, was obliged to abandon the cultivation of his farm. The lands of Italy, which had been originally divided among the families of free and indigent proprietors, were insensibly purchased or usurped by the avarice of the nobles; and in the age which preceded the fall of the republic, it was computed that only two thousand citizens were possessed of any independent substance. Yet as long as the people bestowed by their suffrages the honours of the state, the command of the legions, and the administration of wealthy provinces, their conscious pride alleviated in some measure the hardships of poverty; and their wants were seasonably supplied by the ambitious liberality of the candidates, who aspired to secure a venal majority in the thirty-five tribes, or the hundred and ninety-three centuries, of Rome. But when the prodigal commons had imprudently alienated not only the *use,* but the *inheritance,* of power, they sunk, under the reign of the Cæsars, into a vile and wretched populace, which must, in a few generations, have been totally extinguished, if it had not been continually recruited by the manumission of slaves and the influx of strangers. As early as the time of Hadrian it was the just complaint of the ingenuous natives that the capital had attracted the vices of the universe and the manners of the most opposite nations. The intemperance of the Gauls, the cunning and levity of the Greeks, the savage obstinacy of the Egyptians and Jews, the servile temper of the Asiatics, and the dissolute, effeminate prostitution of the Syrians, were mingled in the various multitude, which, under the proud and false denomination of Romans, presumed to despise their fellow-subjects, and even their sovereigns, who dwelt beyond the precincts of the ETERNAL CITY.

Yet the name of that city was still pronounced with respect: the frequent and capricious tumults of its inhabitants were indulged with impunity; and the successors of Constantine, instead of crushing the last remains of the democracy by the strong arm of military power, embraced the mild policy of Augustus, and studied to relieve the poverty and to amuse the idleness of an innumerable people. I. For the convenience of the lazy plebeians, the monthly distributions of corn were converted into a daily allowance of bread; a great number of ovens were constructed and maintained at the public expense; and at the appointed hour, each citizen, who was furnished with a ticket, ascended the flight of steps which had been assigned to his peculiar quarter or division, and received, either as a gift or at a very low price, a loaf of bread of the weight of three pounds for the use of his family. II. The forests of Lucania, whose acorns fattened large droves of wild hogs, afforded, as a species of tribute, a plentiful supply of cheap and wholesome meat. During five months of the year a regular allowance of bacon was distributed to the poorer citizens; and the annual consumption of the capital, at a time when it was much declined from its former lustre, was ascertained, by an edict of Valentinian the Third, at three millions six hundred and twenty-eight thousand pounds. III. In the manners of antiquity the use of oil was indispensable for the lamp as well as for the bath, and the annual tax which was imposed on Africa for the benefit of Rome amounted to the weight of three millions of pounds, to the measure, perhaps, of three hundred thousand English gallons. IV. The anxiety of Augustus to provide the metropolis with sufficient plenty of corn was not extended beyond that necessary article of human subsistence; and when the popular clamour accused the dearness and scarcity of wine, a proclamation was issued by the grave reformer to remind his subjects that no man could reasonably complain of thirst, since the aqueducts of Agrippa had introduced into the city so many copious streams of pure and salubrious water. This rigid sobriety was insensibly relaxed; and, although the generous design of Aurelian does not appear to have been executed in its full extent, the use of wine was allowed on very easy and liberal terms. The administration of the public cellars was delegated to a magistrate of honourable rank; and a considerable part of the vintage of Campania was reserved for the fortunate inhabitants of Rome.

The stupendous aqueducts, so justly celebrated by the praises of Augustus himself, replenished the *Thermæ,* or baths, which had been constructed in every part of the city, with Imperial magnificence. The baths of Antoninus Caracalla, which were open, at stated hours, for the indiscriminate service of the senators and the people, contained above sixteen hundred seats of marble; and more than three thousand were reckoned in the baths of Diocletian. The walls of the lofty apartments were covered with curious mosaics, that imitated the art of the pencil in the elegance of design and the variety of colours. The Egyptian granite was beautifully encrusted with the precious green marble of Numidia; the perpetual stream of hot water was poured into the capacious basons through so many wide mouths of bright and massy silver; and the meanest Roman could purchase, with a small copper coin, the daily enjoyment of a scene of pomp and luxury which might excite the envy of the kings of Asia. From these stately palaces issued a swarm of dirty and ragged plebeians, without shoes and without a mantle; who loitered away whole days in the street or Forum to hear news and to hold disputes; who dissipated in extravagant gaming the miserable pittance of their wives and children; and spent the hours of the night in obscure taverns and brothels in the indulgence of gross and vulgar sensuality.

But the most lively and splendid amusement of the idle multitude depended on the frequent exhibition of public games and spectacles. The piety of Christian princes had suppressed the inhuman combats of gladiators; but the Roman people still considered the Circus as their home, their temple, and the seat of the republic. The impatient crowd rushed at the dawn of day to secure their places, and there were many who passed a sleepless and anxious night in the adjacent porticos. From the morning to the evening, careless of the sun or of the rain, the spectators, who sometimes amounted to the number of four hundred thousand, remained in eager attention; their eyes fixed on the horses and charioteers, their minds agitated with hope and fear for the success of the *colours* which they espoused; and the happiness of Rome appeared to hang on the event of a race. The same immoderate ardour inspired their clamours and their applause as often as they were entertained with the hunting of wild beasts and the various modes of theatrical representation. These representations in modern capitals may deserve to be considered as a pure and elegant school of taste, and perhaps of virtue. But the Tragic and Comic Muse of the Romans, who seldom aspired beyond the imitation of Attic genius, had been almost totally silent since the fall of the republic; and their place was unworthily occupied by licentious farce, effeminate music, and splendid pageantry. The pantomimes, who maintained their reputation from the age of Augustus to the sixth century, expressed, without the use of words, the various fables of the gods and heroes of antiquity; and the perfection of their art, which sometimes disarmed the gravity of the philosopher, always excited the applause and wonder of the people. The vast and magnificent theatres of Rome were filled by three thousand female dancers, and by three thousand singers, with the masters of the respective choruses. Such was the popular favour which they enjoyed, that, in a time of scarcity, when all strangers were banished from the city, the merit of contributing to the public pleasures exempted *them* from a law which was strictly executed against the professors of the liberal arts.

It is said that the foolish curiosity of Elagabalus attempted to discover, from the quantity of spiders' webs, the number of the inhabitants of Rome. A more rational method of inquiry might not have been undeserving of the attention of the wisest princes, who could easily have resolved a question so important for the Roman government and so interesting to succeeding ages. The births and deaths of the citizens were duly registered; and if any writer of antiquity had condescended to mention the annual amount, or the common average, we might now produce some satisfactory calculation which would destroy the extravagant assertions of critics, and perhaps confirm the modest and probable conjectures of philosophers. The most diligent researches have collected only the following circumstances, which, slight and imperfect as they are, may tend in some degree to illustrate the question of the populousness of ancient Rome. I. When the capital of the empire was besieged by the Goths, the circuit of the walls was accurately measured by Ammonius, the mathematician, who found it equal to twenty-one miles. It should not be forgotten that the form of the city was almost that of a circle; the geometrical figure which is known to contain the largest space within any given circumference. II. The architect Vitruvius, who flourished in the Augustan age, and whose evidence, on this occasion, has peculiar weight and authority, observes that the innumerable habitations of the Roman people would have spread themselves far beyond the narrow limits of the city; and that the want of ground, which was probably contracted on every side by gardens and villas, suggested the common, though inconvenient practice of raising the houses to a considerable height in the air. But the loftiness of these buildings, which often consisted of hasty work and insufficient materials, was the cause of frequent and fatal accidents; and it was repeatedly enacted by Augustus, as well as by Nero, that the height of private edifices within the walls of Rome should not exceed the measure of seventy feet from the ground. III. Juvenal laments, as it should seem from his own experience, the hardships of the poorer citizens, to whom he addresses the salutary advice of emigrating, without delay, from the smoke of Rome, since they might purchase in the little towns of Italy a cheerful, commodious dwelling at the same price which they annually paid for a dark and miserable lodging. House-rent was therefore immoderately dear: the rich acquired, at an enormous expense, the ground, which they covered with palaces and gardens; but the body of the Roman people was crowded into a narrow space; and the different floors and apartments of the same house were divided, as it is still the custom of Paris and other cities, among several families of plebeians. IV. The total number of houses in the fourteen regions of the city is accurately stated in the description of Rome composed under the reign of Theodosius, and they amount to forty-eight thousand three hundred and eighty-two. The two classes of *domus* and of *insulæ,* into which they are divided, include all the habitations of the capital, of every rank and condition, from the marble palace of the Anicii, with a numerous establishment of freedmen and slaves, to the lofty and narrow lodging-house where the poet Codrus and his wife were permitted to hire a wretched garret immediately under the tiles. If we adopt the same average which, under similar circumstances, has been found applicable to Paris, and indifferently allow about twenty-five persons for each house, of every degree, we may fairly estimate the inhabitants of Rome at twelve hundred thousand: a number which cannot be thought excessive for the capital of a mighty empire, though it exceeds the populousness of the greatest cities of modern Europe.

THE FIRST SIEGE OF ROME

Such was the state of Rome under the reign of Honorius, at the time when the Gothic army formed the siege, or rather the blockade, of the city. By a skilful disposition of his numerous forces, who impatiently watched the moment of an assault, Alaric encompassed the walls, commanded the

twelve principal gates, intercepted all communication with
the adjacent country, and vigilantly guarded the navigation
of the Tiber, from which the Romans derived the surest and
most plentiful supply of provisions. The first emotions of
the nobles and of the people were those of surprise and indignation, that a vile barbarian should dare to insult the
capital of the world; but their arrogance was soon humbled
by misfortune; and their unmanly rage, instead of being
directed against an enemy in arms, was meanly exercised on
a defenceless and innocent victim. Perhaps in the person of
Serena the Romans might have respected the niece of
Theodosius, the aunt, nay even the adoptive mother, of the
reigning emperor; but they abhorred the widow of Stilicho;
and they listened with credulous passion to the tale of
calumny which accused her of maintaining a secret and
criminal correspondence with the Gothic invader. Actuated,
or overawed, by the same popular frenzy, the senate, without requiring any evidence of her guilt, pronounced the sentence of her death. Serena was ignominiously strangled; and
the infatuated multitude were astonished to find that this
cruel act of injustice did not immediately produce the retreat
of the barbarians and the deliverance of the city. That unfortunate city gradually experienced the distress of scarcity,
and at length the horrid calamities of famine. The daily allowance of three pounds of bread was reduced to one-half,
to one-third, to nothing; and the price of corn still continued
to rise in a rapid and extravagant proportion. The poorer
citizens, who were unable to purchase the necessaries of life,
solicited the precarious charity of the rich; and for a while
the public misery was alleviated by the humanity of Læta,
the widow of the emperor Gratian, who had fixed her residence at Rome, and consecrated, to the use of the indigent,
the princely revenue which she annually received from the
grateful successors of her husband. But these private and
temporary donatives were insufficient to appease the hunger
of a numerous people; and the progress of famine invaded
the marble palaces of the senators themselves. The persons of
both sexes, who had been educated in the enjoyment of ease
and luxury, discovered how little is requisite to supply the
demands of nature; and lavished their unavailing treasures of
gold and silver to obtain the coarse and scanty sustenance
which they would formerly have rejected with disdain. The

food the most repugnant to sense or imagination, the aliments the most unwholesome and pernicious to the constitution, were eagerly devoured, and fiercely disputed, by the rage of hunger. A dark suspicion was entertained that some desperate wretches fed on the bodies of their fellow-creatures whom they had secretly murdered; and even mothers (such was the horrid conflict of the two most powerful instincts implanted by nature in the human breast), even mothers are said to have tasted the flesh of their slaughtered infants! Many thousands of the inhabitants of Rome expired in their houses, or in the streets, for want of sustenance; and as the public sepulchres without the walls were in the power of the enemy, the stench which arose from so many putrid and unburied carcasses infected the air; and the miseries of famine were succeeded and aggravated by the contagion of a pestilential disease. The assurances of speedy and effectual relief, which were repeatedly transmitted from the court of Ravenna, supported, for some time, the fainting resolution of the Romans, till at length the despair of any human aid tempted them to accept the offers of a preternatural deliverance. Pompeianus, prefect of the city, had been persuaded, by the art or fanaticism of some Tuscan diviners, that, by the mysterious force of spells and sacrifices, they could extract the lightning from the clouds, and point those celestial fires against the camp of the barbarians. The important secret was communicated to Innocent, the bishop of Rome; and the successor of St. Peter is accused, perhaps without foundation, of preferring the safety of the republic to the rigid severity of the Christian worship. But when the question was agitated in the senate; when it was proposed, as an essential condition, that those sacrifices should be performed in the Capitol, by the authority, and in the presence, of the magistrates; the majority of that respectable assembly, apprehensive either of the Divine or of the Imperial displeasure, refused to join in an act which appeared almost equivalent to the public restoration of Paganism.

The last resource of the Romans was in the clemency, or at least in the moderation, of the king of the Goths. The senate, who in an emergency assumed the supreme powers of government, appointed two ambassadors to negociate with the enemy. This important trust was delegated to Basilius, a senator of Spanish extraction, and already conspicuous in the administration of provinces; and to John, the first tribune of the notaries, who was peculiarly qualified, by his dexterity in business, as well as by his former intimacy with the Gothic prince. When they were introduced into his presence, they declared, perhaps in a more lofty style than became their abject condition, that the Romans were resolved to maintain their dignity, either in peace or war; and that, if Alaric refused them a fair and honourable capitulation, he might sound his trumpets, and prepare to give battle to an innumerable people, exercised in arms and animated by despair. "The thicker the hay, the easier it is mowed," was the concise reply of the barbarian; and this rustic metaphor was accompanied by a loud and insulting laugh, expressive of his contempt for the menaces of an unwarlike populace, enervated by luxury before they were emaciated by famine. He then condescended to fix the ransom which he would accept as the price of his retreat from the walls of Rome: *all* the gold and silver in the city, whether it were the property of the state, or of individuals; *all* the rich and precious moveables; and *all* the slaves who could prove their title to the name of *barbarians*. The ministers of the senate presumed to ask, in a modest and suppliant tone, "If such, O king! are your demands, what do you intend to leave us?" "YOUR LIVES," replied the haughty conqueror: they trembled and retired. Yet before they retired, a short suspension of arms was granted, which allowed some time for a more temperate negociation. The stern features of Alaric were insensibly relaxed; he abated much of the rigour of his terms; and at length consented to raise the siege, on the immediate payment of five thousand pounds of gold, of thirty thousand pounds of silver, of four thousand robes of silk, of three thousand pieces of fine scarlet cloth, and of three thousand pounds weight of pepper.[1] But the public treasury was exhausted; the annual rents of the great estates in Italy and the provinces were intercepted by the calamities of war; the gold and gems had been exchanged, during the famine, for the vilest sustenance; the hoards of secret wealth were still concealed by the obstinacy of avarice; and some remains of consecrated spoils afforded

---

[1] Pepper was a favourite ingredient of the most expensive Roman cookery, and the best sort commonly sold for fifteen denarii, or ten shillings, the pound. It was brought from India; and the same country, the coast of Malabar, still affords the greatest plenty; but the improvement of trade and navigation has multiplied the quantity and reduced the price.

the only resource that could avert the impending ruin of the city. As soon as the Romans had satisfied the rapacious demands of Alaric, they were restored, in some measure, to the enjoyment of peace and plenty. Several of the gates were cautiously opened; the importation of provisions from the river and the adjacent country was no longer obstructed by the Goths; the citizens resorted in crowds to the free market which was held during three days in the suburbs; and while the merchants who undertook this gainful trade made a considerable profit, the future subsistence of the city was secured by the ample magazines which were deposited in the public and private granaries. A more regular discipline than could have been expected was maintained in the camp of Alaric; and the wise barbarian justified his regard for the faith of treaties, by the just severity with which he chastised a party of licentious Goths who had insulted some Roman citizens on the road to Ostia. His army, enriched by the contributions of the capital, slowly advanced into the fair and fruitful province of Tuscany, where he proposed to establish his winter-quarters; and the Gothic standard became the refuge of forty thousand barbarian slaves, who had broke their chains, and aspired, under the command of their great deliverer, to revenge the injuries and the disgrace of their cruel servitude. About the same time he received a more honourable reinforcement of Goths and Huns, whom Adolphus,[1] the brother of his wife, had conducted, at his pressing invitation, from the banks of the Danube to those of the Tiber, and who had cut their way, with some difficulty and loss, through the superior numbers of the Imperial troops. A victorious leader, who united the daring spirit of a barbarian with the art and discipline of a Roman general, was at the head of an hundred thousand fighting men; and Italy pronounced with terror and respect the formidable name of Alaric.

At the distance of fourteen centuries we may be satisfied with relating the military exploits of the conquerors of Rome, without presuming to investigate the motives of their political conduct. In the midst of his apparent prosperity, Alaric was conscious, perhaps, of some secret weakness, some internal

---

[1] This Gothic chieftain is called, by Jornandes and Isidore, *Athaulphus;* by Zosimus and Orosius, *Ataulphus;* and by Olympiodorus, *Adaoulphus.* I have used the celebrated name of *Adolphus,* which seems to be authorised by the practice of the Swedes, the sons or brothers of the ancient Goths.

defect; or perhaps the moderation which he displayed was intended only to deceive and disarm the easy credulity of the ministers of Honorius. The king of the Goths repeatedly declared that it was his desire to be considered as the friend of peace and of the Romans. Three senators, at his earnest request, were sent ambassadors to the court of Ravenna, to solicit the exchange of hostages and the conclusion of the treaty; and the proposals which he more clearly expressed during the course of the negociations could only inspire a doubt of his sincerity, as they might seem inadequate to the state of his fortune. The barbarian still aspired to the rank of master-general of the armies of the West; he stipulated an annual subsidy of corn and money; and he chose the provinces of Dalmatia, Noricum, and Venetia for the seat of his new kingdom, which would have commanded the important communication between Italy and the Danube. If these modest terms should be rejected, Alaric showed a disposition to relinquish his pecuniary demands, and even to content himself with the possession of Noricum; an exhausted and impoverished country, perpetually exposed to the inroads of the barbarians of Germany. But the hopes of peace were disappointed by the weak obstinacy, or interested views, of the minister Olympius. Without listening to the salutary remonstrances of the senate, he dismissed their ambassadors under the conduct of a military escort, too numerous for a retinue of honour, and too feeble for an army of defence. Six thousand Dalmatians, the flower of the Imperial legions, were ordered to march from Ravenna to Rome, through an open country which was occupied by the formidable myriads of the barbarians. These brave legionaries, encompassed and betrayed, fell a sacrifice to ministerial folly; their general, Valens, with an hundred soldiers, escaped from the field of battle; and one of the ambassadors, who could no longer claim the protection of the law of nations, was obliged to purchase his freedom with a ransom of thirty thousand pieces of gold. Yet Alaric, instead of resenting this act of impotent hostility, immediately renewed his proposals of peace; and the second embassy of the Roman senate, which derived weight and dignity from the presence of Innocent, bishop of the city, was guarded from the dangers of the road by a detachment of Gothic soldiers.

Olympius might have continued to insult the just resentment of a people who loudly accused him as the author of the public calamities, but his power was undermined by the secret intrigues of the palace. The favourite eunuchs transferred the government of Honorius and the empire to Jovius, the Prætorian prefect—an unworthy servant, who did not atone by the merit of personal attachment for the errors and misfortunes of his administration. The exile, or escape, of the guilty Olympius reserved him for more vicissitudes of fortune: he experienced the adventures of an obscure and wandering life; he again rose to power; he fell a second time into disgrace; his ears were cut off—he expired under the lash—and his ignominious death afforded a grateful spectacle to the friends of Stilicho. After the removal of Olympius, whose character was deeply tainted with religious fanaticism, the Pagans and heretics were delivered from the impolitic proscription which excluded them from the dignities of the state. The brave Gennerid, a soldier of barbarian origin, who still adhered to the worship of his ancestors, had been obliged to lay aside the military belt; and though he was repeatedly assured by the emperor himself that laws were not made for persons of his rank or merit, he refused to accept any partial dispensation, and persevered in honourable disgrace till he had extorted a general act of justice from the distress of the Roman government. The conduct of Gennerid in the important station to which he was promoted or restored, of master-general of Dalmatia, Pannonia, Noricum, and Rhætia, seemed to revive the discipline and spirit of the republic. From a life of idleness and want his troops were soon habituated to severe exercise and plentiful subsistence, and his private generosity often supplied the rewards which were denied by the avarice or poverty of the court of Ravenna. The valour of Gennerid, formidable to the adjacent barbarians, was the firmest bulwark of the Illyrian frontier; and his vigilant care assisted the empire with a reinforcement of ten thousand Huns, who arrived on the confines of Italy, attended by such a convoy of provisions, and such a numerous train of sheep and oxen, as might have been sufficient not only for the march of an army but for the settlement of a colony. But the court and councils of Honorius still remained a scene of weakness and distraction, of corruption and anarchy. Instigated by the prefect Jovius, the guards rose in furious mutiny and demanded the heads of two generals and of the two principal eunuchs. The generals, under a perfidious promise of safety, were sent on ship-board and privately executed; while the favour of the eunuchs procured them a mild and secure exile at Milan and Constantinople. Eusebius the eunuch and the barbarian Allobich succeeded to the command of the bed-chamber and of the guards; and the mutual jealousy of the subordinate ministers was the cause of their mutual destruction. By the insolent order of the count of the domestics, the great chamberlain was shamefully beaten to death with sticks before the eyes of the astonished emperor; and the subsequent assassination of Allobich, in the midst of a public procession, is the only circumstance of his life in which Honorius discovered the faintest symptom of courage or resentment. Yet before they fell, Eusebius and Allobich had contributed their part to the ruin of the empire by opposing the conclusion of a treaty which Jovius, from a selfish, and perhaps a criminal motive, had negociated with Alaric, in a personal interview under the walls of Rimini. During the absence of Jovius the emperor was persuaded to assume a lofty tone of inflexible dignity, such as neither his situation nor his character could enable him to support; and a letter, signed with the name of Honorius, was immediately despatched to the Prætorian prefect, granting him a free permission to dispose of the public money, but sternly refusing to prostitute the military honours of Rome to the proud demands of a barbarian. This letter was imprudently communicated to Alaric himself; and the Goth, who in the whole transaction had behaved with temper and decency, expressed in the most outrageous language his lively sense of the insult so wantonly offered to his person and to his nation. The conference of Rimini was hastily interrupted; and the prefect Jovius, on his return to Ravenna, was compelled to adopt, and even to encourage, the fashionable opinions of the court. By his advice and example the principal officers of the state and army were obliged to swear, that, without listening in *any* circumstances to *any* conditions of peace, they would still persevere in perpetual and implacable war against the enemy of the republic. This rash engagement opposed an insuperable bar to all future negociation. The ministers of Honorius were heard to declare, that, if they had only invoked the name of the Deity, they would consult the public safety, and trust their souls to the mercy of Heaven: but they had sworn by the sacred head of the emperor himself; they had touched in solemn ceremony that august seat of majesty and wisdom; and the violation of their oath would expose them to the temporal penalties of sacrilege and rebellion.

THE SECOND SIEGE OF ROME

While the emperor and his court enjoyed with sullen pride the security of the marshes and fortifications of Ravenna, they abandoned Rome, almost without defence, to the resentment of Alaric. Yet such was the moderation which he still preserved, or affected, that as he moved with his army along the Flaminian way he successively despatched the bishops of the towns of Italy to reiterate his offers of peace, and to conjure the emperor that he would save the city and its inhabitants from hostile fire and the sword of the barbarians. These impending calamities were however averted, not indeed by the wisdom of Honorius, but by the prudence or humanity of the Gothic king, who employed a milder, though not less effectual, method of conquest. Instead of assaulting the capital he successfully directed his efforts against the *Port* of Ostia, one of the boldest and most stupendous works of Roman magnificence. The accidents to which the precarious subsistence of the city was continually exposed in a winter navigation and an open road had suggested to the genius of the first Cæsar the useful design which was executed under the reign of Claudius. The artificial moles which formed the narrow entrance advanced far into the sea, and firmly repelled the fury of the waves, while the largest vessels securely rode at anchor within three deep and capacious basons which received the northern branch of the Tiber about two miles from the ancient colony of Ostia.[1] The Roman *Port* insensibly swelled to the size of an episcopal city, where the corn of Africa was deposited in spacious granaries for the use of the capital. As soon as Alaric was

[1] The *Ostia Tiberina*, in the plural number, the two mouths of the Tiber, were separated by the Holy Island, an equilateral triangle, whose sides were each of them computed at about two miles. The colony of Ostia was founded immediately beyond the left, or southern, and the *Port* immediately beyond the right, or northern, branch of the river; and the distance between their remains measures something more than two miles on Cingolani's map. In the time of Strabo the sand and mud deposited by the Tiber had choked the harbour of Ostia; the progress of the same cause had added much to the

in possession of that important place he summoned the city to surrender at discretion; and his demands were enforced by the positive declaration that a refusal, or even a delay, should be instantly followed by the destruction of the magazines on which the life of the Roman people depended. The clamours of that people and the terror of famine subdued the pride of the senate; they listened without reluctance to the proposal of placing a new emperor on the throne of the unworthy Honorius; and the suffrage of the Gothic conqueror bestowed the purple on Attalus, prefect of the city. The grateful monarch immediately acknowledged his protector as master-general of the armies of the West; Adolphus, with the rank of count of the domestics, obtained the custody of the person of Attalus; and the two hostile nations seemed to be united in the closest bands of friendship and alliance.

The gates of the city were thrown open, and the new emperor of the Romans, encompassed on every side by the Gothic arms, was conducted in tumultuous procession to the palace of Augustus and Trajan. After he had distributed the civil and military dignities among his favourites and followers, Attalus convened an assembly of the senate, before whom, in a formal and florid speech, he asserted his resolution of restoring the majesty of the republic, and of uniting to the empire the provinces of Egypt and the East which had once acknowledged the sovereignty of Rome. Such extravagant promises inspired every reasonable citizen with a just contempt for the character of an unwarlike usurper, whose elevation was the deepest and most ignominious wound which the republic had yet sustained from the insolence of the barbarians. But the populace, with their usual levity, applauded the change of masters. The public discontent was favourable to the rival of Honorius; and the sectaries, oppressed by his persecuting edicts, expected some degree of countenance, or at least of toleration, from a prince who, in his native country of Ionia, had been educated in the Pagan superstition, and who had since received the sacrament of baptism from the

size of the Holy Island, and gradually left both Ostia and the Port at a considerable distance from the shore. The dry channels and the large estuaries mark the changes of the river and the efforts of the sea. Consult, for the present state of this dreary and desolate tract, the excellent map of the ecclesiastical state by the mathematicians of Benedict XIV; an actual survey of the *Agro Romano*, in six sheets, by Cingolani, which contains 113,819 *rubbia* (about 570,000 acres); and the large topographical map of Ameti, in eight sheets.

hands of an Arian bishop. The first days of the reign of Attalus were fair and prosperous. An officer of confidence
was sent with an inconsiderable body of troops to secure
the obedience of Africa; the greatest part of Italy submitted
to the terror of the Gothic powers; and though the city of
Bologna made a vigorous and effectual resistance, the people
of Milan, dissatisfied perhaps with the absence of Honorius,
accepted with loud acclamations the choice of the Roman
senate. At the head of a formidable army, Alaric conducted
his royal captive almost to the gates of Ravenna; and a solemn
embassy of the principal ministers—of Jovius the Prætorian
prefect, of Valens, master of the cavalry and infantry, of the
quæstor Potamius, and of Julian, the first of the notaries—
was introduced with martial pomp into the Gothic camp.
In the name of their sovereign they consented to acknowledge the lawful election of his competitor, and to divide the
provinces of Italy and the West between the two emperors.
Their proposals were rejected with disdain; and the refusal
was aggravated by the insulting clemency of Attalus, who
condescended to promise that if Honorius would instantly
resign the purple he should be permitted to pass the remainder
of his life in the peaceful exile of some remote island. So
desperate indeed did the situation of the son of Theodosius
appear to those who were the best acquainted with his strength
and resources, that Jovius and Valens, his minister and his
general, betrayed their trust, infamously deserted the sinking
cause of their benefactor, and devoted their treacherous
allegiance to the service of his more fortunate rival. Astonished by such examples of domestic treason, Honorius
trembled at the approach of every servant, at the arrival of
every messenger. He dreaded the secret enemies who might
lurk in his capital, his palace, his bed-chamber; and some ships
lay ready in the harbour of Ravenna to transport the abdicated
monarch to the dominions of his infant nephew, the emperor
of the East.

But there *is* a Providence (such at least was the opinion
of the historian Procopius) that watches over innocence and
folly, and the pretensions of Honorius to its peculiar care
cannot reasonably be disputed. At the moment when his despair, incapable of any wise or manly resolution, meditated a
shameful flight, a seasonable reinforcement of four thousand
veterans unexpectedly landed in the port of Ravenna. To these

valiant strangers, whose fidelity had not been corrupted by the factions of the court, he committed the walls and gates of the city, and the slumbers of the emperor were no longer disturbed by the apprehension of imminent and internal danger. The favourable intelligence which was received from Africa suddenly changed the opinions of men and the state of public affairs. The troops and officers whom Attalus had sent into the province were defeated and slain, and the active zeal of Heraclian maintained his own allegiance and that of his people. The faithful count of Africa transmitted a large sum of money, which fixed the attachment of the Imperial guards; and his vigilance in preventing the exportation of corn and oil introduced famine, tumult, and discontent into the walls of Rome. The failure of the African expedition was the source of mutual complaint and recrimination in the party of Attalus, and the mind of his protector was insensibly alienated from the interest of a prince who wanted spirit to command or docility to obey. The most imprudent measures were adopted, without the knowledge or against the advice of Alaric, and the obstinate refusal of the senate to allow in the embarkation the mixture even of five hundred Goths, betrayed a suspicious and distrustful temper which in their situation was neither generous nor prudent. The resentment of the Gothic king was exasperated by the malicious arts of Jovius, who had been raised to the rank of patrician, and who afterwards excused his double perfidy by declaring without a blush that he had only *seemed* to abandon the service of Honorius more effectually to ruin the cause of the usurper. In a large plain near Rimini, and in the presence of an innumerable multitude of Romans and barbarians, the wretched Attalus was publicly despoiled of the diadem and purple; and those ensigns of royalty were sent by Alaric as the pledge of peace and friendship to the son of Theodosius. The officers who returned to their duty were reinstated in their employments, and even the merit of a tardy repentance was graciously allowed; but the degraded emperor of the Romans, desirous of life and insensible of disgrace, implored the permission of following the Gothic camp in the train of a haughty and capricious barbarian.

THE THIRD SIEGE AND SACK OF ROME

The degradation of Attalus removed the only real obstacle to the conclusion of the peace, and Alaric advanced within three miles of Ravenna to press the irresolution of the Imperial ministers, whose insolence soon returned with the return of fortune. His indignation was kindled by the report that a rival chieftain, that Sarus, the personal enemy of Adolphus, and the hereditary foe of the house of Balti, had been received into the palace. At the head of three hundred followers that fearless barbarian immediately sallied from the gates of Ravenna, surprised and cut in pieces a considerable body of Goths, re-entered the city in triumph, and was permitted to insult his adversary by the voice of a herald, who publicly declared that the guilt of Alaric had for ever excluded him from the friendship and alliance of the emperor. The crime and folly of the court of Ravenna was expiated a third time by the calamities of Rome. The king of the Goths, who no longer dissembled his appetite for plunder and revenge, appeared in arms under the walls of the capital; and the trembling senate, without any hopes of relief, prepared by a desperate resistance to delay the ruin of their country. But they were unable to guard against the secret conspiracy of their slaves and domestics, who either from birth or interest were attached to the cause of the enemy. At the hour of midnight the Salarian gate was silently opened, and the inhabitants were awakened by the tremendous sound of the Gothic trumpet. Eleven hundred and sixty-three years after the foundation of Rome, the Imperial city, which had subdued and civilised so considerable a part of mankind, was delivered to the licentious fury of the tribes of Germany and Scythia.

The proclamation of Alaric, when he forced his entrance into a vanquished city, discovered, however, some regard for the laws of humanity and religion. He encouraged his troops boldly to seize the rewards of valour, and to enrich themselves with the spoils of a wealthy and effeminate people; but he exhorted them at the same time to spare the lives of the unresisting citizens, and to respect the churches of the apostles of St. Peter and St. Paul as holy and inviolable sanctuaries. Amidst the horrors of a nocturnal tumult several of the Christian Goths displayed the fervour of a recent conversion; and some instances of their uncommon piety and moderation are related, and perhaps adorned, by the zeal of ecclesiastical writers.[1] While the barbarians roamed through the city in quest of prey, the humble dwelling of an aged virgin, who had devoted her life to the service of the altar, was forced open by one of the powerful Goths. He immediately demanded, though in civil language, all the gold and silver in her possession, and was astonished at the readiness with which she conducted him to a splendid hoard of massy plate of the richest materials and the most curious workmanship. The barbarian viewed with wonder and delight this valuable acquisition, till he was interrupted by a serious admonition, addressed to him in the following words: "These," said she, "are the consecrated vessels belonging to St. Peter: if you presume to touch them, the sacrilegious deed will remain on your conscience. For my part, I dare not keep what I am unable to defend." The Gothic captain, struck with reverential awe, despatched a messenger to inform the king of the treasure which he had discovered, and received a peremptory order from Alaric, that all the consecrated plate and ornaments should be transported, without damage or delay, to the church of the apostle. From the extremity, perhaps, of the Quirinal hill to the distant quarter of the Vatican, a numerous detachment of Goths, marching in order of battle through the principal streets, protected with glittering arms the long train of their devout companions who bore aloft on their heads the sacred vessels of gold and silver, and the martial shouts of the barbarians were mingled with the sound of religious psalmody. From all the adjacent houses a crowd of Christians hastened to join this edifying procession, and a multitude of fugitives, without distinction of age or rank, or even of sect, had the good fortune to escape to the secure and hospitable sanctuary of the Vatican. The learned work concerning the *City of God* was professedly composed by St. Augustin, to justify the ways of Providence in the destruction of the Roman greatness. He celebrates with pecul-

---

[1] Orosius applauds the piety of the Christian Goths without seeming to perceive that the greatest part of them were Arian heretics. Jornandes and Isidore of Seville, who were both attached to the Gothic cause, have repeated and embellished these edifying tales. According to Isidore, Alaric himself was heard to say that he waged war with the Romans, and not with the Apostles. Such was the style of the seventh century; two hundred years before, the fame and merit had been ascribed, not to the Apostles, but to Christ.

iar satisfaction this memorable triumph of Christ, and insults his adversaries by challenging them to produce some similar example of a town taken by storm, in which the fabulous gods of antiquity had been able to protect either themselves or their deluded votaries.

In the sack of Rome some rare and extraordinary examples of barbarian virtue have been deservedly applauded. But the holy precincts of the Vatican and the apostolic churches could receive a very small proportion of the Roman people: many thousand warriors, more especially of the Huns who served under the standard of Alaric, were strangers to the name, or at least to the faith of Christ, and we may suspect, without any breach of charity or candour, that in the hour of savage licence, when every passion was inflamed and every restraint was removed, the precepts of the Gospel seldom influenced the behaviour of the Gothic Christians. The writers the best disposed to exaggerate their clemency have freely confessed that a cruel slaughter was made of the Romans, and that the streets of the city were filled with dead bodies, which remained without burial during the general consternation. The despair of the citizens was sometimes converted into fury; and whenever the barbarians were provoked by opposition, they extended the promiscuous massacre to the feeble, the innocent, and the helpless. The private revenge of forty thousand slaves was exercised without pity or remorse; and the ignominious lashes which they had formerly received were washed away in the blood of the guilty or obnoxious families. The matrons and virgins of Rome were exposed to injuries more dreadful, in the apprehension of chastity, than death itself; and the ecclesiastical historian has selected an example of female virtue for the admiration of future ages.[1] A Roman lady, of singular beauty and orthodox faith, had excited the impatient desires of a young Goth, who, according to the sagacious remark of Sozomen, was attached to the Arian heresy. Exasperated by her obstinate resistance, he drew his sword, and, with the anger of a lover, slightly wounded her neck. The bleeding heroine still continued to

---

[1] Augustin intimates that some virgins or matrons actually killed themselves to escape violation; and though he admires their spirit, he is obliged, by his theology, to condemn their rash presumption. Perhaps the good bishop of Hippo was too easy in the belief, as well as too rigid in the censure, of this act of female heroism. The twenty maidens (if they ever existed) who threw themselves into the Elbe when Magdeburg was taken by storm, have been multiplied to the number of twelve hundred.

brave his resentment and to repel his love, till the ravisher desisted from his unavailing efforts, respectfully conducted her to the sanctuary of the Vatican, and gave six pieces of gold to the guards of the church on condition that they should restore her inviolate to the arms of her husband. Such instances of courage and generosity were not extremely common. The brutal soldiers satisfied their sensual appetites without consulting either the inclination or the duties of their female captives; and a nice question of casuistry was seriously agitated, Whether those tender victims, who had inflexibly refused their consent to the violation which they sustained, had lost, by their misfortune, the glorious crown of virginity. There were other losses indeed of a more substantial kind and more general concern. It cannot be presumed that all the barbarians were at all times capable of perpetrating such amorous outrages; and the want of youth, or beauty, or chastity, protected the greatest part of the Roman women from the danger of a rape. But avarice is an insatiate and universal passion; since the enjoyment of almost every object that can afford pleasure to the different tastes and tempers of mankind may be procured by the possession of wealth. In the pillage of Rome a just preference was given to gold and jewels, which contain the greatest value in the smallest compass and weight; but, after these portable riches had been removed by the more diligent robbers, the palaces of Rome were rudely stripped of their splendid and costly furniture. The sideboards of massy plate, and the variegated wardrobes of silk and purple, were irregularly piled in the waggons that always followed the march of a Gothic army. The most exquisite works of art were roughly handled or wantonly destroyed: many a statue was melted for the sake of the precious materials; and many a vase, in the division of the spoil, was shivered into fragments by the stroke of a battle-axe. The acquisition of riches served only to stimulate the avarice of the rapacious barbarians, who proceeded by threats, by blows, and by tortures, to force from their prisoners the confession of hidden treasure. Visible splendour and expense were alleged as the proof of a plentiful fortune; the appearance of poverty was imputed to a parsimonious disposition; and the obstinacy of some misers, who endured the most cruel torments before they would discover the secret object of their affection, was fatal to many unhappy wretches, who expired under the lash for refusing to reveal their imaginary treasures. The edifices of Rome, though the damage has been much exaggerated, received some injury from the violence of the Goths. At their entrance through the Salarian gate they fired the adjacent houses to guide their march and to distract the attention of the citizens; the flames, which encountered no obstacle in the disorder of the night, consumed many private and public buildings, and the ruins of the palace of Sallust remained in the age of Justinian a stately monument of the Gothic conflagration. Yet a contemporary historian has observed that fire could scarcely consume the enormous beams of solid brass, and that the strength of man was insufficient to subvert the foundations of ancient structures. Some truth may possibly be concealed in his devout assertion, that the wrath of Heaven supplied the imperfections of hostile rage, and that the proud Forum of Rome, decorated with the statues of so many gods and heroes, was levelled in the dust by the stroke of lightning.

Whatever might be the numbers, of equestrian or plebeian rank, who perished in the massacre of Rome, it is confidently affirmed that only one senator lost his life by the sword of the enemy. But it was not easy to compute the multitudes who, from an honourable station and a prosperous fortune, were suddenly reduced to the miserable condition of captives and exiles. As the barbarians had more occasion for money than for slaves, they fixed at a moderate price the redemption of their indigent prisoners; and the ransom was often paid by the benevolence of their friends, or the charity of strangers. The captives, who were regularly sold, either in open market, or by private contract, would have legally regained their native freedom, which it was impossible for a citizen to lose or to alienate. But as it was soon discovered that the vindication of their liberty would endanger their lives, and that the Goths, unless they were tempted to sell, might be provoked to murder their useless prisoners, the civil jurisprudence had been already qualified by a wise regulation, that they should be obliged to serve the moderate term of five years, till they had discharged by their labour the price of their redemption. The nations who invaded the Roman empire had driven before them, into Italy, whole troops of hungry and affrighted provincials, less apprehensive of servitude than of famine. The calamities of Rome and Italy dispersed the inhabitants to the most lonely, the most secure, the most distant places of refuge. While the Gothic cavalry spread terror and desolation along the seacoast of Campania and Tuscany, the little island of Igilium, separated by a narrow channel from the Argentarian promontory, repulsed, or eluded, their hostile attempts; and at so small a distance from Rome, great numbers of citizens were securely concealed in the thick woods of the sequestered spot. The ample patrimonies which many senatorian families possessed in Africa invited them, if they had time and prudence to escape from the ruin of their country, to embrace the shelter of that hospitable province. The most illustrious of these fugitives was the noble and pious Proba,[1] the widow of the prefect Petronius. After the death of her husband, the most powerful subject of Rome, she had remained at the head of the Anician family, and successively supplied, from her private fortune, the expense of the consulships of her three sons. When the city was besieged and taken by the Goths, Proba supported with Christian resignation the loss of immense riches; embarked in a small vessel, from whence she beheld, at sea, the flames of her burning palace; and fled with her daughter Læta, and her granddaughter, the celebrated virgin Demetrias, to the coast of Africa. The benevolent profusion with which the matron distributed the fruits or the price of her estates contributed to alleviate the misfortunes of exile and captivity. But even the family of Proba herself was not exempt from the rapacious oppression of Count Heraclian, who basely sold, in matrimonial prostitution, the noblest maidens of Rome to the lust or avarice of the Syrian merchants. The Italian fugitives were dispersed through the provinces, along the coast of Egypt and Asia, as far as Constantinople and Jerusalem; and the village of Bethlem, the solitary residence of St. Jerom and his female converts, was crowded with illustrious beggars, of either sex and every age, who excited the public compassion by the remembrance of their past fortune. This awful catastrophe of Rome filled the astonished empire with grief and terror. So interesting a contrast of greatness and ruin disposed the

---

[1] As the adventures of Proba and her family are connected with the life of St. Augustin, they are diligently illustrated by Tillemont. Some time after their arrival in Africa, Demetrias took the veil and made a vow of virginity; an event which was considered as of the highest importance to Rome and to the world. All the *Saints* wrote congratulatory letters to her; that of Jerom is still extant, and contains a mixture of absurd reasoning, spirited declamation, and curious facts, some of which relate to the siege and sack of Rome.

fond credulity of the people to deplore, and even to exaggerate, the afflictions of the queen of cities. The clergy, who applied to recent events the lofty metaphors of Oriental prophecy, were sometimes tempted to confound the destruction of the capital and the dissolution of the globe.

There exists in human nature a strong propensity to depreciate the advantages, and to magnify the evils, of the present times. Yet, when the first emotions had subsided, and a fair estimate was made of the real damage, the more learned and judicious contemporaries were forced to confess that infant Rome had formerly received more essential injury from the Gauls than she had now sustained from the Goths in her declining age. The experience of eleven centuries had enabled posterity to produce a much more singular parallel; and to affirm with confidence, that the ravages of the barbarians whom Alaric had led from the banks of the Danube were less destructive than the hostilities exercised by the troops of Charles the Fifth, a catholic prince, who styled himself Emperor of the Romans. The Goths evacuated the city at the end of six days, but Rome remained above nine months in the possession of the Imperialists; and every hour was stained by some atrocious act of cruelty, lust, and rapine. The authority of Alaric preserved some order and moderation among the ferocious multitude which acknowledged him for their leader and king; but the constable of Bourbon had gloriously fallen in the attack of the walls; and the death of the general removed every restraint of discipline from an army which consisted of three independent nations, the Italians, the Spaniards, and the Germans. In the beginning of the sixteenth century the manners of Italy exhibited a remarkable scene of the depravity of mankind. They united the sanguinary crimes that prevail in an unsettled state of society, with the polished vices which spring from the abuse of art and luxury; and the loose adventurers, who had violated every prejudice of patriotism and superstition to assault the palace of the Roman pontiff, must deserve to be considered as the most profligate of the *Italians*. At the same era the *Spaniards* were the terror both of the Old and New World; but their high-spirited valour was disgraced by gloomy pride, rapacious avarice, and unrelenting cruelty. Indefatigable in the pursuit of fame and riches, they had improved, by repeated practice, the most exquisite and effectual methods of torturing their prisoners: many of the Castilians who pillaged Rome were familiars of the holy inquisition; and some volunteers, perhaps, were lately returned from the conquest of Mexico. The *Germans* were less corrupt than the Italians, less cruel than the Spaniards; and the rustic, or even savage, aspect of those *Tramontane* warriors often disguised a simple and merciful disposition. But they had imbibed, in the first fervour of the Reformation, the spirit, as well as the principles, of Luther. It was their favourite amusement to insult, or destroy, the consecrated objects of catholic superstition; they indulged, without pity or remorse, a devout hatred against the clergy of every denomination and degree who form so considerable a part of the inhabitants of modern Rome; and their fanatic zeal might aspire to subvert the throne of Antichrist, to purify, with blood and fire, the abominations of the spiritual Babylon.

THE RETREAT OF THE GOTHS AND THE DEATH OF ALARIC

The retreat of the victorious Goths, who evacuated Rome on the sixth day, might be the result of prudence, but it was not surely the effect of fear.[1] At the head of an army encumbered with rich and weighty spoils, their intrepid leader advanced along the Appian Way into the southern provinces of Italy, destroying whatever dared to oppose his passage, and contenting himself with the plunder of the unresisting country. The fate of Capua, the proud and luxurious metropolis of Campania, and which was respected, even in its decay, as the eighth city of the empire, is buried in oblivion; whilst the adjacent town of Nola has been illustrated, on this occasion, by the sanctity of Paulinus, who was successively a consul, a monk, and a bishop. At the age of forty he renounced the enjoyment of wealth and honour, of society and literature, to embrace a life of solitude and penance; and the loud applause of the clergy encouraged him to despise the reproaches of his worldly friends, who ascribed this desperate act to some disorder of the mind or body. An early and passionate attachment determined him to fix his humble dwelling in one of the suburbs of Nola, near the miraculous tomb of St. Felix, which the public devotion had already surrounded with five large

---

[1] Socrates pretends, without any colour of truth or reason, that Alaric fled on the report that the armies of the Eastern empire were in full march to attack him.

and populous churches. The remains of his fortune, and of his understanding, were dedicated to the service of the glorious martyr; whose praise, on the day of his festival, Paulinus never failed to celebrate by a solemn hymn; and in whose name he erected a sixth church, of superior elegance and beauty, which was decorated with many curious pictures from the history of the Old and New Testament. Such assiduous zeal secured the favour of the saint,[1] or at least of the people; and, after fifteen years' retirement, the Roman consul was compelled to accept the bishopric of Nola, a few months before the city was invested by the Goths. During the siege, some religious persons were satisfied that they had seen, either in dreams or visions, the divine form of their tutelar patron; yet it soon appeared by the event, that Felix wanted power, or inclination, to preserve the flock of which he had formerly been the shepherd. Nola was not saved from the general devastation; and the captive bishop was protected only by the general opinion of his innocence and poverty. Above four years elapsed from the successful invasion of Italy by the arms of Alaric, to the voluntary retreat of the Goths under the conduct of his successor Adolphus; and, during the whole time, they reigned without control over a country which, in the opinion of the ancients, had united all the various excellences of nature and art. The prosperity, indeed, which Italy had attained in the auspicious age of the Antonines, had gradually declined with the decline of the empire. The fruits of a long peace perished under the rude grasp of the barbarians; and they themselves were incapable of tasting the more elegant refinements of luxury which had been prepared for the use of the soft and polished Italians. Each soldier, however, claimed an ample portion of the substantial plenty, the corn and cattle, oil and wine, that was daily collected and consumed in the Gothic camp; and the principal warriors insulted the villas and gardens, once inhabited by Lucullus and Cicero, along the beauteous coast of Campania. Their trembling captives, the sons and daughters of Roman senators, presented, in goblets of gold and gems, large draughts of Falernian wine to the haughty victors, who stretched their huge limbs under the shade of plane-trees, artificially disposed to exclude the scorching rays, and to

---

[1] The humble Paulinus once presumed to say that he believed St. Felix *did* love him; at least, as a master loves his little dog.

admit the genial warmth, of the sun. These delights were enhanced by the memory of past hardships: the comparison of their native soil, the bleak and barren hills of Scythia, and the frozen banks of the Elbe and Danube, added new charms to the felicity of the Italian climate.

Whether fame, or conquest, or riches were the object of Alaric, he pursued that object with an indefatigable ardour which could neither be quelled by adversity nor satiated by success. No sooner had he reached the extreme land of Italy than he was attracted by the neighbouring prospect of a fertile and peaceful island. Yet even the possession of Sicily he considered only as an intermediate step to the important expedition which he already meditated against the continent of Africa. The straits of Rhegium and Messina are twelve miles in length, and in the narrowest passage about one mile and a half broad; and the fabulous monsters of the deep, the rocks of Scylla and the whirlpool of Charybdis, could terrify none but the most timid and unskilful mariners. Yet as soon as the first division of the Goths had embarked, a sudden tempest arose, which sunk or scattered many of the transports; their courage was daunted by the terrors of a new element; and the whole design was defeated by the premature death of Alaric, which fixed, after a short illness, the fatal term of his conquests. The ferocious character of the barbarians was displayed in the funeral of a hero whose valour and fortune they celebrated with mournful applause. By the labour of a captive multitude they forcibly diverted the course of the Busentinus, a small river that washes the walls of Consentia. The royal sepulchre, adorned with the splendid spoils and trophies of Rome, was constructed in the vacant bed; the waters were then restored to their natural channel; and the secret spot where the remains of Alaric had been deposited was for ever concealed by the inhuman massacre of the prisoners who had been employed to execute the work.

Adolphus, who now became King of the Goths, concluded a peace with the Romans and married Placidia, the half-sister of Honorius. He marched into Spain to expel an invasion of the Suevi, Vandals, and Alani but was treacherously murdered. His successor, Wallia, recovered Spain for Honorius, confining the Vandals in the northwestern part of the peninsula, and then established the Goths in Aquitaine.

32.

THE REIGN OF ARCADIUS. ST. JOHN CHRYSOSTOM.
DEATH OF ARCADIUS AND SUCCESSION OF THEODOSIUS
THE YOUNGER. ADMINISTRATION OF PULCHERIA.
ADVENTURES OF EUDOCIA

THE DIVISION of the Roman world between the sons of Theodosius marks the final establishment of the empire of the East, which from the reign of Arcadius to the taking of Constantinople by the Turks, subsisted one thousand and fifty-eight years in a state of premature and perpetual decay. The sovereign of that empire assumed and obstinately retained the vain, and at length fictitious, title of Emperor of the ROMANS; and the hereditary appellations of CÆSAR and AUGUSTUS continued to declare that he was the legitimate successor of the first of men, who had reigned over the first of nations. The palace of Constantinople rivalled, and perhaps excelled, the magnificence of Persia; and the eloquent sermons of St. Chrysostom celebrate, while they condemn, the pompous luxury of the reign of Arcadius. "The emperor," says he, "wears on his head either a diadem or a crown of gold, decorated with precious stones of inestimable value. These ornaments and his purple garments are reserved for his sacred person alone; and his robes of silk are embroidered with the figures of golden dragons. His throne is of massy gold. Whenever he appears in public he is surrounded by his courtiers, his guards, and his attendants. Their spears, their shields, their cuirasses, the bridles and trappings of their horses, have either the substance, or the appearance of gold; and the large splendid boss in the midst of their shield is encircled with smaller bosses, which represent the shape of the human eye. The two mules that draw the chariot of the monarch are perfectly white, and shining all over with gold. The chariot itself, of pure and solid gold, attracts the admiration of the spectators, who contemplate the purple curtains, the snowy carpet, the size of the precious stones, and the resplendent plates of gold, that glitter as they are agitated by the motion of the carriage. The Imperial pictures are white, on a blue ground; the emperor appears seated on his throne, with his arms, his horses, and his guards beside him; and his vanquished enemies in chains at his feet." The successors of Constantine established their perpetual residence in the royal city which he had erected on the verge of Europe and Asia. Inaccessible to the menaces of their enemies, and perhaps to the complaints of their people, they received with each wind the tributary productions of every climate; while the impregnable strength of their capital continued for ages to defy the hostile attempts of the barbarians. Their dominions were bounded by the Adriatic and the Tigris; and the whole interval of twenty-five days' navigation, which separated the extreme cold of Scythia from the torrid zone of Ethiopia, was comprehended within the limits of the empire of the East. The populous countries of that empire were the seat of art and learning, of luxury and wealth; and the inhabitants, who had assumed the language and manners of Greeks, styled themselves, with some appearance of truth, the most enlightened and civilised portion of the human species. The form of government was a pure and simple monarchy; the name of the ROMAN REPUBLIC, which so long preserved a faint tradition of freedom, was confined to the Latin provinces; and the princes of Constantinople measured their greatness by the servile obedience of their people. They were ignorant how much this passive disposition enervates and degrades every faculty of the mind. The subjects who had resigned their will to the absolute commands of a master were equally incapable of guarding their lives and fortunes against the assaults of the barbarians, or of defending their reason from the terrors of superstition.

During the first five years of the reign of Arcadius the administration was controlled by his chamberlain, the cruel and avaricious eunuch Eutropius. Eutropius was brought down by a rebellion of the Ostrogoths under Tribigild and Gainas and at the instigation of the Empress Eudoxia. The rebellion was subsequently defeated.

ST. JOHN CHRYSOSTOM

After the death of the indolent Nectarius, the successor of Gregory Nazianzen, the church of Constantinople was distracted by the ambition of rival candidates, who were not ashamed to solicit, with gold or flattery, the suffrage of the people or of the favourite. On this occasion Eutropius seems to have deviated from his ordinary maxims; and his uncorrupted judgment was determined only by the superior merit of a stranger. In a late journey into the East he had admired the sermons of John, a native and presbyter of Antioch, whose name has been distinguished by the epithet of Chrysostom, or the Golden Mouth. A private order was despatched to the governor of Syria; and as the people might be unwilling to resign their favourite preacher, he was transported, with speed and secrecy, in a post-chariot, from Antioch to Constantinople. The unanimous and unsolicited consent of the court, the clergy, and the people ratified the choice of the minister; and, both as a saint and as an orator, the new archbishop surpassed the sanguine expectations of the public. Born of a noble and opulent family in the capital of Syria, Chrysostom had been educated, by the care of a tender mother, under the tradition of the most skilful masters. He studied the art of rhetoric in the school of Libanius; and that celebrated sophist, who soon discovered the talents of his disciple, ingenuously confessed that John would have deserved to succeed him had he not been stolen away by the Christians. His piety soon disposed him to receive the sacrament of baptism; to renounce the lucrative and honourable profession of the law; and to bury himself in the adjacent desert, where he subdued the lusts of the flesh by an austere penance of six years. His infirmities compelled him to return to the society of mankind; and the authority of Meletius devoted his talents to the service of the church: but in the midst of his family, and afterwards on the archiepiscopal throne, Chrysostom still persevered in the practice of the monastic virtues. The ample revenues, which his predecessors had consumed in pomp and luxury, he diligently applied to the establishment of hospitals; and the multitudes who were supported by his charity preferred the eloquent and edifying discourses of their archbishop to the amusements of the theatre or the circus.

The monuments of that eloquence, which was admired near twenty years at Antioch and Constantinople, have been carefully preserved; and the possession of near one thousand sermons or homilies has authorised the critics[1] of succeeding times to appreciate the genuine merit of Chrysostom. They unanimously attribute to the Christian orator the free command of an elegant and copious language; the judgment to conceal the advantages which he derived from the knowledge of rhetoric and philosophy; an inexhaustible fund of metaphors and similitudes, of ideas and images, to vary and illustrate the most familiar topics; the happy art of engaging the passions in the service of virtue, and of exposing the folly as well as the turpitude of vice almost with the truth and spirit of a dramatic representation.

The pastoral labours of the archbishop of Constantinople provoked and gradually united against him two sorts of enemies; the aspiring clergy, who envied his success, and the obstinate sinners, who were offended by his reproofs. When Chrysostom thundered from the pulpit of St. Sophia against the degeneracy of the Christians, his shafts were spent among the crowd, without wounding or even marking the character of any individual. When he declaimed against the peculiar vices of the rich, poverty might obtain a transient consolation from his invectives: but the guilty were still sheltered by their numbers; and the reproach itself was dignified by some ideas of superiority and enjoyment. But as the pyramid rose towards the summit, it insensibly diminished to a point; and the magistrates, the ministers, the favourite eunuchs, the ladies of the court,[2] the empress Eudoxia herself, had a much larger share of guilt to divide among a smaller proportion of criminals. The personal applications of the audience were anticipated or confirmed by the testimony of their own conscience; and the intrepid preacher assumed the dangerous right of exposing

---

[1] As I am *almost* a stranger to the voluminous sermons of Chrysostom, I have given my confidence to the two most judicious and moderate of the ecclesiastical critics, Erasmus and Dupin; yet the good taste of the former is sometimes vitiated by an excessive love of antiquity, and the good sense of the latter is always restrained by prudential considerations.

[2] The females of Constantinople distinguished themselves by their enmity or their attachment to Chrysostom. Three noble and opulent widows—Marsa, Castricia, and Eugraphia—were the leaders of the persecution. It was impossible that they should forgive a preacher who reproached their affectation to conceal, by the ornaments of dress, their age and ugliness. Olympias, by equal zeal, displayed in a more pious cause, has obtained the title of saint.

both the offence and the offender to the public abhorrence.
The secret resentment of the court encouraged the discontent
of the clergy and monks of Constantinople, who were too
hastily reformed by the fervent zeal of their archbishop. He
had condemned from the pulpit the domestic females of the
clergy of Constantinople, who, under the name of servants
or sisters, afforded a perpetual occasion either of sin or of
scandal. The silent and solitary ascetics, who had secluded
themselves from the world, were entitled to the warmest
approbation of Chrysostom; but he despised and stigmatised,
as the disgrace of their holy profession, the crowd of degenerate monks, who, from some unworthy motives of pleasure or
profit, so frequently infested the streets of the capital. To the
voice of persuasion the archbishop was obliged to add the
terrors of authority; and his ardour in the exercise of ecclesiastical jurisdiction was not always exempt from passion; nor
was it always guided by prudence. Chrysostom was naturally
of a choleric disposition.[1] Although he struggled, according
to the precepts of the Gospel, to love his private enemies, he
indulged himself in the privilege of hating the enemies of
God and of the church; and his sentiments were sometimes
delivered with too much energy of countenance and expression.
He still maintained, from some considerations of health or
abstinence, his former habits of taking his repasts alone; and
this inhospitable custom,[2] which his enemies imputed to pride,
contributed at least to nourish the infirmity of a morose and
unsocial humour. Separated from that familiar intercourse
which facilitates the knowledge and the despatch of business,
he reposed an unsuspecting confidence in his deacon Serapion;
and seldom applied his speculative knowledge of human nature
to the particular characters either of his dependents or of his
equals. Conscious of the purity of his intentions, and perhaps
of the superiority of his genius, the archbishop of Constantinople extended the jurisdiction of the Imperial city, that he

---

[1] Sozomen, and more especially Socrates, have defined the real character of
Chrysostom with a temperate and impartial freedom very offensive to his
blind admirers. Those historians lived in the next generation, when party
violence was abated, and had conversed with many persons intimately acquainted with the virtues and imperfections of the saint.

[2] Palladius very seriously defends the archbishop. 1. He never tasted wine.
2. The weakness of his stomach required a peculiar diet. 3. Business, or study,
or devotion, often kept him fasting till sunset. 4. He detested the noise and
levity of great dinners. 5. He saved the expense for the use of the poor. 6.
He was apprehensive, in a capital like Constantinople, of the envy and reproach of partial invitations.

might enlarge the sphere of his pastoral labours; and the conduct which the profane imputed to an ambitious motive, appeared to Chrysostom himself in the light of a sacred and indispensable duty. In his visitation through the Asiatic provinces he deposed thirteen bishops of Lydia and Phrygia; and indiscreetly declared that a deep corruption of simony and licentiousness had infected the whole episcopal order.[1] If those bishops were innocent, such a rash and unjust condemnation must excite a well-grounded discontent. If they were guilty, the numerous associates of their guilt would soon discover that their own safety depended on the ruin of the archbishop, whom they studied to represent as the tyrant of the Eastern church.

This ecclesiastical conspiracy was managed by Theophilus, archbishop of Alexandria, an active and ambitious prelate, who displayed the fruits of rapine in monuments of ostentation. His national dislike to the rising greatness of a city which degraded him from the second to the third rank in the Christian world was exasperated by some personal disputes with Chrysostom himself. By the private invitation of the empress, Theophilus landed at Constantinople, with a stout body of Egyptian mariners, to encounter the populace; and a train of dependent bishops, to secure by their voices the majority of a synod. The synod was convened in the suburb of Chalcedon, surnamed the *Oak*, where Rufinus had erected a stately church and monastery; and their proceedings were continued during fourteen days or sessions. A bishop and a deacon accused the archbishop of Constantinople; but the frivolous or improbable nature of the forty-seven articles which they presented against him may justly be considered as a fair and unexceptionable panegyric. Four successive summons were signified to Chrysostom; but he still refused to trust either his person or his reputation in the hands of his implacable enemies, who, prudently declining the examination of any particular charges, condemned his contumacious disobedience, and hastily pronounced a sentence of deposition. The synod of the *Oak* immediately addressed the emperor to ratify and execute their judgment, and charitably insinuated that the penalties of treason might be inflicted on the audacious preacher, who had reviled, under the name of Jezebel, the

---

[1] Chrysostom declares his free opinion that the number of bishops who might be saved bore a very small proportion to those who would be damned.

empress Eudoxia herself. The archbishop was rudely arrested, and conducted through the city, by one of the Imperial messengers, who landed him, after a short navigation, near the entrance of the Euxine; from whence, before the expiration of two days, he was gloriously recalled.

The first astonishment of his faithful people had been mute and passive: they suddenly rose with unanimous and irresistible fury. Theophilus escaped, but the promiscuous crowd of monks and Egyptian mariners was slaughtered without pity in the streets of Constantinople. A seasonable earthquake justified the interposition of Heaven; the torrent of sedition rolled forwards to the gates of the palace; and the empress, agitated by fear or remorse, threw herself at the feet of Arcadius, and confessed that the public safety could be purchased only by the restoration of Chrysostom. The Bosphorus was covered with innumerable vessels; the shores of Europe and Asia were profusely illuminated; and the acclamations of a victorious people accompanied, from the port to the cathedral, the triumph of the archbishop, who too easily consented to resume the exercise of his functions, before his sentence had been legally reversed by the authority of an ecclesiastical synod. Ignorant, or careless, of the impending danger, Chrysostom indulged his zeal, or perhaps his resentment; declaimed with peculiar asperity against *female* vices; and condemned the profane honours which were addressed, almost in the precincts of St. Sophia, to the statue of the empress. His imprudence tempted his enemies to inflame the haughty spirit of Eudoxia, by reporting, or perhaps inventing, the famous exordium of a sermon, "Herodias is again furious; Herodias again dances; she once more requires the head of John": an insolent allusion, which, as a woman and a sovereign, it was impossible for her to forgive. The short interval of a perfidious truce was employed to concert more effectual measures for the disgrace and ruin of the archbishop. A numerous council of the Eastern prelates, who were guided from a distance by the advice of Theophilus, confirmed the validity, without examining the justice, of the former sentence; and a detachment of barbarian troops was introduced into the city, to suppress the emotions of the people. On the vigil of Easter the solemn administration of baptism was rudely interrupted by the soldiers, who alarmed the modesty of the naked catechumens, and violated, by their presence, the awful mysteries of the Christian worship. Arsacius occupied the church of St. Sophia and the archiepiscopal throne. The catholics retreated to the baths of Constantine, and afterwards to the fields, where they were still pursued and insulted by the guards, the bishops, and the magistrates. The fatal day of the second and final exile of Chrysostom was marked by the conflagration of the cathedral, of the senate-house, and of the adjacent buildings; and this calamity was imputed, without proof, but not without probability, to the despair of a persecuted faction.

Cicero might claim some merit if his voluntary banishment preserved the peace of the republic; but the submission of Chrysostom was the indispensable duty of a Christian and a subject. Instead of listening to his humble prayer that he might be permitted to reside at Cyzicus or Nicomedia, the inflexible empress assigned for his exile the remote and desolate town of Cucusus, among the ridges of Mount Taurus, in the Lesser Armenia. A secret hope was entertained that the archbishop might perish in a difficult and dangerous march of seventy days in the heat of summer, through the provinces of Asia Minor, where he was continually threatened by the hostile attacks of the Isaurians, and the more implacable fury of the monks. Yet Chrysostom arrived in safety at the place of his confinement; and the three years which he spent at Cucusus, and the neighbouring town of Arabissus, were the last and most glorious of his life. His character was consecrated by absence and persecution; the faults of his administration were no longer remembered; but every tongue repeated the praises of his genius and virtue: and the respectful attention of the Christian world was fixed on a desert spot among the mountains of Taurus. From that solitude the archbishop, whose active mind was invigorated by misfortunes, maintained a strict and frequent correspondence with the most distant provinces; exhorted the separate congregation of his faithful adherents to persevere in their allegiance; urged the destruction of the temples of Phœnicia, and the extirpation of heresy in the isle of Cyprus; extended his pastoral care to the missions of Persia and Scythia; negociated, by his ambassadors, with the Roman pontiff and the emperor Honorius; and boldly appealed, from a partial synod, to the supreme tribunal of a free and general council. The mind of the illustrious exile was still independent; but his captive body was exposed to the revenge of the oppressors, who continued to abuse the name and authority of Arcadius. An order was despatched for the instant removal of Chrysostom to the extreme desert of Pityus: and his guards so faithfully obeyed their cruel instructions, that, before he reached the sea-coast of the Euxine, he expired at Comana, in Pontus, in the sixtieth year of his age. The succeeding generation acknowledged his innocence and merit. The archbishops of the East, who might blush that their predecessors had been the enemies of Chrysostom, were gradually disposed, by the firmness of the Roman pontiff, to restore the honours of that venerable name. At the pious solicitation of the clergy and people of Constantinople, his relics, thirty years after his death, were transported from their obscure sepulchre to the royal city. The emperor Theodosius advanced to receive them as far as Chalcedon; and, falling prostrate on the coffin, implored, in the name of his guilty parents, Arcadius and Eudoxia, the forgiveness of the injured saint.

THE DEATH OF ARCADIUS AND SUCCESSION OF
THEODOSIUS THE YOUNGER

Yet a reasonable doubt may be entertained whether any stain of hereditary guilt could be derived from Arcadius to his successor. Eudoxia was a young and beautiful woman, who indulged her passions and despised her husband: Count John enjoyed, at least, the familiar confidence of the empress; and the public named him as the real father of Theodosius the younger. The birth of a son was accepted, however, by the pious husband, as an event the most fortunate and honourable to himself, to his family, and to the Eastern world: and the royal infant, by an unprecedented favour, was invested with the titles of Cæsar and Augustus. In less than four years afterwards, Eudoxia, in the bloom of youth, was destroyed by the consequences of a miscarriage; and this untimely death confounded the prophecy of a holy bishop, who, amidst the universal joy, had ventured to foretell that she should behold the long and auspicious reign of her glorious son. The catholics applauded the justice of Heaven, which avenged the persecution of St. Chrysostom; and perhaps the emperor was the only person who sincerely bewailed the loss of the haughty and rapacious Eudoxia. Such a domestic misfortune afflicted *him* more deeply than the public calamities of the East—the licentious excursions, from Pontus to Palestine, of the Isaurian robbers, whose impunity accused the weakness of the government; and the earthquakes, the conflagrations, the famine, and the flights of locusts, which the popular discontent was equally disposed to attribute to the incapacity of the monarch. At length, in the thirty-first year of his age, after a reign (if we may abuse that word) of thirteen years, three months, and fifteen days, Arcadius expired in the palace of Constantinople. It is impossible to delineate his character; since, in a period very copiously furnished with historical materials, it has not been possible to remark one action that properly belongs to the son of the great Theodosius.

The historian Procopius has indeed illuminated the mind of the dying emperor with a ray of human prudence, or celestial wisdom. Arcadius considered, with anxious foresight, the helpless condition of his son Theodosius, who was no more than seven years of age, the dangerous factions of a minority, and the aspiring spirit of Jezdegerd, the Persian monarch. Instead of tempting the allegiance of an ambitious subject by the participation of supreme power, he boldly appealed to the magnanimity of a king, and placed, by a solemn testament, the sceptre of the East in the hands of Jezdegerd himself. The royal guardian accepted and discharged this honourable trust with unexampled fidelity; and the infancy of Theodosius was protected by the arms and councils of Persia. Such is the singular narrative of Procopius; and his veracity is not disputed by Agathias, while he presumes to dissent from his judgment, and to arraign the wisdom of a Christian emperor, who, so rashly, though so fortunately, committed his son and his dominions to the unknown faith of a stranger, a rival, and a heathen. At the distance of one hundred and fifty years, this political question might be debated in the court of Justinian; but a prudent historian will refuse to examine the *propriety*, till he has ascertained the *truth*, of the testament of Arcadius. As it stands without a parallel in the history of the world, we may justly require that it should be attested by the positive and unanimous evidence of contemporaries. The strange novelty of the event, which excites our distrust, must have attracted their notice; and their universal silence annihilates the vain tradition of the succeeding age.

The maxims of Roman jurisprudence, if they could fairly

be transferred from private property to public dominion, would have adjudged to the emperor Honorius the guardianship of his nephew, till he had attained, at least, the fourteenth year of his age. But the weakness of Honorius, and the calamities of his reign, disqualified him from prosecuting this natural claim; and such was the absolute separation of the two monarchies, both in interest and affection, that Constantinople would have obeyed with less reluctance the orders of the Persian, than those of the Italian court. Under a prince whose weakness is disguised by the external signs of manhood and discretion, the most worthless favourites may secretly dispute the empire of the palace, and dictate to submissive provinces the commands of a master whom they direct and despise. But the ministers of a child, who is incapable of arming them with the sanction of the royal name, must acquire and exercise an independent authority. The great officers of the state and army, who had been appointed before the death of Arcadius, formed an aristocracy, which might have inspired them with the idea of a free republic; and the government of the Eastern empire was fortunately assumed by the prefect Anthemius, who obtained, by his superior abilities, a lasting ascendant over the minds of his equals. The safety of the young emperor proved the merit and integrity of Anthemius; and his prudent firmness sustained the force and reputation of an infant reign. Uldin, with a formidable host of barbarians, was encamped in the heart of Thrace; he proudly rejected all terms of accommodation; and, pointing to the rising sun, declared to the Roman ambassadors that the course of that planet should alone terminate the conquests of the Huns. But the desertion of his confederates, who were privately convinced of the justice and liberality of the Imperial ministers, obliged Uldin to repass the Danube: the tribe of the Scyrri, which composed his rear-guard, was almost extirpated; and many thousand captives were dispersed, to cultivate, with servile labour, the fields of Asia. In the midst of the public triumph, Constantinople was protected by a strong enclosure of new and more extensive walls; the same vigilant care was applied to restore the fortifications of the Illyrian cities; and a plan was judiciously conceived, which, in the space of seven years, would have secured the command of the Danube, by establishing on that river a perpetual fleet of two hundred and fifty armed vessels.

THE ADMINISTRATION OF PULCHERIA

But the Romans had so long been accustomed to the
authority of a monarch, that the first, even among the females
of the Imperial family, who displayed any courage or capacity,
was permitted to ascend the vacant throne of Theodosius.
His sister Pulcheria, who was only two years older than
himself, received at the age of sixteen the title of *Augusta;*
and though her favour might be sometimes clouded by caprice
or intrigue, she continued to govern the Eastern empire near
forty years; during the long minority of her brother, and after
his death in her own name, and in the name of Marcian, her
nominal husband. From a motive either of prudence or religion, she embraced a life of celibacy; and notwithstanding
some aspersions on the chastity of Pulcheria, this resolution,
which she communicated to her sisters Arcadia and Marina,
was celebrated by the Christian world as the sublime effort of
heroic piety. In the presence of the clergy and people the three
daughters of Arcadius dedicated their virginity to God; and
the obligation of their solemn vow was inscribed on a tablet
of gold and gems, which they publicly offered in the great
church of Constantinople. Their palace was converted into a
monastery, and all males—except the guides of their conscience, the saints who had forgotten the distinction of sexes—
were scrupulously excluded from the holy threshold. Pulcheria,
her two sisters, and a chosen train of favourite damsels,
formed a religious community: they renounced the vanity of
dress, interrupted by frequent fasts their simple and frugal
diet, allotted a portion of their time to works of embroidery,
and devoted several hours of the day and night to the exercises of prayer and psalmody. The piety of a Christian virgin
was adorned by the zeal and liberality of an empress. Ecclesiastical history describes the splendid churches which were
built at the expense of Pulcheria in all the provinces of the
East, her charitable foundations for the benefit of strangers
and the poor, the ample donations which she assigned for the
perpetual maintenance of monastic societies, and the active
severity with which she laboured to suppress the opposite
heresies of Nestorius and Eutyches. Such virtues were supposed to deserve the peculiar favour of the Deity: and the
relics of martyrs, as well as the knowledge of future events,

were communicated in visions and revelations to the Imperial saint.[1] Yet the devotion of Pulcheria never diverted her indefatigable attention from temporal affairs; and she alone, among all the descendants of the great Theodosius, appears to have inherited any share of his manly spirit and abilities. The elegant and familiar use which she had acquired both of the Greek and Latin languages was readily applied to the various occasions of speaking or writing on public business: her deliberations were maturely weighed; her actions were prompt and decisive; and while she moved without noise or ostentation the wheel of government, she discreetly attributed to the genius of the emperor the long tranquillity of his reign. In the last years of his peaceful life Europe was indeed afflicted by the arms of Attila; but the more extensive provinces of Asia still continued to enjoy a profound and permanent repose. Theodosius the younger was never reduced to the disgraceful necessity of encountering and punishing a rebellious subject: and since we cannot applaud the vigour, some praise may be due to the mildness and prosperity, of the administration of Pulcheria.

The Roman world was deeply interested in the education of its master. A regular course of study and exercise was judiciously instituted; of the military exercises of riding, and shooting with the bow; of the liberal studies of grammar, rhetoric, and philosophy: the most skilful masters of the East ambitiously solicited the attention of their royal pupil, and several noble youths were introduced into the palace to animate his diligence by the emulation of friendship. Pulcheria alone discharged the important task of instructing her brother in the arts of government; but her precepts may countenance some suspicion of the extent of her capacity or of the purity of her intentions. She taught him to maintain a grave and majestic deportment; to walk, to hold his robes, to seat himself on his throne in a manner worthy of a great prince; to abstain from laughter, to listen with condescension, to return suitable answers; to assume by turns a serious or a placid

---

[1] She was admonished, by repeated dreams, of the place where the relics of the forty martyrs had been buried. The ground had successively belonged to the house and garden of a woman of Constantinople, to a monastery of Macedonian monks, and to a church of St. Thyrsus, erected by Cæsarius, who was consul A.D. 397; and the memory of the relics was almost obliterated. Notwithstanding the charitable wishes of Dr. Jortin, it is not easy to acquit Pulcheria of some share in the pious fraud, which must have been transacted when she was more than five-and-thirty years of age.

countenance; in a word, to represent with grace and dignity the external figure of a Roman emperor. But Theodosius was never excited to support the weight and glory of an illustrious name; and, instead of aspiring to imitate his ancestors, he degenerated (if we may presume to measure the degrees of incapacity) below the weakness of his father and his uncle. Arcadius and Honorius had been assisted by the guardian care of a parent, whose lessons were enforced by his authority and example. But the unfortunate prince who is born in the purple must remain a stranger to the voice of truth; and the son of Arcadius was condemned to pass his perpetual infancy encompassed only by a servile train of women and eunuchs. The ample leisure which he acquired by neglecting the essential duties of his high office was filled by idle amusements and unprofitable studies. Hunting was the only active pursuit that could tempt him beyond the limits of the palace; but he most assiduously laboured, sometimes by the light of a midnight lamp, in the mechanic occupations of painting and carving; and the elegance with which he transcribed religious books entitled the Roman emperor to the singular epithet of *Calligraphes*, or a fair writer. Separated from the world by an impenetrable veil, Theodosius trusted the persons he loved; he loved those who were accustomed to amuse and flatter his indolence; and as he never perused the papers that were presented for the royal signature, the acts of injustice the most repugnant to his character were frequently perpetrated in his name. The emperor himself was chaste, temperate, liberal, and merciful; but these qualities—which can only deserve the name of virtues when they are supported by courage and regulated by discretion—were seldom beneficial, and they sometimes proved mischievous, to mankind. His mind, enervated by a royal education, was oppressed and degraded by abject superstition: he fasted, he sung psalms, he blindly accepted the miracles and doctrines with which his faith was continually nourished. Theodosius devoutly worshipped the dead and living saints of the catholic church; and he once refused to eat till an insolent monk, who had cast an excommunication on his sovereign, condescended to heal the spiritual wound which he had inflicted.

THE ADVENTURES OF EUDOCIA

The story of a fair and virtuous maiden, exalted from a private condition to the Imperial throne, might be deemed an incredible romance, if such a romance had not been verified in the marriage of Theodosius. The celebrated Athenais was educated by her father Leontius in the religion and sciences of the Greeks; and so advantageous was the opinion which the Athenian philosopher entertained of his contemporaries, that he divided his patrimony between his two sons, bequeathing to his daughter a small legacy of one hundred pieces of gold, in the lively confidence that her beauty and merit would be a sufficient portion. The jealousy and avarice of her brothers soon compelled Athenais to seek a refuge at Constantinople, and with some hopes, either of justice or favour, to throw herself at the feet of Pulcheria. That sagacious princess listened to her eloquent complaint, and secretly destined the daughter of the philosopher Leontius for the future wife of the emperor of the East, who had now attained the twentieth year of his age. She easily excited the curiosity of her brother by an interesting picture of the charms of Athenais: large eyes, a well-proportioned nose, a fair complexion, golden locks, a slender person, a graceful demeanour, an understanding improved by study, and a virtue tried by distress. Theodosius, concealed behind a curtain in the apartment of his sister, was permitted to behold the Athenian virgin: the modest youth immediately declared his pure and honourable love, and the royal nuptials were celebrated amidst the acclamations of the capital and the provinces. Athenais, who was easily persuaded to renounce the errors of Paganism, received at her baptism the Christian name of Eudocia: but the cautious Pulcheria withheld the title of Augusta till the wife of Theodosius had approved her fruitfulness by the birth of a daughter, who espoused fifteen years afterwards the emperor of the West. The brothers of Eudocia obeyed, with some anxiety, her Imperial summons; but as she could easily forgive their fortunate unkindness, she indulged the tenderness, or perhaps the vanity, of a sister, by promoting them to the rank of consuls and prefects. In the luxury of the palace she still cultivated those ingenuous arts which had contributed to her greatness, and wisely dedicated her talents to the honour of religion and of

her husband. Eudocia composed a poetical paraphrase of the
first eight books of the Old Testament and of the prophecies
of Daniel and Zachariah; a cento of the verses of Homer, applied to the life and miracles of Christ, the legend of St.
Cyprian, and a panegyric on the Persian victories of Theodosius: and her writings, which were applauded by a servile
and superstitious age, have not been disdained by the candour
of impartial criticism. The fondness of the emperor was not
abated by time and possession; and Eudocia, after the marriage of her daughter, was permitted to discharge her grateful
vows by a solemn pilgrimage to Jerusalem. Her ostentatious
progress through the East may seem inconsistent with the
spirit of Christian humility: she pronounced from a throne
of gold and gems an eloquent oration to the senate of Antioch,
declared her royal intention of enlarging the walls of the city,
bestowed a donative of two hundred pounds of gold to restore
the public baths, and accepted the statues which were de-
creed by the gratitude of Antioch. In the Holy Land her alms
and pious foundations exceeded the munificence of the great
Helena; and though the public treasure might be impoverished
by this excessive liberality, she enjoyed the conscious satisfaction of returning to Constantinople with the chains of St.
Peter, the right arm of St. Stephen, and an undoubted picture
of the Virgin, painted by St. Luke. But this pilgrimage was
the fatal term of the glories of Eudocia. Satiated with empty
pomp, and unmindful perhaps of her obligations to Pulcheria,
she ambitiously aspired to the government of the Eastern
empire: the palace was distracted by female discord; but the
victory was at last decided by the superior ascendant of the
sister of Theodosius. The execution of Paulinus, master of
the offices, and the disgrace of Cyrus, Prætorian prefect of the
East, convinced the public that the favour of Eudocia was
insufficient to protect her most faithful friends, and the uncommon beauty of Paulinus encouraged the secret rumour
that his guilt was that of a successful lover. As soon as the
empress perceived that the affection of Theodosius was irretrievably lost, she requested the permission of retiring to the
distant solitude of Jerusalem. She obtained her request, but
the jealousy of Theodosius, or the vindictive spirit of Pulcheria, pursued her in her last retreat; and Saturninus, count
of the domestics, was directed to punish with death two ecclesiastics, her most favoured servants. Eudocia instantly re-

venged them by the assassination of the count: the furious
passions which she indulged on this suspicious occasion seemed
to justify the severity of Theodosius; and the empress, ignominiously stripped of the honours of her rank, was disgraced,
perhaps unjustly, in the eyes of the world. The remainder
of the life of Eudocia, about sixteen years, was spent in exile
and devotion; and the approach of age, the death of Theodosius, the misfortunes of her only daughter, who was led a
captive from Rome to Carthage, and the society of the Holy
Monks of Palestine, insensibly confirmed the religious temper
of her mind. After a full experience of the vicissitudes of
human life, the daughter of the philosopher Leontius expired
at Jerusalem, in the sixty-seventh year of her age; protesting
with her dying breath that she had never transgressed the
bounds of innocence and friendship.

*An inconclusive war with Persia led to a peace of eighty
years. Armenia was divided between the Persians and the
Romans.*

33.

THE INVASION OF AFRICA BY THE VANDALS.
ST. AUGUSTIN AND THE SIEGE OF HIPPO. SACK OF
CARTHAGE. FABLE OF THE SEVEN SLEEPERS

---

*Honorius died of dropsy in 423. He was eventually succeed-
ed by Valentinian III, the six-year-old son of Galla Placidia
and the general Constantius (whom she had married after the
death of Adolphus) and the cousin of Theodosius the Younger.
Placidia reigned for twenty-five years in her son's name. Her
armies were commanded by Aëtius and Boniface, whom Gibbon describes as "the last of the Romans." After Aëtius had
conspired to discredit him in the eyes of Placidia, Boniface
rashly proposed an alliance with the Vandals in Spain and
invited them to settle in Africa. This invitation, which Boniface regretted too late, was accepted by the savage Vandal
king, Genseric.*

INVASION OF AFRICA BY THE VANDALS

THE LONG and narrow tract of the African coast was filled
with frequent monuments of Roman art and magnificence;
and the respective degrees of improvement might be accurately measured by the distance from Carthage and the Mediterranean. A simple reflection will impress every thinking mind
with the clearest idea of fertility and cultivation: the country
was extremely populous; the inhabitants reserved a liberal
subsistence for their own use; and the annual exportation,
particularly of wheat, was so regular and plentiful, that Africa
deserved the name of the common granary of Rome and of
mankind. On a sudden the seven fruitful provinces, from
Tangier to Tripoli, were overwhelmed by the invasion of the
Vandals, whose destructive rage has perhaps been exaggerated
by popular animosity, religious zeal, and extravagant declamation. War in its fairest form implies a perpetual violation

of humanity and justice; and the hostilities of barbarians are inflamed by the fierce and lawless spirit which incessantly disturbs their peaceful and domestic society. The Vandals, where they found resistance, seldom gave quarter; and the deaths of their valiant countrymen were expiated by the ruin of the cities under whose walls they had fallen. Careless of the distinctions of age, or sex, or rank, they employed every species of indignity and torture to force from the captives a discovery of their hidden wealth. The stern policy of Genseric justified his frequent examples of military execution: he was not always the master of his own passions or of those of his followers; and the calamities of war were aggravated by the licentiousness of the Moors and the fanaticism of the Donatists. Yet I shall not easily be persuaded that it was the common practice of the Vandals to extirpate the olives and other fruit-trees of a country where they intended to settle; nor can I believe that it was a usual stratagem to slaughter great numbers of their prisoners before the walls of a besieged city, for the sole purpose of infecting the air and producing a pestilence, of which they themselves must have been the first victims.[1]

ST. AUGUSTIN AND THE SIEGE OF HIPPO

The generous mind of Count Boniface was tortured by the exquisite distress of beholding the ruin which he had occasioned, and whose rapid progress he was unable to check. After the loss of a battle he retired into Hippo Regius, where he was immediately besieged by an enemy who considered him as the real bulwark of Africa. The maritime colony of *Hippo,* about two hundred miles westward of Carthage, had formerly acquired the distinguishing epithet of *Regius,* from the residence of Numidian kings; and some remains of trade and populousness still adhere to the modern city, which is known in Europe by the corrupted name of Bona. The military labours and anxious reflections of Count Boniface were alleviated by the edifying conversation of his friend St.

---

[1] The original complaints of the desolation of Africa are contained—1. In a letter from Capreolus, bishop of Carthage, to excuse his absence from the council of Ephesus. 2. In the Life of St. Augustin by his friend and colleague Possidius. 3. In the History of the Vandalic Persecution, by Victor Vitensis. The last picture, which was drawn sixty years after the event, is more expressive of the author's passions than of the truth of facts.

Augustin; till that bishop, the light and pillar of the catholic church, was gently released, in the third month of the siege and in the seventy-sixth year of his age, from the actual and the impending calamities of his country. The youth of Augustin had been stained by the vices and errors which he so ingenuously confesses; but from the moment of his conversion to that of his death the manners of the bishop of Hippo were pure and austere, and the most conspicuous of his virtues was an ardent zeal against heretics of every denomination—the Manichæans, the Donatists, and the Pelagians, against whom he waged a perpetual controversy. When the city, some months after his death, was burnt by the Vandals, the library was fortunately saved which contained his voluminous writings—two hundred and thirty-two separate books or treatises on theological subjects, besides a complete exposition of the psalter and the gospel, and a copious magazine of epistles and homilies. According to the judgment of the most impartial critics, the superficial learning of Augustin was confined to the Latin language;[1] and his style, though sometimes animated by the eloquence of passion, is usually clouded by false and affected rhetoric. But he possessed a strong, capacious, argumentative mind; he boldly sounded the dark abyss of grace, predestination, free-will, and original sin; and the rigid system of Christianity which he framed or restored has been entertained with public applause and secret reluctance by the Latin church.[2]

By the skill of Boniface, and perhaps by the ignorance of the Vandals, the siege of Hippo was protracted above fourteen months: the sea was continually open; and when the adjacent country had been exhausted by irregular rapine, the besiegers themselves were compelled by famine to relinquish their enterprise. The importance and danger of Africa were deeply felt by the regent of the West. Placidia implored the

---

[1] In his early youth, St. Augustin disliked and neglected the study of Greek; and he frankly owns that he read the Platonists in a Latin version. Some modern critics have thought that his ignorance of Greek disqualified him from expounding the Scriptures; and Cicero or Quintilian would have required the knowledge of that language in a professor of rhetoric.

[2] The church of Rome has canonised Augustin and reprobated Calvin. Yet, as the *real* difference between them is invisible even to a theological microscope, the Molinists are oppressed by the authority of the saint, and the Jansenists are disgraced by their resemblance to the heretic. In the mean while the Protestant Arminians stand aloof and deride the mutual perplexity of the disputants. Perhaps a reasoner still more independent may smile in *his* turn when he peruses an Arminian Commentary on the Epistle to the Romans.

assistance of her Eastern ally; and the Italian fleet and army were reinforced by Aspar, who sailed from Constantinople with a powerful armament. As soon as the force of the two empires was united under the command of Boniface, he boldly marched against the Vandals; and the loss of a second battle irretrievably decided the fate of Africa. He embarked with the precipitation of despair; and the people of Hippo were permitted, with their families and effects, to occupy the vacant place of the soldiers, the greatest part of whom were either slain or made prisoners by the Vandals. The count, whose fatal credulity had wounded the vitals of the republic, might enter the palace of Ravenna with some anxiety, which was soon removed by the smiles of Placidia. Boniface accepted with gratitude the rank of patrician and the dignity of master-general of the Roman armies; but he must have blushed at the sight of those medals in which he was represented with the name and attributes of victory. The discovery of his fraud, the displeasure of the empress, and the distinguished favour of his rival, exasperated the haughty and perfidious soul of Aëtius. He hastily returned from Gaul to Italy, with a retinue, or rather with an army, of barbarian followers; and such was the weakness of the government, that the two generals decided their private quarrel in a bloody battle. Boniface was successful; but he received in the conflict a mortal wound from the spear of his adversary, of which he expired within a few days, in such Christian and charitable sentiments that he exhorted his wife, a rich heiress of Spain, to accept Aëtius for her second husband. But Aëtius could not derive any immediate advantage from the generosity of his dying enemy: he was proclaimed a rebel by the justice of Placidia; and though he attempted to defend some strong fortresses, erected on his patrimonial estate, the Imperial power soon compelled him to retire into Pannonia, to the tents of his faithful Huns. The republic was deprived by their mutual discord of the service of her two most illustrious champions.

THE SACK OF CARTHAGE

It might naturally be expected, after the retreat of Boniface, that the Vandals would achieve without resistance or delay the conquest of Africa. Eight years however elapsed from the evacuation of Hippo to the reduction of Carthage.

In the midst of that interval the ambitious Genseric, in the full tide of apparent prosperity, negociated a treaty of peace, by which he gave his son Hunneric for an hostage, and consented to leave the Western emperor in the undisturbed possession of the three Mauritanias. This moderation, which cannot be imputed to the justice, must be ascribed to the policy, of the conqueror. His throne was encompassed with domestic enemies, who accused the baseness of his birth, and asserted the legitimate claims of his nephews, the sons of Gonderic. Those nephews, indeed, he sacrificed to his safety; and their mother, the widow of the deceased king, was precipitated by his order into the river Ampsaga. But the public discontent burst forth in dangerous and frequent conspiracies; and the warlike tyrant is supposed to have shed more Vandal blood by the hand of the executioner than in the field of battle. The convulsions of Africa, which had favoured his attack, opposed the firm establishment of his power; and the various seditions of the Moors and Germans, the Donatists and catholics, continually disturbed or threatened the unsettled reign of the conqueror. As he advanced towards Carthage he was forced to withdraw his troops from the Western provinces; the sea-coast was exposed to the naval enterprises of the Romans of Spain and Italy; and, in the heart of Numidia, the strong inland city of Cirta still persisted in obstinate independence. These difficulties were gradually subdued by the spirit, the perseverance, and the cruelty of Genseric; who alternately applied the arts of peace and war to the establishment of his African kingdom. He subscribed a solemn treaty, with the hope of deriving some advantage from the term of its continuance and the moment of its violation. The vigilance of his enemies was relaxed by the protestations of friendship which concealed his hostile approach; and Carthage was at length surprised by the Vandals, five hundred and eighty-five years after the destruction of the city and republic by the younger Scipio.

A new city had arisen from its ruins, with the title of a colony; and though Carthage might yield to the royal prerogatives of Constantinople, and perhaps to the trade of Alexandria, or the splendour of Antioch, she still maintained the second rank in the West; as the *Rome* (if we may use the style of contemporaries) of the African world. That wealthy and opulent metropolis displayed, in a dependent condition, the image of a flourishing republic. Carthage contained the manufactures, the arms, and the treasures of the six provinces. A regular subordination of civil honours gradually ascended from the procurators of the streets and quarters of the city to the tribunal of the supreme magistrate, who, with the title of proconsul, represented the state and dignity of a consul of ancient Rome. Schools and *gymnasia* were instituted for the education of the African youth; and the liberal arts and manners, grammar, rhetoric, and philosophy, were publicly taught in the Greek and Latin languages. The buildings of Carthage were uniform and magnificent: a shady grove was planted in the midst of the capital; the *new* port, a secure and capacious harbour, was subservient to the commercial industry of citizens and strangers; and the splendid games of the circus and theatre were exhibited almost in the presence of the barbarians. The reputation of the Carthaginians was not equal to that of their country, and the reproach of Punic faith still adhered to their subtle and faithless character. The habits of trade and the abuse of luxury had corrupted their manners; but their impious contempt of monks and the shameless practice of unnatural lusts are the two abominations which excite the pious vehemence of Salvian, the preacher of the age.[1] The king of the Vandals severely reformed the vices of a voluptuous people; and the ancient, noble, ingenuous freedom of Carthage (these expressions of Victor are not without energy) was reduced by Genseric into a state of ignominious servitude. After he had permitted his licentious troops to satiate their rage and avarice, he instituted a more regular system of rapine and oppression. An edict was promulgated, which enjoined all persons, without fraud or delay, to deliver their gold, silver, jewels, and valuable furniture or apparel to the royal officers; and the attempt to secrete any part of their patrimony was inexorably punished with death and torture as an act of treason against the state. The lands of the proconsular province, which formed the immediate district

---

[1] He declares that the peculiar vices of each country were collected in the sink of Carthage. In the indulgence of vice the Africans applauded their manly virtue. Et illi se magis virilis fortitudinis esse crederent, qui maxime viros fœminei usus probrositate fregissent. The streets of Carthage were polluted by effeminate wretches, who publicly assumed the countenance, the dress, and the character, of women. If a monk appeared in the city, the holy man was pursued with impious scorn and ridicule; detestantibus ridentium cachinnis.

of Carthage, were accurately measured and divided among the barbarians; and the conqueror reserved for his peculiar domain the fertile territory of Byzacium and the adjacent parts of Numidia and Gætulia.

It was natural enough that Genseric should hate those whom he had injured: the nobility and senators of Carthage were exposed to his jealousy and resentment; and all those who refused the ignominious terms which their honour and religion forbade them to accept were compelled by the Arian tyrant to embrace the condition of perpetual banishment. Rome, Italy, and the provinces of the East, were filled with a crowd of exiles, of fugitives, and of ingenuous captives, who solicited the public compassion: and the benevolent epistles of Theodoret still preserve the names and misfortunes of Cælestian and Maria. The Syrian bishop deplores the misfortunes of Cælestian, who, from the state of a noble and opulent senator of Carthage, was reduced, with his wife and family, and servants, to beg his bread in a foreign country; but he applauds the resignation of the Christian exile, and the philosophic temper which, under the pressure of such calamities, could enjoy more real happiness than was the ordinary lot of wealth and prosperity. The story of Maria, the daughter of the magnificent Eudæmon, is singular and interesting. In the sack of Carthage she was purchased from the Vandals by some merchants of Syria, who afterwards sold her as a slave in their native country. A female attendant, transported in the same ship, and sold in the same family, still continued to respect a mistress whom fortune had reduced to the common level of servitude; and the daughter of Eudæmon received from her grateful affection the domestic services which she had once required from her obedience. This remarkable behaviour divulged the real condition of Maria, who, in the absence of the bishop of Cyrrhus, was redeemed from slavery by the generosity of some soldiers of the garrison. The liberality of Theodoret provided for her decent maintenance; and she passed ten months among the deaconesses of the church, till she was unexpectedly informed that her father, who had escaped from the ruin of Carthage, exercised an honourable office in one of the Western provinces. Her filial impatience was seconded by the pious bishop: Theodoret, in a letter still extant, recommends Maria to the bishop of Ægæ, a maritime city of Cilicia, which was frequented, during the annual fair, by the vessels of the West; most earnestly requesting that his colleague would use the maiden with a tenderness suitable to her birth; and that he would intrust her to the care of such faithful merchants as would esteem it a sufficient gain if they restored a daughter, lost beyond all human hope, to the arms of her afflicted parent.

THE FABLE OF THE SEVEN SLEEPERS

Among the insipid legends of ecclesiastical history, I am tempted to distinguish the memorable fable of the SEVEN SLEEPERS; whose imaginary date corresponds with the reign of the younger Theodosius, and the conquest of Africa by the Vandals. When the emperor Decius persecuted the Christians, seven noble youths of Ephesus concealed themselves in a spacious cavern in the side of an adjacent mountain; where they were doomed to perish by the tyrant, who gave orders that the entrance should be firmly secured with a pile of huge stones. They immediately fell into a deep slumber, which was miraculously prolonged, without injuring the powers of life, during a period of one hundred and eighty-seven years. At the end of that time, the slaves of Adolius, to whom the inheritance of the mountain had descended, removed the stones, to supply materials for some rustic edifice: the light of the sun darted into the cavern, and the Seven Sleepers were permitted to awake. After a slumber, as they thought of a few hours, they were pressed by the calls of hunger; and resolved that Jamblichus, one of their number, should secretly return to the city to purchase bread for the use of his companions. The youth (if we may still employ that appellation) could no longer recognise the once familiar aspect of his native country; and his surprise was increased by the appearance of a large cross, triumphantly erected over the principal gate of Ephesus. His singular dress and obsolete language confounded the baker, to whom he offered an ancient medal of Decius as the current coin of the empire; and Jamblichus, on the suspicion of a secret treasure, was dragged before the judge. Their mutual inquiries produced the amazing discovery that two centuries were almost elapsed since Jamblichus and his friends had escaped from the rage of a Pagan tyrant. The bishop of

Ephesus, the clergy, the magistrates, the people, and, as it is said, the emperor Theodosius himself, hastened to visit the cavern of the Seven Sleepers; who bestowed their benediction, related their story, and at the same instant peaceably expired. The origin of this marvellous fable cannot be ascribed to the pious fraud and credulity of the *modern* Greeks, since the authentic tradition may be traced within half a century of the supposed miracle. James of Sarug, a Syrian bishop, who was born only two years after the death of the younger Theodosius, has devoted one of his two hundred and thirty homilies to the praise of the young men of Ephesus. Their legend, before the end of the sixth century, was translated from the Syriac into the Latin language, by the care of Gregory of Tours. The hostile communions of the East preserve their memory with equal reverence; and their names are honourably inscribed in the Roman, the Abyssinian, and the Russian calendar. Nor has their reputation been confined to the Christian world. This popular tale, which Mahomet might learn when he drove his camels to the fairs of Syria, is introduced, as a divine revelation, into the Koran.[1] The story of the Seven Sleepers has been adopted and adorned by the nations, from Bengal to Africa, who profess the Mahometan religion; and some vestiges of a similar tradition have been discovered in the remote extremities of Scandinavia.[2] This easy and universal belief, so expressive of the sense of mankind, may be ascribed to the genuine merit of the fable itself. We imperceptibly advance from youth to age without observing the gradual, but incessant, change of human affairs; and even in our larger experience of history, the imagination is accustomed, by a perpetual series of causes and effects, to unite the most distant revolutions. But if the interval between two memorable eras could be instantly annihilated; if it were possible, after a momentary slumber of two hundred years, to display the *new* world to the eyes of a spectator who still

---

[1] With such an ample privilege Mahomet has not shown much taste or ingenuity. He has invented the dog (Al Rakim) of the Seven Sleepers; the respect of the sun, who altered his course twice a day that he might not shine into the cavern; and the care of God himself, who preserved their bodies from putrefaction by turning them to the right and left.

[2] Paul, the deacon of Aquileia, who lived towards the end of the eighth century, has placed in a cavern under a rock on the shore of the ocean the Seven Sleepers of the North, whose long repose was respected by the barbarians. Their dress declared them to be Romans; and the deacon conjectures that they were reserved by Providence as the future apostles of those unbelieving countries.

retained a lively and recent impression of the *old,* his surprise and his reflections would furnish the pleasing subject of a philosophical romance. The scene could not be more advantageously placed than in the two centuries which elapsed between the reigns of Decius and of Theodosius the Younger. During this period the seat of government had been transported from Rome to a new city on the banks of the Thracian Bosphorus; and the abuse of military spirit had been suppressed by an artificial system of tame and ceremonious servitude. The throne of the persecuting Decius was filled by a succession of Christian and orthodox princes, who had extirpated the fabulous gods of antiquity: and the public devotion of the age was impatient to exalt the saints and martyrs of the catholic church on the altars of Diana and Hercules. The union of the Roman empire was dissolved; its genius was humbled in the dust; and armies of unknown barbarians, issuing from the frozen regions of the North, had established their victorious reign over the fairest provinces of Europe and Africa.

The End of the
Empire in the West

35.

INVASION OF GAUL AND ITALY BY ATTILA.
FOUNDATION OF VENICE. DEATH OF ATTILA AND
DESTRUCTION OF HIS EMPIRE. MURDER OF AËTIUS
AND DEATH OF VALENTINIAN III. SYMPTOMS OF
DECAY IN THE ROMAN EMPIRE OF THE WEST

The progress of invasions by the Goths and kindred peoples had been accelerated by the pressure in their rear by the Huns. In Chapter 34 Gibbon describes the first appearance of Attila and the establishment of the Huns in modern Hungary. Between 430–440 Persia had been invaded and in 466 Attila, after ravaging Europe as far as Constantinople, signed a treaty with the Eastern empire. Theodosius the Younger died in 450 and was succeeded in the empire of the East by his sister Pulcheria, who thus became the first woman to rule the Romans. She soon however married a senator, Marcian, who was himself invested with the Imperial purple.

Meanwhile Attila, the king of the Huns, prepared to invade Gaul. Here Theodoric, the son of Alaric, had become king of the Visigoths on the death of Wallia. Aëtius, who had previously cultivated an alliance with the Huns, now allied the Romans with the Goths. In 451 Attila invaded Gaul and besieged Orleans. Aëtius and Theodoric marched to its relief.

THE INVASION OF GAUL BY ATTILA

THE FACILITY with which Attila had penetrated into the heart of Gaul may be ascribed to his insidious policy as well as to the terror of his arms. His public declarations were skilfully mitigated by his private assurances; he alternately soothed **and threatened the Romans and the Goths; and the courts of**

609

Ravenna and Toulouse, mutually suspicious of each other's intentions, beheld with supine indifference the approach of their common enemy. Aëtius was the sole guardian of the public safety; but his wisest measures were embarrassed by a faction which, since the death of Placidia, infested the Imperial palace: the youth of Italy trembled at the sound of the trumpet; and the barbarians, who from fear or affection were inclined to the cause of Attila, awaited with doubtful and venal faith the event of the war. The patrician passed the Alps at the head of some troops whose strength and numbers scarcely deserved the name of an army. But on his arrival at Arles or Lyons he was confounded by the intelligence that the Visigoths, refusing to embrace the defence of Gaul, had determined to expect within their own territories the formidable invader whom they professed to despise. The senator Avitus, who after the honourable exercise of the Prætorian prefecture had retired to his estate in Auvergne, was persuaded to accept the important embassy, which he executed with ability and success. He represented to Theodoric that an ambitious conqueror who aspired to the dominion of the earth could be resisted only by the firm and unanimous alliance of the powers whom he laboured to oppress. The lively eloquence of Avitus inflamed the Gothic warriors by the description of the injuries which their ancestors had suffered from the Huns, whose implacable fury still pursued them from the Danube to the foot of the Pyrenees. He strenuously urged that it was the duty of every Christian to save from sacrilegious violation the churches of God and the relics of the saints; that it was the interest of every barbarian who had acquired a settlement in Gaul to defend the fields and vineyards, which were cultivated for his use, against the desolation of the Scythian shepherds. Theodoric yielded to the evidence of truth, adopted the measure at once the most prudent and the most honourable, and declared that as the faithful ally of Aëtius and the Romans he was ready to expose his life and kingdom for the common safety of Gaul. The Visigoths, who at that time were in the mature vigour of their fame and power, obeyed with alacrity the signal of war, prepared their arms and horses, and assembled under the standard of their aged king, who was resolved, with his two eldest sons, Torismond and Theodoric, to command in person his numerous and valiant people. The example of the Goths determined several tribes or nations that seemed to fluctuate between the Huns and the Romans. The indefatigable diligence of the patrician gradually collected the troops of Gaul and Germany, who had formerly acknowledged themselves the subjects or soldiers of the republic, but who now claimed the rewards of voluntary service and the rank of independent allies; the Læti, the Armoricans, the Breones, the Saxons, the Burgundians, the Sarmatians or Alani, the Ripuarians, and the Franks who followed Meroveus as their lawful prince. Such was the various army which, under the conduct of Aëtius and Theodoric, advanced by rapid marches to relieve Orleans, and to give battle to the innumerable host of Attila.

On their approach the king of the Huns immediately raised the siege, and sounded a retreat to recall the foremost of his troops from the pillage of a city which they had already entered. The valour of Attila was always guided by his prudence; and as he foresaw the fatal consequences of a defeat in the heart of Gaul, he repassed the Seine, and expected the enemy in the plains of Châlons, whose smooth and level surface was adapted to the operations of his Scythian cavalry. But in this tumultuary retreat the vanguard of the Romans and their allies continually pressed, and sometimes engaged, the troops whom Attila had posted in the rear; the hostile columns, in the darkness of the night and the perplexity of the roads, might encounter each other without design; and the bloody conflict of the Franks and Gepidæ, in which fifteen thousand barbarians were slain, was a prelude to a more general and decisive action. The Catalaunian fields spread themselves round Châlons, and extend, according to the vague measurement of Jornandes, to the length of one hundred and fifty, and the breadth of one hundred miles, over the whole province, which is entitled to the appellation of a *champaign* country. This spacious plain was distinguished, however, by some inequalities of ground; and the importance of an height which commanded the camp of Attila was understood and disputed by the two generals. The young and valiant Torismond first occupied the summit; the Goths rushed with irresistible weight on the Huns, who laboured to ascend from the opposite side: and the possession of this advantageous post inspired both the troops and their leaders with a fair assurance of victory. The anxiety of Attila prompted him to consult his priests and haruspices. It was reported that, after scrutinising the entrails of victims and scraping their bones, they revealed, in mysterious language, his own defeat, with the death of his principal adversary; and that the barbarian, by accepting the equivalent, expressed his involuntary esteem for the superior merit of Aëtius. But the unusual despondency which seemed to prevail among the Huns engaged Attila to use the expedient, so familiar to the generals of antiquity, of animating his troops by a military oration; and his language was that of a king who had often fought and conquered at their head. He pressed them to consider their past glory, their actual danger, and their future hopes. The same fortune which opened the deserts and morasses of Scythia to their unarmed valour, which had laid so many warlike nations prostrate at their feet, had reserved the *joys* of this memorable field for the consummation of their victories. The cautious steps of their enemies, their strict alliance, and their advantageous posts, he artfully represented as the effects, not of prudence, but of fear. The Visigoths alone were the strength and nerves of the opposite army; and the Huns might securely trample on the degenerate Romans, whose close and compact order betrayed their apprehensions, and who were equally incapable of supporting the dangers or the fatigues of a day of battle. The doctrine of predestination, so favourable to martial virtue, was carefully inculcated by the king of the Huns; who assured his subjects that the warriors, protected by Heaven, were safe and invulnerable amidst the darts of the enemy; but that the unerring Fates would strike their victims in the bosom of inglorious peace. "I myself," continued Attila, "will throw the first javelin, and the wretch who refuses to imitate the example of his sovereign is devoted to inevitable death." The spirit of the barbarians was rekindled by the presence, the voice, and the example of their intrepid leader; and Attila, yielding to their impatience, immediately formed his order of battle. At the head of his brave and faithful Huns, he occupied in person the centre of the line. The nations subject to his empire, the Rugians, the Heruli, the Thuringians, the Franks, the Burgundians, were extended, on either hand, over the ample space of the Catalaunian fields; the right wing was commanded by Ardaric, king of the Gepidæ; and the three valiant brothers who reigned over the Ostrogoths were posted on the left to oppose the kindred tribes of the Visigoths. The disposition of the allies was regulated by a different principle. Sangiban, the faithless king of the Alani, was placed in the centre: where his motions might be strictly watched, and his treachery might be instantly punished. Aëtius assumed the command of the left, and Theodoric of the right wing; while Torismond still continued to occupy the heights which appear to have stretched on the flank, and perhaps the rear, of the Scythian army. The nations from the Volga to the Atlantic were assembled on the plain of Châlons; but many of these nations had been divided by faction, or conquest, or emigration; and the appearance of similar arms and ensigns, which threatened each other, presented the image of a civil war.

The discipline and tactics of the Greeks and Romans form an interesting part of their national manners. The attentive study of the military operations of Xenophon, or Cæsar, or Frederic, when they are described by the same genius which conceived and executed them, may tend to improve (if such improvement can be wished) the art of destroying the human species. But the battle of Châlons [1] can only excite our curiosity by the magnitude of the object; since it was decided by the blind impetuosity of barbarians, and has been related by partial writers, whose civil or ecclesiastical profession secluded them from the knowledge of military affairs. Cassiodorus, however, had familiarly conversed with many Gothic warriors who served in that memorable engagement; "a conflict," as they informed him, "fierce, various, obstinate, and bloody; such as could not be paralleled either in the present or in past ages." The number of the slain amounted to one hundred and sixty-two thousand, or, according to another account, three hundred thousand persons; and these incredible exaggerations suppose a real and effective loss, sufficient to justify the historian's remark that whole generations may be swept away by the madness of kings in the space of a single hour. After the mutual and repeated discharge of missile weapons, in which the archers of Scythia might signalise their superior dexterity, the cavalry and infantry of the two armies were furiously mingled in closer combat. The Huns, who fought under the eyes of their king, pierced through the

---

[1] Gibbon and others after him were mistaken in giving the name of Châlons to the scene of Attila's defeat. It is now accepted that the action occurred in the plain of Maurica.—D.M.L.

feeble and doubtful centre of the allies, separated their wings
from each other, and wheeling, with a rapid effort, to the
left, directed their whole force against the Visigoths. As
Theodoric rode along the ranks to animate his troops, he
received a mortal stroke from the javelin of Andages, a noble
Ostrogoth, and immediately fell from his horse. The wounded
king was oppressed in the general disorder and trampled under
the feet of his own cavalry; and this important death served
to explain the ambiguous prophecy of the haruspices. Attila
already exulted in the confidence of victory, when the valiant
Torismond descended from the hills, and verified the remainder of the prediction. The Visigoths, who had been
thrown into confusion by the flight, or defection, of the Alani,
gradually restored their order of battle; and the Huns were
undoubtedly vanquished, since Attila was compelled to retreat. He had exposed his person with the rashness of a
private soldier; but the intrepid troops of the centre had
pushed forwards beyond the rest of the line; their attack was
faintly supported; their flanks were unguarded; and the conquerors of Scythia and Germany were saved by the approach
of the night from a total defeat. They retired within the
circle of waggons that fortified their camp; and the dismounted
squadrons prepared themselves for a defence to which neither
their arms nor their temper were adapted. The event was
doubtful: but Attila had secured a last and honourable resource. The saddles and rich furniture of the cavalry were
collected by his order into a funeral pile; and the magnani-
mous barbarian had resolved, if his entrenchments should be
forced, to rush headlong into the flames, and to deprive his
enemies of the glory which they might have acquired by the
death or captivity of Attila.

But his enemies had passed the night in equal disorder and
anxiety. The inconsiderate courage of Torismond was tempted
to urge the pursuit, till he unexpectedly found himself, with
a few followers, in the midst of the Scythian waggons. In
the confusion of a nocturnal combat he was thrown from
his horse; and the Gothic prince must have perished like his
father, if his youthful strength and the intrepid zeal of his
companions had not rescued him from this dangerous situation. In the same manner, but on the left of the line, Aëtius
himself, separated from his allies, ignorant of their victory,
and anxious for their fate, encountered and escaped the

hostile troops that were scattered over the plains of Châlons; and at length reached the camp of the Goths, which he could only fortify with a slight rampart of shields till the dawn of day. The Imperial general was soon satisfied of the defeat of Attila, who still remained inactive within his entrenchments; and when he contemplated the bloody scene, he observed, with secret satisfaction, that the loss had principally fallen on the barbarians. The body of Theodoric, pierced with honourable wounds, was discovered under a heap of the slain: his subjects bewailed the death of their king and father; but their tears were mingled with songs and acclamations, and his funeral rites were performed in the face of a vanquished enemy. The Goths, clashing their arms, elevated on a buckler his eldest son Torismond, to whom they justly ascribed the glory of their success; and the new king accepted the obligation of revenge as a sacred portion of his paternal inheritance. Yet the Goths themselves were astonished by the fierce and undaunted aspect of their formidable antagonist; and their historian has compared Attila to a lion encompassed in his den and threatening his hunters with redoubled fury. The kings and nations who might have deserted his standard in the hour of distress were made sensible that the displeasure of their monarch was the most imminent and inevitable danger. All his instruments of martial music incessantly sounded a loud and animating strain of defiance; and the foremost troops, who advanced to the assault, were checked or destroyed by showers of arrows from every side of the entrenchments. It was determined in a general council of war to besiege the king of the Huns in his camp, to intercept his provisions, and to reduce him to the alternative of a disgraceful treaty or an unequal combat. But the impatience of the barbarians soon disdained these cautious and dilatory measures: and the mature policy of Aëtius was apprehensive that, after the extirpation of the Huns, the republic would be oppressed by the pride and power of the Gothic nation. The patrician exerted the superior ascendant of authority and reason to calm the passions which the son of Theodoric considered as a duty; represented, with seeming affection and real truth, the dangers of absence and delay; and persuaded Torismond to disappoint, by his speedy return, the ambitious designs of his brothers, who might occupy the throne and treasures of Toulouse. After the departure of the Goths, and the separation of the allied army, Attila was surprised at the vast silence that reigned over the plains of Châlons: the suspicion of some hostile stratagem detained him several days within the circle of his waggons, and his retreat beyond the Rhine confessed the last victory which was achieved in the name of the Western empire. Meroveus and his Franks, observing a prudent distance, and magnifying the opinion of their strength by the numerous fires which they kindled every night, continued to follow the rear of the Huns till they reached the confines of Thuringia. The Thuringians served in the army of Attila: they traversed, both in their march and in their return, the territories of the Franks; and it was perhaps in this war that they exercised the cruelties which, about fourscore years afterwards, were revenged by the son of Clovis. They massacred their hostages, as well as their captives: two hundred young maidens were tortured with exquisite and unrelenting rage; their bodies were torn asunder by wild horses, or their bones were crushed under the weight of rolling waggons; and their unburied limbs were abandoned on the public roads as a prey to dogs and vultures. Such were those savage ancestors whose imaginary virtues have sometimes excited the praise and envy of civilised ages!

THE INVASION OF ITALY

Neither the spirit, nor the forces, nor the reputation of Attila were impaired by the failure of the Gallic expedition. In the ensuing spring he repeated his demand of the princess Honoria and her patrimonial treasures. The demand was again rejected or eluded; and the indignant lover immediately took the field, passed the Alps, invaded Italy, and besieged Aquileia with an innumerable host of barbarians. Those barbarians were unskilled in the methods of conducting a regular siege, which, even among the ancients, required some knowledge, or at least some practice, of the mechanic arts. But the labour of many thousand provincials and captives, whose lives were sacrificed without pity, might execute the most painful and dangerous work. The skill of the Roman artists might be corrupted to the destruction of their country. The **walls of Aquileia were assaulted by a formidable train of** battering rams, moveable turrets, and engines that threw stones, darts, and fire;[1] and the monarch of the Huns employed the forcible impulse of hope, fear, emulation, and interest, to subvert the only barrier which delayed the conquest of Italy. Aquileia was at that period one of the richest, the most populous, and the strongest of the maritime cities of the Adriatic coast. The Gothic auxiliaries, who appear to have served under their native princes, Alaric and Antala, communicated their intrepid spirit and the citizens still remembered the glorious and successful resistance which their ancestors had opposed to a fierce, inexorable barbarian, who disgraced the majesty of the Roman purple. Three months were consumed without effect in the siege of Aquileia; till the want of provisions and the clamours of his army compelled Attila to relinquish the enterprise, and reluctantly to issue his orders that the troops should strike their tents the next morning, and begin their retreat. But as he rode round the walls, pensive, angry, and disappointed, he observed a stork preparing to leave her nest in one of the towers, and to fly with her infant family towards the country. He seized, with the ready penetration of a statesman, this trifling incident which chance had offered to superstition; and exclaimed, in a loud and cheerful tone, that such a domestic bird, so constantly attached to human society, would never have abandoned her ancient seats unless those towers had been devoted to impending ruin and solitude. The favourable omen inspired an assurance of victory; the siege was renewed, and prosecuted with fresh vigour; a large breach was made in the part of the wall from whence the stork had taken her flight; the Huns mounted to the assault with irresistible fury; and the succeeding generation could scarcely discover the ruins of Aquileia. After this dreadful chastisement, Attila pursued his march; and as he passed, the cities of Altinum, Concordia, and Padua were reduced into heaps of stones and ashes. The inland towns, Vicenza, Verona, and Bergamo, were exposed to the rapacious cruelty of the Huns. Milan and Pavia sub-

---

[1] In the thirteenth century the Moguls battered the cities of China with large engines constructed by the Mahometans or Christians in their service, which threw stones from 150 to 300 pounds weight. In the defence of their country the Chinese used gunpowder, and even bombs, above an hundred years before they were known in Europe; yet even those celestial, or infernal, arms were insufficient to protect a pusillanimous nation.

mitted, without resistance, to the loss of their wealth; and applauded the unusual clemency which preserved from the flames the public as well as private buildings, and spared the lives of the captive multitude. The popular traditions of Comum, Turin, or Modena may justly be suspected; yet they concur with more authentic evidence to prove that Attila spread his ravages over the rich plains of modern Lombardy, which are divided by the Po, and bounded by the Alps and Apennine. When he took possession of the royal palace of Milan, he was surprised and offended at the sight of a picture which represented the Cæsars seated on their throne, and the princes of Scythia prostrate at their feet. The revenge which Attila inflicted on this monument of Roman vanity was harmless and ingenious. He commanded a painter to reverse the figures and the attitudes; and the emperors were delineated on the same canvas approaching in a suppliant posture to empty their bags of tributary gold before the throne of the Scythian monarch. The spectators must have confessed the truth and propriety of the alteration; and were perhaps tempted to apply, on this singular occasion, the well-known fable of the dispute between the lion and the man.

THE FOUNDATION OF VENICE

It is a saying worthy of the ferocious pride of Attila, that the grass never grew on the spot where his horse had trod. Yet the savage destroyer undesignedly laid the foundations of a republic which revived, in the feudal state of Europe, the art and spirit of commercial industry. The celebrated name of Venice, or Venetia, was formerly diffused over a large and fertile province of Italy, from the confines of Pannonia to the river Addua, and from the Po to the Rhætian and Julian Alps. Before the irruption of the barbarians, fifty Venetian cities flourished in peace and prosperity: Aquileia was placed in the most conspicuous station: but the ancient dignity of Padua was supported by agriculture and manufactures; and the property of five hundred citizens, who were entitled to the equestrian rank, must have amounted, at the strictest computation, to one million seven hundred thousand pounds. Many families of Aquileia, Padua, and the adjacent towns, who fled from the sword of the Huns, found a safe, though obscure, refuge in the neighbouring islands.[1] At the extremity of the Gulf, where the Adriatic feebly imitates the tides of the ocean, near an hundred small islands are separated by shallow water from the continent, and protected from the waves by several long slips of land, which admit the entrance of vessels through some secret and narrow channels. Till the middle of the fifth century these remote and sequestered spots remained without cultivation, with few inhabitants, and almost without a name. But the manners of the Venetian fugitives, their arts and their government, were gradually formed by their new situation; and one of the epistles of Cassiodorus, which describes their condition about seventy years afterwards, may be considered as the primitive monument of the republic. The minister of Theodoric compares them, in his quaint declamatory style, to waterfowl, who had fixed their nests on the bosom of the waves; and though he allows that the Venetian provinces had formerly contained many noble families, he insinuates that they were now reduced by misfortune to the same level of humble poverty. Fish was the common, and almost the universal, food of every rank: their only treasure consisted in the plenty of salt which they extracted from the sea: and the exchange of that commodity, so essential to human-life, was substituted in the neighbouring markets to the currency of gold and silver. A people whose habitations might be doubtfully assigned to the earth or water soon became alike familiar with the two elements; and the demands of avarice succeeded to those of necessity. The islanders, who, from Grado to Chiozza, were intimately connected with each other, penetrated into the heart of Italy, by the secure, though laborious, navigation of the rivers and inland canals. Their vessels, which were continually increasing in size and number, visited all the harbours of the Gulf; and the marriage which Venice annually celebrates with the Adriatic was contracted in her early infancy. The epistle of Cassiodorus, the Prætorian prefect, is addressed to the maritime tribunes; and he exhorts them, in a mild tone of authority, to animate the zeal of their countrymen for the public service, which required their assistance to transport the magazines of wine and oil from the

---

[1] Venice is now held to have had its beginnings during the later invasions of the Lombards. There need be no doubt, however, that some people fleeing from Attila took refuge in the Lagoon. Gibbon's description therefore may be accepted with this *caveat*.—D.M.L.

province of Istria to the royal city of Ravenna. The ambiguous office of these magistrates is explained by the tradition, that, in the twelve principal islands, twelve tribunes, or judges, were created by an annual and popular election. The existence of the Venetian republic under the Gothic kingdom of Italy is attested by the same authentic record which annihilates their lofty claim of original and perpetual independence.

The Italians, who had long since renounced the exercise of arms, were surprised, after forty years' peace, by the approach of a formidable barbarian, whom they abhorred as the enemy of their religion as well as of their republic. Amidst the general consternation, Aëtius alone was incapable of fear; but it was impossible that he should achieve alone and unassisted any military exploits worthy of his former renown. The barbarians who had defended Gaul refused to march to the relief of Italy; and the succours promised by the Eastern emperor were distant and doubtful. Since Aëtius, at the head of his domestic troops, still maintained the field, and harassed or retarded the march of Attila, he never showed himself more truly great than at the time when his conduct was blamed by an ignorant and ungrateful people. If the mind of Valentinian had been susceptible of any generous sentiments, he would have chosen such a general for his example and his guide. But the timid grandson of Theodosius, instead of sharing the dangers, escaped from the sound, of war; and his hasty retreat from Ravenna to Rome, from an impregnable fortress to an open capital, betrayed his secret intention of abandoning Italy as soon as the danger should approach his Imperial person. This shameful abdication was suspended, however, by the spirit of doubt and delay which commonly adheres to pusillanimous counsels, and sometimes corrects their pernicious tendency. The Western emperor, with the senate and people of Rome, embraced the more salutary resolution of deprecating, by a solemn and suppliant embassy, the wrath of Attila. This important commission was accepted by Avienus, who, from his birth and riches, his consular dignity, the numerous train of his clients, and his personal abilities, held the first rank in the Roman senate. The specious and artful character of Avienus was admirably qualified to conduct a negociation either of public or private interest: his colleague Trigetius had exercised the Prætorian prefecture of Italy; and Leo, bishop of Rome, consented to

expose his life for the safety of his flock. The genius of Leo
was exercised and displayed in the public misfortunes; and
he has deserved the appellation of *Great* by the successful
zeal with which he laboured to establish his opinions and his
authority, under the venerable names of orthodox faith and
ecclesiastical discipline. The Roman ambassadors were introduced to the tent of Attila, as he lay encamped at the
place where the slow-winding Mincius is lost in the foaming
waves of the lake Benacus, and trampled, with his Scythian
cavalry, the farms of Catullus and Virgil. The barbarian
monarch listened with favourable, and even respectful, attention; and the deliverance of Italy was purchased by the immense ransom or dowry of the princess Honoria. The state of
his army might facilitate the treaty and hasten his retreat.
Their martial spirit was relaxed by the wealth and indolence
of a warm climate. The shepherds of the North, whose ordinary food consisted of milk and raw flesh, indulged themselves
too freely in the use of bread, of wine, and of meat prepared
and seasoned by the arts of cookery; and the progress of
disease revenged in some measure the injuries of the Italians.
When Attila declared his resolution of carrying his victorious
arms to the gates of Rome, he was admonished by his friends,
as well as by his enemies, that Alaric had not long survived
the conquest of the eternal city. His mind, superior to real
danger, was assaulted by imaginary terrors; nor could he
escape the influence of superstition, which had so often been
subservient to his designs. The pressing eloquence of Leo, his
majestic aspect and sacerdotal robes, excited the veneration
of Attila for the spiritual father of the Christians. The apparition of the two apostles St. Peter and St. Paul, who
menaced the barbarian with instant death if he rejected the
prayer of their successor, is one of the noblest legends of
ecclesiastical tradition. The safety of Rome might deserve
the interposition of celestial beings; and some indulgence is
due to a fable which has been represented by the pencil of
Raphael and the chisel of Algardi.

THE DEATH OF ATTILA AND DESTRUCTION OF HIS EMPIRE

Before the king of the Huns evacuated Italy, he threatened
to return more dreadful, and more implacable, if his bride,
the princess Honoria, were not delivered to his ambassadors

within the term stipulated by the treaty. Yet, in the meanwhile, Attila relieved his tender anxiety by adding a beautiful maid, whose name was Ildico, to the list of his innumerable wives. Their marriage was celebrated with barbaric pomp and festivity, at his wooden palace beyond the Danube; and the monarch, oppressed with wine and sleep, retired at a late hour from the banquet to the nuptial bed. His attendants continued to respect his pleasures or his repose the greatest part of the ensuing day, till the unusual silence alarmed their fears and suspicions; and, after attempting to awaken Attila by loud and repeated cries, they at length broke into the royal apartment. They found the trembling bride sitting by the bedside, hiding her face with her veil, and lamenting her own danger, as well as the death of the king, who had expired during the night. An artery had suddenly burst: and as Attila lay in a supine posture, he was suffocated by a torrent of blood, which, instead of finding a passage through the nostrils, regurgitated into the lungs and stomach. His body was solemnly exposed in the midst of the plain, under a silken pavilion; and the chosen squadrons of the Huns, wheeling round in measured evolutions, chanted a funeral song to the memory of a hero, glorious in his life, invincible in his death, the father of his people, the scourge of his enemies, and the terror of the world. According to their national custom, the barbarians cut off a part of their hair, gashed their faces with unseemly wounds, and bewailed their valiant leader as he deserved, not with the tears of women, but with the blood of warriors. The remains of Attila were enclosed within three coffins, of gold, of silver, and of iron, and privately buried in the night: the spoils of nations were thrown into his grave; the captives who had opened the ground were inhumanly massacred; and the same Huns, who had indulged such excessive grief, feasted, with dissolute and intemperate mirth, about the recent sepulchre of their king. It was reported at Constantinople that, on the fortunate night in which he expired, Marcian beheld in a dream the bow of Attila broken asunder: and the report may be allowed to prove how seldom the image of that formidable barbarian was absent from the mind of a Roman emperor.

The revolution which subverted the empire of the Huns established the fame of Attila, whose genius alone had sustained the huge and disjointed fabric. After his death the boldest chieftains aspired to the rank of kings; the most powerful kings refused to acknowledge a superior; and the numerous sons whom so many various mothers bore to the deceased monarch divided and disputed like a private inheritance the sovereign command of the nations of Germany and Scythia. The bold Ardaric felt and represented the disgrace of this servile partition; and his subjects, the warlike Gepidæ, with the Ostrogoths, under the conduct of three valiant brothers, encouraged their allies to vindicate the rights of freedom and royalty. In a bloody and decisive conflict on the banks of the river Netad in Pannonia, the lance of the Gepidæ, the sword of the Goths, the arrows of the Huns, the Suevic infantry, the light arms of the Heruli, and the heavy weapons of the Alani, encountered or supported each other; and the victory of Ardaric was accompanied with the slaughter of thirty thousand of his enemies. Ellac, the eldest son of Attila, lost his life and crown in the memorable battle of Netad: his early valour had raised him to the throne of the Acatzires, a Scythian people, whom he subdued; and his father, who loved the superior merit, would have envied the death, of Ellac. His brother Dengisich, with an army of Huns still formidable in their flight and ruin, maintained his ground above fifteen years on the banks of the Danube. The palace of Attila, with the old country of Dacia, from the Carpathian hills to the Euxine, became the seat of a new power which was erected by Ardaric, king of the Gepidæ. The Pannonian conquests, from Vienna to Sirmium, were occupied by the Ostrogoths; and the settlements of the tribes who had so bravely asserted their native freedom were irregularly distributed according to the measure of their respective strength. Surrounded and oppressed by the multitude of his father's slaves, the kingdom of Dengisich was confined to the circle of his waggons; his desperate courage urged him to invade the Eastern empire: he fell in battle, and his head, ignominiously exposed in the Hippodrome, exhibited a grateful spectacle to the people of Constantinople. Attila had fondly or superstitiously believed that Irnac, the youngest of his sons, was destined to perpetuate the glories of his race. The character of that prince, who attempted to moderate the rashness of his brother Dengisich, was more suitable to the declining condition of the Huns; and Irnac, with his subject hordes, retired into the heart of the Lesser Scythia. They were soon overwhelmed by a torrent of new barbarians, who followed the same road which their own ancestors had formerly discovered. The *Geougen,* or Avares, whose residence is assigned by the Greek writers to the shores of the ocean, impelled the adjacent tribes; till at length the Igours of the North, issuing from the cold Siberian regions which produce the most valuable furs, spread themselves over the desert as far as the Borysthenes and the Caspian gates, and finally extinguished the empire of the Huns.

THE MURDER OF AËTIUS AND DEATH OF VALENTINIAN III

Such an event might contribute to the safety of the Eastern empire under the reign of a prince who conciliated the friendship, without forfeiting the esteem, of the barbarians. But the emperor of the West, the feeble and dissolute Valentinian, who had reached his thirty-fifth year without attaining the age of reason or courage, abused this apparent security to undermine the foundations of his own throne by the murder of the patrician Aëtius. From the instinct of a base and jealous mind, he hated the man who was universally celebrated as the terror of the barbarians and the support of the republic; and his new favourite, the eunuch Heraclius, awakened the emperor from the supine lethargy which might be disguised during the life of Placidia[1] by the excuse of filial piety. The fame of Aëtius, his wealth and dignity, the numerous and martial train of barbarian followers, his powerful dependents who filled the civil offices of the state, and the hopes of his son Gaudentius, who was already contracted to Eudoxia, the emperor's daughter, had raised him above the rank of a subject. The ambitious designs, of which he was secretly accused, excited the fears as well as the resentment of Valentinian. Aëtius himself, supported by the consciousness of his merit, his services, and perhaps his innocence, seems to have maintained a haughty and indiscreet behaviour. The patrician offended his sovereign by an hostile declaration; he aggravated the offence by compelling him to ratify with a solemn oath a treaty of reconciliation and alliance; he proclaimed his sus-

---

[1] Placidia died at Rome, November 27, A.D. 450. She was buried at Ravenna, where her sepulchre, and even her corpse, seated in a chair of cypresswood, were preserved for ages. The empress received many compliments from the orthodox clergy; and St. Peter Chrysologus assured her that her zeal for the Trinity had been recompensed by an august trinity of children.

picions, he neglected his safety; and from a vain confidence that the enemy whom he despised was incapable even of a manly crime, he rashly ventured his person in the palace of Rome. Whilst he urged, perhaps with intemperate vehemence, the marriage of his son, Valentinian, drawing his sword—the first sword he had ever drawn—plunged it in the breast of a general who had saved his empire: his courtiers and eunuchs ambitiously struggled to imitate their master; and Aëtius, pierced with an hundred wounds, fell dead in the royal presence. Boethius, the Prætorian prefect, was killed at the same moment; and before the event could be divulged, the principal friends of the patrician were summoned to the palace and separately murdered. The horrid deed, palliated by the specious names of justice and necessity, was immediately communicated by the emperor to his soldiers, his subjects, and his allies. The nations who were strangers or enemies to Aëtius generously deplored the unworthy fate of a hero; the barbarians who had been attached to his service dissembled their grief and resentment; and the public contempt which had been so long entertained for Valentinian was at once converted into deep and universal abhorrence. Such sentiments seldom pervade the walls of a palace; yet the emperor was confounded by the honest reply of a Roman whose approbation he had not disdained to solicit. "I am ignorant, sir, of your motives or provocations; I only know that you have acted like a man who cuts off his right hand with his left."

The luxury of Rome seems to have attracted the long and frequent visits of Valentinian, who was consequently more despised at Rome than in any other part of his dominions. A republican spirit was insensibly revived in the senate, as their authority, and even their supplies, became necessary for the support of his feeble government. The stately demeanour of an hereditary monarch offended their pride, and the pleasures of Valentinian were injurious to the peace and honour of noble families. The birth of the empress Eudoxia was equal to his own, and her charms and tender affection deserved those testimonies of love which her inconstant husband dissipated in vague and unlawful amours. Petronius Maximus, a wealthy senator of the Anician family, who had been twice consul, was possessed of a chaste and beautiful wife: her obstinate resistance served only to irritate the desires of Valentinian, and he resolved to accomplish them either by stratagem or force. Deep gaming was one of the vices of the court; the emperor, who, by chance or contrivance, had gained from Maximus a considerable sum, uncourteously exacted his ring as a security for the debt, and sent it by a trusty messenger to his wife, with an order in her husband's name that she should immediately attend the empress Eudoxia. The unsuspecting wife of Maximus was conveyed in her litter to the Imperial palace; the emissaries of her impatient lover conducted her to a remote and silent bed-chamber; and Valentinian violated, without remorse, the laws of hospitality. Her tears when she returned home, her deep affliction, and her bitter reproaches against a husband whom she considered as the accomplice of his own shame, excited Maximus to a just revenge; the desire of revenge was stimulated by ambition; and he might reasonably aspire, by the free suffrage of the Roman senate, to the throne of a detested and despicable rival. Valentinian, who supposed that every human breast was devoid like his own of friendship and gratitude, had imprudently admitted among his guards several domestics and followers of Aëtius. Two of these, of barbarian race, were persuaded to execute a sacred and honourable duty by punishing with death the assassin of their patron; and their intrepid courage did not long expect a favourable moment. Whilst Valentinian amused himself in the field of Mars with the spectacle of some military sports, they suddenly rushed upon him with drawn weapons, despatched the guilty Heraclius, and stabbed the emperor to the heart, without the least opposition from his numerous train, who seemed to rejoice in the tyrant's death. Such was the fate of Valentinian the Third, the last Roman emperor of the family of Theodosius. He faithfully imitated the hereditary weakness of his cousin and his two uncles, without inheriting the gentleness, the purity, the innocence, which alleviate in their characters the want of spirit and ability. Valentinian was less excusable, since he had passions without virtues: even his religion was questionable; and though he never deviated into the paths of heresy, he scandalised the pious Christians by his attachment to the profane arts of magic and divination.

SYMPTOMS OF DECAY IN THE ROMAN EMPIRE OF THE WEST

As early as the time of Cicero and Varro it was the opinion of the Roman augurs that the *twelve vultures* which Romulus had seen represented the *twelve centuries* assigned for the fatal period of his city. This prophecy, disregarded perhaps in the season of health and prosperity, inspired the people with gloomy apprehensions when the twelfth century, clouded with disgrace and misfortune, was almost elapsed; and even posterity must acknowledge with some surprise that the arbitrary interpretation of an accidental or fabulous circumstance has been seriously verified in the downfall of the Western empire. But its fall was announced by a clearer omen than the flight of vultures: the Roman government appeared every day less formidable to its enemies, more odious and oppressive to its subjects. The taxes were multiplied with the public distress; economy was neglected in proportion as it became necessary; and the injustice of the rich shifted the unequal burden from themselves to the people, whom they defrauded of the *indulgences* that might sometimes have alleviated their misery. The severe inquisition, which confiscated their goods and tortured their persons, compelled the subjects of Valentinian to prefer the more simple tyranny of the barbarians, to fly to the woods and mountains, or to embrace the vile and abject condition of mercenary servants. They abjured and abhorred the name of Roman citizens, which had formerly excited the ambition of mankind. The Armorican provinces of Gaul and the greatest part of Spain were thrown into a state of disorderly independence by the confederations of the Bagaudæ, and the Imperial ministers pursued with proscriptive laws and ineffectual arms the rebels whom they had made. If all the barbarian conquerors had been annihilated in the same hour, their total destruction would not have restored the empire of the West: and if Rome still survived, she survived the loss of freedom, of virtue, and of honour.

36.

Although the Huns had made but a transitory sojourn in Italy, the organisation of the West was now shaken beyond repair. Within three months of Valentinian's death (455) Genseric (Gaiseric) had brought his fleet to the mouth of the Tiber and sacked Rome.

The next twenty years witnessed the final collapse of the West under a series of emperors who are but names. Some respite was obtained in the short reign (457–461) of Majorian.

THE EMPEROR MAJORIAN

THE SUCCESSOR of Avitus presents the welcome discovery of a great and heroic character, such as sometimes arise, in a degenerate age, to vindicate the honour of the human species. The emperor Majorian has deserved the praises of his contemporaries and of posterity; and these praises may be strongly expressed in the words of a judicious and disinterested historian: "That he was gentle to his subjects; that he was terrible to his enemies; and that he excelled in *every* virtue *all* his predecessors who had reigned over the Romans." Such a testimony may justify at least the panegyric of Sidonius; and we may acquiesce in the assurance that, although the obsequious orator would have flattered with equal zeal the most worthless of princes, the extraordinary merit of his object confined him, on this occasion, within the bounds of truth. Majorian derived his name from his maternal grandfather, who, in the reign of the great Theodosius, had commanded the troops of the Illyrian frontier. He gave his daughter in marriage to the father of Majorian, a respectable officer, who administered the revenues of Gaul with skill and integrity; and generously preferred the friendship of Aëtius to the tempting offers of an insidious court. His son, the future emperor, who was educated in the profession of arms, displayed, from his early youth, intrepid courage, premature wisdom, and unbounded liberality in a scanty fortune. He followed the standard of Aëtius, contributed to his success, shared, and sometimes eclipsed, his glory, and at last excited the jealousy of the patrician, or rather of his wife, who forced him to retire from the service. Majorian, after the death of Aëtius, was recalled and promoted: and his intimate connection with Count Ricimer was the immediate step by which he ascended the throne of the Western empire. During the vacancy that succeeded the abdication of Avitus, the ambitious barbarian, whose birth excluded him from the Imperial dignity, governed Italy, with the title of Patrician; resigned to his friend the conspicuous station of master-general of the cavalry and infantry; and, after an interval of some months, consented to the unanimous wish of the Romans, whose favour Majorian had solicited by a recent victory over the Alemanni. He was invested with the purple at Ravenna: and the epistle which he addressed to the senate will best describe his situation and his sentiments. "Your election, Conscript Fathers! and the ordinance of the most valiant army, have made me your emperor. May the propitious Deity direct and prosper the counsels and events of my administration to your advantage and to the public welfare! For my own part, I did not aspire, I have submitted, to reign; nor should I have discharged the obligations of a citizen if I had refused, with base and selfish ingratitude, to support the weight of those labours which were imposed by the republic. Assist, therefore, the prince whom you have made; partake the duties which you have enjoined; and may our common endeavours promote the happiness of an empire which I have accepted from your hands. Be assured that, in our times, justice shall resume her ancient vigour, and that virtue shall become not only innocent but meritorious. Let none, except the authors themselves, be apprehensive of *delations,* which, as a subject, I have always condemned, and, as a prince, will severely punish. Our own vigilance, and that of our father, the patrician Ricimer, shall regulate all military affairs and provide for the safety of the Roman world, which we have saved from foreign and domestic enemies. You now understand the maxims of my government: you may confide in the faithful love and sincere assurances of a prince who has formerly been the companion of your life and dangers, who still glories in the name of senator, and who is anxious that you should never repent of the judgment which you have pronounced in his favour." The emperor, who, amidst the ruins of the Roman world, revived the ancient language of law and liberty, which Trajan would not have disclaimed, must have derived those generous sentiments from his own heart, since they were not suggested to his imitation by the customs of his age or the example of his predecessors.

The private and public actions of Majorian are very imperfectly known: but his laws, remarkable for an original cast of thought and expression, faithfully represent the character of a sovereign who loved his people, who sympathised in their distress, who had studied the causes of the decline of the empire, and who was capable of applying (as far as such reformation was practicable) judicious and effectual remedies to the public disorders. His regulations concerning the finances manifestly tended to remove, or at least to mitigate, the most intolerable grievances. I. From the first hour of his reign, he was solicitous (I translate his own words) to relieve the *weary* fortunes of the provincials, oppressed by the accumulated weight of indictions and superindictions. With this view, he granted an universal amnesty, a final and absolute discharge of all arrears of tribute, of all debts which, under any pretence, the fiscal officers might demand from the people. This wise dereliction of obsolete, vexatious, and unprofitable claims, improved and purified the sources of the public revenue; and the subject, who could now look back without despair, might labour with hope and gratitude for himself and for his country. II. In the assessment and collection of taxes Majorian restored the ordinary jurisdiction of the provincial magistrates, and suppressed the extraordinary commissions which had been introduced in the name of the emperor himself or of the Prætorian prefects. The favourite servants who obtained such irregular powers were insolent in their behaviour and arbitrary in their demands: they affected to despise the subordinate tribunals, and they were discontented if their fees and profits did not twice exceed the sum which they condescended to pay into the treasury. One instance of their extortion would appear incredible were it not authenticated by the legislator himself. They exacted the whole payment in gold: but they refused the current coin of the empire, and would accept only such ancient pieces as were stamped with the names of Faustina or the Antonines. The subject who was unprovided with these curious medals had recourse to the expedient of compounding with their rapacious demands; or, if he succeeded in the research, his imposition was doubled according to the weight and value of the money of former times. III. "The municipal corporations (says the emperor), the lesser senates (so antiquity has justly styled them), deserve to be considered as the heart of the cities and the sinews of the republic. And yet so low are they now reduced, by the injustice of magistrates and the venality of collectors, that many of their members, renouncing their dignity and their country, have taken refuge in distant and obscure exile." He urges, and even compels, their return to their respective cities; but he removes the grievance which had forced them to desert the exercise of their municipal functions. They are directed, under the authority of the provincial magistrates, to resume their office of levying the tribute; but, instead of being made responsible for the whole sum assessed on their district, they are only required to produce a regular account of the payments which they have actually received, and of the defaulters who are still indebted to the public. IV. But Majorian was not ignorant that these corporate bodies were too much inclined to retaliate the injustice and oppression which they had suffered, and he therefore revives the useful office of the *defenders of cities*. He exhorts the people to elect, in a full and free assembly, some man of discretion and integrity who would dare to assert their privileges, to represent their grievances, to protect the poor from the tyranny of the rich, and to inform the emperor of the abuses that were committed under the sanction of his name and authority.

The spectator who casts a mournful view over the ruins of ancient Rome is tempted to accuse the memory of the Goths and Vandals for the mischief which they had neither leisure, nor power, nor perhaps inclination, to perpetrate. The tempest of war might strike some lofty turrets to the ground; but the destruction which undermined the foundations of those massy fabrics was prosecuted, slowly and silently, during a period of ten centuries; and the motives of interest, that afterwards operated without shame or control, were severely checked by the taste and spirit of the emperor Majorian. The decay of the city had gradually impaired the value of the

public works. The circus and theatres might still excite, but
they seldom gratified, the desires of the people: the temples
which had escaped the zeal of the Christians were no longer
inhabited either by gods or men; the diminished crowds of
the Romans were lost in the immense space of their baths
and porticoes; and the stately libraries and halls of justice
became useless to an indolent generation whose repose was
seldom disturbed either by study or business. The monuments
of consular or Imperial greatness were no longer revered as
the immortal glory of the capital: they were only esteemed as
an inexhaustible mine of materials, cheaper, and more convenient, than the distant quarry. Specious petitions were
continually addressed to the easy magistrates of Rome which
stated the want of stones or bricks for some necessary service:
the fairest forms of architecture were rudely defaced for the
sake of some paltry or pretended repairs; and the degenerate
Romans, who converted the spoil to their own emolument,
demolished, with sacrilegious hands, the labours of their
ancestors. Majorian, who had often sighed over the desolation
of the city, applied a severe remedy to the growing evil. He
reserved to the prince and senate the sole cognizance of the
extreme cases which might justify the destruction of an
ancient edifice; imposed a fine of fifty pounds of gold (two
thousand pounds sterling) on every magistrate who should
presume to grant such illegal and scandalous licence; and
threatened to chastise the criminal obedience of their subordinate officers by a severe whipping and the amputation of
both their hands. In the last instance the legislator might
seem to forget the proportion of guilt and punishment; but
his zeal arose from a generous principle, and Majorian was
anxious to protect the monuments of those ages in which he
would have desired and deserved to live. The emperor conceived that it was his interest to increase the number of his
subjects; that it was his duty to guard the purity of the
marriage-bed: but the means which he employed to accomplish these salutary purposes are of an ambiguous, and perhaps
exceptionable, kind. The pious maids who consecrated their
virginity to Christ were restrained from taking the veil till
they had reached their fortieth year. Widows under that age
were compelled to form a second alliance within the term
of five years, by the forfeiture of half their wealth to their
nearest relations or to the state. Unequal marriages were

condemned or annulled. The punishment of confiscation and exile was deemed so inadequate to the guilt of adultery, that, if the criminal returned to Italy, he might, by the express declaration of Majorian, be slain with impunity.

While the emperor Majorian assiduously laboured to restore the happiness and virtue of the Romans, he encountered the arms of Genseric, from his character and situation their most formidable enemy. A fleet of Vandals and Moors landed at the mouth of the Liris or Garigliano; but the Imperial troops surprised and attacked the disorderly barbarians, who were encumbered with the spoils of Campania; they were chased with slaughter to their ships, and their leader, the king's brother-in-law, was found in the number of the slain. Such vigilance might announce the character of the new reign, but the strictest vigilance and the most numerous forces were insufficient to protect the long-extended coast of Italy from the depredations of a naval war. The public opinion had imposed a nobler and more arduous task on the genius of Majorian. Rome expected from him alone the restitution of Africa, and the design which he formed of attacking the Vandals in their new settlements was the result of bold and judicious policy. If the intrepid emperor could have infused his own spirit into the youth of Italy; if he could have revived in the field of Mars the manly exercises in which he had always surpassed his equals; he might have marched against Genseric at the head of a *Roman* army. Such a reformation of national manners might be embraced by the rising generation; but it is the misfortune of those princes who laboriously sustain a declining monarchy, that, to obtain some immediate advantage, or to avert some impending danger, they are forced to countenance, and even to multiply, the most pernicious abuses. Majorian, like the weakest of his predecessors, was reduced to the disgraceful expedient of substituting barbarian auxiliaries in the place of his unwarlike subjects: and his superior abilities could only be displayed in the vigour and dexterity with which he wielded a dangerous instrument, so apt to recoil on the hand that used it. Besides the confederates who were already engaged in the service of the empire, the fame of his liberality and valour attracted the nations of the Danube, the Borysthenes, and perhaps of the Tanais. Many thousands of the bravest subjects of Attila, the Gepidæ, the Ostrogoths, the Rugians, the Burgundians, the Suevi, the Alani,

assembled in the plains of Liguria, and their formidable
strength was balanced by their mutual animosities. They
passed the Alps in a severe winter. The emperor led the way
on foot and in complete armour, sounding with his long staff
the depth of the ice or snow, and encouraging the Scythians,
who complained of the extreme cold, by the cheerful assurance
that they should be satisfied with the heat of Africa. The
citizens of Lyons had presumed to shut their gates: they soon
implored, and experienced, the clemency of Majorian. He
vanquished Theodoric in the field, and admitted to his friendship and alliance a king whom he had found not unworthy of
his arms. The beneficial though precarious reunion of the
greatest part of Gaul and Spain was the effect of persuasion
as well as of force; and the independent Bagaudæ, who had
escaped or resisted the oppression of former reigns, were
disposed to confide in the virtues of Majorian. His camp
was filled with barbarian allies; his throne was supported by
the zeal of an affectionate people; but the emperor had foreseen that it was impossible without a maritime power to
achieve the conquest of Africa. In the first Punic war the
republic had exerted such incredible diligence, that, within
sixty days after the first stroke of the axe had been given in
the forest, a fleet of one hundred and sixty galleys proudly
rode at anchor in the sea. Under circumstances much less
favourable, Majorian equalled the spirit and perseverance of
the ancient Romans. The woods of the Apennine were felled;
the arsenals and manufactures of Ravenna and Misenum
were restored; Italy and Gaul vied with each other in liberal
contributions to the public service; and the Imperial navy of
three hundred large galleys, with an adequate proportion of
transports and smaller vessels, was collected in the secure
and capacious harbour of Carthagena in Spain. The intrepid
countenance of Majorian animated his troops with a confidence of victory; and if we might credit the historian Procopius, his courage sometimes hurried him beyond the bounds
of prudence. Anxious to explore with his own eyes the state
of the Vandals, he ventured, after disguising the colour of
his hair, to visit Carthage in the character of his own ambassador: and Genseric was afterwards mortified by the discovery
that he had entertained and dismissed the emperor of the
Romans. Such an anecdote may be rejected as an improbable

fiction, but it is a fiction which would not have been imagined unless in the life of a hero.

Without the help of a personal interview, Genseric was sufficiently acquainted with the genius and designs of his adversary. He practised his customary arts of fraud and delay, but he practised them without success. His applications for peace became each hour more submissive, and perhaps more sincere; but the inflexible Majorian had adopted the ancient maxim that Rome could not be safe as long as Carthage existed in a hostile state. The king of the Vandals distrusted the valour of his native subjects, who were enervated by the luxury of the South; he suspected the fidelity of the vanquished people, who abhorred him as an Arian tyrant; and the desperate measure which he executed of reducing Mauritania into a desert could not defeat the operations of the Roman emperor, who was at liberty to land his troops on any part of the African coast. But Genseric was saved from impending and inevitable ruin by the treachery of some powerful subjects, envious or apprehensive of their master's success. Guided by their secret intelligence, he surprised the unguarded fleet in the bay of Carthagena: many of the ships were sunk, or taken, or burnt; and the preparations of three years were destroyed in a single day. After this event the behaviour of the two antagonists showed them superior to their fortune. The Vandal, instead of being elated by this accidental victory, immediately renewed his solicitations for peace. The emperor of the West, who was capable of forming great designs and of supporting heavy disappointments, consented to a treaty, or rather to a suspension of arms, in the full assurance that before he could restore his navy he should be supplied with provocations to justify a second war. Majorian returned to Italy to prosecute his labours for the public happiness; and as he was conscious of his own integrity, he might long remain ignorant of the dark conspiracy which threatened his throne and his life. The recent misfortune of Carthagena sullied the glory which had dazzled the eyes of the multitude: almost every description of civil and military officers were exasperated against the Reformer, since they all derived some advantage from the abuses which he endeavoured to suppress; and the patrician Ricimer impelled the inconstant passions of the barbarians against a prince whom he esteemed and hated. The virtues of Majorian could not protect him from the impetuous sedition which broke out in the camp near Tortona at the foot of the Alps. He was compelled to abdicate the Imperial purple; five days after his abdication it was reported that he died of a dysentery; and the humble tomb which covered his remains was consecrated by the respect and gratitude of succeeding generations. The private character of Majorian inspired love and respect. Malicious calumny and satire excited his indignation, or, if he himself were the object, his contempt; but he protected the freedom of wit, and in the hours which the emperor gave to the familiar society of his friends he could indulge his taste for pleasantry without degrading the majesty of his rank.

Between 461 and 471 Ricimer ruled Italy in fact if not in name. In 471, after disagreement with the Emperor Anthemius, he sacked Rome but died soon after. In 476 Romulus Augustulus became the last emperor. The traditional date of the extinction of the Western Empire is linked with his accidentally significant name. Between 476 and 490 Odoacer established a Gothic kingdom in Italy while nominally acting as vice-gerent for the Emperor in Constantinople.

ODOACER, KING OF ITALY

Odoacer was the first barbarian who reigned in Italy, over a people who had once asserted their just superiority above the rest of mankind. The disgrace of the Romans still excites our respectful compassion, and we fondly sympathise with the imaginary grief and indignation of their degenerate posterity. But the calamities of Italy had gradually subdued the proud consciousness of freedom and glory. In the age of Roman virtue the provinces were subject to the arms, and the citizens to the laws, of the republic, till those laws were subverted by civil discord, and both the city and the provinces became the servile property of a tyrant. The forms of the constitution, which alleviated or disguised their abject slavery, were abolished by time and violence; the Italians alternately lamented the presence or the absence of the sovereigns whom they detested or despised; and the succession of five centuries inflicted the various evils of military licence, capricious despotism, and elaborate oppression. During the same period, the barbarians had emerged from obscurity and contempt,

and the warriors of Germany and Scythia were introduced
into the provinces, as the servants, the allies, and at length
the masters, of the Romans, whom they insulted or protected.
The hatred of the people was suppressed by fear; they
respected the spirit and splendour of the martial chiefs who
were invested with the honours of the empire; and the fate
of Rome had long depended on the sword of those formidable
strangers. The stern Ricimer, who trampled on the ruins of
Italy, had exercised the power, without assuming the title, of
a king; and the patient Romans were insensibly prepared to
acknowledge the royalty of Odoacer and his barbaric successors.

The king of Italy was not unworthy of the high station to
which his valour and fortune had exalted him: his savage
manners were polished by the habits of conversation; and he
respected, though a conqueror and a barbarian, the institutions,
and even the prejudices, of his subjects. After an interval of
seven years, Odoacer restored the consulship of the West.
For himself, he modestly, or proudly, declined an honour
which was still accepted by the emperors of the East; but the
curule chair was successively filled by eleven of the most
illustrious senators; and the list is adorned by the respectable
name of Basilius, whose virtues claimed the friendship and
grateful applause of Sidonius, his client. The laws of the
emperors were strictly enforced, and the civil administration
of Italy was still exercised by the Prætorian prefect and his
subordinate officers. Odoacer devolved on the Roman magistrates the odious and oppressive task of collecting the public
revenue; but he reserved for himself the merit of seasonable
and popular indulgence. Like the rest of the barbarians, he
had been instructed in the Arian heresy; but he revered the
monastic and episcopal characters; and the silence of the
catholics attests the toleration which they enjoyed. The peace
of the city required the interposition of his prefect Basilius in
the choice of a Roman pontiff: the decree which restrained
the clergy from alienating their lands was ultimately designed
for the benefit of the people, whose devotion would have
been taxed to repair the dilapidations of the church. Italy
was protected by the arms of its conqueror; and its frontiers
were respected by the barbarians of Gaul and Germany, who
had so long insulted the feeble race of Theodosius. Odoacer
passed the Adriatic, to chastise the assassins of the emperor

Nepos, and to acquire the maritime province of Dalmatia. He passed the Alps, to rescue the remains of Noricum from Fava, or Feletheus, king of the Rugians, who held his residence beyond the Danube. The king was vanquished in battle, and led away prisoner; a numerous colony of captives and subjects was transplanted into Italy; and Rome, after a long period of defeat and disgrace, might claim the triumph of her barbarian master.

Notwithstanding the prudence and success of Odoacer, his kingdom exhibited the sad prospect of misery and desolation. Since the age of Tiberius, the decay of agriculture had been felt in Italy; and it was a just subject of complaint that the life of the Roman people depended on the accidents of the winds and waves. In the division and the decline of the empire, the tributary harvests of Egypt and Africa were withdrawn; the numbers of the inhabitants continually diminished with the means of subsistence; and the country was exhausted by the irretrievable losses of war, famine, and pestilence. St. Ambrose has deplored the ruin of a populous district, which had been once adorned with the flourishing cities of Bologna, Modena, Rhegium, and Placentia. Pope Gelasius was a subject of Odoacer; and he affirms, with strong exaggeration, that in Æmilia, Tuscany, and the adjacent provinces, the human species was almost extirpated. The plebeians of Rome, who were fed by the hand of their master, perished or disappeared as soon as his liberality was suppressed; the decline of the arts reduced the industrious mechanic to idleness and want; and the senators, who might support with patience the ruin of their country, bewailed their private loss of wealth and luxury. One third of those ample estates, to which the ruin of Italy is originally imputed, was extorted for the use of the conquerors. Injuries were aggravated by insults; the sense of actual sufferings was embittered by the fear of more dreadful evils; and as new lands were allotted to new swarms of barbarians, each senator was apprehensive lest the arbitrary surveyors should approach his favourite villa, or his most profitable farm. The least unfortunate were those who submitted without a murmur to the power which it was impossible to resist. Since they desired to live, they owed some gratitude to the tyrant who had spared their lives; and since he was the absolute master of their fortunes, the portion which he left must be accepted as his pure and voluntary gift. The distress of Italy was mitigated by the prudence and humanity of Odoacer, who had bound himself, as the price of his elevation, to satisfy the demands of a licentious and turbulent multitude. The kings of the barbarians were frequently resisted, deposed, or murdered, by their *native* subjects; and the various bands of Italian mercenaries, who associated under the standard of an elective general, claimed a larger privilege of freedom and rapine. A monarchy destitute of national union and hereditary right hastened to its dissolution. After a reign of fourteen years Odoacer was oppressed by the superior genius of Theodoric, king of the Ostrogoths; a hero alike excellent in the arts of war and of government, who restored an age of peace and prosperity, and whose name still excites and deserves the attention of mankind.

37.

ORIGIN OF THE MONKS. CAUSES OF THE RAPID
PROGRESS OF MONASTICISM. ST. SIMEON STYLITES.
CONVERSION OF THE BARBARIANS TO CHRISTIANITY

THE INDISSOLUBLE connexion of civil and ecclesiastical affairs
had compelled and encouraged me to relate the progress, the
persecutions, the establishment, the divisions, the final triumph,
and the gradual corruption of Christianity. I have purposely
delayed the consideration of two religious events interesting
in the study of human nature, and important in the decline
and fall of the Roman empire. I. The institution of the
monastic life; and, II. The conversion of the northern barbarians.

I. Prosperity and peace introduced the distinction of the
vulgar and the *Ascetic Christians*. The loose and imperfect
practice of religion satisfied the conscience of the multitude.
The prince or magistrate, the soldier or merchant, reconciled
their fervent zeal and implicit faith with the exercise of their
profession, the pursuit of their interest, and the indulgence
of their passions: but the Ascetics, who obeyed and abused
the rigid precepts of the Gospel, were inspired by the savage
enthusiasm which represents man as a criminal, and God as
a tyrant. They seriously renounced the business and the
pleasures of the age; abjured the use of wine, of flesh, and
of marriage; chastised their body, mortified their affections,
and embraced a life of misery, as the price of eternal happiness. In the reign of Constantine the Ascetics fled from a
profane and degenerate world to perpetual solitude or religious
society. Like the first Christians of Jerusalem, they resigned
the use or the property of their temporal possessions; established regular communities of the same sex and a similar
disposition; and assumed the names of *Hermits, Monks,* and
Anachorets, expressive of their lonely retreat in a natural

or artificial desert. They soon acquired the respect of the world, which they despised; and the loudest applause was bestowed on this DIVINE PHILOSOPHY, which surpassed, without the aid of science or reason, the laborious virtues of the Grecian schools. The monks might indeed contend with the Stoics in the contempt of fortune, of pain, and of death: the Pythagorean silence and submission were revived in their servile discipline; and they disdained as firmly as the Cynics themselves all the forms and decencies of civil society. But the votaries of this Divine Philosophy aspired to imitate a purer and more perfect model. They trod in the footsteps of the prophets, who had retired to the desert; and they restored the devout and contemplative life, which had been instituted by the Essenians in Palestine and Egypt. The philosophic eye of Pliny had surveyed with astonishment a solitary people, who dwelt among the palm-trees near the Dead Sea; who subsisted without money; who were propagated without women; and who derived from the disgust and repentance of mankind a perpetual supply of voluntary associates.

Egypt, the fruitful parent of superstition, afforded the first example of the monastic life. Antony, an illiterate youth of the lower parts of Thebais, distributed his patrimony, deserted his family and native home, and executed his *monastic* penance with original and intrepid fanaticism. After a long and painful noviciate, among the tombs, and in a ruined tower, he boldly advanced into the desert three days' journey to the eastward of the Nile; discovered a lonely spot, which possessed the advantages of shade and water; and fixed his last residence on Mount Colzim, near the Red Sea, where an ancient monastery still preserves the name and memory of the saint. The curious devotion of the Christians pursued him to the desert; and when he was obliged to appear at Alexandria, in the face of mankind, he supported his fame with discretion and dignity. He enjoyed the friendship of Athanasius, whose doctrine he approved; and the Egyptian peasant respectfully declined a respectful invitation from the emperor Constantine. The venerable patriarch (for Antony attained the age of one hundred and five years) beheld the numerous progeny which had been formed by his example and his lessons. The prolific colonies of monks multiplied with rapid increase on the sands of Libya, upon the rocks of

Thebais, and in the cities of the Nile. To the south of Alexandria, the mountain, and adjacent desert, of Nitria, was peopled by five thousand anachorets; and the traveller may still investigate the ruins of fifty monasteries, which were planted in that barren soil by the disciples of Antony. In the Upper Thebais, the vacant island of Tabenne was occupied by Pachomius and fourteen hundred of his brethren. That holy abbot successively founded nine monasteries of men, and one of women; and the festival of Easter sometimes collected fifty thousand religious persons, who followed his *angelic* rule of discipline. The stately and populous city of Oxyrhyuchus, the seat of Christian orthodoxy, had devoted the temples, the public edifices, and even the ramparts, to pious and charitable uses; and the bishop, who might preach in twelve churches, computed ten thousand females, and twenty thousand males, of the monastic profession. The Egyptians, who gloried in this marvellous revolution, were disposed to hope, and to believe, that the number of the monks was equal to the remainder of the people; and posterity might repeat the saying which had formerly been applied to the sacred animals of the same country, that in Egypt it was less difficult to find a god than a man.

Athanasius introduced into Rome the knowledge and practice of the monastic life; and a school of this new philosophy was opened by the disciples of Antony, who accompanied their primate to the holy threshold of the Vatican. The strange and savage appearance of these Egyptians excited, at first, horror and contempt, and, at length, applause and zealous imitation. The senators, and more especially the matrons, transformed their palaces and villas into religious houses; and the narrow institution of *six* Vestals was eclipsed by the frequent monasteries, which were seated on the ruins of ancient temples, and in the midst of the Roman forum. Inflamed by the example of Antony, a Syrian youth, whose name was Hilarion,[1] fixed his dreary abode on a sandy beach between the sea and a morass, about seven miles from Gaza. The austere penance, in which he persisted forty-eight years, diffused a similar enthusiasm; and the holy man was followed

---

[1] See the Life of Hilarion, by St. Jerom. The stories of Paul, Hilarion, and Malchus, by the same author, are admirably told; and the only defect of these pleasing compositions is the want of truth and common sense.

by a train of two or three thousand anachorets, whenever he visited the innumerable monasteries of Palestine. The fame of Basil is immortal in the monastic history of the East. With a mind that had tasted the learning and eloquence of Athens; with an ambition scarcely to be satisfied by the archbishopric of Cæsarea, Basil retired to a savage solitude in Pontus; and deigned, for a while, to give laws to the spiritual colonies which he profusely scattered along the coast of the Black Sea. In the West, Martin of Tours,[1] a soldier, an hermit, a bishop, and a saint, established the monasteries of Gaul; two thousand of his disciples followed him to the grave; and his eloquent historian challenges the deserts of Thebais to produce, in a more favourable climate, a champion of equal virtue. The progress of the monks was not less rapid or universal than that of Christianity itself. Every province, and, at last, every city, of the empire, was filled with their increasing multitudes; and the bleak and barren isles, from Lerins to Lipari, that arise out of the Tuscan sea, were chosen by the anachorets for the place of their voluntary exile. An easy and perpetual intercourse by sea and land connected the provinces of the Roman world; and the life of Hilarion displays the facility with which an indigent hermit of Palestine might traverse Egypt, embark for Sicily, escape to Epirus, and finally settle in the island of Cyprus.[2] The Latin Christians embraced the religious institutions of Rome. The pilgrims who visited Jerusalem eagerly copied, in the most distant climates of the earth, the faithful model of the monastic life. The disciples of Antony spread themselves beyond the tropic, over the Christian empire of Ethiopia. The monastery of Banchor, in Flintshire, which contained above two thousand brethren, dispersed a numerous colony among the barbarians of Ireland; and Iona, one of the Hebrides, which was planted by the Irish monks, diffused over the northern regions a doubtful ray of science and superstition.

---

[1] See his Life, and the three Dialogues by Sulpicius Severus, who asserts that the booksellers of Rome were delighted with the quick and ready sale of his popular work.

[2] When Hilarion sailed from Parætonium to Cape Pachynus, he offered to pay his passage with a book of the Gospels. Posthumian, a Gallic monk, who had visited Egypt, found a merchant-ship bound from Alexandria to Marseilles, and performed the voyage in thirty days. Athanasius, who addressed his Life of St. Antony to the foreign monks, was obliged to hasten the composition, that it might be ready for the sailing of the fleets.

CAUSES OF THE RAPID PROGRESS OF MONASTICISM

These unhappy exiles from social life were impelled by the dark and implacable genius of superstition. Their mutual resolution was supported by the example of millions, of either sex, of every age, and of every rank; and each proselyte who entered the gates of a monastery was persuaded that he trod the steep and thorny path of eternal happiness.[1] But the operation of these religious motives was variously determined by the temper and situation of mankind. Reason might subdue, or passion might suspend, their influence; but they acted most forcibly on the infirm minds of children and females; they were strengthened by secret remorse, or accidental misfortune; and they might derive some aid from the temporal consideration of vanity or interest. It was naturally supposed that the pious and humble monks, who had renounced the world to accomplish the work of their salvation, were the best qualified for the spiritual government of the Christians. The reluctant hermit was torn from his cell, and seated, amidst the acclamations of the people, on the episcopal throne: the monasteries of Egypt, of Gaul, and of the East, supplied a regular succession of saints and bishops; and ambition soon discovered the secret road which led to the possession of wealth and honours. The popular monks, whose reputation was connected with the fame and success of the order, assiduously laboured to multiply the number of their fellow-captives. They insinuated themselves into noble and opulent families; and the specious arts of flattery and seduction were employed to secure those proselytes who might bestow wealth or dignity on the monastic profession. The indignant father bewailed the loss, perhaps, of an only son; the credulous maid was betrayed by vanity to violate the laws of nature; and the matron aspired to imaginary perfection by renouncing the virtues of domestic life. Paula yielded to the persuasive elo-

---

[1] Chrysostom has consecrated three books to the praise and defence of the monastic life. He is encouraged, by the example of the ark, to presume that none but the elect (the monks) can possibly be saved. Elsewhere, indeed, he becomes more merciful, and allows different degrees of glory, like the sun, moon, and stars. In his lively comparison of a king and a monk, he supposes (what is hardly fair) that the king will be more sparingly rewarded, and more rigorously punished.

quence of Jerom;[1] and the profane title of mother-in-law of God tempted that illustrious widow to consecrate the virginity of her daughter Eustochium. By the advice, and in the company, of her spiritual guide, Paula abandoned Rome and her infant son; retired to the holy village of Bethlem; founded an hospital and four monasteries; and acquired, by her alms and penance, an eminent and conspicuous station in the catholic church. Such rare and illustrious penitents were celebrated as the glory and example of their age; but the monasteries were filled by a crowd of obscure and abject plebeians, who gained in the cloister much more than they had sacrificed in the world. Peasants, slaves, and mechanics, might escape from poverty and contempt to a safe and honourable profession, whose apparent hardships were mitigated by custom, by popular applause, and by the secret relaxation of discipline.[2] The subjects of Rome, whose persons and fortunes were made responsible for unequal and exorbitant tributes, retired from the oppression of the Imperial government; and the pusillanimous youth preferred the penance of a monastic, to the dangers of a military life. The affrighted provincials of every rank, who fled before the barbarians, found shelter and subsistence; whole legions were buried in these religious sanctuaries; and the same cause which relieved the distress of individuals impaired the strength and fortitude of the empire.

The monastic profession of the ancients was an act of voluntary devotion. The inconstant fanatic was threatened with the eternal vengeance of the God whom he deserted; but the doors of the monastery were still open for repentance. Those monks whose conscience was fortified by reason or passion were at liberty to resume the character of men and citizens; and even the spouses of Christ might accept the legal embraces of an earthly lover. The examples of scandal, and the progress of superstition, suggested the propriety of more forcible restraints. After a sufficient trial, the fidelity of the novice was secured by a solemn and perpetual vow; and his irrevocable engagement was ratified by the laws of the church and state.

[1] Jerom's devout ladies form a very considerable portion of his works: the particular treatise, which he styles the Epitaph of Paula, is an elaborate and extravagant panegyric. The exordium is ridiculously turgid:—"If all the members of my body were changed into tongues, and if all my limbs resounded with a human voice, yet should I be incapable," etc.

[2] A Dominican friar, who lodged at Cadiz in a convent of his brethren, soon understood that their repose was never interrupted by nocturnal devotion; "quoiqu'on ne laisse pas de sonner pour l'édification du peuple."

A guilty fugitive was pursued, arrested, and restored to his perpetual prison, and the interposition of the magistrate oppressed the freedom and merit which had alleviated, in some degree, the abject slavery of the monastic discipline. The actions of a monk, his words, and even his thoughts, were determined by an inflexible rule, or a capricious superior: the slightest offences were corrected by disgrace or confinement, extraordinary fasts, or bloody flagellation; and disobedience, murmur, or delay, were ranked in the catalogue of the most heinous sins.[1] A blind submission to the commands of the abbot, however absurd, or even criminal, they might seem, was the ruling principle, the first virtue of the Egyptian monks; and their patience was frequently exercised by the most extravagant trials. They were directed to remove an enormous rock; assiduously to water a barren staff that was planted in the ground, till, at the end of three years, it should vegetate and blossom like a tree; to walk into a fiery furnace; or to cast their infant into a deep pond; and several saints, or madmen, have been immortalised in monastic story, by their thoughtless and fearless obedience. The freedom of the mind, the source of every generous and rational sentiment, was destroyed by the habits of credulity and submission; and the monk, contracting the vices of a slave, devoutly followed the faith and passions of his ecclesiastical tyrant. The peace of the Eastern church was invaded by a swarm of fanatics, incapable of fear, or reason, or humanity; and the Imperial troops acknowledged, without shame, that they were much less apprehensive of an encounter with the fiercest barbarians.

Superstition has often framed and consecrated the fantastic garments of the monks: but their apparent singularity sometimes proceeds from their uniform attachment to a simple and primitive model, which the revolutions of fashion have made ridiculous in the eyes of mankind. The father of the Benedictines expressly disclaims all idea of choice or merit; and soberly exhorts his disciples to adopt the coarse and convenient dress of the countries which they may inhabit. The monastic

---

[1] The rule of Columbanus, so prevalent in the West, inflicts one hundred lashes for very slight offences. Before the time of Charlemagne the abbots indulged themselves in mutilating their monks, or putting out their eyes—a punishment much less cruel than the tremendous *vade in pace* (the subterraneous dungeon, or sepulchre), which was afterwards invented. See an admirable discourse of the learned Mabillon, who, on this occasion, seems to be inspired by the genius of humanity. For such an effort, I can forgive his defence of the holy tear of Vendôme.

habits of the ancients varied with the climate and the mode of life; and they assumed, with the same indifference, the sheepskin of the Egyptian peasants, or the cloak of the Grecian philosophers. They allowed themselves the use of linen in Egypt, where it was a cheap and domestic manufacture; but in the West they rejected such an expensive article of foreign luxury. It was the practice of the monks either to cut or shave their hair; they wrapped their heads in a cowl, to escape the sight of profane objects; their legs and feet were naked, except in the extreme cold of winter; and their slow and feeble steps were supported by a long staff. The aspect of a genuine anachoret was horrid and disgusting: every sensation that is offensive to man was thought acceptable to God; and the angelic rule of Tabenne condemned the salutary custom of bathing the limbs in water, and of anointing them with oil. The austere monks slept on the ground, on a hard mat, or a rough blanket; and the same bundle of palm-leaves served them as a seat in the day, and a pillow in the night. Their original cells were low narrow huts, built of the slightest materials; which formed, by the regular distribution of the streets, a large and populous village, enclosing, within the common wall, a church, an hospital, perhaps a library, some necessary offices, a garden, and a fountain or reservoir of fresh water. Thirty or forty brethren composed a family of separate discipline and diet; and the great monasteries of Egypt consisted of thirty or forty families.

Pleasure and guilt are synonymous terms in the language of the monks, and they had discovered, by experience, that rigid fasts and abstemious diet are the most effectual preservatives against the impure desires of the flesh. The rules of abstinence which they imposed, or practised, were not uniform or perpetual: the cheerful festival of the Pentecost was balanced by the extraordinary mortification of Lent: the fervour of new monasteries was insensibly relaxed; and the voracious appetite of the Gauls could not imitate the patient and temperate virtue of the Egyptians. The disciples of Antony and Pachomius were satisfied with the daily pittance [1] of twelve ounces of bread, or rather biscuit, which they divided into two frugal repasts, of the afternoon and of the

---

[1] "Those who drink only water, and have no nutritious liquor, ought at least to have a pound and a half (*twenty-four ounces*) of bread every day." State of Prisons, p. 40, by Mr. Howard. [*The State of the Prisons in England and Wales*, 1784.]

evening. It was esteemed a merit, and almost a duty, to abstain from the boiled vegetables which were provided for the refectory; but the extraordinary bounty of the abbot sometimes indulged them with the luxury of cheese, fruit, salad, and the small dried fish of the Nile. A more ample latitude of sea and river fish was gradually allowed or assumed; but the use of flesh was long confined to the sick or travellers: and when it gradually prevailed in the less rigid monasteries of Europe, a singular distinction was introduced; as if birds, whether wild or domestic, had been less profane than the grosser animals of the field. Water was the pure and innocent beverage of the primitive monks; and the founder of the Benedictines regrets the daily portion of half a pint of wine, which had been extorted from him by the intemperance of the age. Such an allowance might be easily supplied by the vineyards of Italy; and his victorious disciples, who passed the Alps, the Rhine, and the Baltic, required, in the place of wine, an adequate compensation of strong beef or cider.

The candidate who aspired to the virtue of evangelical poverty abjured, at his first entrance into a regular community, the idea, and even the name, of all separate or exclusive possession.[1] The brethren were supported by their manual labour; and the duty of labour was strenuously recommended as a penance, as an exercise, and as the most laudable means of securing their daily subsistence. The garden and fields, which the industry of the monks had often rescued from the forest or the morass, were diligently cultivated by their hands. They performed, without reluctance, the menial offices of slaves and domestics; and the several trades that were necessary to provide their habits, their utensils, and their lodging, were exercised within the precincts of the great monasteries. The monastic studies have tended, for the most part, to darken, rather than to dispel, the cloud of superstition. Yet the curiosity or zeal of some learned solitaries has cultivated the ecclesiastical, and even the profane sciences: and posterity must gratefully acknowledge that the monuments of Greek and Roman literature have been preserved and

---

[1] Such expressions as *my* book, *my* cloak, *my* shoes, were not less severely prohibited among the Western monks, and the Rule of Columbanus punished them with six lashes. The ironical author of the *Ordres Monastiques*, who laughs at the foolish nicety of modern convents, seems ignorant that the ancients were equally absurd.

multiplied by their indefatigable pens. But the more humble industry of the monks, especially in Egypt, was contented with the silent, sedentary occupation of making wooden sandals, or of twisting the leaves of the palm-tree into mats and baskets. The superfluous stock, which was not consumed in domestic use, supplied, by trade, the wants of the community: the boats of Tabenne, and the other monasteries of Thebais, descended the Nile as far as Alexandria; and, in a Christian market, the sanctity of the workmen might enhance the intrinsic value of the work.

But the necessity of manual labour was insensibly superseded. The novice was tempted to bestow his fortune on the saints in whose society he was resolved to spend the remainder of his life; and the pernicious indulgence of the laws permitted him to receive, for their use, any future accessions of legacy or inheritance. Melania contributed her plate, three hundred pounds' weight of silver, and Paula contracted an immense debt, for the relief of their favourite monks, who kindly imparted the merits of their prayers and penance to a rich and liberal sinner.[1] Time continually increased, and accidents could seldom diminish, the estates of the popular monasteries, which spread over the adjacent country and cities: and, in the first century of the institution, the infidel Zosimus has maliciously observed, that, for the benefit of the poor, the Christian monks had reduced a great part of mankind to a state of beggary. As long as they maintained their original fervour, they approved themselves, however, the faithful and benevolent stewards of the charity which was intrusted to their care. But their discipline was corrupted by prosperity: they gradually assumed the pride of wealth, and at last indulged the luxury of expense. Their public luxury might be excused by the magnificence of religious worship, and the decent motive of erecting durable habitations for an immortal society. But every age of the church has accused the licentiousness of the degenerate monks; who no longer remembered the object of their institution, embraced the vain and sensual pleasures of the world which they had renounced, and scandalously abused the riches which had been

---

[1] The monk Pambo made a sublime answer to Melania, who wished to specify the value of her gift:—"Do you offer it to me, or to God? If to God, HE who suspends the mountains in a balance need not be informed of the weight of your plate."

acquired by the austere virtues of their founders.[1] Their natural descent, from such painful and dangerous virtue, to the common vices of humanity, will not, perhaps, excite much grief or indignation in the mind of a philosopher.

The lives of the primitive monks were consumed in penance and solitude, undisturbed by the various occupations which fill the time, and exercise the faculties, of reasonable, active, and social beings. Whenever they were permitted to step beyond the precincts of the monastery, two jealous companions were the mutual guards and spies of each other's actions; and, after their return, they were condemned to forget, or, at least, to suppress, whatever they had seen or heard in the world. Strangers, who professed the orthodox faith, were hospitably entertained in a separate apartment; but their dangerous conversation was restricted to some chosen elders of approved discretion and fidelity. Except in their presence, the monastic slave might not receive the visits of his friends or kindred; and it was deemed highly meritorious, if he afflicted a tender sister, or an aged parent, by the obstinate refusal of a word or look. The monks themselves passed their lives, without personal attachments, among a crowd which had been formed by accident, and was detained, in the same prison, by force or prejudice. Recluse fanatics have few ideas or sentiments to communicate: a special licence of the abbot regulated the time and duration of their familiar visits; and, at their silent meals, they were enveloped in their cowls, inaccessible, and almost invisible, to each other. Study is the resource of solitude; but education had not prepared and qualified for any liberal studies the mechanics and peasants who filled the monastic communities. They might work; but the vanity of spiritual perfection was tempted to disdain the exercise of manual labour; and the industry must be faint and languid which is not excited by the sense of personal interest.

According to their faith and zeal, they might employ the day, which they passed in their cells, either in vocal or mental prayer: they assembled in the evening, and they were awakened in the night, for the public worship of the monastery. The precise moment was determined by the stars,

---

[1] I have somewhere heard or read the frank confession of a Benedictine abbot: "My vow of poverty has given me an hundred thousand crowns a year; my vow of obedience has raised me to the rank of a sovereign prince." I forget the consequences of his vow of chastity.

which are seldom clouded in the serene sky of Egypt; and a rustic horn, or trumpet, the signal of devotion, twice interrupted the vast silence of the desert. Even sleep, the last refuge of the unhappy, was rigorously measured: the vacant hours of the monk heavily rolled along, without business or pleasure; and, before the close of each day, he had repeatedly accused the tedious progress of the sun. In this comfortless state, superstition still pursued and tormented her wretched votaries. The repose which they had sought in the cloister was disturbed by tardy repentance, profane doubts, and guilty desires; and, while they considered each natural impulse as an unpardonable sin, they perpetually trembled on the edge of a flaming and bottomless abyss. From the painful struggles of disease and despair, these unhappy victims were sometimes relieved by madness or death; and, in the sixth century, an hospital was founded at Jerusalem for a small portion of the austere penitents who were deprived of their senses. Their visions, before they attained this extreme and acknowledged term of frenzy, have afforded ample materials of supernatural history. It was their firm persuasion that the air which they breathed was peopled with invisible enemies; with innumerable dæmons, who watched every occasion, and assumed every form, to terrify, and above all to tempt, their unguarded virtue. The imagination, and even the senses, were deceived by the illusions of distempered fanaticism; and the hermit, whose midnight prayer was oppressed by involuntary slumber, might easily confound the phantoms of horror or delight which had occupied his sleeping and his waking dreams.

ST. SIMEON STYLITES

The monks were divided into two classes: the *Cænobites*, who lived under a common and regular discipline; and the *Anachorets*, who indulged their unsocial, independent fanaticism. The most devout, or the most ambitious, of the spiritual brethren, renounced the convent, as they had renounced the world. The fervent monasteries of Egypt, Palestine, and Syria, were surrounded by a *Laura*, a distant circle of solitary cells; and the extravagant penance of the Hermits was stimulated by applause and emulation. They sunk under the painful weight of crosses and chains; and their emaciated limbs were confined by collars, bracelets, gauntlets, and greaves of massy and rigid iron. All superfluous incumbrance of dress they contemptuously cast away; and some savage saints of both sexes have been admired, whose naked bodies were only covered by their long hair. They aspired to reduce themselves to the rude and miserable state in which the human brute is scarcely distinguished above his kindred animals; and the numerous sect of Anachorets derived their name from their humble practice of grazing in the fields of Mesopotamia with the common herd. They often usurped the den of some wild beast whom they affected to resemble; they buried themselves in some gloomy cavern, which art or nature had scooped out of the rock; and the marble quarries of Thebais are still inscribed with the monuments of their penance. The most perfect Hermits are supposed to have passed many days without food, many nights without sleep, and many years without speaking; and glorious was the *man* (I abuse that name) who contrived any cell, or seat, of a peculiar construction, which might expose him, in the most inconvenient posture, to the inclemency of the seasons.

Among these heroes of the monastic life, the name and genius of Simeon Stylites have been immortalised by the singular invention of an aërial penance. At the age of thirteen the young Syrian deserted the profession of a shepherd, and threw himself into an austere monastery. After a long and painful noviciate, in which Simeon was repeatedly saved from pious suicide, he established his residence on a mountain, about thirty or forty miles to the east of Antioch. Within the space of a *mandra,* or circle of stones, to which he had attached himself by a ponderous chain, he ascended a column, which was successively raised from the height of nine, to that of sixty, feet from the ground. In this last and lofty station, the Syrian Anachoret resisted the heat of thirty summers, and the cold of as many winters. Habit and exercise instructed him to maintain his dangerous situation without fear or giddiness, and successively to assume the different postures of devotion. He sometimes prayed in an erect attitude, with his outstretched arms in the figure of a cross; but his most familiar practice was that of bending his meagre skeleton from the forehead to the feet; and a curious spectator, after numbering twelve hundred and forty-four repetitions, at length desisted from the endless account. The progress of an ulcer in his thigh [1] might shorten, but it could not disturb, this *celestial* life; and the patient Hermit expired without descending from his column. A prince, who should capriciously inflict such tortures, would be deemed a tyrant; but it would surpass the power of a tyrant to impose a long and miserable existence on the reluctant victims of his cruelty. This voluntary martyrdom must have gradually destroyed the sensibility both of the mind and body; nor can it be presumed that the fanatics who torment themselves are susceptible of any lively affection for the rest of mankind. A cruel unfeeling temper has distinguished the monks of every age and country: their stern indifference, which is seldom mollified by personal friendship, is inflamed by religious hatred; and their merciless zeal has strenuously administered the holy office of the Inquisition.

The monastic saints, who excite only the contempt and pity of a philosopher, were respected and almost adored by the prince and people. Successive crowds of pilgrims from Gaul and India saluted the divine pillar of Simeon; the tribes of Saracens disputed in arms the honour of his benediction; the queens of Arabia and Persia gratefully confessed his supernatural virtue; and the angelic Hermit was consulted by the younger Theodosius in the most important concerns of the church and state. His remains were transported from the mountain of Telenissa, by a solemn procession of the patriarch, the master-general of the East, six bishops, twenty-one counts or tribunes, and six thousand soldiers; and Antioch revered his bones as her glorious ornament and impregnable defence. The fame of the apostles and martyrs was gradually eclipsed by these recent and popular Anachorets; the Christian world fell prostrate before their shrines; and the miracles ascribed to their relics exceeded, at least in number and duration, the spiritual exploits of their lives. But the golden legend of their lives was embellished by the artful credulity of their interested brethren; and a believing age was easily persuaded that the slightest caprice of an Egyptian or a Syrian monk had been sufficient to interrupt the eternal laws of the universe. The favourites of Heaven were accustomed to cure inveterate

---

[1] I must not conceal a piece of ancient scandal concerning the origin of this ulcer. It has been reported that the Devil, assuming an angelic form, invited him to ascend, like Elijah, into a fiery chariot. The saint too hastily raised his foot, and Satan seized the moment of inflicting this chastisement on his vanity.

diseases with a touch, a word, or a distant message; and to expel the most obstinate dæmons from the souls or bodies which they possessed. They familiarly accosted, or imperiously commanded, the lions and serpents of the desert; infused vegetation into a sapless trunk; suspended iron on the surface of the water; passed the Nile on the back of a crocodile; and refreshed themselves in a fiery furnace. These extravagant tales, which display the fiction, without the genius, of poetry, have seriously affected the reason, the faith, and the morals of the Christians. Their credulity debased and vitiated the faculties of the mind: they corrupted the evidence of history; and superstition gradually extinguished the hostile light of philosophy and science. Every mode of religious worship which had been practised by the saints, every mysterious doctrine which they believed, was fortified by the sanction of divine revelation, and all the manly virtues were oppressed by the servile and pusillanimous reign of the monks. If it be possible to measure the interval between the philosophic writings of Cicero and the sacred legend of Theodoret, between the character of Cato and that of Simeon, we may appreciate the memorable revolution which was accomplished in the Roman empire within a period of five hundred years.

II. The progress of Christianity has been marked by two glorious and decisive victories: over the learned and luxurious citizens of the Roman empire; and over the warlike barbarians of Scythia and Germany, who subverted the empire and embraced the religion of the Romans. The Goths were the foremost of these savage proselytes; and the nation was indebted for its conversion to a countryman, or at least to a subject, worthy to be ranked among the inventors of useful arts who have deserved the remembrance and gratitude of posterity. A great number of Roman provincials had been led away into captivity by the Gothic bands who ravaged Asia in the time of Gallienus; and of these captives many were Christians, and several belonged to the ecclesiastical order. Those involuntary missionaries, dispersed as slaves in the villages of Dacia, successively laboured for the salvation of their masters. The seeds which they planted of the evangelic doctrine were gradually propagated; and before the end of a century the pious work was achieved by the labours of Ulphilas, whose ancestors had been transported beyond the Danube from a small town of Cappadocia.

Ulphilas, the bishop and apostle of the Goths, acquired their love and reverence by his blameless life and indefatigable zeal, and they received with implicit confidence the doctrines of truth and virtue which he preached and practised. He executed the arduous task of translating the Scriptures into their native tongue, a dialect of the German or Teutonic language; but he prudently suppressed the four books of Kings, as they might tend to irritate the fierce and sanguinary spirit of the barbarians. The rude, imperfect idiom of soldiers and shepherds, so ill qualified to communicate any spiritual ideas, was improved and modulated by his genius; and Ulphilas, before he could frame his version, was obliged to compose a new alphabet of twenty-four letters; four of which he invented to express the peculiar sounds that were unknown to the Greek and Latin pronunciation. But the prosperous state of the Gothic church was soon afflicted by war and intestine discord, and the chieftains were divided by religion as well as by interest. Fritigern, the friend of the Romans, became the proselyte of Ulphilas; while the haughty soul of Athanaric disdained the yoke of the empire and of the Gospel. The faith of the new converts was tried by the persecution which he excited. A waggon, bearing aloft the shapeless image of Thor, perhaps, or of Woden, was conducted in solemn procession through the streets of the camp, and the rebels who refused to worship the god of their fathers were immediately burnt with their tents and families. The character of Ulphilas recommended him to the esteem of the Eastern court, where he twice appeared as the minister of peace; he pleaded the cause of the distressed Goths, who implored the protection of Valens; and the name of *Moses* was applied to this spiritual guide, who conducted his people through the deep waters of the Danube to the Land of Promise. The devout shepherds, who were attached to his person and tractable to his voice, acquiesced in their settlement at the foot of the Mæsian mountains, in a country of woodlands and pastures, which supported their flocks and herds, and enabled them to purchase the corn and wine of the more plentiful provinces. These harmless barbarians multiplied in obscure peace and the profession of Christianity.

Their fiercer brethren, the formidable Visigoths, universally adopted the religion of the Romans, with whom they maintained a perpetual intercourse of war, of friendship, or of conquest. In their long and victorious march from the Danube to the Atlantic Ocean they converted their allies; they educated the rising generation; and the devotion which reigned in the camp of Alaric, or the court of Toulouse, might edify or disgrace the palaces of Rome and Constantinople. During the same period Christianity was embraced by almost all the barbarians who established their kingdoms on the ruins of the Western empire; the Burgundians in Gaul, the Suevi in Spain, the Vandals in Africa, the Ostrogoths in Pannonia, and the various bands of mercenaries that raised Odoacer to the throne of Italy. The Franks and the Saxons still persevered in the errors of Paganism; but the Franks obtained the monarchy of Gaul by their submission to the example of Clovis; and the Saxon conquerors of Britain were reclaimed from their savage superstitions by the missionaries of Rome. These barbarian proselytes displayed an ardent and successful zeal in the propagation of the faith. The Merovingian kings and their successors, Charlemagne and the Othos, extended by their laws and victories the dominion of the cross. England produced the apostle of Germany; and the evangelic light was gradually diffused from the neighbourhood of the Rhine to the nations of the Elbe, the Vistula, and the Baltic.

The different motives which influenced the reason of the passions of the barbarian converts cannot easily be ascertained. They were often capricious and accidental; a dream, an omen, the report of a miracle, the example of some priest or hero, the charms of a believing wife, and, above all, the fortunate event of a prayer or vow which, in a moment of danger, they had addressed to the God of the Christians. The early prejudices of education were insensibly erased by the habits of frequent and familiar society; the moral precepts of the Gospel were protected by the extravagant virtues of the monks; and a spiritual theology was supported by the visible power of relics, and the pomp of religious worship. But the rational and ingenious mode of persuasion which a Saxon bishop suggested to a popular saint might sometimes be employed by the missionaries who laboured for the conversion of infidels. "Admit," says the sagacious disputant, "whatever they are pleased to assert of the fabulous and carnal genealogy of their gods and goddesses, who are propagated from each other. From this principle deduce their imperfect nature and human infirmities, the assurance they were *born*, and the probability that they will *die*. At what time, by what means, from what cause, were the eldest of the gods or goddesses produced? Do they still continue, or have they ceased, to propagate? If they have ceased, summon your antagonists to declare the reason of this strange alteration. If they still continue, the number of the gods must become infinite; and shall we not risk, by the indiscreet worship of some impotent deity, to excite the resentment of his jealous superior? The visible heavens and earth, the whole system of the universe, which may be conceived by the mind, is it created or eternal? If created, how or where could the gods themselves exist before the creation? If eternal, how could they assume the empire of an independent and pre-existing world? Urge these arguments with temper and moderation; insinuate, at seasonable intervals, the truth and beauty of the Christian revelation; and endeavour to make the unbelievers ashamed without making them angry." This metaphysical reasoning, too refined perhaps for the barbarians of Germany, was fortified by the grosser weight of authority and popular consent. The advantage of temporal prosperity had deserted the Pagan cause and passed over to the service of Christianity. The Romans themselves, the most powerful and enlightened nation of the globe, had renounced their ancient superstition; and if the ruin of their empire seemed to accuse the efficacy of the new faith, the disgrace was already retrieved by the conversion of the victorious Goths. The valiant and fortunate barbarians who subdued the provinces of the West successively received and reflected the same edifying example. Before the age of Charlemagne, the Christian nations of Europe might exult in the exclusive possession of the temperate climates, of the fertile lands which produced corn, wine, and oil; while the savage idolaters and their helpless idols were confined to the extremities of the earth, the dark and frozen regions of the North.

Christianity, which opened the gates of Heaven to the barbarians, introduced an important change in their moral and political condition. They received, at the same time, the use of letters, so essential to a religion whose doctrines are contained in a sacred book; and while they studied the divine truth, their minds were insensibly enlarged by the distant view of history, of nature, of the arts, and of society.

The version of the Scriptures into their native tongue, which had facilitated their conversion, must excite, among their clergy, some curiosity to read the original text, to understand the sacred liturgy of the church, and to examine, in the writings of the fathers, the chain of ecclesiastical tradition. These spiritual gifts were preserved in the Greek and Latin languages which concealed the inestimable monuments of ancient learning. The immortal productions of Virgil, Cicero, and Livy, which were accessible to the Christian barbarians, maintained a silent intercourse between the reign of Augustus and the times of Clovis and Charlemagne. The emulation of mankind was encouraged by the remembrance of a more perfect state; and the flame of science was secretly kept alive, to warm and enlighten the mature age of the Western world. In the most corrupt state of Christianity the barbarians might learn justice from the *law,* and mercy from the *gospel;* and if the knowledge of their duty was insufficient to guide their actions or to regulate their passions, they were sometimes restrained by conscience, and frequently punished by remorse. But the direct authority of religion was less effectual than holy communion, which united them with their Christian brethren in spiritual friendship. The influence of these sentiments contributed to secure their fidelity in the service or the alliance of the Romans, to alleviate the horrors of war, to moderate the insolence of conquest, and to preserve, in the downfall of the empire, a permanent respect for the name and institutions of Rome. In the days of Paganism the priests of Gaul and Germany reigned over the people, and controlled the jurisdiction of the magistrates; and the zealous proselytes transferred an equal, or more ample, measure of devout obedience to the pontiffs of the Christian faith. The sacred character of the bishops was supported by their temporal possessions; they obtained an honourable seat in the legislative assemblies of soldiers and freemen; and it was their interest, as well as their duty, to mollify by peaceful counsels the fierce spirit of the barbarians. The perpetual correspondence of the Latin clergy, the frequent pilgrimages to Rome and Jerusalem, and the growing authority of the popes, cemented the union of the Christian republic, and gradually produced the similar manners and common jurisprudence which have distinguished from the rest of mankind the independent, and even hostile, nations of modern Europe.

38.

Between 476 and 496 Clovis, king of the Franks, established his power in Gaul and was converted to Christianity. After the conquests of Aquitaine and Burgundy a French monarchy was founded in Gaul in 536. The Visigoths, expelled from Gaul, achieved the conquest of Spain. The Saxons established themselves in Britain in 455–582.

FALL OF THE ROMAN EMPIRE IN THE WEST

I HAVE now accomplished the laborious narrative of the decline and fall of the Roman empire, from the fortunate age of Trajan and the Antonines to its total extinction in the West, about five centuries after the Christian era. At that unhappy period the Saxons fiercely struggled with the natives for the possession of Britain: Gaul and Spain were divided between the powerful monarchies of the Franks and Visigoths and the dependent kingdoms of the Suevi and Burgundians: Africa was exposed to the cruel persecution of the Vandals and the savage insults of the Moors: Rome and Italy, as far as the banks of the Danube, were afflicted by an army of barbarian mercenaries, whose lawless tyranny was succeeded by the reign of Theodoric the Ostrogoth. All the subjects of the empire, who, by the use of the Latin language, more particularly deserved the name and privileges of Romans, were oppressed by the disgrace and calamities of foreign conquest; and the victorious nations of Germany established a new system of manners and government in the western countries of Europe. The majesty of Rome was faintly represented by the princes of Constantinople, the feeble and imaginary successors of Augustus. Yet they continued to reign over the East, from the Danube to the Nile and Tigris; the Gothic and Vandal kingdoms of Italy and Africa were subverted by the arms of Justinian; and the history of the *Greek* emperors may still afford a long series of instructive lessons and interesting revolutions.

GENERAL OBSERVATIONS ON THE FALL OF THE ROMAN EMPIRE IN THE WEST

The Greeks, after their country had been reduced into a province, imputed the triumphs of Rome, not to the merit, but to the FORTUNE, of the republic. The inconstant goddess, who so blindly distributes and resumes her favours, had *now* consented (such was the language of envious flattery) to resign her wings, to descend from her globe, and to fix her firm and immutable throne on the banks of the Tiber. A wiser Greek, who has composed, with a philosophic spirit, the memorable history of his own times, deprived his countrymen of this vain and delusive comfort, by opening to their view the deep foundations of the greatness of Rome. The fidelity of the citizens to each other and to the state was confirmed by the habits of education and the prejudices of religion. Honour, as well as virtue, was the principle of the republic; the ambitious citizens laboured to deserve the solemn glories of a triumph; and the ardour of the Roman youth was kindled into active emulation as often as they beheld the domestic images of their ancestors. The temperate struggles of the patricians and plebeians had finally established the firm and equal balance of the constitution, which united the freedom of popular assemblies with the authority and wisdom of a senate and the executive powers of a regal magistrate. When the consul displayed the standard of the republic, each citizen bound himself, by the obligation of an oath, to draw his sword in the cause of his country till he had discharged the sacred duty by a military service of ten years. This wise institution continually poured into the field the rising generations of freemen and soldiers; and their numbers were reinforced by the warlike and populous states of Italy, who, after a brave resistance, had yielded to the valour and embraced the alliance of the Romans. The sage historian, who excited the virtue of the younger Scipio and beheld the ruin of Carthage, has accurately described their military system; their levies, arms, exercises, subordination, marches, encampments; and the invincible legion, superior in active strength to the Macedonian phalanx of Philip and Alexander. From these institutions of peace and war Polybius has deduced the spirit and success of a people incapable of fear and impatient of repose. The ambitious design of conquest, which might have been defeated by the seasonable conspiracy of mankind, was attempted and achieved; and the perpetual violation of justice was maintained by the political virtues of prudence and courage. The arms of the republic, sometimes vanquished in battle, always victorious in war, advanced with rapid steps to the Euphrates, the Danube, the Rhine, and the Ocean; and the images of gold, or silver, or brass, that might serve to represent the nations and their kings, were successively broken by the *iron* monarchy of Rome.

The rise of a city, which swelled into an empire, may deserve, as a singular prodigy, the reflection of a philosophic mind. But the decline of Rome was the natural and inevitable effect of immoderate greatness. Prosperity ripened the principle of decay; the causes of destruction multiplied with the extent of conquest; and as soon as time or accident had removed the artificial supports, the stupendous fabric yielded to the pressure of its own weight. The story of its ruin is simple and obvious; and instead of inquiring *why* the Roman empire was destroyed, we should rather be surprised that it had subsisted so long. The victorious legions, who, in distant wars, acquired the vices of strangers and mercenaries, first oppressed the freedom of the republic, and afterwards violated the majesty of the purple. The emperors, anxious for their personal safety and the public peace, were reduced to the base expedient of corrupting the discipline which rendered them alike formidable to their sovereign and to the enemy; the vigour of the military government was relaxed and finally dissolved by the partial institutions of Constantine; and the Roman world was overwhelmed by a deluge of barbarians.

The decay of Rome has been frequently ascribed to the translation of the seat of empire; but this history has already shown that the powers of government were *divided*, rather than *removed*. The throne of Constantinople was erected in the East; while the West was still possessed by a series of emperors who held their residence in Italy, and claimed their equal inheritance of the legions and provinces. This dangerous novelty impaired the strength and fomented the vices of a double reign: the instruments of an oppressive and arbitrary system were multiplied; and a vain emulation of luxury, not of merit, was introduced and supported between the degenerate successors of Theodosius. Extreme distress, which unites the virtue of a free people, embitters the factions of a declining monarchy. The hostile favourites of Arcadius and Honorius betrayed the republic to its common enemies; and the Byzantine court beheld with indifference, perhaps with pleasure, the disgrace of Rome, the misfortunes of Italy, and the loss of the West. Under the succeeding reigns the alliance of the two empires was restored; but the aid of the Oriental Romans was tardy, doubtful, and ineffectual; and the national schism of the Greeks and Latins was enlarged by the perpetual difference of language and manners, of interests, and even of religion. Yet the salutary event approved in some measure the judgment of Constantine. During a long period of decay his impregnable city repelled the victorious armies of barbarism, protected the wealth of Asia, and commanded, both in peace and war, the important straits which connect the Euxine and Mediterranean seas. The foundation of Constantinople more essentially contributed to the preservation of the East than to the ruin of the West.

As the happiness of a *future* life is the great object of religion, we may hear without surprise or scandal that the introduction, or at least the abuse of Christianity, had some influence on the decline and fall of the Roman empire. The clergy successfully preached the doctrines of patience and pusillanimity; the active virtues of society were discouraged; and the last remains of military spirit were buried in the cloister: a large portion of public and private wealth was consecrated to the specious demands of charity and devotion; and the soldiers' pay was lavished on the useless multitudes of both sexes who could only plead the merits of abstinence and chastity. Faith, zeal, curiosity, and the more earthly passions of malice and ambition, kindled the flame of theological discord; the church, and even the state, were distracted by religious factions, whose conflicts were sometimes bloody and always implacable; the attention of the emperors was diverted from camps to synods; the Roman world was oppressed by a new species of tyranny; and the persecuted sects became the secret enemies of their country. Yet party-spirit, however pernicious or absurd, is a principle of union as well as of dissension. The bishops, from eighteen hundred pulpits, inculcated the duty of passive obedience to a lawful and orthodox sovereign; their frequent assemblies and perpetual correspondence maintained the communion of distant churches; and the benevolent temper of the Gospel was strengthened, though confined, by the spiritual alliance of the catholics. The sacred indolence of the monks was devoutly embraced by a servile and effeminate age; but if superstition had not afforded a decent retreat, the same vices would have tempted the unworthy Romans to desert, from baser motives, the standard of the republic. Religious precepts are easily obeyed which indulge and sanctify the natural inclinations of their votaries; but the pure and genuine influence of Christianity may be traced in its beneficial, though imperfect, effects on the barbarian proselytes of the North. If the decline of the Roman empire was hastened by the conversion of Constantine, his victorious religion broke the violence of the fall, and mollified the ferocious temper of the conquerors.

This awful revolution may be usefully applied to the instruction of the present age. It is the duty of a patriot to prefer and promote the exclusive interest and glory of his native country: but a philosopher may be permitted to enlarge his views, and to consider Europe as one great republic, whose various inhabitants have attained almost the same level of politeness and cultivation. The balance of power will continue to fluctuate, and the prosperity of our own or the neighbouring kingdoms may be alternately exalted or depressed; but these partial events cannot essentially injure our general state of happiness, the system of arts, and laws, and manners, which so advantageously distinguish, above the rest of mankind, the Europeans and their colonies. The savage nations of the globe are the common enemies of civilised society; and we may inquire, with anxious curiosity, whether Europe is still threatened with a repetition of those calamities which formerly oppressed the arms and institutions of Rome. Perhaps the same reflections will illustrate the fall of that mighty empire, and explain the probable causes of our actual security.

I. The Romans were ignorant of the extent of their danger and the number of their enemies. Beyond the Rhine and Danube the northern countries of Europe and Asia were filled with innumerable tribes of hunters and shepherds, poor, voracious, and turbulent; bold in arms, and impatient to ravish the fruits of industry. The barbarian world was agitated by the rapid impulse of war; and the peace of Gaul or Italy was shaken by the distant revolutions of China. The Huns, who fled before a victorious enemy, directed their march towards the West; and the torrent was swelled by the gradual accession of captives and allies. The flying tribes who yielded to the Huns assumed in *their* turn the spirit of conquest; the endless column of barbarians pressed on the Roman empire with accumulated weight; and, if the foremost were destroyed, the vacant space was instantly replenished by new assailants. Such formidable emigrations no longer issue from the North; and the long repose, which has been imputed to the decrease of population, is the happy consequence of the progress of arts and agriculture. Instead of some rude villages thinly scattered among its woods and morasses, Germany now produces a list of two thousand three hundred walled towns: the Christian kingdoms of Denmark, Sweden, and Poland have been successively established; and the Hanse merchants, with the Teutonic knights, have extended their colonies along the coast of the Baltic as far as the Gulf of Finland. From the Gulf of Finland to the Eastern Ocean, Russia now assumes the form of a powerful and civilised empire. The plough, the loom, and the forge are introduced on the banks of the Volga, the Oby, and the Lena; and the fiercest of the Tartar hordes have been taught to tremble and obey. The reign of independent barbarism is now contracted to a narrow span; and the remnant of Calmucks or Uzbecks, whose forces may be almost numbered, cannot seriously excite the apprehensions of the great republic of Europe. Yet this apparent security should not tempt us to forget that new enemies and unknown dangers may *possibly* arise from some obscure people, scarcely visible in the map of the world. The Arabs or Saracens, who spread their conquests from India to Spain, had languished in poverty and contempt till Mahomet breathed into those savage bodies the soul of enthusiasm.

II. The empire of Rome was firmly established by the singular and perfect coalition of its members. The subject nations, resigning the hope and even the wish of independence, embraced the character of Roman citizens; and the provinces of the West were reluctantly torn by the barbarians from the bosom of their mother country. But this union was purchased by the loss of national freedom and military spirit; and the servile provinces, destitute of life and motion, expected their safety from the mercenary troops and governors who were directed by the orders of a distant court. The happiness of an hundred millions depended on the personal merit of one or two men, perhaps children, whose minds were corrupted by education, luxury, and despotic power. The deepest wounds were inflicted on the empire during the minorities of the sons and grandsons of Theodosius; and, after those incapable princes seemed to attain the age of manhood, they abandoned the church to the bishops, the state to the eunuchs, and the provinces to the barbarians. Europe is now divided into twelve powerful, though unequal kingdoms, three respectable commonwealths, and a variety of smaller, though independent states: the chances of royal and ministerial talents are multiplied, at least, with the number of its rulers; and a Julian, or Semiramis, may reign in the North, while Arcadius and Honorius again slumber on the thrones of the South. The abuses of tyranny are restrained by the mutual influence of fear and shame; republics have acquired order and stability; monarchies have imbibed the principles of freedom, or, at least, of moderation; and some sense of honour and justice is introduced into the most defective constitutions by the general manners of the times. In peace, the progress of knowledge and industry is accelerated by the emulation of so many active rivals: in war, the European forces are exercised by temperate and undecisive contests. If a savage conqueror should issue from the deserts of Tartary, he must repeatedly vanquish the robust peasants of Russia, the numerous armies of Germany, the gallant nobles of France, and the intrepid freemen of Britain; who, perhaps, might confederate for their common defence. Should the victorious barbarians carry slavery and desolation as far as the Atlantic Ocean, ten thousand vessels would transport beyond their pursuit the remains of civilised society; and

Europe would revive and flourish in the American world, which is already filled with her colonies and institutions.[1]

III. Cold, poverty, and a life of danger and fatigue fortify the strength and courage of barbarians. In every age they have oppressed the polite and peaceful nations of China, India, and Persia, who neglected, and still neglect, to counterbalance these natural powers by the resources of military art. The warlike states of antiquity, Greece, Macedonia, and Rome, educated a race of soldiers; exercised their bodies, disciplined their courage, multiplied their forces by regular evolutions, and converted the iron which they possessed into strong and serviceable weapons. But this superiority insensibly declined with their laws and manners: and the feeble policy of Constantine and his successors armed and instructed, for the ruin of the empire, the rude valour of the barbarian mercenaries. The military art has been changed by the invention of gunpowder; which enables man to command the two most powerful agents of nature, air and fire. Mathematics, chemistry, mechanics, architecture, have been applied to the service of war; and the adverse parties oppose to each other the most elaborate modes of attack and of defence. Historians may indignantly observe that the preparations of a siege would found and maintain a flourishing colony; yet we cannot be displeased that the subversion of a city should be a work of cost and difficulty; or that an industrious people should be protected by those arts which survive and supply the decay of military virtue. Cannon and fortifications now form an impregnable barrier against the Tartar horse; and Europe is secure from any future irruption of barbarians; since, before they can conquer, they must cease to be barbarous. Their gradual advances in the science of war would always be accompanied, as we may learn from the example of Russia, with a proportionable improvement in the arts of peace and civil policy; and they themselves must deserve a place among the polished nations whom they subdue.

Should these speculations be found doubtful or fallacious, there still remains a more humble source of comfort and

---

[1] America now contains about six millions of European blood and descent; and their numbers, at least in the North, are continually increasing. Whatever may be the changes of their political situation, they must preserve the manners of Europe; and we may reflect with some pleasure that the English language will probably be diffused over an immense and populous continent.

hope. The discoveries of ancient and modern navigators, and the domestic history or tradition of the most enlightened nations, represent the *human savage* naked both in mind and body, and destitute of laws, of arts, of ideas, and almost of language.[1] From this abject condition, perhaps the primitive and universal state of man, he has gradually arisen to command the animals, to fertilise the earth, to traverse the ocean, and to measure the heavens. His progress in the improvement and exercise of his mental and corporeal faculties has been irregular and various; infinitely slow in the beginning, and increasing by degrees with redoubled velocity: ages of laborious ascent have been followed by a moment of rapid downfall; and the several climates of the globe have felt the vicissitudes of light and darkness. Yet the experience of four thousand years should enlarge our hopes and diminish our apprehensions: we cannot determine to what height the human species may aspire in their advances towards perfection; but it may safely be presumed that no people, unless the face of nature is changed, will relapse into their original barbarism. The improvements of society may be viewed under a threefold aspect. 1. The poet or philosopher illustrates his age and country by the efforts of a *single* mind; but these superior powers of reason or fancy are rare and spontaneous productions; and the genius of Homer, or Cicero, or Newton, would excite less admiration if they could be created by the will of a prince or the lessons of a preceptor. 2. The benefits of law and policy, of trade and manufactures, of arts and sciences, are more solid and permanent; and *many* individuals may be qualified, by education and discipline, to promote, in their respective stations, the interest of the community. But this general order is the effect of skill and labour; and the complex machinery may be decayed by time, or injured by violence. 3. Fortunately for mankind, the more useful, or, at least, more necessary arts, can be performed without superior talents or national subordination; without the powers of *one*, or the union of *many*. Each village, each family, each individual, must always possess both ability and in-

---

[1] It would be an easy, though tedious, task to produce the authorities of poets, philosophers, and historians. I shall therefore content myself with appealing to the decisive and authentic testimony of Diodorus Siculus. The Ichthyophagi, who in his time wandered along the shores of the Red Sea, can only be compared to the natives of New Holland. Fancy, or perhaps reason, may still suppose an extreme and absolute state of nature far below the level of these savages, who had acquired some arts and instruments.

clination to perpetuate the use of fire and of metals; the propagation and service of domestic animals; the methods of hunting and fishing; the rudiments of navigation; the imperfect cultivation of corn or other nutritive grain; and the simple practice of the mechanic trades. Private genius and public industry may be extirpated; but these hardy plants survive the tempest, and strike an everlasting root into the most unfavourable soil. The splendid days of Augustus and Trajan were eclipsed by a cloud of ignorance; and the barbarians subverted the laws and palaces of Rome. But the scythe, the invention or emblem of Saturn, still continued annually to mow the harvests of Italy; and the human feasts of the Læstrigons have never been renewed on the coast of Campania.

Since the first discovery of the arts, war, commerce, and religious zeal have diffused among the savages of the Old and New World these inestimable gifts: they have been successively propagated; they can never be lost. We may therefore acquiesce in the pleasing conclusion that every age of the world has increased and still increases the real wealth, the happiness, the knowledge, and perhaps the virtue, of the human race.[1]

---

[1] The merit of discovery has too often been stained with avarice, cruelty, and fanaticism; and the intercourse of nations has produced the communication of disease and prejudice. A singular exception is due to the virtue of our own times and country. The five great voyages, successively undertaken by the command of his present Majesty, were inspired by the pure and generous love of science and of mankind. The same prince, adapting his benefactions to the different stages of society, has founded a school of painting in his capital, and has introduced into the islands of the South Sea the vegetables and animals most useful to human life.

39.

THE REIGN OF THEODORIC THE OSTROGOTH.
PROSPERITY OF ROME AND ITALY. ARIANISM OF
THEODORIC. EXECUTION OF BOETHIUS.
DEATH OF THEODORIC

With the approval of Zeno, the emperor of the East,
Theodoric invaded Italy and defeated Odoacer. Odoacer was
murdered in 493. In the same year Zeno was succeeded in
Constantinople by Anastasius. Theodoric reigned over a
Gothic kingdom in Italy, 494–526.

THE REIGN OF THEODORIC

AMONG THE BARBARIANS of the West the victory of Theodoric
had spread a general alarm. But as soon as it appeared that
he was satisfied with conquest and desirous of peace, terror
was changed into respect, and they submitted to a powerful
mediation, which was uniformly employed for the best purposes of reconciling their quarrels and civilising their manners.
The ambassadors who resorted to Ravenna from the most
distant countries of Europe admired his wisdom, magnificence,
and courtesy; and if he sometimes accepted either slaves
or arms, white horses or strange animals, the gift of a sun-
dial, a water-clock, or a musician, admonished even the
princes of Gaul of the superior art and industry of his Italian
subjects. His domestic alliances, a wife, two daughters, a
sister, and a niece, united the family of Theodoric with the
kings of the Franks, the Burgundians, the Visigoths, the
Vandals, and the Thuringians, and contributed to maintain
the harmony, or at least the balance, of the great republic
of the West. It is difficult in the dark forests of Germany and
Poland to pursue the emigrations of the Heruli, a fierce people

who disdained the use of armour, and who condemned their widows and aged parents not to survive the loss of their husbands or the decay of their strength. The king of these savage warriors solicited the friendship of Theodoric, and was elevated to the rank of his son, according to the barbaric rites of a military adoption. From the shores of the Baltic the Æstians or Livonians laid their offerings of native amber at the feet of a prince whose fame had excited them to undertake an unknown and dangerous journey of fifteen hundred miles. With the country from whence the Gothic nation derived their origin he maintained a frequent and friendly correspondence: the Italians were clothed in the rich sables of Sweden; and one of its sovereigns, after a voluntary or reluctant abdication, found an hospitable retreat in the palace of Ravenna. He had reigned over one of the thirteen populous tribes who cultivated a small portion of the great island or peninsula of Scandinavia, to which the vague appellation of Thule has been sometimes applied. That northern region was peopled, or had been explored, as high as the sixty-eighth degree of latitude, where the natives of the polar circle enjoy and lose the presence of the sun at each summer and winter solstice during an equal period of forty days. The long night of his absence or death was the mournful season of distress and anxiety, till the messengers, who had been sent to the mountain tops, descried the first rays of returning light, and proclaimed to the plain below the festival of his resurrection.

The life of Theodoric represents the rare and meritorious example of a barbarian who sheathed his sword in the pride of victory and the vigour of his age. A reign of three and thirty years was consecrated to the duties of civil government, and the hostilities, in which he was sometimes involved, were speedily terminated by the conduct of his lieutenants, the discipline of his troops, the arms of his allies, and even by the terror of his name. He reduced, under a strong and regular government, the unprofitable countries of Rhætia, Noricum, Dalmatia, and Pannonia, from the source of the Danube and the territory of the Bavarians to the petty kingdom erected by the Gepidæ on the ruins of Sirmium. His prudence could not safely intrust the bulwark of Italy to such feeble and turbulent neighbours; and his justice might claim the lands which they oppressed, either as a part of his kingdom, or as the inheritance of his father. The greatness of a servant, who was named perfidious because he was successful, awakened the jealousy of the emperor Anastasius; and a war was kindled on the Dacian frontier, by the protection which the Gothic king, in the vicissitude of human affairs, had granted to one of the descendants of Attila. Sabinian, a general illustrious by his own and father's merit, advanced at the head of ten thousand Romans; and the provisions and arms, which filled a long train of waggons, were distributed to the fiercest of the Bulgarian tribes. But in the fields of Margus the Eastern powers were defeated by the inferior forces of the Goths and Huns; the flower and even the hope of the Roman armies was irretrievably destroyed; and such was the temperance with which Theodoric had inspired his victorious troops, that, as their leader had not given the signal of pillage, the rich spoils of the enemy lay untouched at their feet. Exasperated by this disgrace, the Byzantine court despatched two hundred ships and eight thousand men to plunder the sea-coast of Calabria and Apulia: they assaulted the ancient city of Tarentum, interrupted the trade and agriculture of an happy country, and sailed back to the Hellespont, proud of their piratical victory over a people whom they still presumed to consider as their *Roman* brethren. Their retreat was possibly hastened by the activity of Theodoric; Italy was covered by a fleet of a thousand light vessels, which he constructed with incredible despatch; and his firm moderation was soon rewarded by a solid and honourable peace. He maintained with a powerful hand the balance of the West, till it was at length overthrown by the ambition of Clovis; and although unable to assist his rash and unfortunate kinsman, the king of the Visigoths, he saved the remains of his family and people, and checked the Franks in the midst of their victorious career. I am not desirous to prolong or repeat this narrative of military events, the least interesting of the reign of Theodoric; and shall be content to add that the Alemanni were protected, that an inroad of the Burgundians was severely chastised, and that the conquest of Arles and Marseilles opened a free communication with the Visigoths, who revered him both as their national protector, and as the guardian of his grandchild, the infant son of Alaric. Under this respectable character, the king of Italy restored the Prætorian prefecture of the Gauls, reformed some abuses in the civil government of Spain, and accepted the annual tribute and apparent submission of its military governor, who wisely refused to trust his person in the palace of Ravenna. The Gothic sovereignty was established from Sicily to the Danube, from Sirmium or Belgrade to the Atlantic Ocean; and the Greeks themselves have acknowledged that Theodoric reigned over the fairest portion of the Western empire.

The union of the Goths and Romans might have fixed for ages the transient happiness of Italy; and the first of nations, a new people of free subjects and enlightened soldiers, might have gradually arisen from the mutual emulation of their respective virtues. But the sublime merit of guiding or second-ing such a revolution was not reserved for the reign of Theodoric: he wanted either the genius or the opportunities of a legislator; and while he indulged the Goths in the enjoyment of rude liberty, he servilely copied the institutions, and even the abuses, of the political system which had been framed by Constantine and his successors. From a tender regard to the expiring prejudices of Rome, the barbarian declined the name, the purple, and the diadem of the emperors; but he assumed, under the hereditary title of king, the whole substance and plenitude of Imperial prerogative. His addresses to the Eastern throne were respectful and ambiguous: he celebrated in pomp-ous style the harmony of the two republics, applauded his own government as the perfect similitude of a sole and un-divided empire, and claimed above the kings of the earth the same pre-eminence which he modestly allowed to the person or rank of Anastasius. The alliance of the East and West was annually declared by the unanimous choice of two consuls; but it should seem that the Italian candidate, who was named by Theodoric, accepted a formal confirmation from the sovereign of Constantinople. The Gothic palace of Ravenna reflected the image of the court of Theodosius or Valentinian. The Prætorian prefect, the prefect of Rome, the quæstor, the master of the offices, with the public and patri-monial treasurers, whose functions àre painted in gaudy colours by the rhetoric of Cassiodorus, still continued to act as the ministers of state. And the subordinate care of justice and the revenue was delegated to seven consulars, three cor-rectors, and five presidents, who governed the fifteen *regions* of Italy according to the principles, and even the forms, of Roman jurisprudence. The violence of the conquerors was abated or eluded by the slow artifice of judicial proceedings; the civil administration, with its honours and emoluments, was confined to the Italians; and the people still preserved their dress and language, their laws and customs, their personal freedom, and two-thirds of their landed property. It had been the object of Augustus to conceal the introduction of monarchy; it was the policy of Theodoric to disguise the reign of a barbarian. If his subjects were sometimes awakened from this pleasing vision of a Roman government, they derived more substantial comfort from the character of a Gothic prince who had penetration to discern, and firmness to pursue, his own and the public interest. Theodoric loved the virtues which he possessed, and the talents of which he was destitute. Liberius was promoted to the office of Prætorian prefect for his unshaken fidelity to the unfortunate cause of Odoacer. The ministers of Theodoric, Cassiodorus and Boethius, have reflected on his reign the lustre of their genius and learning. More prudent or more fortunate than his colleague, Cassiodorus preserved his own esteem without forfeiting the royal favour; and after passing thirty years in the honours of the world, he was blessed with an equal term of repose in the devout and studious solitude of Squillace.

PROSPERITY OF ROME AND ITALY

As the patron of the republic, it was the interest and duty of the Gothic king to cultivate the affections of the senate and people. The nobles of Rome were flattered by sonorous epithets and formal professions of respect, which had been more justly applied to the merit and authority of their ancestors. The people enjoyed, without fear or danger, the three blessings of a capital, order, plenty, and public amusements. A visible diminution of their numbers may be found even in the measure of liberality; yet Apulia, Calabria, and Sicily poured their tribute of corn into the granaries of Rome; an allowance of bread and meat was distributed to the indigent citizens; and every office was deemed honourable which was consecrated to the care of their health and happiness. The public games, such as a Greek ambassador might politely applaud, exhibited a faint and feeble copy of the magnificence of the Cæsars: yet the musical, the gymnastic, and the pantomime arts, had not totally sunk in oblivion; the wild beasts of Africa still exercised in the amphitheatre the courage and dexterity of the hunters; and the indulgent Goth either patiently tolerated or gently restrained the blue and green factions, whose contests so often filled the circus with clamour, and even with blood. In the seventh year of his peaceful reign, Theodoric visited the old capital of the world; the senate and people advanced in solemn procession to salute a second Trajan, a new Valentinian; and he nobly supported that character, by the assurance of a just and legal government, in a discourse which he was not afraid to pronounce in public, and to inscribe on a tablet of brass. Rome, in this august ceremony, shot a last ray of declining glory; and a saint, the spectator of this pompous scene, could only hope, in his pious fancy, that it was excelled by the celestial splendour of the New Jerusalem. During a residence of six months, the fame, the person, and the courteous demeanour of the Gothic king, excited the admiration of the Romans, and he contemplated, with equal curiosity and surprise, the monuments that remained of their ancient greatness. He imprinted the footsteps of a conqueror on the Capitoline hill, and frankly confessed that each day he viewed with fresh wonder the forum of Trajan and his lofty column. The theatre of Pompey appeared, even in its decay, as a huge mountain artificially hollowed and polished, and adorned by human industry; and he vaguely computed that a river of gold must have been drained to erect the colossal amphitheatre of Titus. From the mouths of fourteen aqueducts a pure and copious stream was diffused into every part of the city; among these the Claudian water, which arose at the distance of thirty-eight miles in the Sabine mountains, was conveyed along a gentle though constant declivity of solid arches, till it descended on the summit of the Aventine hill. The long and spacious vaults which had been constructed for the purpose of common sewers subsisted after twelve centuries in their pristine strength; and these subterraneous channels have been preferred to all the visible wonders of Rome. The Gothic kings, so injuriously accused of the ruin of antiquity, were anxious to preserve the monuments of the nation whom they had subdued. The royal edicts were framed to prevent the abuses, the neglect, or the depredations of the citizens themselves; and a professed architect, the annual sum of two hundred pounds of gold, twenty-five thousand tiles, and the receipt of customs from the Lucrine port, were assigned for the ordinary repairs of the walls and public edifices. A similar care was extended to the statues of metal or marble of men or animals. The spirit of the horses which have given a modern name to the Quirinal was applauded by the barbarians; the brazen elephants of the *Via sacra* were diligently restored; the famous heifer of Myron deceived the cattle, as they were driven through the forum of peace; and an officer was created to protect those works of art, which Theodoric considered as the noblest ornament of his kingdom.

After the example of the last emperors, Theodoric preferred the residence of Ravenna, where he cultivated an orchard with his own hands. As often as the peace of his kingdom was threatened (for it was never invaded) by the barbarians, he removed his court to Verona on the northern frontier, and the image of his palace, still extant on a coin, represents the oldest and most authentic model of Gothic architecture. These two capitals, as well as Pavia, Spoleto, Naples, and the rest of the Italian cities, acquired under his reign the useful or splendid decorations of churches, aqueducts, baths, porticoes, and palaces. But the happiness of the subject was more truly conspicuous in the busy scene of labour and luxury, in the rapid increase and bold enjoyment of national wealth. From the shades of Tibur and Præneste, the Roman senators still retired in the winter season to the warm sun and salubrious springs of Baiæ; and their villas, which advanced on solid moles into the bay of Naples, commanded the various prospect of the sky, the earth, and the water. On the eastern side of the Adriatic a new Campania was formed in the fair and fruitful province of Istria, which communicated with the palace of Ravenna by an easy navigation of one hundred miles. The rich productions of Lucania and the adjacent provinces were exchanged at the Marcilian fountain, in a populous fair annually dedicated to trade, intemperance, and superstition. In the solitude of Comum, which had once been animated by the mild genius of Pliny, a transparent basin above sixty miles in length still reflected the rural seats which encompassed the margin of the Larian lake; and the gradual ascent of the hills was covered by a triple plantation of olives, of vines, and of chestnut-trees. Agriculture revived under the shadow of peace, and the number of husbandmen was multiplied by the redemption of captives.[1] The iron-mines of Dalmatia, a gold-mine in Bruttium, were carefully explored, and the Pomptine marshes, as well as those of Spoleto, were drained and cultivated by private undertakers, whose distant reward must depend on the continuance of the public prosperity. Whenever the seasons were less propitious, the doubtful precautions of forming magazines of corn, fixing the price, and prohibiting the exportation, attested at least the benevolence of the state; but such was the extraordinary plenty which an industrious people produced from a grateful soil, that a gallon of wine was sometimes sold in Italy for less than three farthings, and a quarter of wheat at about five shillings and sixpence. A country possessed of so many valuable objects of exchange soon attracted the merchants of the world, whose beneficial traffic was encouraged and protected by the liberal spirit of Theodoric. The free intercourse of the provinces by land and water was restored and extended; the city gates were never shut either by day or by night; and the common saying, that a purse of gold might be safely left in the fields, was expressive of the conscious security of the inhabitants.

ARIANISM OF THEODORIC

A difference of religion is always pernicious and often fatal to the harmony of the prince and people: the Gothic conqueror had been educated in the profession of Arianism, and Italy was devoutly attached to the Nicene faith. But the persuasion of Theodoric was not infected by zeal: and he piously adhered to the heresy of his fathers, without condescending to balance the subtile arguments of theological metaphysics. Satisfied with the private toleration of his Arian sectaries, he justly conceived himself to be the guardian of the public worship, and his external reverence for a superstition which he despised may have nourished in his mind the salutary indifference of a statesman or philosopher. The catholics of his dominions acknowledged, perhaps with reluctance, the peace of the church; their clergy, according to the degrees of rank or merit, were honourably entertained in the palace of Theodoric; he esteemed the living sanctity of

---

[1] St. Epiphanius of Pavia redeemed by prayer or ransom 600 captives from the Burgundians of Lyons and Savoy. Such deeds are the best of miracles.

Cæsarius and Epiphanius, the orthodox bishops of Arles and
Pavia; and presented a decent offering on the tomb of St.
Peter, without any scrupulous inquiry into the creed of the
apostle. His favourite Goths, and even his mother, were permitted to retain or embrace the Athanasian faith, and his
long reign could not afford the example of an Italian catholic
who, either from choice or compulsion, had deviated into the
religion of the conqueror. The people, and the barbarians
themselves, were edified by the pomp and order of religious
worship; the magistrates were instructed to defend the just
immunities of ecclesiastical persons and possessions; the bishops held their synods, the metropolitans exercised their
jurisdiction, and the privileges of sanctuary were maintained
or moderated according to the spirit of the Roman jurisprudence. With the protection, Theodoric assumed the legal
supremacy, of the church; and his firm administration restored
or extended some useful prerogatives which had been neglected
by the feeble emperors of the West. He was not ignorant of
the dignity and importance of the Roman pontiff, to whom
the venerable name of POPE was now appropriated. The peace
or the revolt of Italy might depend on the character of a
wealthy and popular bishop, who claimed such ample dominion
both in heaven and earth; who had been declared in a
numerous synod to be pure from all sin, and exempt from
all judgment. When the chair of St. Peter was disputed by
Symmachus and Laurence, they appeared at his summons
before the tribunal of an Arian monarch, and he confirmed
the election of the most worthy or the most obsequious candidate. At the end of his life, in a moment of jealousy and
resentment, he prevented the choice of the Romans, by
nominating a pope in the palace of Ravenna. The danger and
furious contests of a schism were mildly restrained, and the
last decree of the senate was enacted to extinguish, if it were
possible, the scandalous venality of the papal elections.

I have descanted with pleasure on the fortunate condition
of Italy, but our fancy must not hastily conceive that the
golden age of the poets, a race of men without vice or misery,
was realised under the Gothic conquest. The fair prospect was
sometimes overcast with clouds; the wisdom of Theodoric
might be deceived, his power might be resisted, and the
declining age of the monarch was sullied with popular hatred
and patrician blood. In the first insolence of victory he had

been tempted to deprive the whole party of Odoacer of the civil and even the natural rights of society; a tax, unseasonably imposed after the calamities of war, would have crushed the rising agriculture of Liguria; a rigid pre-emption of corn, which was intended for the public relief, must have aggravated the distress of Campania. These dangerous projects were defeated by the virtue and eloquence of Epiphanius and Boethius, who, in the presence of Theodoric himself, successfully pleaded the cause of the people: but, if the royal ear was open to the voice of truth, a saint and a philosopher are not always to be found at the ear of kings. The privileges of rank, or office, or favour were too frequently abused by Italian fraud and Gothic violence, and the avarice of the king's nephew was publicly exposed, at first by the usurpation, and afterwards by the restitution, of the estates which he had unjustly extorted from his Tuscan neighbours. Two hundred thousand barbarians, formidable even to their master, were seated in the heart of Italy; they indignantly supported the restraints of peace and discipline; the disorders of their march were always felt and sometimes compensated; and where it was dangerous to punish, it might be prudent to dissemble, the sallies of their native fierceness. When the indulgence of Theodoric had remitted two-thirds of the Ligurian tribute, he condescended to explain the difficulties of his situation, and to lament the heavy though inevitable burdens which he imposed on his subjects for their own defence. These ungrateful subjects could never be cordially reconciled to the origin, the religion, or even the virtues, of the Gothic conqueror; past calamities were forgotten, and the sense or suspicion of injuries was rendered still more exquisite by the present felicity of the times.

Even the religious toleration which Theodoric had the glory of introducing into the Christian world was painful and offensive to the orthodox zeal of the Italians. They respected the armed heresy of the Goths; but their pious rage was safely pointed against the rich and defenceless Jews, who had formed their establishments at Naples, Rome, Ravenna, Milan, and Genoa, for the benefit of trade, and under the sanction of the laws. Their persons were insulted, their effects were pillaged, and their synagogues were burnt by the mad populace of Ravenna and Rome, inflamed, as it should seem, by the most frivolous or extravagant pretences. The government which could neglect, would have deserved such an outrage. A legal inquiry was instantly directed; and, as the authors of the tumult had escaped in the crowd, the whole community was condemned to repair the damage, and the obstinate bigots, who refused their contributions, were whipped through the streets by the hand of the executioner. This simple act of justice exasperated the discontent of the catholics, who applauded the merit and patience of these holy confessors. Three hundred pulpits deplored the persecution of the church; and if the chapel of St. Stephen at Verona was demolished by the command of Theodoric, it is probable that some miracle hostile to his name and dignity had been performed on that sacred theatre. At the close of a glorious life, the king of Italy discovered that he had excited the hatred of a people whose happiness he had so assiduously laboured to promote; and his mind was soured by indignation, jealousy, and the bitterness of unrequited love. The Gothic conqueror condescended to disarm the unwarlike natives of Italy, interdicting all weapons of offence, and excepting only a small knife for domestic use. The deliverer of Rome was accused of conspiring with the vilest informers against the lives of senators whom he suspected of a secret and treasonable correspondence with the Byzantine court. After the death of Anastasius, the diadem had been placed on the head of a feeble old man, but the powers of government were assumed by his nephew Justinian, who already meditated the extirpation of heresy and the conquest of Italy and Africa. A rigorous law, which was published at Constantinople, to reduce the Arians, by the dread of punishment, within the pale of the church, awakened the just resentment of Theodoric, who claimed for his distressed brethren of the East the same indulgence which he had so long granted to the catholics of his dominions. At his stern command the Roman pontiff, with four *illustrious* senators, embarked on an embassy of which he must have alike dreaded the failure or the success. The singular veneration shown to the first pope who had visited Constantinople was punished as a crime by his jealous monarch; the artful or peremptory refusal of the Byzantine court might excuse an equal, and would provoke a larger, measure of retaliation; and a mandate was prepared in Italy to prohibit, after a stated day, the exercise of the catholic worship. By the bigotry of his subjects and enemies the most tolerant of princes was driven to the brink of persecution, and the life of Theodoric was too long, since he lived to condemn the virtue of Boethius and Symmachus.

THE EXECUTION OF BOETHIUS

The senator Boethius is the last of the Romans whom Cato or Tully could have acknowledged for their countryman. As a wealthy orphan, he inherited the patrimony and honours of the Anician family, a name ambitiously assumed by the kings and emperors of the age, and the appellation of Manlius asserted his genuine or fabulous descent from a race of consuls and dictators who had repulsed the Gauls from the Capitol, and sacrificed their sons to the discipline of the republic. In the youth of Boethius the studies of Rome were not totally abandoned; a Virgil is now extant corrected by the hand of a consul; and the professors of grammar, rhetoric, and jurisprudence were maintained in their privileges and pensions by the liberality of the Goths. But the erudition of the Latin language was insufficient to satiate his ardent curiosity; and Boethius is said to have employed eighteen laborious years in the schools of Athens, which were supported by the zeal, the learning, and the diligence of Proclus and his disciples. The reason and piety of their Roman pupil were fortunately saved from the contagion of mystery and magic which polluted the groves of the Academy; but he imbibed the spirit, and imitated the method, of his dead and living masters, who attempted to reconcile the strong and subtle sense of Aristotle with the devout contemplation and sublime fancy of Plato. After his return to Rome, and his marriage with the daughter of his friend the patrician Symmachus, Boethius still continued, in a palace of ivory and marble, to prosecute the same studies. The church was edified by his profound defence of the orthodox creed against the Arian, the Eutychian, and the Nestorian heresies; and the catholic unity was explained or exposed in a formal treatise by the *indifference* of three distinct though consubstantial persons. For the benefit of his Latin readers, his genius submitted to teach the first elements of the arts and sciences of Greece. The geometry of Euclid, the music of Pythagoras, the arithmetic of Nicomachus, the mechanics of Archimedes, the astronomy of Ptolemy, the theology of Plato, and the logic of Aristotle, with the commentary of Porphyry, were translated and illustrated by the indefatigable pen of the Roman senator. And he alone was esteemed capable of describing the wonders of art, a sun-dial, a water-clock, or a sphere which represented the motions of the planets. From these abstruse speculations Boethius stooped—or, to speak more truly, he rose—to the social duties of public and private life; the indigent were relieved by his liberality, and his eloquence, which flattery might compare to the voice of Demosthenes or Cicero, was uniformly exerted in the cause of innocence and humanity. Such conspicuous merit was felt and rewarded by a discerning prince: the dignity of Boethius was adorned with the titles of consul and patrician, and his talents were usefully employed in the important station of master of the offices. Notwithstanding the equal claims of the East and West, his two sons were created, in their tender youth, the consuls of the same year. On the memorable day of their inauguration they proceeded in solemn pomp from their palace to the forum amidst the applause of the senate and people; and their joyful father, the true consul of Rome, after pronouncing an oration in the praise of his royal benefactor, distributed a triumphal largess in the games of the circus. Prosperous in his fame and fortunes, in his public honours and private alliances, in the cultivation of science and the consciousness of virtue, Boethius might have been styled happy, if that precarious epithet could be safely applied before the last term of the life of man.

A philosopher, liberal of his wealth and parsimonious of his time, might be insensible to the common allurements of ambition, the thirst of gold and employment. And some credit may be due to the asseveration of Boethius, that he had reluctantly obeyed the divine Plato, who enjoins every virtuous citizen to rescue the state from the usurpation of vice and ignorance. For the integrity of his public conduct he appeals to the memory of his country. His authority had restrained the pride and oppression of the royal officers, and his eloquence had delivered Paulianus from the dogs of the palace. He had always pitied, and often relieved, the distress of the provincials, whose fortunes were exhausted by public and private rapine; and Boethius alone had courage to oppose the tyranny of the barbarians, elated by conquest, excited by avarice, and, as he complains, encouraged by impunity. In these honourable contests his spirit soared above the consideration of danger, and perhaps of prudence; and we may learn from the example of Cato that a character of pure and inflexible virtue is the most apt to be misled by prejudice, to be heated by enthusiasm, and to confound private enmities with public justice. The disciple of Plato might exaggerate the infirmities of nature and the imperfections of society; and the mildest form of a Gothic kingdom, even the weight of allegiance and gratitude, must be insupportable to the free spirit of a Roman patriot. But the favour and fidelity of Boethius declined in just proportion with the public happiness, and an unworthy colleague was imposed to divide and control the power of the master of the offices. In the last gloomy season of Theodoric he indignantly felt that he was a slave; but as his master had only power over his life, he stood, without arms and without fear, against the face of an angry barbarian, who had been provoked to believe that the safety of the senate was incompatible with his own. The senator Albinus was accused and already convicted on the presumption of *hoping*, as it was said, the liberty of Rome. "If Albinus be criminal," exclaimed the orator, "the senate and myself are all guilty of the same crime. If we are innocent, Albinus is equally entitled to the protection of the laws." These laws might not have punished the simple and barren wish of an unattainable blessing; but they would have shown less indulgence to the rash confession of Boethius, that, had he known of a conspiracy, the tyrant never should. The advocate of Albinus was soon involved in the danger and perhaps the guilt of his client; their signature (which they denied as a forgery) was affixed to the original address inviting the emperor to deliver Italy from the Goths; and three witnesses of honourable rank, perhaps of infamous reputation, attested the treasonable designs of the Roman patrician. Yet his innocence must be presumed, since he was deprived by Theodoric of the means of justification, and rigorously confined in the tower of Pavia, while the senate, at the distance of five hundred miles, pronounced a sentence of confiscation and death against the most illustrious of its members. At the command of the barbarians, the occult science of a philosopher was stigmatised with the names of sacrilege and magic.[1] A devout and dutiful attachment to the senate was condemned as criminal by the trembling voices of the senators themselves; and their ingratitude deserved the wish or prediction of Boethius, that, after him, none should be found guilty of the same offence.

While Boethius, oppressed with fetters, expected each moment the sentence or the stroke of death, he composed in the tower of Pavia the *Consolation of Philosophy;* a golden volume not unworthy of the leisure of Plato or Tully, but which claims incomparable merit from the barbarism of the times and the situation of the author. The celestial guide whom he had so long invoked at Rome and Athens now condescended to illumine his dungeon, to revive his courage, and to pour into his wounds her salutary balm. She taught him to compare his long prosperity and his recent distress, and to conceive new hopes from the inconstancy of fortune. Reason had informed him of the precarious condition of her gifts; experience had satisfied him of their real value; he had enjoyed them without guilt, he might resign them without a sigh, and calmly disdain the impotent malice of his enemies, who had left him happiness, since they had left him virtue. From the earth Boethius ascended to heaven in search of the SUPREME GOOD; explored the metaphysical labyrinth of chance and destiny, of prescience and free-will, of time and eternity; and generously attempted to reconcile the perfect attributes of the Deity with the apparent disorders of his moral and physical government. Such topics of consolation, so obvious, so vague, or so abstruse, are ineffectual to subdue the feelings of human nature. Yet the sense of misfortune may be diverted by the labour of thought; and the sage who could artfully combine in the same work the various riches of philosophy, poetry, and eloquence, must already have possessed the intrepid calmness which he affected to seek. Suspense, the worst of evils, was at length determined by the ministers of death, who executed, and perhaps exceeded, the inhuman mandate of Theodoric. A strong cord was fastened round the head of Boethius, and forcibly tightened till his eyes almost started from their sockets; and some mercy may

---

[1] A severe inquiry was instituted into the crime of magic; and it was believed that many necromancers had escaped by making their gaolers mad: for *mad,* I should read *drunk.*

be discovered in the milder torture of beating him with clubs till he expired. But his genius survived to diffuse a ray of knowledge over the darkest ages of the Latin world; the writings of the philosopher were translated by the most glorious of the English kings, and the third emperor of the name of Otho removed to a more honourable tomb the bones of a catholic saint who, from his Arian persecutors, had acquired the honours of martyrdom and the fame of miracles.[1] In the last hours of Boethius he derived some comfort from the safety of his two sons, of his wife, and of his father-in-law, the venerable Symmachus. But the grief of Symmachus was indiscreet, and perhaps disrespectful: he had presumed to lament, he might dare to revenge, the death of an injured friend. He was dragged in chains from Rome to the palace of Ravenna, and the suspicions of Theodoric could only be appeased by the blood of an innocent and aged senator.

THE DEATH OF THEODORIC

Humanity will be disposed to encourage any report which testifies the jurisdiction of conscience and the remorse of kings; and philosophy is not ignorant that the most horrid spectres are sometimes created by the powers of a disordered fancy, and the weakness of a distempered body. After a life of virtue and glory, Theodoric was now descending with shame and guilt into the grave: his mind was humbled by the contrast of the past, and justly alarmed by the invisible terrors of futurity. One evening, as it is related, when the head of a large fish was served on the royal table, he suddenly exclaimed that he beheld the angry countenance of Symmachus, his eyes glaring fury and revenge, and his mouth armed with long sharp teeth, which threatened to devour him. The monarch instantly retired to his chamber, and, as he lay trembling with aguish cold under a weight of bed-clothes, he expressed in broken murmurs to his physician Elpidius his deep repentance for the murders of

---

[1] The inscription on his new tomb was composed by the preceptor of Otho the Third, the learned pope Silvester II, who, like Boethius himself, was styled a magician by the ignorance of the times. The catholic martyr had carried his head in his hands a considerable way; yet on a similar tale, a lady of my acquaintance once observed, "La distance n'y fait rien; il n'y a que le premier pas qui coûte." [Madame du Deffand. She was speaking of the similar miracle of St. Denis.—D.M.L.]

Boethius and Symmachus. His malady increased, and, after a dysentery which continued three days, he expired in the palace of Ravenna, in the thirty-third, or, if we compute from the invasion of Italy, in the thirty-seventh year of his reign. Conscious of his approaching end, he divided his treasures and provinces between his two grandsons, and fixed the Rhône as their common boundary. Amalaric was restored to the throne of Spain. Italy, with all the conquests of the Ostrogoths, was bequeathed to Athalaric, whose age did not exceed ten years, but who was cherished as the last male offspring of the line of Amali, by the short-lived marriage of his mother Amalasuntha with a royal fugitive of the same blood. In the presence of the dying monarch the Gothic chiefs and Italian magistrates mutually engaged their faith and loyalty to the young prince and to his guardian mother; and received, in the same awful moment, his last salutary advice to maintain the laws, to love the senate and people of Rome, and to cultivate with decent reverence the friendship of the emperor. The monument of Theodoric was erected by his daughter Amalasuntha in a conspicuous situation, which commanded the city of Ravenna, the harbour, and the adjacent coast. A chapel of a circular form, thirty feet in diameter, is crowned by a dome of one entire piece of granite: from the centre of the dome four columns arose, which supported in a vase of porphyry the remains of the Gothic king, surrounded by the brazen statues of the twelve apostles. His spirit, after some previous expiation, might have been permitted to mingle with the benefactors of mankind, if an Italian hermit had not been witness in a vision to the damnation of Theodoric, whose soul was plunged by the ministers of divine vengeance into the volcano of Lipari, one of the flaming mouths of the infernal world.

40.

THE EMPEROR Justinian was born near the ruins of Sardica (the modern Sophia), of an obscure race of barbarians, the inhabitants of a wild and desolate country, to which the names of Dardania, of Dacia, and of Bulgaria, have been successively applied. His elevation was prepared by the adventurous spirit of his uncle Justin, who, with two other peasants of the same village, deserted for the profession of arms the more useful employment of husbandmen or shepherds. On foot, with a scanty provision of biscuit in their knapsacks, the three youths followed the high road of Constantinople, and were soon enrolled, for their strength and stature, among the guards of the emperor Leo. Under the two succeeding reigns, the fortunate peasant emerged to wealth and honours; and his escape from some dangers which threatened his life was afterwards ascribed to the guardian angel who watches over the fate of kings. His long and laudable service in the Isaurian and Persian wars would not have preserved from oblivion the name of Justin; yet they might warrant the military promotion which, in the course of fifty years, he gradually obtained—the rank of tribune, of count, and of general, the dignity of senator, and the command of the guards, who obeyed him as their chief at the important crisis when the emperor Anastasius was removed from the world. The powerful kinsmen whom he had raised and enriched were excluded from the throne; and the eunuch Amantius, who reigned in the palace, had secretly resolved to fix the diadem on the head of the most obsequious of his creatures. A liberal donative, to conciliate the suffrage of the guards, was entrusted for that purpose in the hands of their commander. But these weighty arguments were treacherously employed by Justin in his own favour; and as no competitor presumed to appear, the Dacian peasant was invested with the purple by the unanimous consent of the soldiers, who knew him to be brave and gentle; of the clergy and people, who believed him to be orthodox; and of the provincials, who yielded a blind and implicit submission to the will of the capital. The elder Justin, as he is distinguished from another emperor of the same family and name, ascended the Byzantine throne at the age of sixty-eight years; and, had he been left to his own guidance, every moment of a nine-years' reign must have exposed to his subjects the impropriety of their choice. His ignorance was similar to that of Theodoric; and it is remarkable that, in an age not destitute of learning, two contemporary monarchs had never been instructed in the knowledge of the alphabet. But the genius of Justin was far inferior to that of the Gothic king: the experience of a soldier had not qualified him for the government of an empire; and though personally brave, the consciousness of his own weakness was naturally attended with doubt, distrust, and political apprehension. But the official business of the state was diligently and faithfully transacted by the quæstor Proclus; and the aged emperor adopted the talents and ambition of his nephew Justinian, an aspiring youth, whom his uncle had drawn from the rustic solitude of Dacia, and educated at Constantinople as the heir of his private fortune, and at length of the Eastern empire.

Since the eunuch Amantius had been defrauded of his money, it became necessary to deprive him of his life. The task was easily accomplished by the charge of a real or fictitious conspiracy; and the judges were informed, as an accumulation of guilt, that he was secretly addicted to the Manichæan heresy. Amantius lost his head; three of his companions, the first domestics of the palace, were punished either with death or exile; and their unfortunate candidate for the purple was cast into a deep dungeon, overwhelmed with stones, and ignominiously thrown without burial into the sea. The ruin of Vitalian was a work of more difficulty and danger. That Gothic chief had rendered himself popular by the civil war which he boldly waged against Anastasius for the defence of the orthodox faith; and after the conclusion of an advantageous treaty, he still remained in the neighbourhood of Constantinople at the head of a formidable and victorious army of barbarians. By the frail security of oaths he was tempted to relinquish this advantageous situation, and to trust his person within the walls of a city whose inhabitants, particularly the *blue* faction, were artfully incensed against him by the remembrance even of his pious hostilities. The emperor and his nephew embraced him as the faithful and worthy champion of the church and state, and gratefully adorned their favourite with the titles of consul and general; but in the seventh month of his consulship Vitalian was stabbed with seventeen wounds at the royal banquet, and Justinian, who inherited the spoil, was accused as the assassin of a spiritual brother, to whom he had recently pledged his faith in the participation of the Christian mysteries. After the fall of his rival, he was promoted, without any claim of military service, to the office of master-general of the Eastern armies, whom it was his duty to lead into the field against the public enemy. But, in the pursuit of fame, Justinian might have lost his present dominion over the age and weakness of his uncle; and instead of acquiring by Scythian or Persian trophies the applause of his countrymen, the prudent warrior solicited their favour in the churches, the circus, and the senate of Constantinople. The catholics were attached to the nephew of Justin, who between the Nestorian and Eutychian heresies, trod the narrow path of inflexible and intolerant orthodoxy. In the first days of the new reign he prompted and gratified the popular enthusiasm against the memory of the deceased emperor. After a schism of thirty-four years, he reconciled the proud and angry spirit of the Roman pontiff, and spread among the Latins a favourable report of his pious respect for the apostolic see. The thrones of the East were filled with catholic bishops devoted to his interest, the clergy and the monks were gained by his liberality, and the people were taught to pray for their future sovereign, the hope and pillar of the true religion. The magnificence of Justinian was displayed in the superior pomp of his public spectacles, an object not less sacred and important in the eyes of the multitude than the creed of Nice or Chalcedon: the expense of his consulship was esteemed at two hundred and eighty-eight thousand pieces

of gold; twenty lions and thirty leopards were produced at
the same time in the amphitheatre; and a numerous train of
horses, with their rich trappings, was bestowed as an extraordinary gift on the victorious charioteers of the circus. While
he indulged the people of Constantinople, and received the
addresses of foreign kings, the nephew of Justin assiduously
cultivated the friendship of the senate. That venerable name
seemed to qualify its members to declare the sense of the
nation, and to regulate the succession of the Imperial throne.
The feeble Anastasius had permitted the vigour of government to degenerate into the form or substance of an aristocracy, and the military officers who had obtained the senatorial
rank were followed by their domestic guards, a band of
veterans whose arms or acclamations might fix in a tumultuous
moment the diadem of the East. The treasures of the state
were lavished to procure the voices of the senators, and their
unanimous wish that he would be pleased to adopt Justinian
for his colleague was communicated to the emperor. But this
request, which too clearly admonished him of his approaching
end, was unwelcome to the jealous temper of an aged monarch
desirous to retain the power which he was incapable of
exercising; and Justin, holding his purple with both his hands,
advised them to prefer, since an election was so profitable,
some older candidate. Notwithstanding this reproach, the
senate proceeded to decorate Justinian with the royal epithet
of *nobilissimus;* and their decree was ratified by the affection
or the fears of his uncle. After some time the languor of
mind and body to which he was reduced by an incurable
wound in his thigh indispensably required the aid of a guardian. He summoned the patriarch and senators, and in their
presence solemnly placed the diadem on the head of his
nephew, who was conducted from the palace to the circus,
and saluted by the loud and joyful applause of the people.
The life of Justin was prolonged about four months; but
from the instant of this ceremony he was considered as dead
to the empire, which acknowledged Justinian, in the forty-
ninth year of his age, for the lawful sovereign of the East.

From his elevation to his death, Justinian governed the
Roman empire thirty-eight years, seven months, and thirteen
days. The events of his reign, which excite our curious attention by their number, variety, and importance, are diligently
related by the secretary of Belisarius, a rhetorician, whom

eloquence had promoted to the rank of senator and prefect of Constantinople. According to the vicissitudes of courage or servitude, of favour or disgrace, Procopius successively composed the *history*, the *panegyric*, and the *satire* of his own times. The eight books of the Persian, Vandalic, and Gothic wars, which are continued in the five books of Agathias, deserve our esteem as a laborious and successful imitation of the Attic, or at least of the Asiatic, writers of ancient Greece. His facts are collected from the personal experience and free conversation of a soldier, a statesman, and a traveller; his style continually aspires, and often attains to the merit of strength and elegance; his reflections, more especially in the speeches, which he too frequently inserts, contain a rich fund of political knowledge; and the historian, excited by the generous ambition of pleasing and instructing posterity, appears to disdain the prejudices of the people and the flattery of courts. The writings of Procopius were read and applauded by his contemporaries: but, although he respectfully laid them at the foot of the throne, the pride of Justinian must have been wounded by the praise of an hero who perpetually eclipses the glory of his inactive sovereign. The conscious dignity of independence was subdued by the hopes and fears of a slave; and the secretary of Belisarius laboured for pardon and reward in the six books of the Imperial *edifices*. He had dexterously chosen a subject of apparent splendour, in which he could loudly celebrate the genius, the magnificence, and the piety of a prince who, both as a conqueror and legislator, has surpassed the puerile virtues of Themistocles and Cyrus. Disappointment might urge the flatterer to secret revenge; and the first glance of favour might again tempt him to suspend and suppress a libel in which the Roman Cyrus is degraded into an odious and contemptible tyrant, in which both the emperor and his consort Theodora are seriously represented as two dæmons who had assumed an human form for the destruction of mankind.[1] Such base inconsistency must doubtless sully the reputation, and detract from the credit, of Procopius: yet after the venom of his malignity has been

---

[1] Justinian an ass—the perfect likeness of Domitian—Theodora's lovers driven from her bed by rival dæmons—her marriage foretold with a great dæmon—a monk saw the prince of the dæmons, instead of Justinian, on the throne—the servants who watched beheld a face without features, a body walking without an head, etc. etc. Procopius declares his own and his friends' belief in these diabolical stories.

suffered to exhale, the residue of the *anecdotes,* even the most disgraceful facts, some of which had been tenderly hinted in his public history, are established by their internal evidence, or the authentic monuments of the times. From these various materials I shall now proceed to describe the reign of Justinian, which will deserve and occupy an ample space. The present chapter will explain the elevation and character of Theodora, the factions of the circus, and the peaceful administration of the sovereign of the East. In the three succeeding chapters I shall relate the wars of Justinian, which achieved the conquest of Africa and Italy; and I shall follow the victories of Belisarius and Narses, without disguising the vanity of their triumphs, or the hostile virtue of the Persian and Gothic heroes. The series of this volume will embrace the jurisprudence and theology of the emperor; the controversies and sects which still divide the Oriental church; the reformation of the Roman law which is obeyed or respected by the nations of modern Europe.

THE EMPRESS THEODORA

In the exercise of supreme power, the first act of Justinian was to divide it with the woman whom he loved, the famous Theodora, whose strange elevation cannot be applauded as the triumph of female virtue. Under the reign of Anastasius, the care of the wild beasts maintained by the green faction at Constantinople was intrusted to Acacius, a native of the isle of Cyprus, who, from his employment, was surnamed the master of the bears. This honourable office was given after his death to another candidate, notwithstanding the diligence of his widow, who had already provided a husband and a successor. Acacius had left three daughters, Comito, THEODORA, and Anastasia, the eldest of whom did not then exceed the age of seven years. On a solemn festival, these helpless orphans were sent by their distressed and indignant mother, in the garb of suppliants, into the midst of the theatre: the green faction received them with contempt, the blues with compassion; and this difference, which sunk deep into the mind of Theodora, was felt long afterwards in the administration of the empire. As they improved in age and beauty, the three sisters were successively devoted to the public and private pleasures of the Byzantine people; and Theodora, after follow-

ing Comito on the stage, in the dress of a slave, with a stool
on her head, was at length permitted to exercise her independent talents. She neither danced, nor sung, nor played on the
flute; her skill was confined to the pantomime arts; she excelled in buffoon characters; and as often as the comedian
swelled her cheeks, and complained with a ridiculous tone
and gesture of the blows that were inflicted, the whole theatre
of Constantinople resounded with laughter and applause. The
beauty of Theodora was the subject of more flattering praise,
and the source of more exquisite delight. Her features were
delicate and regular; her complexion, though somewhat pale,
was tinged with a natural colour; every sensation was instantly
expressed by the vivacity of her eyes; her easy motions displayed the graces of a small but elegant figure; and either
love or adulation might proclaim that painting and poetry were
incapable of delineating the matchless excellence of her form.
But this form was degraded by the facility with which it was
exposed to the public eye, and prostituted to licentious desire.
Her venal charms were abandoned to a promiscuous crowd of
citizens and strangers, of every rank and of every profession:
the fortunate lover who had been promised a night of enjoyment was often driven from her bed by a stronger or more
wealthy favourite; and when she passed through the streets,
her presence was avoided by all who wished to escape either
the scandal or the temptation. The satirical historian has not
blushed to describe the naked scenes which Theodora was
not ashamed to exhibit in the theatre. After exhausting the
arts of sensual pleasure, she most ungratefully murmured
against the parsimony of Nature; but her murmurs, her
pleasures, and her arts, must be veiled in the obscurity of a
learned language. After reigning for some time the delight and
contempt of the capital, she condescended to accompany
Ecebolus, a native of Tyre, who had obtained the government of the African Pentapolis. But this union was frail
and transient: Ecebolus soon rejected an expensive or faithless concubine; she was reduced at Alexandria to extreme
distress; and in her laborious return to Constantinople, every
city of the East admired and enjoyed the fair Cyprian, whose
merit appeared to justify her descent from the peculiar island
of Venus. The vague commerce of Theodora, and the most
detestable precautions, preserved her from the danger which
she feared; yet once, and once only, she became a mother.

The infant was saved and educated in Arabia by his father, who imparted to him on his death-bed that he was the son of an empress. Filled with ambitious hopes, the unsuspecting youth immediately hastened to the palace of Constantinople, and was admitted to the presence of his mother. As he was never more seen, even after the decease of Theodora, she deserved the foul imputation of extinguishing with his life a secret so offensive to her imperial virtue.

In the most abject state of her fortune and reputation, some vision, either of sleep or of fancy, had whispered to Theodora the pleasing assurance that she was destined to become the spouse of a potent monarch. Conscious of her approaching greatness, she returned from Paphlagonia to Constantinople; assumed, like a skilful actress, a more decent character; relieved her poverty by the laudable industry of spinning wool; and affected a life of chastity and solitude in a small house, which she afterwards changed into a magnificent temple. Her beauty, assisted by art or accident, soon attracted, captivated, and fixed, the patrician Justinian, who already reigned with absolute sway under the name of his uncle. Perhaps she contrived to enhance the value of a gift which she had so often lavished on the meanest of mankind; perhaps she inflamed, at first by modest delays, and at last by sensual allurements, the desires of a lover who, from nature or devotion, was addicted to long vigils and abstemious diet. When his first transports had subsided, she still maintained the same ascendant over his mind by the more solid merit of temper and understanding. Justinian delighted to ennoble and enrich the object of his affection: the treasures of the East were poured at her feet, and the nephew of Justin was determined, perhaps by religious scruples, to bestow on his concubine the sacred and legal character of a wife. But the laws of Rome expressly prohibited the marriage of a senator with any female who had been dishonoured by a servile origin or theatrical profession: the empress Lupicina or Euphemia, a barbarian of rustic manners, but of irreproachable virtue, refused to accept a prostitute for her niece; and even Vigilantia, the superstitious mother of Justinian, though she acknowledged the wit and beauty of Theodora, was seriously apprehensive lest the levity and arrogance of that artful paramour might corrupt the piety and happiness of her son. These obstacles were removed by the inflexible constancy of Justinian. He patiently expected the death of the empress; he despised the tears of his mother, who soon sunk under the weight of her affliction; and a law was promulgated, in the name of the emperor Justin, which abolished the rigid jurisprudence of antiquity. A glorious repentance (the words of the edict) was left open for the unhappy females who had prostituted their persons on the theatre, and they were permitted to contract a legal union with the most illustrious of the Romans. This indulgence was speedily followed by the solemn nuptials of Justinian and Theodora; her dignity was gradually exalted with that of her lover; and, as soon as Justin had invested his nephew with the purple, the patriarch of Constantinople placed the diadem on the heads of the emperor and empress of the East. But the usual honours which the severity of Roman manners had allowed to the wives of princes could not satisfy either the ambition of Theodora or the fondness of Justinian. He seated her on the throne as an equal and independent colleague in the sovereignty of the empire, and an oath of allegiance was imposed on the governors of the provinces in the joint names of Justinian and Theodora. The Eastern world fell prostrate before the genius and fortune of the daughter of Acacius. The prostitute who, in the presence of innumerable spectators, had polluted the theatre of Constantinople, was adorned as a queen in the same city, by grave magistrates, orthodox bishops, victorious generals, and captive monarchs.[1]

Those who believe that the female mind is totally depraved by the loss of chastity will eagerly listen to all the invectives of private envy or popular resentment, which have dissembled the virtues of Theodora, exaggerated her vices, and condemned with rigour the venal or voluntary sins of the youthful harlot. From a motive of shame or contempt, she often declined the servile homage of the multitude, escaped from the odious light of the capital, and passed the greatest part of the year in the palaces and gardens which were pleasantly seated on the sea-coast of the Propontis and the Bosphorus. Her private hours were devoted to the prudent as well as grateful care

---

[1] "Let greatness own her, and she's mean no more," etc. Without Warburton's critical telescope I should never have seen, in this general picture of triumphant vice, any personal allusion to Theodora.

of her beauty, the luxury of the bath and table, and the long slumber of the evening and the morning. Her secret apartments were occupied by the favourite women and eunuchs, whose interests and passions she indulged at the expense of justice: the most illustrious personages of the state were crowded into a dark and sultry antechamber; and when at last, after tedious attendance, they were admitted to kiss the feet of Theodora, they experienced, as her humour might suggest, the silent arrogance of an empress or the capricious levity of a comedian. Her rapacious avarice to accumulate an immense treasure may be excused by the apprehension of her husband's death, which could leave no alternative between ruin and the throne; and fear as well as ambition might exasperate Theodora against two generals who, during a malady of the emperor, had rashly declared that they were not disposed to acquiesce in the choice of the capital. But the reproach of cruelty, so repugnant even to her softer vices, has left an indelible stain on the memory of Theodora. Her numerous spies observed and zealously reported every action, or word, or look, injurious to their royal mistress. Whomsoever they accused were cast into her peculiar prisons, inaccessible to the inquirers of justice; and it was rumoured that the torture of the rack or scourge had been inflicted in the presence of a female tyrant, insensible to the voice of prayer or of pity. Some of these unhappy victims perished in deep unwholesome dungeons, while others were permitted, after the loss of their limbs, their reason, or their fortune, to appear in the world, the living monuments of her vengeance, which was commonly extended to the children of those whom she had suspected or injured. The senator or bishop whose death or exile Theodora had pronounced, was delivered to a trusty messenger, and his diligence was quickened by a menace from her own mouth. "If you fail in the execution of my commands, I swear by him who liveth for ever that your skin shall be flayed from your body."

If the creed of Theodora had not been tainted with heresy, her exemplary devotion might have atoned, in the opinion of her contemporaries, for pride, avarice, and cruelty; but if she employed her influence to assuage the intolerant fury of the emperor, the present age will allow some merit to her religion, and much indulgence to her speculative errors. The name of Theodora was introduced, with equal honour, in all the pious and charitable foundations of Justinian; and the most benevolent institution of his reign may be ascribed to the sympathy of the empress for her less fortunate sisters, who had been seduced or compelled to embrace the trade of prostitution. A palace, on the Asiatic side of the Bosphorus, was converted into a stately and spacious monastery, and a liberal maintenance was assigned to five hundred women who had been collected from the streets and brothels of Constantinople. In this safe and holy retreat they were devoted to perpetual confinement; and the despair of some, who threw themselves headlong into the sea, was lost in the gratitude of the penitents who had been delivered from sin and misery by the generous benefactress. The prudence of Theodora is celebrated by Justinian himself; and his laws are attributed to the sage counsels of his most reverend wife, whom he had received as the gift of the Deity. Her courage was displayed amidst the tumult of the people and the terrors of the court. Her chastity, from the moment of her union with Justinian, is founded on the silence of her implacable enemies; and although the daughter of Acacius might be satiated with love, yet some applause is due to the firmness of a mind which could sacrifice pleasure and habit to the stronger sense either of duty or interest. The wishes and prayers of Theodora could never obtain the blessing of a lawful son, and she buried an infant daughter, the sole offspring of her marriage. Notwithstanding this disappointment, her dominion was permanent and absolute; she preserved, by art or merit, the affections of Justinian; and their seeming dissensions were always fatal to the courtiers who believed them to be sincere. Perhaps her health had been impaired by the licentiousness of her youth; but it was always delicate, and she was directed by her physicians to use the Pythian warm-baths. In this journey the empress was followed by the Prætorian prefect, the great treasurer, several counts and patricians, and a splendid train of four thousand attendants: the highways were repaired at her approach; a palace was erected for her reception; and as she passed through Bithynia she distributed liberal alms to the churches, the monasteries, and the hospitals, that they might implore Heaven for the restoration of her health. At length, in the twenty-fourth year of her marriage, and the twenty-second of her reign, she was consumed by a cancer; and the irreparable loss was deplored by her husband, who, in the room of a theatrical prostitute, might have selected the purest and most noble virgin of the East.

THE *NIKA* RIOTS

A material difference may be observed in the games of antiquity; the most eminent of the Greeks were actors, the Romans were merely spectators. The Olympic stadium was open to wealth, merit, and ambition; and if the candidates could depend on their personal skill and activity, they might pursue the footsteps of Diomedes and Menelaus, and conduct their own horses in the rapid career. Ten, twenty, forty chariots, were allowed to start at the same instant; a crown of leaves was the reward of the victor, and his fame, with that of his family and country, was chanted in lyric strains more durable than monuments of brass and marble. But a senator, or even a citizen, conscious of his dignity, would have blushed to expose his person or his horse in the circus of Rome. The games were exhibited at the expense of the republic, the magistrates, or the emperors; but the reins were abandoned to servile hands; and if the profits of a favourite charioteer sometimes exceeded those of an advocate, they must be considered as the effects of popular extravagance, and the high wages of a disgraceful profession. The race, in its first institution, was a simple contest of two chariots, whose drivers were distinguished by *white* and *red* liveries: two additional colours, a light *green* and a cærulean *blue*, were afterwards introduced; and, as the races were repeated twenty-five times, one hundred chariots contributed in the same day to the pomp of the circus. The four *factions* soon acquired a legal establishment and a mysterious origin, and their fanciful colours were derived from the various appearances of nature in the four seasons of the year; the red dog-star of summer, the snows of winter, the deep shades of autumn, and the cheerful verdure of the spring. Another interpretation preferred the elements to the seasons, and the struggle of the green and blue was supposed to represent the conflict of the earth and sea. Their respective victories announced either a plentiful harvest or a prosperous navigation, and the hostility of the husbandmen and mariners was somewhat less absurd than the blind ardour of the Roman people, who devoted their lives and fortunes to the colour which they had espoused.

Such folly was disdained and indulged by the wisest princes; but the names of Caligula, Nero, Vitellius, Verus, Commodus, Caracalla, and Elagabalus, were enrolled in the blue or green factions of the circus: they frequented their stables, applauded their favourites, chastised their antagonists, and deserved the esteem of the populace by the natural or affected imitation of their manners. The bloody and tumultuous contest continued to disturb the public festivity till the last age of the spectacles of Rome; and Theodoric, from a motive of justice or affection, interposed his authority to protect the greens against the violence of a consul and a patrician who were passionately addicted to the blue faction of the circus.

Constantinople adopted the follies, though not the virtues, of ancient Rome; and the same factions which had agitated the circus raged with redoubled fury in the hippodrome. Under the reign of Anastasius, this popular frenzy was inflamed by religious zeal; and the greens, who had treacherously concealed stones and daggers under baskets of fruit, massacred at a solemn festival three thousand of their blue adversaries. From the capital this pestilence was diffused into the provinces and cities of the East, and the sportive distinction of two colours produced two strong and irreconcilable factions, which shook the foundations of a feeble government. The popular dissensions, founded on the most serious interest or holy pretence, have scarcely equalled the obstinacy of this wanton discord, which invaded the peace of families, divided friends and brothers, and tempted the female sex, though seldom seen in the circus, to espouse the inclinations of their lovers, or to contradict the wishes of their husbands. Every law, either human or divine, was trampled under foot; and as long as the party was successful, its deluded followers appeared careless of private distress or public calamity. The licence, without the freedom, of democracy, was revived at Antioch and Constantinople, and the support of a faction became necessary to every candidate for civil or ecclesiastical honours. A secret attachment to the family or sect of Anastasius was imputed to the greens; the blues were zealously devoted to the cause of orthodoxy and Justinian, and their grateful patron protected, above five years, the disorders of a faction whose seasonable tumults overawed the palace, the senate, and the capitals of the East. Insolent with royal favour, the blues affected to strike terror by a peculiar and barbaric dress—the long hair of the Huns, their close sleeves and ample garments, a lofty step, and a sonorous voice. In the day they concealed the two-edged poniards, but in the night they boldly assembled in arms and in numerous bands, prepared for every act of violence and rapine. Their adversaries of the green faction, or even inoffensive citizens, were stripped and often murdered by these nocturnal robbers, and it became dangerous to wear any gold buttons or girdles, or to appear at a late hour in the streets of a peaceful capital. A daring spirit, rising with impunity, proceeded to violate the safeguard of private houses; and fire was employed to facilitate the attack, or to conceal the crimes, of these factious rioters. No place was safe or sacred from their depredations; to gratify either avarice or revenge they profusely spilt the blood of the innocent; churches and altars were polluted by atrocious murders, and it was the boast of the assassins that their dexterity could always inflict a mortal wound with a single stroke of their dagger. The dissolute youth of Constantinople adopted the blue livery of disorder; the laws were silent, and the bonds of society were relaxed; creditors were compelled to resign their obligations; judges to reverse their sentences; masters to enfranchise their slaves; fathers to supply the extravagance of their children; noble matrons were prostituted to the lust of their servants; beautiful boys were torn from the arms of their parents; and wives, unless they preferred a voluntary death, were ravished in the presence of their husbands. The despair of the greens, who were persecuted by their enemies and deserted by the magistrate, assumed the privilege of defence, perhaps of retaliation; but those who survived the combat were dragged to execution, and the unhappy fugitives, escaping to woods and caverns, preyed without mercy on the society from whence they were expelled. Those ministers of justice who had courage to punish the crimes and to brave the resentment of the blues became the victims of their indiscreet zeal: a prefect of Constantinople fled for refuge to the holy sepulchre, a count of the East was ignominiously whipped, and a governor of Cilicia was hanged, by the order of Theodora, on the tomb of two assassins whom he had condemned for the murder of his groom, and a daring attack upon his own life. An aspiring candidate may be tempted to build his greatness on the public confusion, but it is the interest as well as duty of a sovereign to maintain the authority of the laws. The first edict of Justinian, which was often repeated and sometimes executed, announced his firm resolution to support the innocent, and to chastise the guilty, of every denomination and *colour*. Yet the balance of justice was still inclined in favour of the blue faction, by the secret affection, the habits, and the fears of the emperor; his equity, after an apparent struggle, submitted without reluctance to the implacable passions of Theodora, and the empress never forgot or forgave the injuries of the comedian. At the accession of the younger Justin, the proclamation of equal and rigorous justice indirectly condemned the partiality of the former reign. "Ye blues, Justinian is no more! ye greens, he is still alive!"

A sedition, which almost laid Constantinople in ashes, was excited by the mutual hatred and momentary reconciliation of the two factions.[1] In the fifth year of his reign Justinian celebrated the festival of the ides of January: the games were incessantly disturbed by the clamorous discontent of the greens; till the twenty-second race the emperor maintained his silent gravity; at length, yielding to his impatience, he condescended to hold, in abrupt sentences, and by the voice of a crier, the most singular dialogue that ever passed between a prince and his subjects. Their first complaints were respectful and modest; they accused the subordinate ministers of oppression, and proclaimed their wishes for the long life and victory of the emperor. "Be patient and attentive, ye insolent railers!" exclaimed Justinian; "be mute, ye Jews, Samaritans, and Manichæans!" The greens still attempted to awaken his compassion. "We are poor, we are innocent, we are injured, we dare not pass through the streets: a general persecution is exercised against our name and colour. Let us die, O emperor! but let us die by your command, and for your service!" But the repetition of partial and passionate invectives degraded, in their eyes, the majesty of the purple; they renounced allegiance to the prince who refused justice to his people, lamented that the father of Justinian had been born, and branded his son with the opprobrious names of an homicide, an ass, and a perjured tyrant. "Do you despise

[1] The real cause of the *Nika* riots was resentment at the extortions of Justinian's reckless administration. Gibbon does not bring this out nor was he aware that the factions of the Circus were in fact the atrophied demes or parishes of the city. They were therefore to some extent still the constitutional means of communication between the people and the emperor.—D.M.L.

your lives?" cried the indignant monarch. The blues rose with fury from their seats, their hostile clamours thundered in the hippodrome, and their adversaries, deserting the unequal contest, spread terror and despair through the streets of Constantinople. At this dangerous moment, seven notorious assassins of both factions, who had been condemned by the prefect, were carried round the city, and afterwards transported to the place of execution in the suburb of Pera. Four were immediately beheaded; a fifth was hanged; but, when the same punishment was inflicted on the remaining two, the rope broke, they fell alive to the ground, the populace applauded their escape, and the monks of St. Conon, issuing from the neighbouring convent, conveyed them in a boat to the sanctuary of the church. As one of these criminals was of the blue, and the other of the green, livery, the two factions were equally provoked by the cruelty of their oppressor or the ingratitude of their patron, and a short truce was concluded till they had delivered their prisoners and satisfied their revenge. The palace of the prefect, who withstood the seditious torrent, was instantly burnt, his officers and guards were massacred, the prisons were forced open, and freedom was restored to those who could use it for the public destruction. A military force which had been despatched to the aid of the civil magistrate was fiercely encountered by an armed multitude, whose numbers and boldness continually increased: and the Heruli, the wildest barbarians in the service of the empire, overturned the priests and their relics, which, from a pious motive, had been rashly interposed to separate the bloody conflict. The tumult was exasperated by this sacrilege; the people fought with enthusiasm in the cause of God; the women, from the roofs and windows, showered stones on the heads of the soldiers, who darted firebrands against the houses; and the various flames, which had been kindled by the hands of citizens and strangers, spread without control over the face of the city. The conflagration involved the cathedral of St. Sophia, the baths of Zeuxippus, a part of the palace from the first entrance to the altar of Mars, and the long portico from the palace to the forum of Constantine: a large hospital, with the sick patients, was consumed; many churches and stately edifices were destroyed; and an immense treasure of gold and silver was either melted or lost. From such scenes of horror and distress the wise and wealthy citizens escaped over the Bosphorus to the Asiatic side, and during five days Constantinople was abandoned to the factions, whose watchword, NIKA, *vanquish!* has given a name to this memorable sedition.

As long as the factions were divided, the triumphant blues and desponding greens appeared to behold with the same indifference the disorders of the state. They agreed to censure the corrupt management of justice and the finance; and the two responsible ministers, the artful Tribonian and the rapacious John of Cappadocia, were loudly arraigned as the authors of the public misery. The peaceful murmurs of the people would have been disregarded: they were heard with respect when the city was in flames; the quæstor and the prefect were instantly removed, and their offices were filled by two senators of blameless integrity. After this popular concession Justinian proceeded to the hippodrome to confess his own errors, and to accept the repentance of his grateful subjects; but they distrusted his assurances, though solemnly pronounced in the presence of the holy gospels; and the emperor, alarmed by their distrust, retreated with precipitation to the strong fortress of the palace. The obstinacy of the tumult was now imputed to a secret and ambitious conspiracy, and a suspicion was entertained that the insurgents, more especially the green faction, had been supplied with arms and money by Hypatius and Pompey, two patricians who could neither forget with honour, nor remember with safety, that they were the nephews of the emperor Anastasius. Capriciously trusted, disgraced, and pardoned by the jealous levity of the monarch, they had appeared as loyal servants before the throne, and, during five days of the tumult, they were detained as important hostages; till at length, the fears of Justinian prevailing over his prudence, he viewed the two brothers in the light of spies, perhaps of assassins, and sternly commanded them to depart from the palace. After a fruitless representation that obedience might lead to involuntary treason, they retired to their houses, and in the morning of the sixth day Hypatius was surrounded and seized by the people, who, regardless of his virtuous resistance and the tears of his wife, transported their favourite to the forum of Constantine, and, instead of a diadem, placed a rich collar on his head. If the usurper, who afterwards pleaded the merit of his delay, had complied with the advice of his senate, and urged the fury of the multitude, their first irresistible effort might have oppressed or expelled his trembling competitor. The Byzantine palace enjoyed a free communication with the sea, vessels lay ready at the garden-stairs, and a secret resolution was already formed to convey the emperor with his family and treasures to a safe retreat at some distance from the capital.

Justinian was lost, if the prostitute whom he raised from the theatre had not renounced the timidity as well as the virtues of her sex. In the midst of a council where Belisarius was present, Theodora alone displayed the spirit of an hero, and she alone, without apprehending his future hatred, could save the emperor from the imminent danger and his un-worthy fears. "If flight," said the consort of Justinian, "were the only means of safety, yet I should disdain to fly. Death is the condition of our birth, but they who have reigned should never survive the loss of dignity and dominion. I implore Heaven that I may never be seen, not a day, without my diadem and purple; that I may no longer behold the light when I cease to be saluted with the name of queen. If you resolve, O Cæsar! to fly, you have treasures; behold the sea, you have ships; but tremble lest the desire of life should expose you to wretched exile and ignominious death. For my own part, I adhere to the maxim of antiquity, that the throne is a glori-ous sepulchre." The firmness of a woman restored the courage to deliberate and act, and courage soon discovers the resources of the most desperate situation. It was an easy and a decisive measure to revive the animosity of the factions; the blues were astonished at their own guilt and folly, that a trifling injury should provoke them to conspire with their implacable enemies against a gracious and liberal benefactor; they again proclaimed the majesty of Justinian; and the greens, with their upstart emperor, were left alone in the hippodrome. The fidelity of the guards was doubtful; but the military force of Justinian consisted in three thousand veterans, who had been trained to valour and discipline in the Persian and Illyrian wars. Under the command of Belisarius and Mundus, they silently marched in two divisions from the palace, forced their obscure way through narrow passages, expiring flames, and falling edifices, and burst open at the same moment the two opposite gates of the hippodrome. In this narrow space the disorderly and affrighted crowd was incapable of resisting on either side a firm and regular attack; the blues signalised the fury of their repentance, and it is computed that above thirty thousand persons were slain in the merciless and promiscuous carnage of the day. Hypatius was dragged from his throne, and conducted with his brother Pompey to the feet of the emperor; they implored his clemency, but their crime was manifest, their innocence uncertain, and Justinian had been too much terrified to forgive. The next morning the two nephews of Anastasius, with eighteen *illustrious* accomplices, of patrician or consular rank, were privately executed by the soldiers, their bodies were thrown into the sea, their palaces razed, and their fortunes confiscated. The hippodrome itself was condemned, during several years, to a mournful silence; with the restoration of the games the same disorders revived, and the blue and green factions continued to afflict the reign of Justinian, and to disturb the tranquillity of the Eastern empire.

IMPORTATION OF SILK FROM CHINA

That empire, after Rome was barbarous, still embraced the nations whom she had conquered beyond the Adriatic, and as far as the frontiers of Ethiopia and Persia. Justinian reigned over sixty-four provinces and nine hundred and thirty-five cities; his dominions were blessed by nature with the advantages of soil, situation, and climate, and the improvements of human art had been perpetually diffused along the coast of the Mediterranean and the banks of the Nile from ancient Troy to the Egyptian Thebes. Abraham had been relieved by the well-known plenty of Egypt; the same country, a small and populous tract, was still capable of exporting each year two hundred and sixty thousand quarters of wheat for the use of Constantinople; and the capital of Justinian was supplied with the manufactures of Sidon fifteen centuries after they had been celebrated in the poems of Homer. The annual powers of vegetation, instead of being exhausted by two thousand harvests, were renewed and invigorated by skilful husbandry, rich manure, and seasonable repose. The breed of domestic animals was infinitely multiplied. Plantations, buildings, and the instruments of labour and luxury, which are more durable than the term of human life, were accumulated by the care of successive generations. Tradition preserved, and experience simplified, the humble practice of the arts; ...ty was enriched by the division of labour and the facility

of exchange; and every Roman was lodged, clothed, and subsisted by the industry of a thousand hands. The invention of
the loom and distaff has been piously ascribed to the gods.
In every age a variety of animal and vegetable productions,
hair, skins, wool, flax, cotton, and at length *silk*, have been
skilfully manufactured to hide or adorn the human body;
they were stained with an infusion of permanent colours, and
the pencil was successfully employed to improve the labours
of the loom. In the choice of those colours which imitate the
beauties of nature, the freedom of taste and fashion was indulged; but the deep purple which the Phœnicians extracted
from a shell-fish was restrained to the sacred person and
palace of the emperor, and the penalties of treason were denounced against the ambitious subjects who dared to usurp
the prerogative of the throne.

I need not explain that *silk* [1] is originally spun from the
bowels of a caterpillar, and that it composes the golden tomb
from whence a worm emerges in the form of a butterfly. Till
the reign of Justinian, the silkworms who feed on the leaves
of the white mulberry-tree were confined to China; those of
the pine, the oak, and the ash were common in the forests
both of Asia and Europe; but as their education is more difficult, and their produce more uncertain, they were generally
neglected, except in the little island of Ceos, near the coast
of Attica. A thin gauze was procured from their webs, and
this Cean manufacture, the invention of a woman, for female
use, was long admired both in the East and at Rome. Whatever suspicions may be raised by the garments of the Medes
and Assyrians, Virgil is the most ancient writer who expressly mentions the soft wool which was combed from the trees
of the Seres or Chinese; and this natural error, less marvellous
than the truth, was slowly corrected by the knowledge of a
valuable insect, the first artificer of the luxury of nations.
That rare and elegant luxury was censured, in the reign of
Tiberius, by the gravest of the Romans; and Pliny, in affected
though forcible language, has condemned the thirst of gain,
which explored the last confines of the earth for the pernicious

---

[1] In the history of insects (far more wonderful than Ovid's Metamorphoses)
the silkworm holds a conspicuous place. The bombyx of the isle of Ceos, as
described by Pliny, may be illustrated by a similar species in China; but
our silkworm, as well as the white mulberry-tree, was unknown to
Theophrastus and Pliny. [Gibbon has confused Cos with Ceos. Aristotle was
the first Greek writer to mention silk. It is probable that raw silk was brought
from Asia to Cos and there manufactured.—D.M.L.]

purpose of exposing to the public eye naked draperies and transparent matrons. A dress which showed the turn of the limbs and colour of the skin might gratify vanity or provoke desire; the silks which had been closely woven in China were sometimes unravelled by the Phœnician women, and the precious materials were multiplied by a looser texture, and the intermixture of linen threads. Two hundred years after the age of Pliny the use of pure or even of mixed silks was confined to the female sex, till the opulent citizens of Rome and the provinces were insensibly familiarised with the example of Elagabalus, the first who, by this effeminate habit, had sullied the dignity of an emperor and a man. Aurelian complained that a pound of silk was sold at Rome for twelve ounces of gold; but the supply increased with the demand, and the price diminished with the supply. If accident or monopoly sometimes raised the value even above the standard of Aurelian, the manufacturers of Tyre and Berytus were sometimes compelled, by the operation of the same causes, to content themselves with a ninth part of that extravagant rate. A law was thought necessary to discriminate the dress of comedians from that of senators, and of the silk exported from its native country the far greater part was consumed by the subjects of Justinian. They were still more intimately acquainted with a shell-fish of the Mediterranean, surnamed the silkworm of the sea: the fine wool or hair by which the mother-of-pearl affixes itself to the rock is now manufactured for curiosity rather than use; and a robe obtained from the same singular materials was the gift of the Roman emperor to the satraps of Armenia.

A valuable merchandise of small bulk is capable of defraying the expense of land-carriage, and the caravans traversed the whole latitude of Asia in two hundred and forty-three days from the Chinese ocean to the sea-coast of Syria. Silk was immediately delivered to the Romans by the Persian merchants, who frequented the fairs of Armenia and Nisibis; but this trade, which in the intervals of truce was oppressed by avarice and jealousy, was totally interrupted by the long wars of the rival monarchies. The Great King might proudly number Sogdiana, and even *Serica*, among the provinces of his empire, but his real dominion was bounded by the Oxus, and his useful intercourse with the Sogdoites, beyond the river, depended on the pleasure of their conquerors, the white Huns and the Turks, who successively reigned over that industrious people. Yet the most savage dominion has not extirpated the seeds of agriculture and commerce in a region which is celebrated as one of the four gardens of Asia; the cities of Samarcand and Bochara are advantageously seated for the exchange of its various productions, and their merchants purchased from the Chinese [1] the raw or manufactured silk which they transported into Persia for the use of the Roman empire. In the vain capital of China the Sogdian caravans were entertained as the suppliant embassies of tributary kingdoms, and, if they returned in safety, the bold adventure was rewarded with exorbitant gain. But the difficult and perilous march from Samarcand to the first town of Shensi could not be performed in less than sixty, eighty, or one hundred days; as soon as they had passed the Jaxartes they entered the desert, and the wandering hordes, unless they are restrained by armies and garrisons, have always considered the citizen and the traveller as the objects of lawful rapine. To escape the Tartar robbers and the tyrants of Persia, the silk-caravans explored a more southern road: they traversed the mountains of Thibet, descended the streams of the Ganges or the Indus, and patiently expected, in the ports of Guzerat and Malabar, the annual fleets of the West.[2] But the dangers of the desert were found less intolerable than toil, hunger, and the loss of time; the attempt was seldom renewed, and the only European who has passed that unfrequented way applauds his own diligence that, in nine months after his departure from Pekin, he reached the mouth of the Indus. The ocean, however, was open to the free communication of mankind. From the great river to the tropic of Cancer the provinces of China were subdued and civilised by the emperors of the North; they were filled about the time of the Christian era with cities and men, mulberry-trees and their precious inhabitants; and if the Chinese, with the knowledge of the compass, had pos-

---

[1] The blind admiration of the Jesuits confounds the different periods of the Chinese history. They are more critically distinguished by M. de Guignes, who discovers the gradual progress of the truth of the annals and the extent of the monarchy, till the Christian era. He has searched with a curious eye the connexions of the Chinese with the nations of the West; but these connexions are slight, casual, and obscure; nor did the Romans entertain a suspicion that the Seres or Sinæ possessed an empire not inferior to their own.

[2] The roads from China to Persia and Hindostan may be investigated in the relations of Hackluyt and Thevenot. A communication through Thibet has been lately explored by the English sovereigns of Bengal.

sessed the genius of the Greeks or Phœnicians, they might have spread their discoveries over the southern hemisphere. I am not qualified to examine, and I am not disposed to believe, their distant voyages to the Persian Gulf or the Cape of Good Hope; but their ancestors might equal the labours and success of the present race, and the sphere of their navigation might extend from the isles of Japan to the straits of Malacca, the Pillars, if we may apply that name, of an Oriental Hercules. Without losing sight of land, they might sail along the coast to the extreme promontory of Achin, which is annually visited by ten or twelve ships laden with the productions, the manufactures, and even the artificers of China; the island of Sumatra and the opposite peninsula are faintly delineated as the regions of gold and silver, and the trading cities named in the geography of Ptolemy may indicate that this wealth was not solely derived from the mines. The direct interval between Sumatra and Ceylon is about three hundred leagues; the Chinese and Indian navigators were conducted by the flight of birds and periodical winds, and the ocean might be securely traversed in square-built ships, which instead of iron, were sewed together with the strong thread of the cocoa-nut. Ceylon, Serendib, or Taprobana was divided between two hostile princes, one of whom possessed the mountains, the elephants, and the luminous carbuncle, and the other enjoyed the more solid riches of domestic industry, foreign trade, and the capacious harbour of Trinquemale, which received and dismissed the fleets of the East and West. In this hospitable isle, at an equal distance (as it was computed) from their respective countries, the silk-merchants of China, who had collected in their voyages aloes, cloves, nutmeg, and sandal-wood, maintained a free and beneficial commerce with the inhabitants of the Persian Gulf. The subjects of the Great King exalted, without a rival, his power and magnificence; and the Roman, who confounded their vanity by comparing his paltry coin with a gold medal of the emperor Anastasius, had sailed to Ceylon, in an Ethiopian ship, as a simple passenger.

As silk became of indispensable use, the emperor Justinian saw with concern that the Persians had occupied by land and sea the monopoly of this important supply, and that the wealth of his subjects was continually drained by a nation of enemies and idolaters. An active government would have restored the trade of Egypt and the navigation of the Red Sea, which had decayed with the prosperity of the empire; and the Roman vessels might have sailed for the purchase of silk to the ports of Ceylon, of Malacca, or even of China. Justinian embraced a more humble expedient, and solicited the aid of his Christian allies, the Ethiopians of Abyssinia, who had recently acquired the arts of navigation, the spirit of trade, and the seaport of Adulis, still decorated with the trophies of a Grecian conqueror. Along the African coast they penetrated to the equator in search of gold, emeralds, and aromatics; but they wisely declined an unequal competition, in which they must be always prevented by the vicinity of the Persians to the markets of India: and the emperor submitted to the disappointment till his wishes were gratified by an unexpected event. The Gospel had been preached to the Indians: a bishop already governed the Christians of St. Thomas on the pepper-coast of Malabar; a church was planted in Ceylon, and the missionaries pursued the footsteps of commerce to the extremities of Asia. Two Persian monks had long resided in China, perhaps in the royal city of Nankin, the seat of a monarch addicted to foreign superstitions, and who actually received an embassy from the isle of Ceylon. Amidst their pious occupations they viewed with a curious eye the common dress of the Chinese, the manufactures of silk, and the myriads of silkworms, whose education (either on trees or in houses) had once been considered as the labour of queens. They soon discovered that it was impracticable to transport the short-lived insect, but that in the eggs a numerous progeny might be preserved and multiplied in a distant climate. Religion or interest had more power over the Persian monks than the love of their country: after a long journey they arrived at Constantinople, imparted their project to the emperor, and were liberally encouraged by the gifts and promises of Justinian. To the historians of that prince a campaign at the foot of Mount Caucasus has seemed more deserving of a minute relation than the labours of these missionaries of commerce, who again entered China, deceived a jealous people by concealing the eggs of the silkworm in a hollow cane, and returned in triumph with the spoils of the East. Under their direction the eggs were hatched at the proper season by the artificial heat of dung; the worms were fed with mulberry-leaves; they lived and laboured in a foreign climate; a sufficient number of butterflies was saved to propagate the race, and trees were planted to supply the nourishment of the rising generations. Experience and reflection corrected the errors of a new attempt, and the Sogdoite ambassadors acknowledged in the succeeding reign that the Romans were not inferior to the natives of China in the education of the insects and the manufactures of silk, in which both China and Constantinople have been surpassed by the industry of modern Europe. I am not insensible of the benefits of elegant luxury; yet I reflect with some pain that if the importers of silk had introduced the art of printing, already practised by the Chinese, the comedies of Menander and the entire decads of Livy would have been perpetuated in the editions of the sixth century. A larger view of the globe might at least have promoted the improvement of speculative science; but the Christian geography was forcibly extracted from texts of Scripture, and the study of nature was the surest symptom of an unbelieving mind. The orthodox faith confined the habitable world to *one* temperate zone, and represented the earth as an oblong surface, four hundred days' journey in length, two hundred in breadth, encompassed by the ocean and covered by the solid crystal of the firmament.

*   *   *   *   *

THE CHURCH OF ST. SOPHIA

The *edifices* of Justinian were cemented with the blood and treasure of his people; but those stately structures appeared to announce the prosperity of the empire, and actually displayed the skill of their architects. Both the theory and practice of the arts which depend on mathematical science and mechanical power were cultivated under the patronage of the emperors; the fame of Archimedes was rivalled by Proclus and Anthemius; and if their *miracles* had been related by intelligent spectators, they might now enlarge the speculations, instead of exciting the distrust, of philosophers. A tradition has prevailed that the Roman fleet was reduced to ashes in the port of Syracuse by the burning-glasses of Archimedes; and it is asserted that a similar expedient was employed by Proclus to destroy the Gothic vessels in the harbour of Constantinople, and to protect his benefactor Anastasius against the bold enterprise of Vitalian. A machine was fixed on the walls of the city, consisting of an hexagon mirror of polished brass, with many smaller and moveable polygons to receive and reflect the rays of the meridian sun; and a consuming flame was darted, to the distance, perhaps, of two hundred feet. The truth of these two extraordinary facts is invalidated by the silence of the most authentic historians; and the use of burning-glasses was never adopted in the attack or defence of places. Yet the admirable experiments of a French philosopher have demonstrated the possibility of such a mirror; and, since it is possible, I am more disposed to attribute the art to the greatest mathematicians of antiquity, than to give the merit of the fiction to the idle fancy of a monk or a sophist. According to another story, Proclus applied sulphur to the destruction of the Gothic fleet; in a modern imagination, the name of sulphur is instantly connected with the suspicion of gunpowder, and that suspicion is propagated by the secret arts of his disciple Anthemius. A citizen of Tralles in Asia had five sons, who were all distinguished in their respective professions by merit and success. Olympius excelled in the knowledge and practice of the Roman jurisprudence. Dioscorus and Alexander became learned physicians; but the skill of the former was exercised for the benefit of his fellow-citizens, while his more ambitious brother acquired wealth and reputation at Rome. The fame of Metrodorus the grammarian, and of Anthemius the mathematician and architect, reached the ears of the emperor Justinian, who invited them to Constantinople; and while the one instructed the rising generation in the schools of eloquence, the other filled the capital and provinces with more lasting monuments of his art. In a trifling dispute relative to the walls or windows of their contiguous houses, he had been vanquished by the eloquence of his neighbour Zeno; but the orator was defeated in his turn by the master of mechanics, whose malicious, though harmless, stratagems are darkly represented by the ignorance of Agathias. In a lower room, Anthemius arranged several vessels or caldrons of water, each of them covered by the wide bottom of a leathern tube, which rose to a narrow top, and was artificially conveyed among the joists and rafters of the adjacent building. A fire was kindled beneath the caldron; the steam of the boiling water ascended through the tubes; the house was shaken by the efforts of imprisoned air, and its trembling inhabitants might wonder that the city was unconscious of the earthquake which they had felt. At another time, the friends of Zeno, as they sat at table, were dazzled by the intolerable light which flashed in their eyes from the reflecting mirrors of Anthemius; they were astonished by the noise which he produced from the collision of certain minute and sonorous particles; and the orator declared in tragic style to the senate, that a mere mortal must yield to the power of an antagonist who shook the earth with the trident of Neptune, and imitated the thunder and lightning of Jove himself. The genius of Anthemius, and his colleague Isidore the Milesian, was excited and employed by a prince whose taste for architecture had degenerated into a mischievous and costly passion. His favourite architects submitted their designs and difficulties to Justinian, and discreetly confessed how much their laborious meditations were surpassed by the intuitive knowledge or celestial inspiration of an emperor whose views were always directed to the benefit of his people, the glory of his reign, and the salvation of his soul.

The principal church, which was dedicated by the founder of Constantinople to Saint Sophia, or the eternal wisdom, had been twice destroyed by fire; after the exile of John Chrysostom, and during the *Nika* of the blue and green factions. No sooner did the tumult subside than the Christian populace deplored their sacrilegious rashness; but they might have rejoiced in the calamity, had they foreseen the glory of the new temple, which at the end of forty days was strenuously undertaken by the piety of Justinian. The ruins were cleared away, a more spacious plan was described, and, as it required the consent of some proprietors of ground, they obtained the most exorbitant terms from the eager desires and timorous conscience of the monarch. Anthemius formed the design, and his genius directed the hands of ten thousand workmen, whose payment in pieces of fine silver was never delayed beyond the evening. The emperor himself, clad in a linen tunic, surveyed each day their rapid progress, and encouraged their diligence by his familiarity, his zeal, and his rewards. The new cathedral of St. Sophia was consecrated by the patriarch, five years, eleven months, and ten days from the first foundation; and in the midst of the solemn festival Justinian exclaimed with devout vanity, "Glory be to God, who hath thought me worthy to accomplish so great a work;

I have vanquished thee, O Solomon!" But the pride of the
Roman Solomon, before twenty years had elapsed, was humbled by an earthquake, which overthrew the eastern part of
the dome. Its splendour was again restored by the perseverance
of the same prince; and in the thirty-sixth year of his reign
Justinian celebrated the second dedication of a temple which
remains, after twelve centuries, a stately monument of his
fame. The architecture of St. Sophia, which is now converted
into the principal mosque, has been imitated by the Turkish
sultans, and that venerable pile continues to excite the fond
admiration of the Greeks, and the more rational curiosity of
European travellers. The eye of the spectator is disappointed
by an irregular prospect of half-domes and shelving roofs:
the western front, the principal approach, is destitute of
simplicity and magnificence; and the scale of dimensions has
been much surpassed by several of the Latin cathedrals. But
the architect who first erected an *aërial* cupola is entitled to
the praise of bold design and skilful execution. The dome of
St. Sophia, illuminated by four-and-twenty windows, is formed
with so small a curve, that the depth is equal only to one-
sixth of its diameter; the measure of that diameter is one
hundred and fifteen feet, and the lofty centre, where a crescent
has supplanted the cross, rises to the perpendicular height of
one hundred and eighty feet above the pavement. The circle
which encompasses the dome lightly reposes on four strong
arches, and their weight is firmly supported by four massy
piles, whose strength is assisted on the northern and southern
sides by four columns of Egyptian granite. A Greek cross,
inscribed in a quadrangle, represents the form of the edifice;
the exact breadth is two hundred and forty-three feet, and
two hundred and sixty-nine may be assigned for the extreme
length, from the sanctuary in the east to the nine western
doors which open into the vestibule, and from thence into
the *narthex* or exterior portico. That portico was the humble
station of the penitents. The nave or body of the church was
filled by the congregation of the faithful; but the two sexes
were prudently distinguished, and the upper and lower galleries were allotted for the more private devotion of the
women. Beyond the northern and southern piles, a balustrade,
terminated on either side by the thrones of the emperor and
the patriarch, divided the nave from the choir; and the space,
as far as the steps of the altar, was occupied by the clergy

and singers. The altar itself, a name which insensibly became familiar to Christian ears, was placed in the eastern recess, artificially built in the form of a demicylinder; and this sanctuary communicated by several doors with the sacristy, the vestry, the baptistery, and the contiguous buildings, subservient either to the pomp of worship, or the private use of the ecclesiastical ministers. The memory of past calamities inspired Justinian with a wise resolution, that no wood, except for the doors, should be admitted into the new edifice; and the choice of the materials was applied to the strength, the lightness, or the splendour of the respective parts. The solid piles which sustained the cupola were composed of huge blocks of freestone, hewn into squares and triangles, fortified by circles of iron, and firmly cemented by the infusion of lead and quicklime; but the weight of the cupola was diminished by the levity of its substance, which consists either of pumice-stone that floats in the water, or of brick, from the isle of Rhodes, five times less ponderous than the ordinary sort. The whole frame of the edifice was constructed of brick; but those base materials were concealed by a crust of marble; and the inside of St. Sophia, the cupola, the two larger and the six smaller semidomes, the walls, the hundred columns, and the pavement, delight even the eyes of barbarians with a rich and variegated picture.

A poet, who beheld the primitive lustre of St. Sophia, enumerates the colours, the shades, and the spots of ten or twelve marbles, jaspers, and porphyries, which nature had profusely diversified, and which were blended and contrasted as it were by a skilful painter. The triumph of Christ was adorned with the last spoils of Paganism, but the greater part of these costly stones was extracted from the quarries of Asia Minor, the isles and continent of Greece, Egypt, Africa, and Gaul. Eight columns of porphyry, which Aurelian had placed in the Temple of the Sun, were offered by the piety of a Roman matron; eight others of green marble were presented by the ambitious zeal of the magistrates of Ephesus: both are admirable by their size and beauty, but every order of architecture disclaims their fantastic capitals. A variety of ornaments and figures was curiously expressed in mosaic; and the images of Christ, of the Virgin, of saints, and of angels, which have been defaced by Turkish fanaticism, were dangerously exposed to the superstition of the Greeks. According to the sanctity of each object, the precious metals were distributed in thin leaves or in solid masses. The balustrade of the choir, the capitals of the pillars, the ornaments of the doors and galleries, were of gilt bronze. The spectator was dazzled by the glittering aspect of the cupola. The sanctuary contained forty thousand pound weight of silver, and the holy vases and vestments of the altar were of the purest gold, enriched with inestimable gems. Before the structure of the church had arisen two cubits above the ground, forty-five thousand two hundred pounds were already consumed, and the whole expense amounted to three hundred and twenty thousand. Each reader, according to the measure of his belief, may estimate their value either in gold or silver; but the sum of one million sterling is the result of the lowest computation. A magnificent temple is a laudable monument of national taste and religion, and the enthusiast who entered the dome of St. Sophia might be tempted to suppose that it was the residence, or even the workmanship, of the Deity. Yet how dull is the artifice, how insignificant is the labour, if it be compared with the formation of the vilest insect that crawls upon the surface of the temple!

So minute a description of an edifice which time has respected may attest the truth and excuse the relation of the innumerable works, both in the capital and provinces, which Justinian constructed on a smaller scale and less durable foundations. In Constantinople alone, and the adjacent suburbs, he dedicated twenty-five churches to the honour of Christ, the Virgin, and the saints. Most of these churches were decorated with marble and gold; and their various situation was skilfully chosen in a populous square or a pleasant grove, on the margin of the sea-shore, or on some lofty eminence which overlooked the continents of Europe and Asia. The church of the Holy Apostles at Constantinople, and that of St. John at Ephesus, appear to have been framed on the same model: their domes aspired to imitate the cupolas of St. Sophia, but the altar was more judiciously placed under the centre of the dome, at the junction of four stately porticoes, which more accurately expressed the figure of the Greek cross. The Virgin of Jerusalem might exult in the temple erected by her imperial votary on a most ungrateful spot, which afforded neither ground nor materials to the architect. A level was formed by raising part of a deep valley to the height of the mountain. The stones of a neighbouring quarry were hewn into regular forms; each block was fixed on a peculiar carriage drawn by forty of the strongest oxen, and the roads were widened for the passage of such enormous weights. Lebanon furnished her loftiest cedars for the timbers of the church; and the seasonable discovery of a vein of red marble supplied its beautiful columns, two of which, the supporters of the exterior portico, were esteemed the largest in the world. The pious munificence of the emperor was diffused over the Holy Land; and if reason should condemn the monasteries of both sexes which were built or restored by Justinian, yet charity must applaud the wells which he sunk, and the hospitals which he founded, for the relief of the weary pilgrims. The schismatical temper of Egypt was ill entitled to the royal bounty; but in Syria and Africa some remedies were applied to the disasters of wars and earthquakes, and both Carthage and Antioch, emerging from their ruins, might revere the name of their gracious benefactor. Almost every saint in the calendar acquired the honours of a temple—almost every city of the empire obtained the solid advantages of bridges, hospitals, and aqueducts; but the severe liberality of the monarch disdained to indulge his subjects in the popular luxury of baths and theatres. While Justinian laboured for the public service, he was not unmindful of his own dignity and ease. The Byzantine palace, which had been damaged by the conflagration, was restored with new magnificence; and some notion may be conceived of the whole edifice by the vestibule or hall, which, from the doors perhaps, or the roof, was surnamed *chalce*, or the brazen. The dome of a spacious quadrangle was supported by massy pillars; the pavement and walls were incrusted with many-coloured marbles—the emerald green of Laconia, the fiery red, and the white Phrygian stone, intersected with veins of a sea-green hue. The mosaic paintings of the dome and sides represented the glories of the African and Italian triumphs. On the Asiatic shore of the Propontis, at a small distance to the east of Chalcedon, the costly palace and gardens of Heræum were prepared for the summer residence of Justinian, and more especially of Theodora. The poets of the age have celebrated the rare alliance of nature and art, the harmony of the nymphs of the groves, the fountains and the waves; yet the crowd of attendants who followed the court complained of their inconvenient lodgings, and the nymphs were too often alarmed by the famous Porphyrio, a whale of ten cubits in breadth and thirty in length, who was stranded at the mouth of the river Sangaris after he had infested more than half a century the seas of Constantinople.

*   *   *   *   *

SUPPRESSION OF THE SCHOOLS OF ATHENS

Justinian suppressed the schools of Athens and the consulship of Rome, which had given so many sages and heroes to mankind. Both these institutions had long since degenerated from their primitive glory, yet some reproach may be justly inflicted on the avarice and jealousy of a prince by whose hand such venerable ruins were destroyed.

Athens, after her Persian triumphs, adopted the philosophy of Ionia and the rhetoric of Sicily; and these studies became the patrimony of a city whose inhabitants, about thirty thousand males, condensed, within the period of a single life, the genius of ages and millions. Our sense of the dignity of human nature is exalted by the simple recollection that Isocrates was the companion of Plato and Xenophon; that he assisted, perhaps with the historian Thucydides, at the first representations of the Œdipus of Sophocles and the Iphigenia of Euripides; and that his pupils Æschines and Demosthenes contended for the crown of patriotism in the presence of Aristotle, the master of Theophrastus, who taught at Athens with the founders of the Stoic and Epicurean sects. The ingenuous youth of Attica enjoyed the benefits of their domestic education, which was communicated without envy to the rival cities. Two thousand disciples heard the lessons of Theophrastus; the schools of rhetoric must have been still more populous than those of philosophy; and a rapid succession of students diffused the fame of their teachers as far as the utmost limits of the Grecian language and name. Those limits were enlarged by the victories of Alexander; the arts of Athens survived her freedom and dominion; and the Greek colonies which the Macedonians planted in Egypt, and scattered over Asia, undertook long and frequent pilgrimages to worship the Muses in their favourite temple on the banks of the Ilissus. The Latin conquerors respectfully listened to the instructions of their subjects and captives; the names of Cicero and Horace were enrolled in the schools of Athens; and after the perfect settlement of the Roman empire, the natives of Italy, of Africa, and of Britain, conversed in the groves of the Academy with their fellow-students of the East. The studies of philosophy and eloquence are congenial to a popular state, which encourages the freedom of inquiry, and submits only to the force of persuasion. In the republics of Greece and Rome the art of speaking was the powerful engine of patriotism or ambition; and the schools of rhetoric poured forth a colony of statesmen and legislators. When the liberty of public debate was suppressed, the orator, in the honourable profession of an advocate, might plead the cause of innocence and justice; he might abuse his talents in the more profitable trade of panegyric; and the same precepts continued to dictate the fanciful declamations of the sophist, and the chaster beauties of historical composition. The systems which professed to unfold the nature of God, of man, and of the universe, entertained the curiosity of the philosophic student; and according to the temper of his mind, he might doubt with the Sceptics, or decide with the Stoics, sublimely speculate with Plato, or severely argue with Aristotle. The pride of the adverse sects had fixed an unattainable term of moral happiness and perfection: but the race was glorious and salutary; the disciples of Zeno, and even those of Epicurus, were taught both to act and to suffer; and the death of Petronius was not less effectual than that of Seneca to humble a tyrant by the discovery of his impotence. The light of science could not indeed be confined within the walls of Athens. Her incomparable writers address themselves to the human race; the living masters emigrated to Italy and Asia; Berytus, in later times, was devoted to the study of the law; astronomy and physic were cultivated in the musæum of Alexandria; but the Attic schools of rhetoric and philosophy maintained their superior reputation from the Peloponnesian war to the reign of Justinian. Athens, though situate in a barren soil, possessed a pure air, a free navigation, and the monuments of ancient art. That sacred retirement was seldom disturbed by the business of trade or government; and the last of the Athenians were distinguished by their wit, the purity of their taste and language, their social manners, and some traces, at least in discourse, of the magnanimity of their fathers. In the suburbs of the city, the *Academy* of the Platonists, the *Ly-*

cæum of the Peripatetics, the *Portico* of the Stoics, and the *Garden* of the Epicureans, were planted with trees and decorated with statues; and the philosophers, instead of being immured in a cloister, delivered their instructions in spacious and pleasant walks, which, at different hours, were consecrated to the exercises of the mind and body. The genius of the founders still lived in those venerable seats; the ambition of succeeding to the masters of human reason excited a generous emulation; and the merit of the candidates was determined, on each vacancy, by the free voices of an enlightened people. The Athenian professors were paid by their disciples: according to their mutual wants and abilities, the price appears to have varied from a mina to a talent; and Isocrates himself, who derides the avarice of the sophists, required, in his school of rhetoric, about thirty pounds from each of his hundred pupils. The wages of industry are just and honourable, yet the same Isocrates shed tears at the first receipt of a stipend: the Stoic might blush when he was hired to preach the contempt of money; and I should be sorry to discover that Aristotle or Plato so far degenerated from the example of Socrates as to exchange knowledge for gold. But some property of lands and houses was settled, by the permission of the laws, and the legacies of deceased friends, on the philosophic chairs of Athens. Epicurus bequeathed to his disciples the gardens which he had purchased for eighty minæ or two hundred and fifty pounds, with a fund sufficient for their frugal subsistence and monthly festivals; and the patrimony of Plato afforded an annual rent, which, in eight centuries, was gradually increased from three to one thousand pieces of gold. The schools of Athens were protected by the wisest and most virtuous of the Roman princes. The library, which Hadrian founded, was placed in a portico adorned with pictures, statues, and a roof of alabaster, and supported by one hundred columns of Phrygian marble. The public salaries were assigned by the generous spirit of the Antonines; and each professor, of politics, of rhetoric, of the Platonic, the Peripatetic, the Stoic, and the Epicurean philosophy, received an annual stipend of ten thousand drachmæ, or more than three hundred pounds sterling. After the death of Marcus, these liberal donations, and the privileges attached to the *thrones* of science, were abolished and revived, diminished and enlarged; but some vestige of royal bounty may be

found under the successors of Constantine; and their arbitrary
choice of an unworthy candidate might tempt the philosophers of Athens to regret the days of independence and
poverty. It is remarkable that the impartial favour of the
Antonines was bestowed on the four adverse sects of philosophy, which they considered as equally useful, or at least
as equally innocent. Socrates had formerly been the glory and
the reproach of his country; and the first lessons of Epicurus
so strangely scandalised the pious ears of the Athenians,
that by his exile, and that of his antagonists, they silenced all
vain disputes concerning the nature of the gods. But in the
ensuing year they recalled the hasty decree, restored the
liberty of the schools, and were convinced by the experience
of ages that the moral character of philosophers is not
affected by the diversity of their theological speculations.

The Gothic arms were less fatal to the schools of Athens
than the establishment of a new religion, whose ministers
superseded the exercise of reason, resolved every question by
an article of faith, and condemned the infidel or sceptic to
eternal flames. In many a volume of laborious controversy
they exposed the weakness of the understanding and the
corruption of the heart, insulted human nature in the sages
of antiquity, and proscribed the spirit of philosophical inquiry, so repugnant to the doctrine, or at least to the temper,
of an humble believer. The surviving sect of the Platonists,
whom Plato would have blushed to acknowledge, extravagant-
ly mingled a sublime theory with the practice of superstition
and magic; and as they remained alone in the midst of a
Christian world, they indulged a secret rancour against the
government of the church and state, whose severity was still
suspended over their heads. About a century after the reign
of Julian, Proclus was permitted to teach in the philosophic
chair of the Academy; and such was his industry, that he
frequently, in the same day, pronounced five lessons, and
composed seven hundred lines. His sagacious mind explored
the deepest questions of morals and metaphysics, and he ventured to urge eighteen arguments against the Christian doctrine of the creation of the world. But in the intervals of
study he *personally* conversed with Pan, Æsculapius, and
Minerva, in whose mysteries he was secretly initiated, and
whose prostrate statues he adored; in the devout persuasion
that the philosopher, who is a citizen of the universe, should

be the priest of its various deities. An eclipse of the sun announced his approaching end; and his Life, with that of his scholar Isidore, compiled by two of their most learned disciples, exhibits a deplorable picture of the second childhood of human reason. Yet the golden chain, as it was fondly styled, of the Platonic succession, continued forty-four years from the death of Proclus to the edict of Justinian, which imposed a perpetual silence on the schools of Athens, and excited the grief and indignation of the few remaining votaries of Grecian science and superstition. Seven friends and philosophers, Diogenes and Hermias, Eulalius and Priscian, Damascius, Isidore, and Simplicius, who dissented from the religion of their sovereign, embraced the resolution of seeking in a foreign land the freedom which was denied in their native country. They had heard, and they credulously believed, that the republic of Plato was realised in the despotic government of Persia, and that a patriot king reigned over the happiest and most virtuous of nations. They were soon astonished by the natural discovery that Persia resembled the other countries of the globe; that Chosroes, who affected the name of a philosopher, was vain, cruel, and ambitious; that bigotry, and a spirit of intolerance, prevailed among the Magi; that the nobles were haughty, the courtiers servile, and the magistrates unjust; that the guilty sometimes escaped, and that the innocent were often oppressed. The disappointment of the philosophers provoked them to overlook the real virtues of the Persians; and they were scandalised, more deeply perhaps than became their profession, with the plurality of wives and concubines, the incestuous marriages, and the custom of exposing dead bodies to the dogs and vultures, instead of hiding them in the earth, or consuming them with fire. Their repentance was expressed by a precipitate return, and they loudly declared that they had rather die on the borders of the empire than enjoy the wealth and favour of the barbarian. From this journey, however, they derived a benefit which reflects the purest lustre on the character of Chosroes. He required that the seven sages who had visited the court of Persia should be exempted from the penal laws which Justinian enacted against his Pagan subjects; and this privilege, expressly stipulated in a treaty of peace, was guarded by the vigilance of a powerful mediator. Simplicius and his companions ended their lives in peace and obscurity; and as they left no disciples, they terminate the long list of Grecian philosophers, who may be justly praised, notwithstanding their defects, as the wisest and most virtuous of their contemporaries. The writings of Simplicius are now extant. His physical and metaphysical commentaries on Aristotle have passed away with the fashion of the times; but his moral interpretation of Epictetus is preserved in the library of nations, as a classic book, most excellently adapted to direct the will, to purify the heart, and to confirm the understanding, by a just confidence in the nature both of God and man.

EXTINCTION OF THE ROMAN CONSULSHIP

About the same time that Pythagoras first invented the appellation of philosopher, liberty and the consulship were founded at Rome by the elder Brutus. The revolutions of the consular office, which may be viewed in the successive lights of a substance, a shadow, and a name, have been occasionally mentioned in the present history. The first magistrates of the republic had been chosen by the people, to exercise, in the senate and in the camp, the powers of peace and war, which were afterwards translated to the emperors. But the tradition of ancient dignity was long revered by the Romans and barbarians. A Gothic historian applauds the consulship of Theodoric as the height of all temporal glory and greatness; the king of Italy himself congratulates those annual favourites of fortune who, without the cares, enjoyed the splendour of the throne; and at the end of a thousand years, two consuls were created by the sovereigns of Rome and Constantinople for the sole purpose of giving a date to the year and a festival to the people. But the expenses of this festival, in which the wealthy and the vain aspired to surpass their predecessors, insensibly arose to the enormous sum of fourscore thousand pounds; the wisest senators declined an useless honour which involved the certain ruin of their families, and to this reluctance I should impute the frequent chasms in the last age of the consular *Fasti*. The predecessors of Justinian had assisted from the public treasures the dignity of the less opulent candidates; the avarice of that prince preferred the cheaper and more convenient method of advice and regulation. Seven *processions* or spectacles were the number to which his edict confined the horse and chariot races, the athletic sports, the music and pantomimes of the theatre, and the hunting of wild beasts; and small pieces of silver were discreetly substituted for the gold medals, which had always excited tumult and drunkenness when they were scattered with a profuse hand among the populace. Notwithstanding these precautions and his own example, the succession of consuls finally ceased in the thirteenth year of Justinian, whose despotic temper might be gratified by the silent extinction of a title which admonished the Romans of their ancient freedom. Yet the annual consulship still lived in the minds of the people; they fondly expected its speedy restoration; they applauded the gracious condescension of successive princes, by whom it was assumed in the first year of their reign; and three centuries elapsed, after the death of Justinian, before that obsolete dignity, which had been suppressed by custom, could be abolished by law. The imperfect mode of distinguishing each year by the name of a magistrate was usefully supplied by the date of a permanent era: the creation of the world, according to the Septuagint version, was adopted by the Greeks; and the Latins, since the age of Charlemagne, have computed their time from the birth of Christ.

Under the glories of Justinian's reign lay two fatally unsound conditions. One was his economic extravagance. The other was that theologically and politically he failed to reconcile the eastern and western provinces. His very able wife Theodora had been a Monophysite. After her death in 548 Justinian tried to conciliate the Monophysite elements. Had he been successful he might have retained the allegiance of the eastern provinces. But in fact Monophysite doctrines were so much akin to those of Islam that when that power arose the eastern provinces easily and inevitably fell away.

In Chapter 41 Gibbon describes Justinian's Conquests (533–540). Through his generals Belisarius and Narses Justinian held the eastern frontier, recovered Africa and part of Spain from the Vandals and made the Mediterranean a Roman sea once more. Belisarius overthrew the Ostrogothic power in Italy, recovering Rome and successfully resisting a siege of Rome by the Goths, and subsequently besieging and taking Ravenna.

In Chapter 42 Gibbon relates the rise of the Lombards and the appearance of Slav and Turkish peoples.

43.

LAST VICTORY AND DEATH OF BELISARIUS.
CHARACTER AND DEATH OF JUSTINIAN. COMETS,
EARTHQUAKES, AND PLAGUE DURING THE
REIGN OF JUSTINIAN

The Goths revolted under Totila and took Rome in 546. It was recovered by Belisarius but taken again after his recall. In 552 the eunuch Narses defeated Totila and liberated Rome. He subsequently defeated Totila's successor, Teias, the last king of the Goths, and crushed an invasion of the Franks and Alemanni. The throne of the Gothic kings was now filled by the exarchs of Ravenna, the representatives of the emperor in Constantinople. Narses himself became the first exarch and administered the entire kingdom of Italy for over fifteen years.

THE LAST VICTORY AND DEATH OF BELISARIUS

I DESIRE to believe, but I dare not affirm, that Belisarius sincerely rejoiced in the triumph of Narses. Yet the consciousness of his own exploits might teach him to esteem, without jealousy, the merit of a rival; and the repose of the aged warrior was crowned by a last victory, which saved the emperor and the capital. The barbarians, who annually visited the provinces of Europe, were less discouraged by some accidental defeats than they were excited by the double hope of spoil and of subsidy. In the thirty-second winter of Justinian's reign the Danube was deeply frozen; Zabergan led the cavalry of the Bulgarians, and his standard was followed by a promiscuous multitude of Sclavonians. The savage chief passed, without opposition, the river and the mountains, spread his troops over Macedonia and Thrace, and advanced with no more than seven thousand horse to the long walls which should have defended the territory of Constantinople.

But the works of man are impotent against the assaults of nature: a recent earthquake had shaken the foundations of the walls; and the forces of the empire were employed on the distant frontiers of Italy, Africa, and Persia. The seven *schools,* or companies, of the guards or domestic troops, had been augmented to the number of five thousand five hundred men, whose ordinary station was in the peaceful cities of Asia. But the places of the brave Armenians were insensibly supplied by lazy citizens, who purchased an exemption from the duties of civil life without being exposed to the dangers of military service. Of such soldiers few could be tempted to sally from the gates; and none could be persuaded to remain in the field, unless they wanted strength and speed to escape from the Bulgarians. The report of the fugitives exaggerated the numbers and fierceness of an enemy who had polluted holy virgins and abandoned new-born infants to the dogs and vultures; a crowd of rustics, imploring food and protection, increased the consternation of the city; and the tents of Zabergan were pitched at the distance of twenty miles, on the banks of a small river which encircles Melanthias and afterwards falls into the Propontis. Justinian trembled: and those who had only seen the emperor in his old age were pleased to suppose that he had *lost* the alacrity and vigour of his youth. By his command the vessels of gold and silver were removed from the churches in the neighbourhood, and even the suburbs, of Constantinople: the ramparts were lined with trembling spectators; the golden gate was crowded with useless generals and tribunes; and the senate shared the fatigues and the apprehensions of the populace.

But the eyes of the prince and people were directed to a feeble veteran, who was compelled by the public danger to resume the armour in which he had entered Carthage and defended Rome. The horses of the royal stables, of private citizens, and even of the circus, were hastily collected; the emulation of the old and young was roused by the name of Belisarius, and his first encampment was in the presence of a victorious enemy. His prudence, and the labour of the friendly peasants, secured, with a ditch and rampart, the repose of the night; innumerable fires and clouds of dust were artfully contrived to magnify the opinion of his strength; his soldiers suddenly passed from despondency to presumption; and, while ten thousand voices demanded the battle, Belisarius dissembled his knowledge that in the hour of trial he must depend on the firmness of three hundred veterans. The next morning the Bulgarian cavalry advanced to the charge. But they heard the shouts of multitudes, they beheld the arms and discipline of the front; they were assaulted on the flanks by two ambuscades which rose from the woods; their foremost warriors fell by the hand of the aged hero and his guards; and the swiftness of their evolutions was rendered useless by the close attack and rapid pursuit of the Romans. In this action (so speedy was their flight) the Bulgarians lost only four hundred horse: but Constantinople was saved; and Zabergan, who felt the hand of a master, withdrew to a respectful distance. But his friends were numerous in the councils of the emperor, and Belisarius obeyed with reluctance the commands of envy and Justinian, which forbade him to achieve the deliverance of his country. On his return to the city, the people, still conscious of their danger, accompanied his triumph with acclamations of joy and gratitude, which were imputed as a crime to the victorious general. But when he entered the palace the courtiers were silent, and the emperor, after a cold and thankless embrace, dismissed him to mingle with the train of slaves. Yet so deep was the impression of his glory on the minds of men, that Justinian, in the seventy-seventh year of his age, was encouraged to advance near forty miles from the capital, and to inspect in person the restoration of the long wall. The Bulgarians wasted the summer in the plains of Thrace; but they were inclined to peace by the failure of their rash attempts on Greece and the Chersonesus. A menace of killing their prisoners quickened the payment of heavy ransoms; and the departure of Zabergan was hastened by the report that double-prowed vessels were built on the Danube to intercept his passage. The danger was soon forgotten; and a vain question, whether their sovereign had shown more wisdom or weakness, amused the idleness of the city.

About two years after the last victory of Belisarius, the emperor returned from a Thracian journey of health, or business, or devotion. Justinian was afflicted by a pain in his head; and his private entry countenanced the rumour of his death. Before the third hour of the day, the bakers' shops were plundered of their bread, the houses were shut, and every citizen, with hope or terror, prepared for the impending tumult. The senators themselves, fearful and suspicious, were convened at the ninth hour; and the prefect received their commands to visit every quarter of the city and proclaim a general illumination for the recovery of the emperor's health. The ferment subsided; but every accident betrayed the impotence of the government and the factious temper of the people: the guards were disposed to mutiny as often as their quarters were changed, or their pay was withheld: the frequent calamities of fires and earthquakes afforded the opportunities of disorder; the disputes of the blues and greens, of the orthodox and heretics, degenerated into bloody battles; and, in the presence of the Persian ambassador, Justinian blushed for himself and for his subjects. Capricious pardon and arbitrary punishment embittered the irksomeness and discontent of a long reign: a conspiracy was formed in the palace; and, unless we are deceived by the names of Marcellus and Sergius, the most virtuous and the most profligate of the courtiers were associated in the same designs. They had fixed the time of the execution; their rank gave them access to the royal banquet; and their black slaves were stationed in the vestibule and porticoes to announce the death of the tyrant, and to excite a sedition in the capital. But the indiscretion of an accomplice saved the poor remnant of the days of Justinian. The conspirators were detected and seized with daggers hidden under their garments; Marcellus died by his own hand, and Sergius was dragged from the sanctuary. Pressed by remorse, or tempted by the hopes of safety, he accused two officers of the household of Belisarius, and torture forced them to declare that they had acted according to the secret instructions of their patron. Posterity will not hastily believe that an hero who in the vigour of life had disdained the fairest offers of ambition and revenge should stoop to the murder of his prince, whom he could not long expect to survive. His followers were impatient to fly; but flight must have been supported by rebellion, and he had lived enough for nature and for glory. Belisarius appeared before the council with less fear than indignation: after forty years' service the emperor had prejudged his guilt; and injustice was sanctified by the presence and authority of the patriarch. The life of Belisarius was graciously spared, but his fortunes were sequestered; and, from December to July, he was guarded as a prisoner in his own palace. At length his innocence was acknowledged; his freedom and honours were restored; and death, which might be hastened by resentment and grief, removed him from the world about eight months after his deliverance. The name of Belisarius can never die: but, instead of the funeral, the monuments, the statues, so justly due to his memory, I only read that his treasures, the spoils of the Goths and Vandals, were immediately confiscated by the emperor. Some decent portion was reserved, however, for the use of his widow: and as Antonina had much to repent, she devoted the last remains of her life and fortune to the foundation of a convent. Such is the simple and genuine narrative of the fall of Belisarius, and the ingratitude of Justinian. That he was deprived of his eyes, and reduced by envy to beg his bread, "Give a penny to Belisarius the general!" is a fiction of later times, which has obtained credit, or rather favour, as a strange example of the vicissitudes of fortune.

THE CHARACTER AND DEATH OF JUSTINIAN

If the emperor could rejoice in the death of Belisarius, he enjoyed the base satisfaction only eight months, the last period of a reign of thirty-eight and a life of eighty-three years. It would be difficult to trace the character of a prince who is not the most conspicuous object of his own times: but the confessions of an enemy may be received as the safest evidence of his virtues. The resemblance of Justinian to the bust of Domitian is maliciously urged, with the acknowledgement, however, of a well-proportioned figure, a ruddy complexion, and a pleasing countenance. The emperor was easy of access, patient of hearing, courteous and affable in discourse, and a master of the angry passions which rage with such destructive violence in the breast of a despot. Procopius praises his temper, to reproach him with calm and deliberate cruelty: but in the conspiracies which attacked his authority and person, a more candid judge will approve the justice, or admire the clemency, of Justinian. He excelled in the private virtues of chastity and temperance; but the impartial love of beauty would have been less mischievous than his conjugal tenderness for Theodora; and his abstemious diet was regulated, not by the prudence of a philosopher, but the superstition of a monk. His repasts were short and frugal: on solemn fasts he contented himself with water and vegetables;

and such was his strength as well as fervour, that he frequently passed two days, and as many nights, without tasting any food. The measure of his sleep was not less rigorous: after the repose of a single hour, the body was awakened by the soul, and, to the astonishment of his chamberlains, Justinian walked or studied till the morning light. Such restless application prolonged his time for the acquisition of knowledge and the despatch of business; and he might seriously deserve the reproach of confounding, by minute and preposterous diligence, the general order of his administration. The emperor professed himself a musician and architect, a poet and philosopher, a lawyer and theologian; and if he failed in the enterprise of reconciling the Christian sects, the review of the Roman jurisprudence is a noble monument of his spirit and industry. In the government of the empire he was less wise, or less successful: the age was unfortunate; the people was oppressed and discontented; Theodora abused her power; a succession of bad ministers disgraced his judgment; and Justinian was neither beloved in his life nor regretted at his death. The love of fame was deeply implanted in his breast, but he condescended to the poor ambition of titles, honours, and contemporary praise; and while he laboured to fix the admiration, he forfeited the esteem and affection, of the Romans. The design of the African and Italian wars was boldly conceived and executed; and his penetration discovered the talents of Belisarius in the camp, of Narses in the palace. But the name of the emperor is eclipsed by the names of his victorious generals; and Belisarius still lives, to upbraid the envy and ingratitude of his sovereign. The partial favour of mankind applauds the genius of a conqueror who leads and directs his subjects in the exercise of arms. The characters of Philip the Second and of Justinian are distinguished by the cold ambition which delights in war, and declines the dangers of the field. Yet a colossal statue of bronze represented the emperor on horseback, preparing to march against the Persians in the habit and armour of Achilles. In the great square before the church of St. Sophia, this monument was raised on a brass column and a stone pedestal of seven steps; and the pillar of Theodosius, which weighed seven thousand four hundred pounds of silver, was removed from the same place by the avarice and vanity of Justinian. Future princes were more just or indulgent to *his* memory; the elder Andronicus, in the beginning of the fourteenth century, repaired and beautified his equestrian statue: since the fall of the empire it has been melted into cannon by the victorious Turks.

COMETS

I shall conclude this chapter with the comets, the earthquakes, and the plague, which astonished or afflicted the age of Justinian.

In the fifth year of his reign, and in the month of September, a comet was seen during twenty days in the western quarter of the heavens, and which shot its rays into the north. Eight years afterwards, while the sun was in Capricorn, another comet appeared to follow in the Sagittary: the size was gradually increasing; the head was in the east, the tail in the west, and it remained visible above forty days. The nations, who gazed with astonishment, expected wars and calamities from their baleful influence; and these expectations were abundantly fulfilled. The astronomers dissembled their ignorance of the nature of these blazing stars, which they affected to represent as the floating meteors of the air; and few among them embraced the simple notion of Seneca and the Chaldæans, that they are only planets of a longer period and more eccentric motion. Time and science have justified the conjectures and predictions of the Roman sage: the telescope has opened new worlds to the eyes of astronomers; and, in the narrow space of history and fable, one and the same comet is already found to have revisited the earth in *seven* equal revolutions of five hundred and seventy-five years. The *first*, which ascends beyond the Christian era one thousand seven hundred and sixty-seven years, is coëval with Ogyges, the father of Grecian antiquity. And this appearance explains the tradition which Varro has preserved, that under his reign the planet Venus changed her colour, size, figure, and course; a prodigy without example either in past or succeeding ages. The *second* visit, in the year eleven hundred and ninety-three, is darkly implied in the fable of Electra, the seventh of the Pleiads, who have been reduced to six since the time of the Trojan war. That nymph, the wife of Dardanus, was unable to support the ruin of her country: she abandoned the dances of her sister orbs, fled from the zodiac to the north pole, and obtained, from her dishevelled locks, the name of the *comet*. The *third* period expires in the year six hundred and eighteen, a date that exactly agrees with the tremendous comet of the Sibyl, and perhaps of Pliny, which arose in the West two generations before the reign of Cyrus. The *fourth* apparition, forty-four years before the birth of Christ, is of all others the most splendid and important. After the death of Cæsar, a long-haired star was conspicuous to Rome and to the nations during the games which were exhibited by young Octavian in honour of Venus and his uncle. The vulgar opinion, that it conveyed to heaven the divine soul of the dictator, was cherished and consecrated by the piety of a statesman; while his secret superstition referred the comet to the glory of his own times. The *fifth* visit has been already ascribed to the fifth year of Justinian, which coincides with the five hundred and thirty-first of the Christian era. And it may deserve notice, that in this, as in the preceding instance, the comet was followed, though at a longer interval, by a remarkable paleness of the sun. The *sixth* return, in the year eleven hundred and six, is recorded by the chronicles of Europe and China: and in the first fervour of the Crusades, the Christians and the Mahometans might surmise, with equal reason, that it portended the destruction of the Infidels. The *seventh* phenomenon, of one thousand six hundred and eighty, was presented to the eyes of an enlightened age. The philosophy of Bayle dispelled a prejudice which Milton's muse had so recently adorned, that the comet, "from its horrid hair shakes pestilence and war." Its road in the heavens was observed with exquisite skill by Flamsteed and Cassini: and the mathematical science of Bernoulli, Newton, and Halley investigated the laws of its revolutions. At the *eighth* period, in the year two thousand three hundred and fifty-five, their calculations may perhaps be verified by the astronomers of some future capital in the Siberian or American wilderness.

EARTHQUAKES

The near approach of a comet may injure or destroy the globe which we inhabit; but the changes on its surface have been hitherto produced by the action of volcanoes and earthquakes. The nature of the soil may indicate the countries most exposed to these formidable concussions, since they are caused by subterraneous fires, and such fires are kindled by the union and fermentation of iron and sulphur. But their times and effects appear to lie beyond the reach of human curiosity; and the philosopher will discreetly abstain from the prediction of earthquakes, till he has counted the drops of water that silently filtrate on the inflammable mineral, and measured the caverns which increase by resistance the explosion of the imprisoned air. Without assigning the cause, history will distinguish the periods in which these calamitous events have been rare or frequent, and will observe that this fever of the earth raged with uncommon violence during the reign of Justinian. Each year is marked by the repetition of earthquakes, of such duration that Constantinople has been shaken above forty days; of such extent that the shock has been communicated to the whole surface of the globe, or at least of the Roman empire. An impulsive or vibratory motion was felt, enormous chasms were opened, huge and heavy bodies were discharged into the air, the sea alternately advanced and retreated beyond its ordinary bounds, and a mountain was torn from Libanus and cast into the waves where it protected, as a mole, the new harbour of Botrys in Phœnicia. The stroke that agitates an ant-hill may crush the insect-myriads in the dust; yet truth must extort a confession that man has industriously laboured for his own destruction. The institution of great cities, which include a nation within the limits of a wall, almost realises the wish of Caligula that the Roman people had but one neck. Two hundred and fifty thousand persons are said to have perished in the earthquake of Antioch, whose domestic multitudes were swelled by the conflux of strangers to the festival of the Ascension. The loss of Berytus was of smaller account, but of much greater value. That city, on the coast of Phœnicia, was illustrated by the study of the civil law, which opened the surest road to wealth and dignity: the schools of Berytus were filled with the rising spirits of the age, and many a youth was lost in the earthquake who might have lived to be the scourge or the guardian of his country. In these disasters the architect becomes the enemy of mankind. The hut of a savage, or the tent of an Arab, may be thrown down without injury to the inhabitant; and the Peruvians had reason to deride the folly of their Spanish conquerors, who with so much cost and labour erected their own sepulchres. The rich marbles of a patrician

are dashed on his own head; a whole people is buried under
the ruins of public and private edifices; and the conflagration
is kindled and propagated by the innumerable fires which are
necessary for the subsistence and manufactures of a great
city. Instead of the mutual sympathy which might comfort
and assist the distressed, they dreadfully experience the vices
and passions which are released from the fear of punishment:
the tottering houses are pillaged by intrepid avarice; revenge
embraces the moment and selects the victim; and the earth
often swallows the assassin, or the ravisher, in the consummation of their crimes. Superstition involves the present
danger with invisible terrors; and if the image of death may
sometimes be subservient to the virtue or repentance of individuals, an affrighted people is more forcibly moved to expect the end of the world, or to deprecate with servile homage
the wrath of an avenging Deity.

THE PLAGUE

Ethiopia and Egypt have been stigmatised in every age as
the original source and seminary of the plague. In a damp,
hot, stagnating air, this African fever is generated from the
putrefaction of animal substances, and especially from the
swarms of locusts, not less destructive to mankind in their
death than in their lives. The fatal disease which depopulated
the earth in the time of Justinian and his successors first
appeared in the neighbourhood of Pelusium, between the
Serbonian bog and the eastern channel of the Nile. From
thence, tracing as it were a double path, it spread to the East,
over Syria, Persia, and the Indies, and penetrated to the West,
along the coast of Africa and over the continent of Europe.
In the spring of the second year Constantinople, during three
or four months, was visited by the pestilence; and Procopius,
who observed its progress and symptoms with the eyes of a
physician, has emulated the skill and diligence of Thucydides
in the description of the plague of Athens. The infection was
sometimes announced by the visions of a distempered fancy,
and the victim despaired as soon as he had heard the menace
and felt the stroke of an invisible spectre. But the greater number, in their beds, in the streets, in their usual occupation,
were surprised by a slight fever; so slight, indeed, that neither
the pulse nor the colour of the patient gave any signs of the

approaching danger. The same, the next, or the succeeding day, it was declared by the swelling of the glands, particularly those of the groin, of the armpits, and under the ear; and when these buboes or tumours were opened, they were found to contain a *coal*, or black substance, of the size of a lentil. If they came to a just swelling and suppuration, the patient was saved by this kind of natural discharge of the morbid humour; but if they continued hard and dry, a mortification quickly ensued, and the fifth day was commonly the term of his life. The fever was often accompanied with lethargy or delirium; the bodies of the sick were covered with black pustules or carbuncles, the symptoms of immediate death; and in the constitutions too feeble to produce an eruption, the vomiting of blood was followed by a mortification of the bowels. To pregnant women the plague was generally mortal; yet one infant was drawn alive from his dead mother, and three mothers survived the loss of their infected fœtus. Youth was the most perilous season, and the female sex was less susceptible than the male; but every rank and profession was attacked with indiscriminate rage, and many of those who escaped were deprived of the use of their speech, without being secure from a return of the disorder. The physicians of Constantinople were zealous and skilful; but their art was baffled by the various symptoms and pertinacious vehemence of the disease: the same remedies were productive of contrary effects, and the event capriciously disappointed their prognostics of death or recovery. The order of funerals and the right of sepulchres were confounded; those who were left without friends or servants lay unburied in the streets, or in their desolate houses; and a magistrate was authorised to collect the promiscuous heaps of dead bodies, to transport them by land or water, and to inter them in deep pits beyond the precincts of the city. Their own danger and the prospect of public distress awakened some remorse in the minds of the most vicious of mankind: the confidence of health again revived their passions and habits; but philosophy must disdain the observation of Procopius, that the lives of such men were guarded by the peculiar favour of fortune or Providence. He forgot, or perhaps he secretly recollected, that the plague had touched the person of Justinian himself; but the abstemious diet of the emperor may suggest, as in the case of Socrates, a more rational and honourable cause for his recovery.[1] During his sickness the public consternation was expressed in the habits of the citizens; and their idleness and despondence occasioned a general scarcity in the capital of the East.

Contagion is the inseparable symptom of the plague; which, by mutual respiration, is transfused from the infected persons to the lungs and stomach of those who approach them. While philosophers believe and tremble, it is singular that the existence of a real danger should have been denied by a people most prone to vain and imaginary terrors.[2] Yet the fellow-citizens of Procopius were satisfied, by some short and partial experience, that the infection could not be gained by the closest conversation; and this persuasion might support the assiduity of friends or physicians in the care of the sick, whom inhuman prudence would have condemned to solitude and despair. But the fatal security, like the predestination of the Turks, must have aided the progress of the contagion; and those salutary precautions to which Europe is indebted for her safety were unknown to the government of Justinian. No restraints were imposed on the free and frequent inter-course of the Roman provinces: from Persia to France the nations were mingled and infected by wars and emigrations; and the pestilential odour which lurks for years in a bale of cotton was imported, by the abuse of trade, into the most distant regions. The mode of its propagation is explained by the remark of Procopius himself, that it always spread from the sea-coast to the inland country: the most sequestered islands and mountains were successively visited; the places which had escaped the fury of its first passage were alone exposed to the contagion of the ensuing year. The winds might diffuse that subtle venom; but unless the atmosphere be previously disposed for its reception, the plague would soon expire in the cold or temperate climates of the earth. Such was the universal corruption of the air, that the pestilence which burst forth in the fifteenth year of Justinian was

---

[1] It was thus that Socrates had been saved by his temperance, in the plague of Athens. Dr. Mead accounts for the peculiar salubrity of religious houses by the two advantages of seclusion and abstinence.

[2] Mead proves that the plague is contagious, from Thucydides, Lucretius, Aristotle, Galen, and common experience; and he refutes the contrary opinion of the French physicians who visited Marseilles in the year 1720. Yet these were the recent and enlightened spectators of a plague which, in a few months, swept away 50,000 inhabitants of a city that, in the present hour of prosperity and trade, contains no more than 90,000 souls.

not checked or alleviated by any difference of the seasons. In time its first malignity was abated and dispersed; the disease alternately languished and revived; but it was not till the end of a calamitous period of fifty-two years that mankind recovered their health, or the air resumed its pure and salubrious quality. No facts have been preserved to sustain an account, or even a conjecture, of the numbers that perished in this extraordinary mortality. I only find that, during three months, five and at length ten thousand persons died each day at Constantinople; that many cities of the East were left vacant; and that in several districts of Italy the harvest and the vintage withered on the ground. The triple scourge of war, pestilence, and famine, afflicted the subjects of Justinian; and his reign is disgraced by a visible decrease of the human species, which has never been repaired in some of the fairest countries of the globe.

The supreme achievement of Justinian's reign was the codification of the Roman law. This is described by Gibbon in Chapter 44, omitted here.

45.

---

*Between 568 and 570, after the death of Narses, the
Lombards under Alboin conquered the greater part of Italy.
For two hundred years Italy was divided between the Lombard
kingdom and the exarchate of Ravenna.*

MISERY OF ROME AT THE CLOSE OF THE SIXTH CENTURY

AMIDST the arms of the Lombards, and under the despotism
of the Greeks, we again inquire into the fate of Rome, which
had reached, about the close of the sixth century, the lowest
period of her depression. By the removal of the seat of empire and the successive loss of the provinces, the sources of
public and private opulence were exhausted: the lofty tree,
under whose shade the nations of the earth had reposed, was
deprived of its leaves and branches, and the sapless trunk was
left to wither on the ground. The ministers of command and
the messengers of victory no longer met on the Appian or
Flaminian way, and the hostile approach of the Lombards
was often felt and continually feared. The inhabitants of a
potent and peaceful capital, who visit without an anxious
thought the garden of the adjacent country, will faintly picture
in their fancy the distress of the Romans: they shut or opened
their gates with a trembling hand, beheld from the walls the
flames of their houses, and heard the lamentations of their
brethren, who were coupled together like dogs, and dragged
away into distant slavery beyond the sea and the mountains.
Such incessant alarms must annihilate the pleasures and interrupt the labours of a rural life; and the Campagna of Rome
was speedily reduced to the state of a dreary wilderness, in
which the land is barren, the waters are impure, and the air

is infectious. Curiosity and ambition no longer attracted the nations to the capital of the world; but, if chance or necessity directed the steps of a wandering stranger, he contemplated with horror the vacancy and solitude of the city, and might be tempted to ask, where is the senate, and where are the people? In a season of excessive rains the Tiber swelled above its banks, and rushed with irresistible violence into the valleys of the seven hills. A pestilential disease arose from the stagnation of the deluge, and so rapid was the contagion that fourscore persons expired in an hour in the midst of a solemn procession which implored the mercy of Heaven. A society in which marriage is encouraged and industry prevails soon repairs the accidental losses of pestilence and war; but, as the far greater part of the Romans was condemned to hopeless indigence and celibacy, the depopulation was constant and visible, and the gloomy enthusiasts might expect the approaching failure of the human race. Yet the number of citizens still exceeded the measure of subsistence: their precarious food was supplied from the harvests of Sicily or Egypt, and the frequent repetition of famine betrays the inattention of the emperor to a distant province. The edifices of Rome were exposed to the same ruin and decay; the mouldering fabrics were easily overthrown by inundations, tempests, and earthquakes; and the monks, who had occupied the most advantageous stations, exulted in their base triumph over the ruins of antiquity. It is commonly believed that pope Gregory the First attacked the temples and mutilated the statues of the city; that, by the command of the barbarian, the Palatine library was reduced to ashes, and that the history of Livy was the peculiar mark of his absurd and mischievous fanaticism. The writings of Gregory himself reveal his implacable aversion to the monuments of classic genius, and he points his severest censure against the profane learning of a bishop who taught the art of grammar, studied the Latin poets, and pronounced with the same voice the praises of Jupiter and those of Christ. But the evidence of his destructive rage is doubtful and recent: the Temple of Peace or the Theatre of Marcellus have been demolished by the slow operation of ages, and a formal proscription would have multiplied the copies of Virgil and Livy in the countries which were subject to the ecclesiastical dictator.

THE PONTIFICATE OF GREGORY THE GREAT

Like Thebes, or Babylon, or Carthage, the name of Rome might have been erased from the earth, if the city had not been animated by a vital principle, which again restored her to honour and dominion. A vague tradition was embraced, that two Jewish teachers, a tent-maker and a fisherman, had formerly been executed in the circus of Nero, and at the end of five hundred years their genuine or fictitious relics were adored as the Palladium of Christian Rome. The pilgrims of the East and West resorted to the holy threshold; but the shrines of the apostles were guarded by miracles and invisible terrors, and it was not without fear that the pious catholic approached the object of his worship. It was fatal to touch, it was dangerous to behold, the bodies of the saints; and those who, from the purest motives, presumed to disturb the repose of the sanctuary were affrighted by visions or punished with sudden death. The unreasonable request of an empress, who wished to deprive the Romans of their sacred treasure, the head of St. Paul, was rejected with the deepest abhorrence; and the pope asserted, most probably with truth, that a linen which had been sanctified in the neighbourhood of his body, or the filings of his chain, which it was sometimes easy and sometimes impossible to obtain, possessed an equal degree of miraculous virtue. But the power as well as virtue of the apostles resided with living energy in the breast of their successors: and the chair of St. Peter was filled under the reign of Maurice by the first and greatest of the name of Gregory. His grandfather Felix had himself been pope, and, as the bishops were already bound by the law of celibacy, his consecration must have been preceded by the death of his wife. The parents of Gregory, Sylvia and Gordian, were the noblest of the senate, and the most pious of the church of Rome; his female relations were numbered among the saints and virgins, and his own figure, with those of his father and mother, were represented near three hundred years in a family portrait which he offered to the monastery of St. Andrew. The design and colouring of this picture afford an honourable testimony that the art of painting was cultivated by the Italians of the sixth century; but the most abject ideas must be entertained of their taste and learning, since the epistles of Gregory, his sermons, and his dialogues, are the work of a man who was second in erudition to none of his contemporaries: his birth and abilities had raised him to the office of prefect of the city, and he enjoyed the merit of renouncing the pomp and vanities of this world. His ample patrimony was dedicated to the foundation of seven monasteries, one in Rome and six in Sicily; and it was the wish of Gregory that he might be unknown in this life, and glorious only in the next. Yet his devotion, and it might be sincere, pursued the path which would have been chosen by a crafty and ambitious statesman. The talents of Gregory, and the splendour which accompanied his retreat, rendered him dear and useful to the church, and implicit obedience has been always inculcated as the first duty of a monk. As soon as he had received the character of deacon, Gregory was sent to reside at the Byzantine court, the nuncio or minister of the apostolic see; and he boldly assumed, in the name of St. Peter, a tone of independent dignity which would have been criminal and dangerous in the most illustrious layman of the empire. He returned to Rome with a just increase of reputation, and, after a short exercise of the monastic virtues, he was dragged from the cloister to the papal throne by the unanimous voice of the clergy, the senate, and the people. He alone resisted, or seemed to resist, his own elevation; and his humble petition that Maurice would be pleased to reject the choice of the Romans could only serve to exalt his character in the eyes of the emperor and the public. When the fatal mandate was proclaimed, Gregory solicited the aid of some friendly merchants to convey him in a basket beyond the gates of Rome, and modestly concealed himself some days among the woods and mountains, till his retreat was discovered, as it is said, by a celestial light.

The pontificate of Gregory the *Great*, which lasted thirteen years, six months, and ten days, is one of the most edifying periods of the history of the church. His virtues, and even his faults, a singular mixture of simplicity and cunning, of pride and humility, of sense and superstition, were happily suited to his station and to the temper of the times. In his rival, the patriarch of Constantinople, he condemned the antichristian title of universal bishop, which the successor of St. Peter was too haughty to concede and too feeble to assume; and the ecclesiastical jurisdiction of Gregory was confined to the triple character of Bishop of Rome, Primate of Italy, and Apostle of the West. He frequently ascended the pulpit, and kindled, by his rude though pathetic eloquence, the congenial passions of his audience: the language of the Jewish prophets was interpreted and applied; and the minds of a people depressed by their present calamities were directed to the hopes and fears of the invisible world. His precepts and example defined the model of the Roman liturgy; the distribution of the parishes, the calendar of festivals, the order of processions, the service of the priests and deacons, the variety and change of sacerdotal garments. Till the last days of his life he officiated in the canon of the mass, which continued above three hours: the Gregorian chant has preserved the vocal and instrumental music of the theatre, and the rough voices of the barbarians attempted to imitate the melody of the Roman school. Experience had shown him the efficacy of these solemn and pompous rites to soothe the distress, to confirm the faith, to mitigate the fierceness, and to dispel the dark enthusiasm of the vulgar, and he readily forgave their tendency to promote the reign of priesthood and superstition. The bishops of Italy and the adjacent islands acknowledged the Roman pontiff as their special metropolitan. Even the existence, the union, or the translation of episcopal seats was decided by his absolute discretion: and his successful inroads into the provinces of Greece, of Spain, and of Gaul, might countenance the more lofty pretensions of succeeding popes. He interposed to prevent the abuses of popular elections; his jealous care maintained the purity of faith and discipline; and the apostolic shepherd assiduously watched over the faith and discipline of the subordinate pastors. Under his reign the Arians of Italy and Spain were reconciled to the catholic church, and the conquest of Britain reflects less glory on the name of Cæsar than on that of Gregory the First. Instead of six legions, forty monks were embarked for that distant island, and the pontiff lamented the austere duties which forbade him to partake the perils of their spiritual warfare. In less than two years he could announce to the archbishop of Alexandria that they had baptised the king of Kent with ten thousand of his Anglo-Saxons; and that the Roman missionaries, like those of the primitive church, were armed only with spiritual and supernatural powers. The credulity or the prudence of Gregory was always disposed to confirm the truths of religion by the evidence of ghosts, miracles, and resurrections; and posterity has paid to *his* memory the same tribute which he freely granted to the virtue of his own or the preceding generation. The celestial honours have been liberally bestowed by the authority of the popes, but Gregory is the last of their own order whom they have presumed to inscribe in the calendar of saints.

Their temporal power insensibly arose from the calamities of the times; and the Roman bishops, who have deluged Europe and Asia with blood, were compelled to reign as the ministers of charity and peace. I. The church of Rome, as it has been formerly observed, was endowed with ample possessions in Italy, Sicily, and the more distant provinces; and her agents, who were commonly subdeacons, had acquired a civil and even criminal jurisdiction over their tenants and husbandmen. The successor of St. Peter administered his patrimony with the temper of a vigilant and moderate landlord; and the epistles of Gregory are filled with salutary instructions to abstain from doubtful or vexatious lawsuits, to preserve the integrity of weights and measures, to grant every reasonable delay, and to reduce the capitation of the slaves of the glebe, who purchased the right of marriage by the payment of an arbitrary fine. The rent or the produce of these estates was transported to the mouth of the Tiber, at the risk and expense of the pope: in the use of wealth he acted like a faithful steward of the church and the poor, and liberally applied to their wants the inexhaustible resources of abstinence and order. The voluminous account of his receipts and disbursements was kept above three hundred years in the Lateran, as the model of Christian economy. On the four great festivals he divided their quarterly allowance to the clergy, to his domestics, to the monasteries, the churches, the places of burial, the almshouses, and the hospitals of Rome, and the rest of the diocese. On the first day of every month he distributed to the poor, according to the season, their stated portion of corn, wine, cheese, vegetables, oil, fish, fresh provisions, clothes, and money; and his treasurers were continually summoned to satisfy, in his name, the extraordinary demands of indigence and merit. The instant distress of the sick and helpless, of strangers and pilgrims, was relieved by the bounty of each day and of every hour; nor would the pontiff indulge himself in a frugal repast till he had sent the dishes from his own table to some objects deserving of his compassion. The misery of the times had reduced the nobles and matrons of Rome to accept, without a blush, the benevolence of the church: three thousand virgins received their food and raiment from the hand of their benefactor; and many bishops of Italy escaped from the barbarians to the hospitable threshold of the Vatican. Gregory might justly be styled the Father of his country; and such was the extreme sensibility of his conscience, that, for the death of a beggar who had perished in the streets, he interdicted himself during several days from the exercise of sacerdotal functions. II. The misfortunes of Rome involved the apostolical pastor in the business of peace and war; and it might be doubtful to himself whether piety or ambition prompted him to supply the place of his absent sovereign. Gregory awakened the emperor from a long slumber; exposed the guilt or incapacity of the exarch and his inferior ministers; complained that the veterans were withdrawn from Rome for the defence of Spoleto; encouraged the Italians to guard their cities and altars; and condescended, in the crisis of danger, to name the tribunes and to direct the operations of the provincial troops. But the martial spirit of the pope was checked by the scruples of humanity and religion: the imposition of tribute, though it was employed in the Italian war, he freely condemned as odious and oppressive; whilst he protected, against the Imperial edicts, the pious cowardice of the soldiers who deserted a military for a monastic life. If we may credit his own declarations, it would have been easy for Gregory to exterminate the Lombards by their domestic factions, without leaving a king, a duke, or a count, to save that unfortunate nation from the vengeance of their foes. As a Christian bishop, he preferred the salutary offices of peace; his mediation appeased the tumult of arms; but he was too conscious of the arts of the Greeks and the passions of the Lombards to engage his sacred promise for the observance of the truce. Disappointed in the hope of a general and lasting treaty, he presumed to save his country without the consent of the emperor or the exarch. The sword of the enemy was suspended over Rome; it was averted by the mild eloquence and seasonable gifts of the pontiff, who commanded the respect of heretics and barbarians. The merits of Gregory were treated by the Byzantine court with reproach and insult; but in the attachment of a grateful people he found the purest reward of a citizen, and the best right of a sovereign.

In the following chapter, 46, Gibbon describes the end of the dynasty of Justinian and the beginning of the new dynasty of Heraclius.

The end of the dynasty of Justinian first under Maurice (582–602) and then Phocas (602–610) witnessed a progress from extreme weakness almost to sheer anarchy with foreign invasions and internal disruption.

During the reign of Heraclius (610–642) the Persians in a long war sacked Jerusalem, invaded Egypt and with the Avars nearly took Constantinople. The Persian power, however, was crushed forever in 628 by Heraclius, who also held the Slavs in the Balkans in check.

The key to the endless theories of the Incarnation which Gibbon discusses in Chapter 47 is the difference between the Nicaean Doctrine and that of the Monophysites. The latter appealed widely to the peoples of the eastern provinces, who recognised in Jesus simply a god incarnate. The body was of human form but the nature was single and divine.

47.

HISTORY OF THE DOCTRINE OF THE INCARNATION.
THE EBIONITES AND GNOSTICS. OPPOSITE THEORIES
OF CERINTHUS AND APOLLINARIS, CYRIL, NESTORIUS
AND THE FIRST COUNCIL OF EPHESUS. HERESY
OF EUTYCHES AND THE SECOND COUNCIL OF
EPHESUS. THE COUNCIL OF CHALCEDON. THE
HENOTICON OF ZENO. THEOLOGY OF JUSTINIAN

AFTER THE EXTINCTION of paganism, the Christians in peace and piety might have enjoyed their solitary triumph. But the principle of discord was alive in their bosom, and they were more solicitous to explore the nature, than to practise the laws, of their founder. I have already observed that the disputes of the TRINITY were succeeded by those of the INCARNATION; alike scandalous to the church, alike pernicious to the state, still more minute in their origin, still more durable in their effects. It is my design to comprise in the present chapter a religious war of two hundred and fifty years, to represent the ecclesiastical and political schism of the Oriental sects, and to introduce their clamorous or sanguinary contests, by a modest inquiry into the doctrines of the primitive church.

THE EBIONITES

I. A laudable regard for the honour of the first proselytes has countenanced the belief, the hope, the wish, that the Ebionites, or at least the Nazarenes, were distinguished only by their obstinate perseverance in the practice of the Mosaic rites. Their churches have disappeared, their books are obliterated: their obscure freedom might allow a latitude of faith, and the softness of their infant creed would be variously moulded by the zeal or prudence of three hundred years. Yet the most charitable criticism must refuse these sectaries any knowledge of the pure and proper divinity of Christ. Educated in the school of Jewish prophecy and prejudice, they had never been taught to elevate their hopes above an human and temporal Messiah. If they had courage to hail their king when he appeared in a plebeian garb, their grosser apprehensions were incapable of discerning their God, who had studiously disguised his celestial character under the name and person of a mortal.[1] The familiar companions of Jesus of Nazareth conversed with their friend and countryman, who, in all the actions of rational and animal life, appeared of the same species with themselves. His progress from infancy to youth and manhood was marked by a regular increase in stature and wisdom; and after a painful agony of mind and body, he expired on the cross. He lived and died for the service of mankind: but the life and death of Socrates had likewise been devoted to the cause of religion and justice; and although the stoic or the hero may disdain the humble virtues of Jesus, the tears which he shed over his friend and country may be esteemed the purest evidence of his humanity. The miracles of the gospel could not astonish a people who held with intrepid faith the more splendid prodigies of the Mosaic law. The prophets of ancient days had cured diseases, raised the dead, divided the sea, stopped the sun, and ascended to heaven in a fiery chariot. And the metaphorical style of the Hebrews might ascribe to a saint and martyr the adoptive title of SON OF GOD.

Yet in the insufficient creed of the Nazarenes and the Ebionites a distinction is faintly noticed between the heretics, who confounded the generation of Christ in the common order of nature, and the less guilty schismatics, who revered the virginity of his mother, and excluded the aid of an earthly father. The incredulity of the former was countenanced by the visible circumstances of his birth, the legal marriage of his reputed parents, Joseph and Mary, and his lineal claim to the kingdom of David and the inheritance of Judah. But the secret and authentic history has been recorded in several copies of the Gospel according to St. Matthew, which these sectaries long preserved in the original Hebrew, as the sole evidence of their faith. The natural suspicions of the husband,

---

[1] Chrysostom and Athanasius are obliged to confess that the divinity of Christ is rarely mentioned by himself or his apostles.

conscious of his own chastity, were dispelled by the assurance (in a dream) that his wife was pregnant of the Holy Ghost: and as this distant and domestic prodigy could not fall under the personal observation of the historian, he must have listened to the same voice which dictated to Isaiah the future conception of a virgin. The son of a virgin, generated by the ineffable operation of the Holy Spirit, was a creature without example or resemblance, superior in every attribute of mind and body to the children of Adam. Since the introduction of the Greek or Chaldean philosophy, the Jews were persuaded of the pre-existence, transmigration, and immortality of souls; and Providence was justified by a supposition that they were confined in their earthly prisons to expiate the stains which they had contracted in a former state. But the degrees of purity and corruption are almost immeasurable. It might be fairly presumed that the most sublime and virtuous of human spirits was infused into the offspring of Mary and the Holy Ghost; that his abasement was the result of his voluntary choice; and that the object of his mission was to purify, not his own, but the sins of the world. On his return to his native skies he received the immense reward of his obedience: the everlasting kingdom of the Messiah, which had been darkly foretold by the prophets, under the carnal images of peace, of conquest, and of dominion. Omnipotence could enlarge the human faculties of Christ to the extent of his celestial office. In the language of antiquity, the title of God has not been severely confined to the first parent; and his incomparable minister, his only begotten Son, might claim, without presumption, the religious, though secondary, worship of a subject world.

THE GNOSTICS

II. The seeds of the faith, which had slowly arisen in the rocky and ungrateful soil of Judea, were transplanted, in full maturity, to the happier climes of the Gentiles; and the strangers of Rome or Asia, who never beheld the manhood, were the more readily disposed to embrace the divinity, of Christ. The polytheist and the philosopher, the Greek and the barbarian, were alike accustomed to conceive a long succession, an infinite chain of angels, or dæmons, or deities, or æons, or emanations, issuing from the throne of light. Nor

could it seem strange or incredible that the first of these
æons, the *Logos*, or Word of God, of the same substance
with the Father, should descend upon earth, to deliver the
human race from vice and error, and to conduct them in the
paths of life and immortality. But the prevailing doctrine
of the eternity and inherent pravity of matter infected the
primitive churches of the East. Many among the Gentile
proselytes refused to believe that a celestial spirit, an un-
divided portion of the first essence, had been personally
united with a mass of impure and contaminated flesh: and,
in their zeal for the divinity, they piously abjured the humanity, of Christ. While his blood was still recent on Mount
Calvary, the *Docetes*, a numerous and learned sect of Asiatics,
invented the *phantastic* system, which was afterwards propagated by the Marcionites, the Manichæans, and the various
names of the Gnostic heresy. They denied the truth and
authenticity of the gospels, as far as they relate the conception of Mary, the birth of Christ, and the thirty years that
preceded the exercise of his ministry. He first appeared on the
banks of the Jordan in the form of perfect manhood; but it
was a form only, and not a substance; an human figure
created by the hand of Omnipotence to imitate the faculties
and actions of a man, and to impose a perpetual illusion on
the senses of his friends and enemies. Articulate sounds vi-
brated on the ears of the disciples; but the image which was
impressed on their optic nerve eluded the more stubborn
evidence of the touch; and they enjoyed the spiritual, not the
corporeal, presence of the Son of God. The rage of the Jews
was idly wasted against an impassive phantom; and the
mystic scenes of the passion and death, the resurrection and
ascension of Christ, were represented on the theatre of
Jerusalem for the benefit of mankind. If it were urged that
such ideal mimicry, such incessant deception, was unworthy
of the God of truth, the Docetes agreed with too many of
their orthodox brethren in the justification of pious falsehood.
In the system of the Gnostics the Jehovah of Israel, the
Creator of this lower world, was a rebellious, or at least an
ignorant, spirit. The Son of God descended upon earth to
abolish his temple and his law; and, for the accomplishment
of this salutary end, he dexterously transferred to his own
person the hope and prediction of a temporal Messiah.

One of the most subtle disputants of the Manichæan school

has pressed the danger and indecency of supposing that the God of the Christians, in the state of an human fœtus, emerged at the end of nine months from a female womb. The pious horror of his antagonists provoked them to disclaim all sensual circumstances of conception and delivery; to maintain that the divinity passed through Mary like a sunbeam through a plate of glass; and to assert that the seal of her virginity remained unbroken even at the moment when she became the mother of Christ. But the rashness of these concessions has encouraged a milder sentiment of those Docetes who taught, not that Christ was a phantom, but that he was clothed with an impassible and incorruptible body. Such, indeed, in the more orthodox system, he has acquired since his resurrection, and such he must have always possessed, if it were capable of pervading, without resistance or injury, the density of intermediate matter. Devoid of its most essential properties, it might be exempt from the attributes and infirmities of the flesh. A fœtus that could increase from an invisible point to its full maturity; a child that could attain the stature of perfect manhood, without deriving any nourishment from the ordinary sources, might continue to exist without repairing a daily waste by a daily supply of external matter. Jesus might share the repasts of his disciples without being subject to the calls of thirst or hunger; and his virgin purity was never sullied by the involuntary stains of sensual concupiscence. Of a body thus singularly constituted, a question would arise, by what means and of what materials it was originally framed; and our sounder theology is startled by an answer which was not peculiar to the Gnostics, that both the form and the substance proceeded from the divine essence. The idea of pure and absolute spirit is a refinement of modern philosophy: the incorporeal essence, ascribed by the ancients to human souls, celestial beings, and even the Deity himself, does not exclude the notion of extended space; and their imagination was satisfied with a subtle nature of air, or fire, or æther, incomparably more perfect than the grossness of the material world. If we define the place, we must describe the figure, of the Deity. Our experience, perhaps our vanity, represents the powers of reason and virtue under an human form. The Anthropomorphites, who swarmed among the monks of Egypt and the Catholics of Africa, could produce the express declaration of Scripture, that man was made after the image of his Creator. The venerable Serapion, one of the saints of the Nitrian desert, relinquished, with many a tear, his darling prejudice; and bewailed, like an infant, his unlucky conversion, which had stolen away his God, and left his mind without any visible object of faith or devotion.

OPPOSITE THEORIES OF CERINTHUS AND APOLLINARIS

III. Such were the fleeting shadows of the Docetes. A more substantial, though less simple hypothesis, was contrived by Cerinthus of Asia,[1] who dared to oppose the last of the apostles. Placed on the confines of the Jewish and Gentile world, he laboured to reconcile the Gnostic with the Ebionite, by confessing in the same Messiah the supernatural union of a man and a God; and this mystic doctrine was adopted with many fanciful improvements by Carpocrates, Basilides, and Valentine, the heretics of the Egyptian school. In their eyes JESUS of Nazareth was a mere mortal, the legitimate son of Joseph and Mary: but he was the best and wisest of the human race, selected as the worthy instrument to restore upon earth the worship of the true and supreme Deity. When he was baptized in the Jordan, the CHRIST, the first of the æons, the Son of God himself, descended on Jesus in the form of a dove, to inhabit his mind and direct his actions during the allotted period of his ministry. When the Messiah was delivered into the hands of the Jews, the Christ, an immortal and impassible being, forsook his earthly tabernacle, flew back to the *pleroma* or world of spirits, and left the solitary Jesus to suffer, to complain, and to expire. But the justice and generosity of such a desertion are strongly questionable; and the fate of an innocent martyr, at first impelled, and at length abandoned, by his divine companion, might provoke the pity and indignation of the profane. Their murmurs were variously silenced by the sectaries who espoused and modified the double system of Cerinthus. It was alleged that, when Jesus was nailed to the cross, he was endowed with a miraculous apathy of mind and body, which rendered him

---

[1] St. John and Cerinthus accidentally met in the public bath of Ephesus; but the apostle fled from the heretic lest the building should tumble on their heads. This foolish story, reprobated by Dr. Middleton, is related however by Irenæus, on the evidence of Polycarp, and was probably suited to the time and residence of Cerinthus. The obsolete, yet probably the true, reading of 1 John iv. 3—ὃ λύει τὸν Ἰησοῦ—alludes to the double nature of that primitive heretic.

insensible of his apparent sufferings. It was affirmed that these momentary, though real pangs, would be abundantly repaid by the temporal reign of a thousand years reserved for the Messiah in his kingdom of the new Jerusalem. It was insinuated that if he suffered, he deserved to suffer; that human nature is never absolutely perfect; and that the cross and passion might serve to expiate the venial transgressions of the son of Joseph, before his mysterious union with the Son of God.

IV. All those who believe the immateriality of the soul, a specious and noble tenet, must confess, from their present experience, the incomprehensible union of mind and matter. A similar union is not inconsistent with a much higher, or even with the highest, degree of mental faculties; and the incarnation of an æon or archangel, the most perfect of created spirits, does not involve any positive contradiction or absurdity. In the age of religious freedom, which was determined by the council of Nice, the dignity of Christ was measured by private judgment according to the indefinite rule of Scripture, or reason, or tradition. But when his pure and proper divinity had been established on the ruins of Arianism, the faith of the Catholics trembled on the edge of a precipice where it was impossible to recede, dangerous to stand, dreadful to fall; and the manifold inconveniences of their creed were aggravated by the sublime character of their theology. They hesitated to pronounce—*that* God himself, the second person of an equal and consubstantial trinity, was manifested in the flesh;[1] *that* a being who pervades the universe had been confined in the womb of Mary; *that* his eternal duration had been marked by the days, and months, and years of human existence; *that* the Almighty had been scourged and crucified; *that* his impassible essence had felt pain and anguish; *that* his omniscience was not exempt from ignorance; and *that* the

---

[1] This strong expression might be justified by the language of St. Paul (1 Tim. iii. 16); but we are deceived by our modern Bibles. The word ő (which) was altered to θεός (God) at Constantinople in the beginning of the sixth century: the true reading, which is visible in the Latin and Syriac versions, still exists in the reasoning of the Greek as well as of the Latin fathers; and this fraud, with that of the *three witnesses of St. John,* is admirably detected by Sir Isaac Newton. I have weighed the arguments, and may yield to the authority of the first of philosophers, who was deeply skilled in critical and theological studies. [It should be ős. The weight of authority is so much against the common reading on both these points, that they are no longer urged by prudent controversialists. Would Gibbon's deference for the *first of philosophers* have extended to *all* his theological conclusions?—Milman.]

source of life and immortality expired on Mount Calvary.
These alarming consequences were affirmed with unblushing
simplicity by Apollinaris, bishop of Laodicea, and one of
the luminaries of the church. The son of a learned grammarian, he was skilled in all the sciences of Greece; eloquence,
erudition, and philosophy, conspicuous in the volumes of
Apollinaris, were humbly devoted to the service of religion.
The worthy friend of Athanasius, the worthy antagonist of
Julian, he bravely wrestled with the Arians and Polytheists,
and, though he affected the rigour of geometrical demonstration, his commentaries revealed the literal and allegorical
sense of the Scriptures. A mystery which had long floated
in the looseness of popular belief was defined by his perverse
diligence in a technical form; and he first proclaimed the
memorable words, "One incarnate nature of Christ," which
are still re-echoed with hostile clamours in the churches of
Asia, Egypt, and Ethiopia. He taught that the Godhead
was united or mingled with the body of a man; and that the
Logos, the eternal wisdom, supplied in the flesh the place
and office of an human soul. Yet, as the profound doctor had
been terrified at his own rashness, Apollinaris was heard to
mutter some faint accents of excuse and explanation. He
acquiesced in the old distinction of the Greek philosophers
between the rational and sensitive soul of man; that he might
reserve the *Logos* for intellectual functions, and employ the
subordinate human principle in the meaner actions of animal
life. With the moderate Docetes he revered Mary as the
spiritual, rather than as the carnal, mother of Christ, whose
body either came from heaven, impassible and incorruptible,
or was absorbed, and as it were transformed, into the essence
of the Deity. The system of Apollinaris was strenuously encountered by the Asiatic and Syrian divines, whose schools
are honoured by the names of Basil, Gregory, and Chrysostom,
and tainted by those of Diodorus, Theodore, and Nestorius.
But the person of the aged bishop of Laodicea, his character
and dignity, remained inviolate; and his rivals, since we may
not suspect them of the weakness of toleration, were astonished, perhaps, by the novelty of the argument, and diffi-
dent of the final sentence of the Catholic church. Her
judgment at length inclined in their favour; the heresy of
Apollinaris was condemned, and the separate congregations
of his disciples were proscribed by the Imperial laws. But

his principles were secretly entertained in the monasteries of Egypt, and his enemies felt the hatred of Theophilus and Cyril, the successive patriarchs of Alexandria.

V. The grovelling Ebionite and the fantastic Docetes were rejected and forgotten: the recent zeal against the errors of Apollinaris reduced the Catholics to a seeming agreement with the double nature of Cerinthus. But instead of a temporary and occasional alliance, *they* established, and *we* still embrace, the substantial, indissoluble, and everlasting union of a perfect God with a perfect man, of the second person of the trinity with a reasonable soul and human flesh. In the beginning of the fifth century the *unity* of the *two natures* was the prevailing doctrine of the church. On all sides it was confessed that the mode of their coexistence could neither be represented by our ideas nor expressed by our language. Yet a secret and incurable discord was cherished between those who were most apprehensive of confounding, and those who were most fearful of separating, the divinity and the humanity of Christ. Impelled by religious frenzy, they fled with adverse haste from the error which they mutually deemed most destructive of truth and salvation. On either hand they were anxious to guard, they were jealous to defend, the union and the distinction of the two natures, and to invent such forms of speech, such symbols of doctrine, as were least susceptible of doubt or ambiguity. The poverty of ideas and language tempted them to ransack art and nature for every possible comparison, and each comparison misled their fancy in the explanation of an incomparable mystery. In the polemic microscope an atom is enlarged to a monster, and each party was skilful to exaggerate the absurd or impious conclusions that might be extorted from the principles of their adversaries. To escape from each other they wandered through many a dark and devious thicket, till they were astonished by the horrid phantoms of Cerinthus and Apollinaris, who guarded the opposite issues of the theological labyrinth. As soon as they beheld the twilight of sense and heresy, they started, measured back their steps, and were again involved in the gloom of impenetrable orthodoxy. To purge themselves from the guilt or reproach of damnable error, they disavowed their consequences, explained their principles, excused their indiscretions, and unanimously pronounced the sounds of concord and faith. Yet a latent and almost invisible spark still lurked among the embers of controversy: by the breath of prejudice and passion it was quickly kindled to a mighty flame, and the verbal disputes of the Oriental sects have shaken the pillars of the church and state.

CYRIL, NESTORIUS AND THE FIRST COUNCILS OF EPHESUS

The name of CYRIL of Alexandria is famous in controversial story, and the title of *saint* is a mark that his opinions and his party have finally prevailed. In the house of his uncle, the archbishop Theophilus, he imbibed the orthodox lessons of zeal and dominion, and five years of his youth were profitably spent in the adjacent monasteries of Nitria. Under the tuition of the abbot Serapion, he applied himself to ecclesiastical studies with such indefatigable ardour, that in the course of *one* sleepless night he had perused the four gospels, the catholic epistles, and the epistle to the Romans. Origen he detested; but the writings of Clemens and Dionysius, of Athanasius and Basil, were continually in his hands: by the theory and practice of dispute, his faith was confirmed and his wit was sharpened; he extended round his cell the cobwebs of scholastic theology, and meditated the works of allegory and metaphysics, whose remains, in seven verbose folios, now peaceably slumber by the side of their rivals. Cyril prayed and fasted in the desert, but his thoughts (it is the reproach of a friend) were still fixed on the world; and the call of Theophilus, who summoned him to the tumult of cities and synods, was too readily obeyed by the aspiring hermit. With the approbation of his uncle he assumed the office and acquired the fame of a popular preacher. His comely person adorned the pulpit; the harmony of his voice resounded in the cathedral; his friends were stationed to lead or second the applause of the congregation; and the hasty notes of the scribes preserved his discourses, which, in their effect, though not in their composition, might be compared with those of the Athenian orators. The death of Theophilus expanded and realised the hopes of his nephew. The clergy of Alexandria was divided; the soldiers and their general supported the claims of the archdeacon; but a resistless multitude, with voices and with hands, asserted the cause of their favourite; and after a period of thirty-nine years Cyril was seated on the throne of Athanasius.

The prize was not unworthy of his ambition. At a distance from the court, and at the head of an immense capital, the patriarch, as he was now styled, of Alexandria had gradually usurped the state and authority of a civil magistrate. The public and private charities of the city were managed by his discretion; his voice inflamed or appeased the passions of the multitude; his commands were blindly obeyed by his numerous and fanatic *parabolani*, familiarised in their daily office with scenes of death; and the prefects of Egypt were awed or provoked by the temporal power of these Christian pontiffs. Ardent in the prosecution of heresy, Cyril auspiciously opened his reign by oppressing the Novatians, the most innocent and harmless of the sectaries. The interdiction of their religious worship appeared in his eyes a just and meritorious act; and he confiscated their holy vessels, without apprehending the guilt of sacrilege. The toleration, and even the privileges of the Jews, who had multiplied to the number of forty thousand, were secured by the laws of the Cæsars and Ptolemies, and a long prescription of seven hundred years since the foundation of Alexandria. Without any legal sentence, without any royal mandate, the patriarch, at the dawn of day, led a seditious multitude to the attack of the synagogues. Unarmed and unprepared, the Jews were incapable of resistance; their houses of prayer were levelled with the ground, and the episcopal warrior, after rewarding his troops with the plunder of their goods, expelled from the city the remnant of the unbelieving nation. Perhaps he might plead the insolence of their prosperity, and their deadly hatred of the Christians, whose blood they had recently shed in a malicious or accidental tumult. Such crimes would have deserved the animadversion of the magistrate; but in this promiscuous outrage the innocent were confounded with the guilty, and Alexandria was impoverished by the loss of a wealthy and industrious colony. The zeal of Cyril exposed him to the penalties of the Julian law; but in a feeble government and a superstitious age he was secure of impunity, and even of praise. Orestes complained; but his just complaints were too quickly forgotten by the ministers of Theodosius, and too deeply remembered by a priest who affected to pardon, and continued to hate, the prefect of Egypt. As he passed through the streets his chariot was assaulted by a band of five hundred of the Nitrian monks; his guards fled from the wild beasts of

the desert; his protestations that he was a Christian and ;
Catholic were answered by a volley of stones, and the fac
of Orestes was covered with blood. The loyal citizens o:
Alexandria hastened to his rescue; he instantly satisfied hi:
justice and revenge against the monk by whose hand he ha
been wounded, and Ammonius expired under the rod of th
lictor. At the command of Cyril his body was raised from th
ground, and transported in solemn procession to the cathedral
the name of Ammonius was changed to that of Thaumasius
the *wonderful;* his tomb was decorated with the trophies o
martyrdom; and the patriarch ascended the pulpit to cele
brate the magnanimity of an assassin and a rebel. Such honour
might incite the faithful to combat and die under the banner
of the saint; and he soon prompted, or accepted, the sacrific
of a virgin, who professed the religion of the Greeks, an
cultivated the friendship of Orestes. Hypatia, the daughter o
Theon the mathematician, was initiated in her father's studies
her learned comments have elucidated the geometry of Apol
lonius and Diophantus; and she publicly taught, both a
Athens and Alexandria, the philosophy of Plato and Aristotle
In the bloom of beauty, and in the maturity of wisdom
the modest maid refused her lovers and instructed her disciples
the persons most illustrious for their rank or merit wer
impatient to visit the female philosopher; and Cyril behel
with a jealous eye the gorgeous train of horses and slaves wh
crowded the door of her academy. A rumour was sprea
among the Christians that the daughter of Theon was th
only obstacle to the reconciliation of the prefect and the arch
bishop; and that obstacle was speedily removed. On a fata
day, in the holy season of Lent, Hypatia was torn from he
chariot, stripped naked, dragged to the church, and inhumanl
butchered by the hands of Peter the reader and a troo|
of savage and merciless fanatics: her flesh was scraped fron
her bones with sharp oyster-shells, and her quivering limb
were delivered to the flames. The just progress of inquiry an
punishment was stopped by seasonable gifts; but the murde
of Hypatia has imprinted an indelible stain on the characte
and religion of Cyril of Alexandria.

Superstition, perhaps, would more gently expiate the bloo
of a virgin than the banishment of a saint; and Cyril had
accompanied his uncle to the iniquitous synod of the Oak
When the memory of Chrysostom was restored and con

ecrated, the nephew of Theophilus, at the head of a dying faction, still maintained the justice of his sentence; nor was it till after a tedious delay and an obstinate resistance that he yielded to the consent of the Catholic world. His enmity to the Byzantine pontiffs was a sense of interest, not a sally of passion: he envied their fortunate station in the sunshine of the Imperial court; and he dreaded their upstart ambition, which oppressed the metropolitans of Europe and Asia, invaded the provinces of Antioch and Alexandria, and measured their diocese by the limits of the empire. The long moderation of Atticus, the mild usurper of the throne of Chrysostom, suspended the animosities of the Eastern patriarchs; but Cyril was at length awakened by the exaltation of a rival more worthy of his esteem and hatred. After the short and troubled reign of Sisinnius, bishop of Constantinople, the factions of the clergy and people were appeased by the choice of the emperor, who, on this occasion, consulted the voice of fame, and invited the merit of a stranger. Nestorius, a native of Germanicia, and a monk of Antioch, was recommended by the austerity of his life and the eloquence of his sermons; but the first homily which he preached before the devout Theodosius betrayed the acrimony and impatience of his zeal. "Give me, O Cæsar!" he exclaimed, "give me the earth purged of heretics, and I will give you in exchange the kingdom of heaven. Exterminate with me the heretics, and with you I will exterminate the Persians." On the fifth day, as if the treaty had been already signed, the patriarch of Constantinople discovered, surprised, and attacked a secret conventicle of the Arians; they preferred death to submission; the flames that were kindled by their despair soon spread to the neighbouring houses, and the triumph of Nestorius was clouded by the name of *incendiary*. On either side of the Hellespont his episcopal vigour imposed a rigid formulary of faith and discipline—a chronological error concerning the festival of Easter was punished as an offence against the church and state. Lydia and Caria, Sardes and Miletus, were purified with the blood of the obstinate Quartodecimans; and the edict of the emperor, or rather of the patriarch, enumerates three-and-twenty degrees and denominations in the guilt and punishment of heresy. But the sword of persecution which Nestorius so furiously wielded was soon turned against his own breast. Religion was the pretence; but, in the judgment of a contem-

porary saint, ambition was the genuine motive of episcopal
warfare.

In the Syrian school Nestorius had been taught to abhor
the confusion of the two natures, and nicely to discriminate
the humanity of his *master* Christ from the divinity of the
Lord Jesus. The Blessed Virgin he revered as the mother of
Christ, but his ears were offended with the rash and recent
title of mother of God, which had been insensibly adopted
since the origin of the Arian controversy. From the pulpit of
Constantinople, a friend of the patriarch, and afterwards the
patriarch himself, repeatedly preached against the use, or the
abuse, of a word unknown to the apostles, unauthorised by
the church, and which could only tend to alarm the timorous,
to mislead the simple, to amuse the profane, and to justify
by a seeming resemblance, the old genealogy of Olympus. In
his calmer moments Nestorius confessed that it might be
tolerated or excused by the union of the two natures, and
the communication of their *idioms:* but he was exasperated
by contradiction to disclaim the worship of a new-born, an
infant Deity, to draw his inadequate similes from the conjugal
or civil partnerships of life, and to describe the manhood of
Christ as the robe, the instrument, the tabernacle of his Godhead. At these blasphemous sounds the pillars of the sanctuary
were shaken. The unsuccessful competitors of Nestorius indulged their pious or personal resentment, the Byzantine clergy
was secretly displeased with the intrusion of a stranger: whatever is superstitious or absurd might claim the protection of
the monks; and the people was interested in the glory of their
virgin patroness. The sermons of the archbishop, and the
service of the altar, were disturbed by seditious clamour; his
authority and doctrine were renounced by separate congregations; every wind scattered round the empire the leaves of
controversy; and the voice of the combatants on a sonorous
theatre re-echoed in the cells of Palestine and Egypt. It was
the duty of Cyril to enlighten the zeal and ignorance of his
innumerable monks: in the school of Alexandria he had
imbibed and professed the incarnation of one nature; and the
successor of Athanasius consulted his pride and ambition
when he rose in arms against another Arius, more formidable
and more guilty, on the second throne of the hierarchy.
After a short correspondence, in which the rival prelates
disguised their hatred in the hollow language of respect and

charity, the patriarch of Alexandria denounced to the prince and people, to the East and to the West, the damnable errors of the Byzantine pontiff. From the East, more especially from Antioch, he obtained the ambiguous counsels of toleration and silence, which were addressed to both parties while they favoured the causes of Nestorius. But the Vatican received with open arms the messengers of Egypt. The vanity of Celestine was flattered by the appeal; and the partial version of a monk decided the faith of the pope, who, with his Latin clergy, was ignorant of the language, the arts, and the theology of the Greeks. At the head of an Italian synod, Celestine weighed the merits of the cause, approved the creed of Cyril, condemned the sentiments and person of Nestorius, degraded the heretic from his episcopal dignity, allowed a respite of ten days for recantation and penance, and delegated to his enemy the execution of this rash and illegal sentence. But the patriarch of Alexandria, whilst he darted the thunders of a god, exposed the errors and passions of a mortal; and his twelve anathemas still torture the orthodox slaves who adore the memory of a saint without forfeiting their allegiance to the synod of Chalcedon. These bold assertions are indelibly tinged with the colours of the Apollinarian heresy; but the serious, and perhaps the sincere, professions of Nestorius have satisfied the wiser and less partial theologians of the present times.

Yet neither the emperor nor the primate of the East were disposed to obey the mandate of an Italian priest; and a synod of the Catholic, or rather of the Greek, church was unanimously demanded as the sole remedy that could appease or decide this ecclesiastical quarrel. Ephesus, on all sides accessible by sea and land, was chosen for the place, the festival of Pentecost for the day, of a meeting; a writ of summons was despatched to each metropolitan, and a guard was stationed to protect and confine the fathers till they should settle the mysteries of heaven and the faith of the earth. Nestorius appeared not as a criminal, but as a judge; he depended on the weight rather than the number of his prelates, and his sturdy slaves from the baths of Zeuxippus were armed for every service of injury or defence. But his adversary Cyril was more powerful in the weapons both of the flesh and of the spirit. Disobedient to the letter, or at least to the meaning, of the royal summons, he was attended by fifty Egyptian bishops, who expected from their patriarch's nod the inspiration of the Holy Ghost. He had contracted an intimate alliance with Memnon bishop of Ephesus. The despotic primate of Asia disposed of the ready succours of thirty or forty episcopal votes: a crowd of peasants, the slaves of the church, was poured into the city to support with blows and clamours a metaphysical argument; and the people zealously asserted the honour of the Virgin, whose body reposed within the walls of Ephesus.[1] The fleet which had transported Cyril from Alexandria was laden with the riches of Egypt; and he disembarked a numerous body of mariners, slaves, and fanatics, enlisted with blind obedience under the banner of St. Mark and the mother of God. The fathers, and even the guards, of the church were awed by this martial array; the adversaries of Cyril and Mary were insulted in the streets, or threatened in their houses; his eloquence and liberality made a daily increase in the number of his adherents; and the Egyptian soon computed that he might command the attendance and the voices of two hundred bishops. But the author of the twelve anathemas foresaw and dreaded the opposition of John of Antioch, who, with a small though respectable train of metropolitans and divines, was advancing by slow journeys from the distant capital of the East. Impatient of a delay which he stigmatised as voluntary and culpable, Cyril announced the opening of the synod sixteen days after the festival of Pentecost. Nestorius, who depended on the near approach of his Eastern friends, persisted, like his predecessor Chrysostom, to disclaim the jurisdiction, and to disobey the summons, of his enemies: they hastened his trial, and his accuser presided in the seat of judgment. Sixty-eight bishops, twenty-two of metropolitan rank, defended his cause by a modest and temperate protest: they were excluded from the councils of their brethren. Candidian, in the emperor's name, requested a delay of four days; the profane magistrate was driven with outrage and insult from the assembly of the saints. The whole of this momentous transaction was crowded into the compass of a summer's day: the bishops delivered their separate opinions; but the uniformity of style reveals the influence or the hand of a master, who has been accused

---

[1] The Christians of the four first centuries were ignorant of the death and burial of Mary. The tradition of Ephesus is affirmed by the synod; yet it has been superseded by the claim of Jerusalem; and her *empty* sepulchre, as it was shown to the pilgrims, produced the fable of her resurrection and assumption, in which the Greek and Latin churches have piously acquiesced.

of corrupting the public evidence of their acts and subscriptions. Without a dissenting voice they recognised in the
epistles of Cyril the Nicene creed and the doctrine of the
fathers: but the partial extracts from the letters and homilies
of Nestorius were interrupted by curses and anathemas; and
the heretic was degraded from his episcopal and ecclesiastical
dignity. The sentence, maliciously inscribed to the new
Judas, was affixed and proclaimed in the streets of Ephesus:
the weary prelates, as they issued from the church of the
mother of God, were saluted as her champions; and her
victory was celebrated by the illuminations, the songs, and
the tumult of the night.

On the fifth day the triumph was clouded by the arrival
and indignation of the Eastern bishops. In a chamber of the
inn, before he had wiped the dust from his shoes, John of
Antioch gave audience to Candidian the Imperial minister,
who related his ineffectual efforts to prevent or to annul the
hasty violence of the Egyptian. With equal haste and violence
the Oriental synod of fifty bishops degraded Cyril and
Memnon from their episcopal honours; condemned, in the
twelve anathemas, the purest venom of the Apollinarian
heresy; and described the Alexandrian primate as a monster,
born and educated for the destruction of the church. *His*
throne was distant and inaccessible; but they instantly resolved
to bestow on the flock of Ephesus the blessing of a faithful
shepherd. By the vigilance of Memnon the churches were
shut against them, and a strong garrison was thrown into the
cathedral. The troops, under the command of Candidian,
advanced to the assault; the outguards were routed and put
to the sword, but the place was impregnable: the besiegers
retired; their retreat was pursued by a vigorous sally; they
lost their horses, and many of the soldiers were dangerously
wounded with clubs and stones. Ephesus, the city of the
Virgin, was defiled with rage and clamour, with sedition and
blood; the rival synods darted anathemas and excommuni-
cations from their spiritual engines; and the court of Theodosius was perplexed by the adverse and contradictory narratives of the Syrian and Egyptian factions. During a busy
period of three months the emperor tried every method,
except the most effectual means of indifference and contempt,
to reconcile this theological quarrel. He attempted to remove
or intimidate the leaders by a common sentence of acquittal or

condemnation; he invested his representatives at Ephesus with ample power and military force; he summoned from either party eight chosen deputies to a free and candid conference in the neighbourhood of the capital, far from the contagion of popular frenzy. But the Orientals refused to yield, and the Catholics, proud of their numbers and of their Latin allies, rejected all terms of union or toleration. The patience of the meek Theodosius was provoked, and he dissolved in anger this episcopal tumult, which at the distance of thirteen centuries assumes the venerable aspect of the third œcumenical council. "God is my witness," said the pious prince, "that I am not the author of this confusion. His providence will discern and punish the guilty. Return to your provinces, and may your private virtues repair the mischief and scandal of your meeting." They returned to their provinces; but the same passions which had distracted the synod of Ephesus were diffused over the Eastern world. After three obstinate and equal campaigns, John of Antioch and Cyril of Alexandria condescended to explain and embrace; but their seeming re-union must be imputed rather to prudence than to reason, to the mutual lassitude rather than to the Christian charity of the patriarchs.

The Byzantine pontiff had instilled into the royal ear a baleful prejudice against the character and conduct of his Egyptian rival. An epistle of menace and invective, which accompanied the summons, accused him as a busy, insolent, and envious priest, who perplexed the simplicity of the faith, violated the peace of the church and state, and, by his artful and separate addresses to the wife and sister of Theodosius, presumed to suppose, or to scatter, the seeds of discord in the Imperial family. At the stern command of his sovereign, Cyril had repaired to Ephesus, where he was resisted, threatened, and confined, by the magistrates in the interest of Nestorius and the Orientals, who assembled the troops of Lydia and Ionia to suppress the fanatic and disorderly train of the patriarch. Without expecting the royal licence, he escaped from his guards, precipitately embarked, deserted the imperfect synod, and retired to his episcopal fortress of safety and independence. But his artful emissaries, both in the court and city, successfully laboured to appease the resentment, and to conciliate the favour, of the emperor. The feeble son of Arcadius was alternately swayed by his wife and sister, by the eunuchs and women of the palace: superstition and avarice were their ruling passions; and the orthodox chiefs were assiduous in their endeavours to alarm the former and to gratify the latter. Constantinople and the suburbs were sanctified with frequent monasteries, and the holy abbots, Dalmatius and Eutyches, had devoted their zeal and fidelity to the cause of Cyril, the worship of Mary, and the unity of Christ. From the first moment of their monastic life they had never mingled with the world, or trod the profane ground of the city. But in this awful moment of the danger of the church, their vow was superseded by a more sublime and indispensable duty. At the head of a long order of monks and hermits, who carried burning tapers in their hands, and chanted litanies to the mother of God, they proceeded from their monasteries to the palace. The people was edified and inflamed by this extraordinary spectacle, and the trembling monarch listened to the prayers and adjurations of the saints, who boldly pronounced that none could hope for salvation unless they embraced the person and the creed of the orthodox successor of Athanasius. At the same time every avenue of the throne was assaulted with gold. Under the decent names of *eulogies* and *benedictions,* the courtiers of both sexes were bribed according to the measure of their power and rapaciousness. But their incessant demands despoiled the sanctuaries of Constantinople and Alexandria; and the authority of the patriarch was unable to silence the just murmur of his clergy, that a debt of sixty thousand pounds had already been contracted to support the expense of this scandalous corruption. Pulcheria, who relieved her brother from the weight of an empire, was the firmest pillar of orthodoxy; and so intimate was the alliance between the thunders of the synod and the whispers of the court, that Cyril was assured of success if he could displace one eunuch, and substitute another in the favour of Theodosius. Yet the Egyptian could not boast of a glorious or decisive victory. The emperor, with unaccustomed firmness, adhered to his promise of protecting the innocence of the Oriental bishops; and Cyril softened his anathemas, and confessed, with ambiguity and reluctance, a twofold nature of Christ, before he was permitted to satiate his revenge against the unfortunate Nestorius.

The rash and obstinate Nestorius, before the end of the synod, was oppressed by Cyril, betrayed by the court, and

faintly supported by his Eastern friends. A sentiment of fear
or indignation prompted him, while it was yet time, to affect
the glory of a voluntary abdication: his wish, or at least his
request, was readily granted; he was conducted with honour
from Ephesus to his old monastery of Antioch; and, after a
short pause, his successors, Maximian and Proclus, were
acknowledged as the lawful bishops of Constantinople. But in
the silence of his cell the degraded patriarch could no longer
resume the innocence and security of a private monk. The
past he regretted, he was discontented with the present, and
the future he had reason to dread: the Oriental bishops
successively disengaged their cause from his unpopular name,
and each day decreased the number of the schismatics who
revered Nestorius as the confessor of the faith. After a
residence at Antioch of four years, the hand of Theodosius
subscribed an edict which ranked him with Simon the magician, proscribed his opinions and followers, condemned his
writings to the flames, and banished his person first to Petra
in Arabia, and at length to Oasis, one of the *islands* of the
Libyan desert. Secluded from the church and from the world,
the exile was still pursued by the rage of bigotry and war.
A wandering tribe of the Blemmyes or Nubians invaded his
solitary prison: in their retreat they dismissed a crowd of
useless captives; but no sooner had Nestorius reached the
banks of the Nile, than he would gladly have escaped from
a Roman and orthodox city to the milder servitude of the
savages. His flight was punished as a new crime: the soul of
the patriarch inspired the civil and ecclesiastical powers of
Egypt; the magistrates, the soldiers, the monks, devoutly
tortured the enemy of Christ and St. Cyril; and, as far as the
confines of Ethiopia, the heretic was alternately dragged and
recalled, till his aged body was broken by the hardships and
accidents of these reiterated journeys. Yet his mind was still
independent and erect; the president of Thebais was awed
by his pastoral letters; he survived the Catholic tyrant of
Alexandria, and, after sixteen years' banishment, the synod
of Chalcedon would perhaps have restored him to the honours,
or at least to the communion, of the church. The death of
Nestorius prevented his obedience to their welcome summons;
and his disease might afford some colour to the scandalous
report, that his tongue, the organ of blasphemy, had been
eaten by the worms. He was buried in a city of Upper Egypt,

known by the names of Chemnis, or Panopolis, or Akmim; but the immortal malice of the Jacobites has persevered for ages to cast stones against his sepulchre, and to propagate the foolish tradition that it was never watered by the rain of heaven, which equally descends on the righteous and the ungodly. Humanity may drop a tear on the fate of Nestorius; yet justice must observe that he suffered the persecution which he had approved and inflicted.

HERESY OF EUTYCHES AND SECOND COUNCIL OF EPHESUS

The death of the Alexandrian primate, after a reign of thirty-two years, abandoned the Catholics to the intemperance of zeal and the abuse of victory. The *monophysite* doctrine (one incarnate nature) was rigorously preached in the churches of Egypt and the monasteries of the East; the primitive creed of Apollinaris was protected by the sanctity of Cyril; and the name of EUTYCHES, his venerable friend, has been applied to the sect most adverse to the Syrian heresy of Nestorius. His rival Eutyches was the abbot, or archimandrite, or superior of three hundred monks; but the opinions of a simple and illiterate recluse might have expired in the cell where he had slept above seventy years, if the resentment or indiscretion of Flavian, the Byzantine pontiff, had not exposed the scandal to the eyes of the Christian world. His domestic synod was instantly convened, their proceedings were sullied with clamour and artifice, and the aged heretic was surprised into a seeming confession that Christ had not derived his body from the substance of the Virgin Mary. From their partial decree Eutyches appealed to a general council; and his cause was vigorously asserted by his godson Chrysaphius, the reigning eunuch of the palace, and his accomplice Dioscorus, who had succeeded to the throne, the creed, the talents, and the vices of the nephew of Theophilus. By the special summons of Theodosius, the second synod of Ephesus was judiciously composed of ten metropolitans and ten bishops from each of the six dioceses of the Eastern empire: some exceptions of favour or merit enlarged the number to one hundred and thirty-five; and the Syrian Barsumas, as the chief and representative of the monks, was invited to sit and vote with the successors of the apostles. But the despotism of the Alexandrian patriarch again oppressed the freedom of debate: the same spiritual and carnal weapons were again drawn from the arsenals of Egypt; the Asiatic veterans, a band of archers, served under the orders of Dioscorus; and the more formidable monks, whose minds were inaccessible to reason or mercy, besieged the doors of the cathedral. The general, and, as it should seem, the unconstrained voice of the fathers accepted the faith and even the anathemas of Cyril; and the heresy of the two natures was formally condemned in the persons and writings of the most learned Orientals. "May those who divide Christ be divided with the sword, may they be hewn in pieces, may they be burned alive!" were the charitable wishes of a Christian synod. The innocence and sanctity of Eutyches were acknowledged without hesitation; but the prelates, more especially those of Thrace and Asia, were unwilling to depose their patriarch for the use or even the abuse of his lawful jurisdiction. They embraced the knees of Dioscorus, as he stood with a threatening aspect on the footstool of his throne, and conjured him to forgive the offences and to respect the dignity of his brother. "Do you mean to raise a sedition?" exclaimed the relentless tyrant. "Where are the officers?" At these words a furious multitude of monks and soldiers, with staves, and swords, and chains, burst into the church: the trembling bishops hid themselves behind the altar, or under the benches; and as they were not inspired with the zeal of martyrdom, they successively subscribed a blank paper, which was afterwards filled with the condemnation of the Byzantine pontiff. Flavian was instantly delivered to the wild beasts of this spiritual amphitheatre: the monks were stimulated by the voice and example of Barsumas to avenge the injuries of Christ: it is said that the patriarch of Alexandria reviled, and buffeted, and kicked, and trampled his brother of Constantinople: it is certain that the victim, before he could reach the place of his exile, expired on the third day of the wounds and bruises which he had received at Ephesus. The second synod has been justly branded as a gang of robbers and assassins; yet the accusers of Dioscorus would magnify his violence, to alleviate the cowardice and inconstancy of their own behaviour.

THE COUNCIL OF CHALCEDON

The faith of Egypt had prevailed: but the vanquished party was supported by the same pope who encountered without fear the hostile rage of Attila and Genseric. The theology of Leo, his famous *tome* or epistle on the mystery of the incarnation, had been disregarded by the synod of Ephesus: his authority, and that of the Latin church, was insulted in his legates, who escaped from slavery and death to relate the melancholy tale of the tyranny of Dioscorus and the martyrdom of Flavian. His provincial synod annulled the irregular proceedings of Ephesus; but as this step was itself irregular, he solicited the convocation of a general council in the free and orthodox provinces of Italy. From his independent throne the Roman bishop spoke and acted without danger as the head of the Christians, and his dictates were obsequiously transcribed by Placidia and her son Valentinian, who addressed their Eastern colleague to restore the peace and unity of the church. But the pageant of Oriental royalty was moved with equal dexterity by the hand of the eunuch; and Theodosius could pronounce, without hesitation, that the church was already peaceful and triumphant, and that the recent flame had been extinguished by the just punishment of the Nestorians. Perhaps the Greeks would be still involved in the heresy of the Monophysites, if the emperor's horse had not fortunately stumbled; Theodosius expired; his orthodox sister, Pulcheria, with a nominal husband, succeeded to the throne; Chrysaphius was burnt, Dioscorus was disgraced, the exiles were recalled, and the *tome* of Leo was subscribed by the Oriental bishops. Yet the pope was disappointed in his favourite project of a Latin council: he disdained to preside in the Greek synod which was speedily assembled at Nice in Bithynia; his legates required in a peremptory tone the presence of the emperor; and the weary fathers were transported to Chalcedon under the immediate eye of Marcian and the senate of Constantinople. A quarter of a mile from the Thracian Bosphorus the church of St. Euphemia was built on the summit of a gentle though lofty ascent: the triple structure was celebrated as a prodigy of art, and the boundless prospect of the land and sea might have raised the mind of a sectary to the contemplation of the God of

the universe. Six hundred and thirty bishops were ranged in
order in the nave of the church; but the patriarchs of the
East were preceded by the legates, of whom the third was
a simple priest; and the place of honour was reserved for
twenty laymen of consular or senatorian rank. The gospel
was ostentatiously displayed in the centre, but the rule of
faith was defined by the papal and imperial ministers, who
moderated the thirteen sessions of the council of Chalcedon.
Their partial interposition silenced the intemperate shouts and
execrations which degraded the episcopal gravity; but, on the
formal accusation of the legates, Dioscorus was compelled
to descend from his throne to the rank of a criminal, already
condemned in the opinion of his judges. The Orientals, less
adverse to Nestorius than to Cyril, accepted the Romans as
their deliverers: Thrace, and Pontus, and Asia, were exasperated against the murderer of Flavian, and the new patriarchs
of Constantinople and Antioch secured their places by the
sacrifice of their benefactor. The bishops of Palestine, Macedonia, and Greece were attached to the faith of Cyril; but
in the face of the synod, in the heat of the battle, the leaders,
with their obsequious train, passed from the right to the left
wing, and decided the victory by this seasonable desertion. Of
the seventeen suffragans who sailed from Alexandria, four
were tempted from their allegiance, and the thirteen, falling
prostrate on the ground, implored the mercy of the council,
with sighs and tears, and a pathetic declaration, that, if they
yielded, they should be massacred, on their return to Egypt,
by the indignant people. A tardy repentance was allowed
to expiate the guilt or error of the accomplices of Dioscorus:
but their sins were accumulated on his head; he neither asked
nor hoped for pardon, and the moderation of those who
pleaded for a general amnesty was drowned in the prevailing
cry of victory and revenge. To save the reputation of his
late adherents, some *personal* offences were skilfully detected;
his rash and illegal excommunication of the pope, and his
contumacious refusal (while he was detained a prisoner) to
attend the summons of the synod. Witnesses were introduced
to prove the special facts of his pride, avarice, and cruelty;
and the fathers heard with abhorrence that the alms of the
church were lavished on the female dancers, that his palace,
and even his bath, was open to the prostitutes of Alexandria,

and that the infamous Pansophia, or Irene, was publicly entertained as the concubine of the patriarch.

For these scandalous offences Dioscorus was deposed by the synod, and banished by the emperor; but the purity of his faith was declared in the presence, and with the tacit approbation, of the fathers. Their prudence supposed rather than pronounced the heresy of Eutyches, who was never summoned before their tribunal; and they sat silent and abashed, when a bold Monophysite, casting at their feet a volume of Cyril, challenged them to anathematise in his person the doctrine of the saint. If we fairly peruse the acts of Chalcedon as they are recorded by the orthodox party, we shall find that a great majority of the bishops embraced the unity of Christ; and the ambiguous concession that he was formed OF or FROM two natures might imply either their previous existence, or their subsequent confusion, or some dangerous interval between the conception of the man and the assumption of the God. The Roman theology, more positive and precise, adopted the term most offensive to the ears of the Egyptians, that Christ existed IN two natures; and this momentous particle (which the memory, rather than the understanding, must retain) had almost produced a schism among the Catholic bishops. The *tome* of Leo had been respectfully, perhaps sincerely, subscribed; but they protested, in two successive debates, that it was neither expedient nor lawful to transgress the sacred landmarks which had been fixed at Nice, Constantinople, and Ephesus, according to the rule of Scripture and tradition. At length they yielded to the importunities of their masters, but their infallible decree, after it had been ratified with deliberate votes and vehement acclamations, was overturned in the next session by the opposition of the legates and their Oriental friends. It was in vain that a multitude of episcopal voices repeated in chorus, "The definition of the fathers is orthodox and immutable! The heretics are now discovered! Anathema to the Nestorians! Let them depart from the synod! Let them repair to Rome." The legates threatened, the emperor was absolute, and a committee of eighteen bishops prepared a new decree, which was imposed on the reluctant assembly. In the name of the fourth general council, the Christ in one person, but *in* two natures, was announced to the Catholic world: an invisible line was drawn between the heresy of Apollinaris and the faith of St. Cyril; and the road to paradise, a bridge as sharp as a razor, was suspended over the abyss by the master-hand of the theological artist. During ten centuries of blindness and servitude Europe received her religious opinions from the oracle of the Vatican; and the same doctrine, already varnished with the rust of antiquity, was admitted without dispute into the creed of the reformers, who disclaimed the supremacy of the Roman pontiff. The synod of Chalcedon still triumphs in the Protestant churches; but the ferment of controversy has subsided, and the most pious Christians of the present day are ignorant, or careless, of their own belief concerning the mystery of the incarnation.

Far different was the temper of the Greeks and Egyptians under the orthodox reigns of Leo and Marcian. Those pious emperors enforced with arms and edicts the symbol of their faith; and it was declared by the conscience or honour of five hundred bishops, that the decrees of the synod of Chalcedon might be lawfully supported, even with blood. The Catholics observed with satisfaction that the same synod was odious both to the Nestorians and the Monophysites; but the Nestorians were less angry, or less powerful, and the East was distracted by the obstinate and sanguinary zeal of the Monophysites. Jerusalem was occupied by an army of monks; in the name of the one incarnate nature, they pillaged, they burnt, they murdered; the sepulchre of Christ was defiled with blood; and the gates of the city were guarded in tumultuous rebellion against the troops of the emperor. After the disgrace and exile of Dioscorus, the Egyptians still regretted their spiritual father, and detested the usurpation of his successor, who was introduced by the fathers of Chalcedon. The throne of Proterius was supported by a guard of two thousand soldiers; he waged a five years' war against the people of Alexandria; and on the first intelligence of the death of Marcian, he became the victim of their zeal. On the third day before the festival of Easter the patriarch was besieged in the cathedral, and murdered in the baptistery. The remains of his mangled corpse were delivered to the flames, and his ashes to the wind: and the deed was inspired by the vision of a pretended angel; an ambitious monk who, under the name of Timothy the Cat, succeeded to the place and opinions of Dioscorus. This deadly superstition was inflamed on either side by the principle and the practice of retaliation: in the pursuit of a metaphysical quarrel many thousands were slain, and the Christians of every degree were deprived of the substantial enjoyments of social life, and of the invisible gifts of baptism and the holy communion. Perhaps an extravagant fable of the times may conceal an allegorical picture of these fanatics, who tortured each other and themselves. "Under the consulship of Venantius and Celer," says a grave bishop, "the people of Alexandria, and all Egypt, were seized with a strange and diabolical frenzy: great and small, slaves and freedmen, monks and clergy, the natives of the land, who opposed the synod of Chalcedon, lost their speech and reason, barked like dogs, and tore, with their own teeth, the flesh from their hands and arms."

THE *HENOTICON* OF ZENO

The disorders of thirty years at length produced the famous HENOTICON of the emperor Zeno, which in his reign, and in that of Anastasius, was signed by all the bishops of the East, under the penalty of degradation and exile if they rejected or infringed this salutary and fundamental law. The clergy may smile or groan at the presumption of a layman who defines the articles of faith; yet, if he stoops to the humiliating task, his mind is less infected by prejudice or interest, and the authority of the magistrate can only be maintained by the concord of the people. It is in ecclesiastical story that Zeno appears least contemptible; and I am not able to discern any Manichæan or Eutychian guilt in the generous saying of Anastasius, That it was unworthy of an emperor to persecute the worshippers of Christ and the citizens of Rome. The Henoticon was most pleasing to the Egyptians; yet the smallest blemish has not been descried by the jealous and even jaundiced eyes of our orthodox schoolmen, and it accurately represents the Catholic faith of the incarnation, without adopting or disclaiming the peculiar terms or tenets of the hostile sects. A solemn anathema is pronounced against Nestorius and Eutyches; against all heretics by whom Christ is divided, or confounded, or reduced to a phantom. Without defining the number or the article of the word *nature*, the pure system of St. Cyril, the faith of Nice, Constantinople, and Ephesus, is respectfully confirmed; but, instead of bowing at the name of the fourth council, the subject is dismissed by the censure of all contrary doctrines, *if* any such have been taught either elsewhere or at Chalcedon. Under this ambiguous expression the friends and the enemies of the last synod might unite in a silent embrace. The most reasonable Christians acquiesced in this mode of toleration; but their reason was feeble and inconstant, and their obedience was despised as timid and servile by the vehement spirit of their brethren. On a subject which engrossed the thoughts and discourses of men, it was difficult to preserve an exact neutrality; a book, a sermon, a prayer, rekindled the flame of controversy; and the bonds of communion were alternately broken and renewed by the private animosity of the bishops. The space between Nestorius and Eutyches was filled by a thousand shades of language and opinion; the *acephali* of Egypt, and the Roman pontiffs, of equal valour, though of unequal strength, may be found at the two extremities of the theological scale. The acephali, without a king or a bishop, were separated above three hundred years from the patriarchs of Alexandria, who had accepted the communion of Constantinople, without exacting a formal condemnation of the synod of Chalcedon. For accepting the communion of Alexandria, without a formal approbation of the same synod, the patriarchs of Constantinople were anathematised by the popes. Their inflexible despotism involved the most orthodox of the Greek churches in this spiritual contagion, denied or doubted the validity of their sacraments, and fomented, thirty-five years, the schism of the East and West, till they finally abolished the memory of four Byzantine pontiffs who had dared to oppose the supremacy of St. Peter. Before that period the precarious truce of Constantinople and Egypt had been violated by the zeal of the rival prelates. Macedonius, who was suspected of the Nestorian heresy, asserted, in disgrace and exile, the synod of Chalcedon, while the successor of Cyril would have purchased its overthrow with a bribe of two thousand pounds of gold.

In the fever of the times the sense, or rather the sound of a syllable, was sufficient to disturb the peace of an empire. The TRISAGION (thrice holy), "Holy, holy, holy, Lord God of Hosts!" is supposed by the Greeks to be the identical hymn which the angels and cherubim eternally repeat before the throne of God, and which, about the middle of the fifth century, was miraculously revealed to the church of Constantinople. The devotion of Antioch soon added, "who was crucified for us!" and this grateful address, either to Christ alone, or to the whole Trinity, may be justified by the rules of theology, and has been gradually adopted by the Catholics of the East and West. But it had been imagined by a Monophysite bishop; the gift of an enemy was at first rejected as a dire and dangerous blasphemy, and the rash innovation had nearly cost the emperor Anastasius his throne and his life. The people of Constantinople was devoid of any rational principles of freedom; but they held, as a lawful cause of rebellion, the colour of a livery in the races, or the colour of a mystery in the schools. The Trisagion, with and without this obnoxious addition, was chanted in the cathedral by two adverse choirs, and, when their lungs were exhausted, they had recourse to the more solid arguments of sticks and stones; the aggressors were punished by the emperor, and defended by the patriarch; and the crown and mitre were staked on the event of this momentous quarrel. The streets were instantly crowded with innumerable swarms of men, women, and children; the legions of monks, in regular array, marched, and shouted, and fought at their head. "Christians! this is the day of martyrdom: let us not desert our spiritual father; anathema to the Manichæan tyrant! he is unworthy to reign." Such was the Catholic cry; and the galleys of Anastasius lay upon their oars before the palace, till the patriarch had pardoned his penitent, and hushed the waves of the troubled multitude. The triumph of Macedonius was checked by a speedy exile; but the zeal of his flock was again exasperated by the same question, "Whether one of the Trinity had been crucified?" On this momentous occasion the blue and green factions of Constantinople suspended their discord, and the civil and military powers were annihilated in their presence. The keys of the city, and the standards of the guards, were deposited in the forum of Constantine, the principal station and camp of the faithful. Day and night they were incessantly busied either in singing hymns to the honour of their God, or in pillaging and murdering the servants of their prince. The head of his favourite monk, the friend, as they styled him, of the enemy of the Holy Trinity, was borne aloft on a spear; and the fire-brands, which had been darted against heretical structures, diffused the undistinguishing flames over the most orthodox buildings. The statues of the emperor were broken, and his person was concealed in a suburb, till, at the end of three days, he dared to implore the mercy of his subjects. Without his diadem, and in the posture of a suppliant, Anastasius appeared on the throne of the circus. The Catholics, before his face, rehearsed their genuine Trisagion; they exulted in the offer which he proclaimed by the voice of a herald of abdicating the purple; they listened to the admonition, that, since *all* could not reign, they should previously agree in the choice of a sovereign: and they accepted the blood of two unpopular ministers, whom their master without hesitation condemned to the lions. These furious but transient seditions were encouraged by the success of Vitalian, who, with an army of Huns and Bulgarians, for the most part idolaters, declared himself the champion of the Catholic faith. In this pious rebellion he depopulated Thrace, besieged Constantinople, exterminated sixty-five thousand of his fellow-Christians, till he obtained the recall of the bishops, the satisfaction of the pope, and the establishment of the council of Chalcedon, an orthodox treaty, reluctantly signed by the dying Anastasius, and more faithfully performed by the uncle of Justinian. And such was the event of the *first* of the religious wars which have been waged in the name and by the disciples of the God of Peace.

THEOLOGY OF JUSTINIAN

Justinian has been already seen in the various lights of a prince, a conqueror, and a lawgiver: the theologian still remains, and it affords an unfavourable prejudice that his theology should form a very prominent feature of his portrait. The sovereign sympathised with his subjects in their superstitious reverence for living and departed saints: his Code, and more especially his Novels, confirm and enlarge the privileges of the clergy; and in every dispute between a monk and a layman, the partial judge was inclined to pronounce that truth and innocence and justice were always on the side of the church. In his public and private devotions the emperor was assiduous and exemplary; his prayers, vigils, and fasts displayed the austere penance of a monk; his fancy was amused by the hope or belief of personal inspiration; he had secured the patronage of the Virgin and St. Michael the archangel; and his recovery from a dangerous disease was ascribed to the miraculous succour of the holy martyrs Cosmas and Damian. The capital and the provinces of the East were decorated with the monuments of his religion; and though the far greater part of these costly structures may be attributed to his taste or ostentation, the zeal of the royal architect was probably quickened by a genuine sense of love and gratitude towards his invisible benefactors. Among the titles of Imperial greatness the name of *Pious* was most pleasing to his ear; to promote the temporal and spiritual interest of the church was the serious business of his life; and the duty of father of his country was often sacrificed to that of defender of the faith. The controversies of the times were congenial to his temper and understanding; and the theological professors must inwardly deride the diligence of a stranger who cultivated their art and neglected his own. "What can ye fear," said a bold conspirator to his associates, "from your bigoted tyrant? Sleepless and unarmed he sits whole nights in his closet debating with reverend greybeards, and turning over the pages of ecclesiastical volumes." The fruits of these lucubrations were displayed in many a conference, where Justinian might shine as the loudest and most subtle of the disputants; in many a sermon, which, under the name of edicts and epistles, proclaimed to the empire the theology of their master. While the barbarians invaded the provinces, while the victorious legions marched under the banners of Belisarius and Narses, the successor of Trajan, unknown to the camp, was content to vanquish at the head of a synod. Had he invited to these synods a disinterested and rational spectator, Justinian might have learned "*that* religious controversy is the offspring of arrogance and folly; *that* true piety is most laudably expressed by silence and submission; *that* man, ignorant of his own nature, should not presume to scrutinise the nature of his God; and *that* it is sufficient for us to know that power and benevolence are the perfect attributes of the Deity."

Toleration was not the virtue of the times, and indulgence to rebels has seldom been the virtue of princes. But when the prince descends to the narrow and peevish character of a disputant, he is easily provoked to supply the defect of argument by the plenitude of power, and to chastise without mercy the perverse blindness of those who wilfully shut their eyes against the light of demonstration. The reign of Justinian was an uniform yet various scene of persecution; and he appears to have surpassed his indolent predecessors, both in the contrivance of his laws and the rigour of their execution. The insufficient term of three months was assigned for the conversion or exile of all heretics; and if he still connived at their precarious stay, they were deprived, under his iron yoke, not only of the benefits of society, but of the common birthright of men and Christians. At the end of four hundred years the Montanists of Phrygia still breathed the wild enthusiasm of perfection and prophecy which they had imbibed from their male and female apostles, the special organs of the Paraclete. On the approach of the Catholic priests and soldiers, they grasped with alacrity the crown of martyrdom; the conventicle and the congregation perished in the flames, but these primitive fanatics were not extinguished three hundred years after the death of their tyrant. Under the protection of the Gothic confederates, the church of the Arians at Constantinople had braved the severity of the laws: their clergy equalled the wealth and magnificence of the senate; and the gold and silver which were seized by the rapacious hand of Justinian might perhaps be claimed as the spoils of the provinces and the trophies of the barbarians. A secret remnant of pagans, who still lurked in the most refined and most rustic conditions of mankind, excited the indignation of the Christians, who were perhaps unwilling that any strangers should be the witnesses of their intestine quarrels. A bishop was named as the inquisitor of the faith, and his diligence soon discovered, in the court and city, the magistrates, lawyers, physicians, and sophists, who still cherished the superstition of the Greeks. They were sternly informed that they must choose without delay between the displeasure of Jupiter or Justinian, and that their aversion to the gospel could no longer be disguised under the scandalous mask of indifference or impiety. The patrician Photius perhaps alone was resolved to live and to die like his ancestors: he enfranchised himself with the stroke of a dagger, and left his tyrant the poor consolation of exposing with ignominy the lifeless corpse of the fugitive. His weaker brethren submitted to their earthly monarch, underwent the ceremony of baptism, and laboured, by their extraordinary zeal, to erase the suspicion, or to expiate the guilt, of idolatry. The native country of Homer, and the theatre of the Trojan war, still retained the last sparks of his mythology: by the care of the same bishop, seventy thousand pagans were detected and converted in Asia, Phrygia, Lydia, and Caria; ninety-six churches were built for the new proselytes; and linen vestments, bibles and liturgies, and vases of gold and silver, were supplied by the pious munificence of Justinian. The Jews, who had been gradually stripped of their immunities, were oppressed by a vexatious law, which compelled them to observe the festival of Easter the same day on which it was celebrated by the Christians. And they might complain with the more reason, since the Catholics themselves did not agree with the astronomical calculations of their sovereign: the people of Constantinople delayed the beginning of their Lent a whole week after it had been ordained by authority; and they had the pleasure of fasting seven days, while meat was exposed for sale by the command of the emperor. The Samaritans of Palestine were a motley race, an ambiguous sect, rejected as Jews by the pagans, by the Jews as schismatics, and by the Christians as idolaters. The abomination of the cross had already been planted on their holy mount of Garizim, but the persecution of Justinian offered only the alternative of baptism or rebellion. They chose the latter: under the standard of a desperate leader they rose in arms, and retaliated their wrongs on the lives, the property, and the temples of a defenceless people. The Samaritans were finally subdued by the regular forces of the East: twenty thousand were slain, twenty thousand were sold by the Arabs to the infidels of Persia and India, and the remains of that unhappy nation atoned for the crime of treason by the sin of hypocrisy. It has been computed that one hundred thousand Roman subjects were extirpated in the Samaritan war, which converted the once fruitful province into a desolate and smoking wilderness. But in the creed of Justinian the guilt of murder could not be applied to the slaughter of unbelievers; and he piously laboured to establish with fire and sword the unity of the Christian faith.

With these sentiments, it was incumbent on him, at least, to be always in the right. In the first years of his administration he signalised his zeal as the disciple and patron of orthodoxy: the reconciliation of the Greeks and Latins established the *tome* of St. Leo as the creed of the emperor and the empire; the Nestorians and Eutychians were exposed, on either side, to the double edge of persecution; and the four synods, of Nice, Constantinople, Ephesus, and *Chalcedon*, were ratified

by the code of a Catholic lawgiver. But while Justinian strove
to maintain the uniformity of faith and worship, his wife
Theodora, whose vices were not incompatible with devotion,
had listened to the Monophysite teachers; and the open or
clandestine enemies of the church revived and multiplied at
the smile of their gracious patroness. The capital, the palace,
the nuptial bed, were torn by spiritual discord; yet so doubtful was the sincerity of the royal consorts, that their seeming
disagreement was imputed by many to a secret mischievous
confederacy against the religion and happiness of their people.
The famous dispute of the THREE CHAPTERS, which has filled
more volumes than it deserves lines, is deeply marked with
this subtle and disingenuous spirit. It was now three hundred
years since the body of Origen had been eaten by the worms:
his soul, of which he held the pre-existence, was in the hands
of its Creator; but his writings were eagerly perused by the
monks of Palestine. In these writings the piercing eye of Justinian descried more than ten metaphysical errors; and the
primitive doctor, in the company of Pythagoras and Plato,
was devoted by the clergy to the *eternity* of hell-fire, which he
had presumed to deny. Under the cover of this precedent a
treacherous blow was aimed at the council of Chalcedon. The
fathers had listened without impatience to the praise of Theodore of Mopsuestia; and their justice or indulgence had restored both Theodoret of Cyrrhus and Ibas of Edessa to the
communion of the church. But the characters of these Oriental bishops were tainted with the reproach of heresy; the first
had been the master, the two others were the friends, of
Nestorius: their most suspicious passages were accused under
the title of the *three chapters;* and the condemnation of their
memory must involve the honour of a synod whose name was
pronounced with sincere or affected reverence by the Catholic
world. If these bishops, whether innocent or guilty, were
annihilated in the sleep of death, they would not probably be
awakened by the clamour which, after an hundred years, was
raised over their grave. If they were already in the fangs of
the dæmon, their torments could neither be aggravated nor
assuaged by human industry. If in the company of saints and
angels they enjoyed the rewards of piety, they must have
smiled at the idle fury of the theological insects who still
crawled on the surface of the earth. The foremost of these
insects, the emperor of the Romans, darted his sting, and dis-

tilled his venom, perhaps without discerning the true motives of Theodora and her ecclesiastical faction. The victims were no longer subject to his power, and the vehement style of his edicts could only proclaim their damnation, and invite the clergy of the East to join in a full chorus of curses and anathemas. The East, with some hesitation, consented to the voice of her sovereign: the fifth general council, of three patriarchs and one hundred and sixty-five bishops, was held at Constantinople; and the authors, as well as the defenders of the three chapters, were separated from the communion of the saints, and solemnly delivered to the prince of darkness. But the Latin churches were more jealous of the honour of Leo and the synod of Chalcedon; and if they had fought as they usually did under the standard of Rome, they might have prevailed in the cause of reason and humanity. But their chief was a prisoner in the hands of the enemy; the throne of St. Peter, which had been disgraced by the simony, was betrayed by the cowardice, of Vigilius, who yielded, after a long and inconsistent struggle, to the despotism of Justinian and the sophistry of the Greeks. His apostasy provoked the indignation of the Latins, and no more than two bishops could be found who would impose their hands on his deacon and successor Pelagius. Yet the perseverance of the popes insensibly transferred to their adversaries the appellation of schismatics; the Illyrian, African, and Italian churches were oppressed by the civil and ecclesiastical powers, not without some effort of military force; the distant barbarians transcribed the creed of the Vatican, and, in the period of a century, the schism of the three chapters expired in an obscure angle of the Venetian province. But the religious discontent of the Italians had already promoted the conquests of the Lombards, and the Romans themselves were accustomed to suspect the faith, and to detest the government, of their Byzantine tyrant.

Justinian was neither steady nor consistent in the nice process of fixing his volatile opinions and those of his subjects. In his youth he was offended by the slightest deviation from the orthodox line; in his old age he transgressed the measure of temperate heresy, and the Jacobites, not less than the Catholics, were scandalised by his declaration that the body of Christ was incorruptible, and that his manhood was never subject to any wants and infirmities, the inheritance of our mortal flesh. This *fantastic* opinion was announced in the last edicts of Justinian; and at the moment of his seasonable departure, the clergy had refused to subscribe, the prince was prepared to persecute, and the people were resolved to suffer or resist. A bishop of Treves, secure beyond the limits of his power, addressed the monarch of the East in the language of authority and affection. "Most gracious Justinian, remember your baptism and your creed. Let not your grey hairs be defiled with heresy. Recall your fathers from exile, and your followers from perdition. You cannot be ignorant that Italy and Gaul, Spain and Africa, already deplore your fall, and anathematise your name. Unless, without delay, you destroy what you have taught; unless you exclaim with a loud voice, I have erred, I have sinned, anathema to Nestorius, anathema to Eutyches, you deliver your soul to the same flames in which they will eternally burn." He died and made no sign. His death restored in some degree the peace of the church, and the reigns of his four successors, Justin, Tiberius, Maurice, and Phocas, are distinguished by a rare, though fortunate, vacancy in the ecclesiastical history of the East.

Heraclius tried to conciliate the Monophysites by the monothelite doctrine, the proposition that Christ had only one will. His victory and diplomatic theology came too late. The Arabian invasions were imminent.

In Chapter 48, which is omitted here, Gibbon outlined the plan of his last two quarto volumes and gave a conspectus of the imperial succession in four main dynasties from Heraclius (610–641) to the Latin conquest of Constantinople in 1204.

The following table is offered in its place.

HERACLIAN DYNASTY A.D. 610–717

Heraclius defeated the Persians and made a first stand against Islam. His defeat in 636 on the banks of the Yarmak resulted in the loss of Syria to the Empire. Jerusalem was captured in 638 and Alexandria in 647 (see below, Chapter 51).

In 679 the Bulgars crossed the Danube, and the latter end of the Heraclian dynasty was a period of decline.

ISAURIAN DYNASTY A.D. 717–867, THE ICONOCLASTS

Leo III the Isurian, 717–740, foiled a large-scale attack by the Arabs on Constantinople.

In 754 the Seventh Ecumenical Council held at Constantinople condemned the worship of images.

The Empress Irene (797–802) temporarily restored the use of images which was finally re-established by Theodora in 843 (see below, Chapter 49).

The disputes about images tend to obscure the fact that the Iconoclasts gave the empire a new civil and military organisation, and tried to adapt Roman law to current needs and to free the civil power from the influence of the monks.

The Isaurian dynasty ended with the murder of Leo V (813–820) and was followed by the short Phrygian dynasty (820–867).

THE MACEDONIAN DYNASTY A.D. 867–1057

Basil I, 867–886, established this dynasty. Among his successors may be noted Constantine VII Porphyrogenitus, 912–959, and his stepfather Romanus I Lecapenus (919–944), and John I Zimisces (969–970), who left three daughters, Eudoxia a nun, Theodora, and Zoe. The personal and political complications of the last two ladies dominated the imperial scene until Theodora's death in 1056. The dynasty survived for one more year with Michael Stratioticus, her nominee.

During this period a new political antithesis arose in Europe between the Emperor and the Patriarch in the East and the Emperor and the Pope in the West. Schism was created between the churches and became final in 1054. Politically the Slav nations became more important to the Roman Empire than the nations of the West.

The ninth and tenth centuries brought about some recovery of power and territory. Constantine VII initiated reforms of law and an intellectual revival (see below, Chapter 53). Nicephorus Phocas in 963–969 and John Zimisces (969–976) recovered Syria and Mesopotamia from Islam. Basil II Bulgaroctonus, i.e. the slayer of the Bulgars (963–1025), broke the power of the Slavs. After his death the power and prosperity of the Empire declined once more.

THE COMNENIAN DYNASTY A.D. 1057–1204

Isaac I Comnenus, 1057–1059, abdicated and was followed by a disastrous period marked by the victory of the Seljuk Turks at Manzikert in 1071, the prelude to the total loss of Asia Minor (see below, Chapter 57). Isaac's nephew founded a dynasty in 1081 and inaugurated a period of reform. Appeals were now made to the West, and the West in various ways recognised advantages to be got from the East. In 1095 the First Crusade began. A mortal blow to the Empire was dealt in 1204 when the Fourth Crusade captured and sacked Constantinople and ended the Comnenian dynasty. (See below, Chapter 60.)

49.

THE WORSHIP OF IMAGES. LEO THE ICONOCLAST.
REVOLT OF ITALY. RELATIONS OF PEPIN AND
CHARLEMAGNE WITH THE POPES. RESTORATION OF
IMAGES IN THE EAST. FINAL SEPARATION OF THE POPES FROM
THE EASTERN EMPIRE. REIGN AND CHARACTER OF
CHARLEMAGNE. REIGN OF CHARLES IV AND
COMPARISON WITH AUGUSTUS

IN THE CONNECTION of the church and state I have considered the former as subservient only, and relative, to the latter; a salutary maxim, if in fact as well as in narrative it had ever been held sacred. The oriental philosophy of the Gnostics, the dark abyss of predestination and grace, and the strange transformation of the Eucharist from the sign to the substance of Christ's body, I have purposely abandoned to the curiosity of speculative divines. But I have reviewed with diligence and pleasure the objects of ecclesiastical history by which the decline and fall of the Roman empire were materially affected, the propagation of Christianity, the constitution of the Catholic church, the ruin of Paganism, and the sects that arose from the mysterious controversies concerning the Trinity and incarnation. At the head of this class we may justly rank the worship of images, so fiercely disputed in the eighth and ninth centuries; since a question of popular superstition produced the revolt of Italy, the temporal power of the popes, and the restoration of the Roman empire in the West.

The primitive Christians were possessed with an unconquerable repugnance to the use and abuse of images; and this aversion may be ascribed to their descent from the Jews, and their enmity to the Greeks. The Mosaic law had severely proscribed all representations of the Deity; and that precept was firmly established in the principles and practice of the chosen people. The wit of the Christian apologists was pointed against the foolish idolaters who bowed before the workmanship of their own hands; the images of brass and marble, which, had

they been endowed with sense and motion, should have started rather from the pedestal to adore the creative powers of
the artist. Perhaps some recent and imperfect converts of the
Gnostic tribe might crown the statues of Christ and St. Paul
with the profane honours which they paid to those of Aristotle
and Pythagoras; but the public religion of the Catholics was
uniformly simple and spiritual; and the first notice of the use
of pictures is in the censure of the council of Illiberis, three
hundred years after the Christian era. Under the successors
of Constantine, in the peace and luxury of the triumphant
church, the more prudent bishops condescended to indulge
a visible superstition for the benefit of the multitude; and
after the ruin of Paganism they were no longer restrained by
the apprehension of an odious parallel. The first introduction
of a symbolic worship was in the veneration of the cross and
of relics. The saints and martyrs, whose intercession was implored, were seated on the right hand of God; but the gracious and often supernatural favours which, in the popular
belief, were showered round their tomb, conveyed an unquestionable sanction of the devout pilgrims who visited, and
touched, and kissed these lifeless remains, the memorials
of their merits and sufferings. But a memorial more interesting
than the skull or the sandals of a departed worthy is the
faithful copy of his person and features, delineated by the
arts of painting or sculpture. In every age such copies, so
congenial to human feelings, have been cherished by the zeal
of private friendship or public esteem: the images of the
Roman emperors were adored with civil and almost religious
honours; a reverence less ostentatious, but more sincere, was
applied to the statues of sages and patriots; and these profane virtues, these splendid sins, disappeared in the presence
of the holy men who had died for their celestial and everlasting country. At first the experiment was made with caution
and scruple; and the venerable pictures were discreetly allowed
to instruct the ignorant, to awaken the cold, and to gratify
the prejudices of the heathen proselytes. By a slow though
inevitable progression the honours of the original were transferred to the copy: the devout Christian prayed before the
image of a saint; and the Pagan rites of genuflexion, luminaries, and incense again stole into the Catholic church. The
scruples of reason or piety were silenced by the strong evidence of visions and miracles; and the pictures which speak,

and move, and bleed, must be endowed with a divine energy, and may be considered as the proper objects of religious adoration. The most audacious pencil might tremble in the rash attempt of defining by forms and colours the infinite Spirit, the eternal Father, who pervades and sustains the universe. But the superstitious mind was more easily reconciled to paint and to worship the angels, and, above all, the Son of God, under the human shape which on earth they have condescended to assume. The second person of the Trinity had been clothed with a real and mortal body; but that body had ascended into heaven: and had not some similitude been presented to the eyes of his disciples, the spiritual worship of Christ might have been obliterated by the visible relics and representations of the saints. A similar indulgence was requisite and propitious for the Virgin Mary: the place of her burial was unknown; and the assumption of her soul and body into heaven was adopted by the credulity of the Greeks and Latins. The use, and even the worship, of images was firmly established before the end of the sixth century: they were fondly cherished by the warm imagination of the Greeks and Asiatics: the Pantheon and Vatican were adorned with the emblems of a new superstition; but this semblance of idolatry was more coldly entertained by the rude barbarians and the Arian clergy of the West. The bolder forms of sculpture, in brass or marble, which peopled the temples of antiquity, were offensive to the fancy or conscience of the Christian Greeks; and a smooth surface of colours has ever been esteemed a more decent and harmless mode of imitation.

The merit and effect of a copy depends on its resemblance with the original; but the primitive Christians were ignorant of the genuine features of the Son of God, his mother, and his apostles: the statue of Christ at Paneas, in Palestine, was more probably that of some temporal saviour; the Gnostics and their profane monuments were reprobated, and the fancy of the Christian artists could only be guided by the clandestine imitation of some heathen model. In this distress a bold and dexterous invention assured at once the likeness of the image and the innocence of the worship. A new superstructure of fable was raised on the popular basis of a Syrian legend on the correspondence of Christ and Abgarus, so famous in the days of Eusebius, so reluctantly deserted by our modern advocates. The bishop of Cæsarea records the epistle, but he most strangely forgets the picture of Christ—the perfect impression of his face on a linen, with which he gratified the faith of the royal stranger who had invoked his healing power, and offered the strong city of Edessa to protect him against the malice of the Jews. The ignorance of the primitive church is explained by the long imprisonment of the image in a niche of the wall, from whence, after an oblivion of five hundred years, it was released by some prudent bishop, and seasonably presented to the devotion of the times. Its first and most glorious exploit was the deliverance of the city from the arms of Chosroes Nushirvan; and it was soon revered as a pledge of the divine promise that Edessa should never be taken by a foreign enemy. It is true, indeed, that the text of Procopius ascribes the double deliverance of Edessa to the wealth and valour of her citizens, who purchased the absence and repelled the assaults of the Persian monarch. He was ignorant, the profane historian, of the testimony which he is compelled to deliver in the ecclesiastical page of Evagrius, that the Palladium was exposed on the rampart, and that the water which had been sprinkled on the holy face, instead of quenching, added new fuel to the flames of the besieged. After this important service the image of Edessa was preserved with respect and gratitude; and if the Armenians rejected the legend, the more credulous Greeks adored the similitude, which was not the work of any mortal pencil, but the immediate creation of the divine original. The style and sentiments of a Byzantine hymn will declare how far their worship was removed from the grossest idolatry. "How can we with mortal eyes contemplate this image, whose celestial splendour the host of heaven presumes not to behold? HE who dwells in heaven condescends this day to visit us by his venerable image; HE who is seated on the cherubim visits us this day by a picture, which the Father has delineated with his immaculate hand, which he has formed in an ineffable manner, and which we sanctify by adoring it with fear and love." Before the end of the sixth century these images, *made without hands* (in Greek it is a single word), were propagated in the camps and cities of the Eastern empire; they were the objects of worship, and the instruments of miracles; and in the hour of danger or tumult their venerable presence could revive the hope, rekindle the courage, or repress the fury of the Roman legions. Of these pictures the far greater part, the transcripts of a human pencil, could only pretend to a secondary likeness and improper title; but there were some of higher descent, who derived their resemblance from an immediate contact with the original, endowed for that purpose with a miraculous and prolific virtue. The most ambitious aspired from a filial to a fraternal relation with the image of Edessa; and such is the *veronica* of Rome, or Spain, or Jerusalem, which Christ in his agony and bloody sweat applied to his face, and delivered to a holy matron. The fruitful precedent was speedily transferred to the Virgin Mary, and the saints and martyrs. In the church of Diospolis, in Palestine, the features of the Mother of God were deeply inscribed in a marble column: the East and West have been decorated by the pencil of St. Luke; and the Evangelist, who was perhaps a physician, has been forced to exercise the occupation of a painter, so profane and odious in the eyes of the primitive Christians. The Olympian Jove, created by the muse of Homer and the chisel of Phidias, might inspire a philosophic mind with momentary devotion; but these Catholic images were faintly and flatly delineated by monkish artists in the last degeneracy of taste and genius.[1]

LEO THE ICONOCLAST

The worship of images had stolen into the church by insensible degrees, and each petty step was pleasing to the superstitious mind, as productive of comfort and innocent of sin. But in the beginning of the eighth century, in the full magnitude of the abuse, the more timorous Greeks were awakened by an apprehension that, under the mask of Christianity, they had restored the religion of their fathers: they heard, with grief and impatience, the name of idolaters—the incessant charge of the Jews and Mahometans, who derived from the Law and the Koran an immortal hatred to graven images and all relative worship. The servitude of the Jews might curb their zeal and depreciate their authority; but the triumphant Musulmans, who reigned at Damascus, and threatened Constantinople, cast into the scale of reproach the accumulated weight of truth and victory. The cities of Syria,

---

[1] "Your scandalous figures stand quite out from the canvas: they are as bad as a group of statues!" It was thus that the ignorance and bigotry of a Greek priest applauded the pictures of Titian, which he had ordered, and refused to accept.

Palestine, and Egypt had been fortified with the images of Christ, his mother, and his saints; and each city presumed on the hope or promise of miraculous defence. In a rapid conquest of ten years the Arabs subdued those cities and these images; and, in their opinion, the Lord of Hosts pronounced a decisive judgment between the adoration and contempt of these mute and inanimate idols. For a while Edessa had braved the Persian assaults; but the chosen city, the spouse of Christ, was involved in the common ruin; and his divine resemblance became the slave and trophy of the infidels. After a servitude of three hundred years, the Palladium was yielded to the devotion of Constantinople, for a ransom of twelve thousand pounds of silver, the redemption of two hundred Musulmans, and a perpetual truce for the territory of Edessa. In this season of distress and dismay the eloquence of the monks was exercised in the defence of images; and they attempted to prove that the sin and schism of the greatest part of the Orientals had forfeited the favour and annihilated the virtue of these precious symbols. But they were now opposed by the murmurs of many simple or rational Christians, who appealed to the evidence of texts, of facts, and of the primitive times, and secretly desired the reformation of the church. As the worship of images had never been established by any general or positive law, its progress in the Eastern empire had been retarded, or accelerated, by the differences of men and manners, the local degrees of refinement, and the personal characters of the bishops. The splendid devotion was fondly cherished by the levity of the capital and the inventive genius of the Byzantine clergy; while the rude and remote districts of Asia were strangers to this innovation of sacred luxury. Many large congregations of Gnostics and Arians maintained, after their conversion, the simple worship which had preceded their separation; and the Armenians, the most warlike subjects of Rome, were not reconciled, in the twelfth century, to the sight of images. These various denominations of men afforded a fund of prejudice and aversion, of small account in the villages of Anatolia or Thrace, but which, in the fortune of a soldier, a prelate, or an eunuch, might be often connected with the powers of the church and state.

Of such adventurers the most fortunate was the emperor Leo the Third, who, from the mountains of Isauria, ascended the throne of the East. He was ignorant of sacred and profane letters; but his education, his reason, perhaps his intercourse with the Jews and Arabs, had inspired the martial peasant with an hatred of images; and it was held to be the duty of a prince to impose on his subjects the dictates of his own conscience. But in the outset of an unsettled reign, during ten years of toil and danger, Leo submitted to the meanness of hypocrisy, bowed before the idols which he despised, and satisfied the Roman pontiff with the annual professions of his orthodoxy and zeal. In the reformation of religion his first steps were moderate and cautious: he assembled a great council of senators and bishops, and enacted, with their consent, that all the images should be removed from the sanctuary and altar to a proper height in the churches, where they might be visible to the eyes, and inaccessible to the superstition, of the people. But it was impossible on either side to check the rapid though adverse impulse of veneration and abhorrence: in their lofty position the sacred images still edified their votaries and reproached the tyrant. He was himself provoked by resistance and invective; and his own party accused him of an imperfect discharge of his duty, and urged for his imitation the example of the Jewish king, who had broken without scruple the brazen serpent of the temple. By a second edict he proscribed the existence as well as the use of religious pictures; the churches of Constantinople and the provinces were cleansed from idolatry; the images of Christ, the Virgin, and the saints were demolished, or a smooth surface of plaster was spread over the walls of the edifice. The sect of the Iconoclasts was supported by the zeal and despotism of six emperors, and the East and West were involved in a noisy conflict of one hundred and twenty years. It was the design of Leo the Isaurian to pronounce the condemnation of images as an article of faith, and by the authority of a general council: but the convocation of such an assembly was reserved for his son Constantine; and though it is stigmatised by triumphant bigotry as a meeting of fools and atheists, their own partial and mutilated acts betray many symptoms of reason and piety. The debates and decrees of many provincial synods introduced the summons of the general council which met in the suburbs of Constantinople, and was composed of the respectable number of three hundred and thirty-eight bishops of Europe and Anatolia; for the patriarchs of Antioch and Alexandria were the slaves of the caliph, and the Roman pontiff had withdrawn the churches of Italy and the West from the communion of the Greeks. This Byzantine synod assumed the rank and powers of the seventh general council; yet even this title was a recognition of the six preceding assemblies, which had laboriously built the structure of the Catholic faith. After a serious deliberation of six months, the three hundred and thirty-eight bishops pronounced and subscribed an unanimous decree, that all visible symbols of Christ, except in the Eucharist, were either blasphemous or heretical; that image-worship was a corruption of Christianity and a renewal of Paganism; that all such monuments of idolatry should be broken or erased; and that those who should refuse to deliver the objects of their private superstition were guilty of disobedience to the authority of the church and of the emperor. In their loud and loyal acclamations they celebrated the merits of their temporal redeemer; and to his zeal and justice they intrusted the execution of their spiritual censures. At Constantinople, as in the former councils, the will of the prince was the rule of episcopal faith; but on this occasion I am inclined to suspect that a large majority of the prelates sacrificed their secret conscience to the temptations of hope and fear. In the long night of superstition the Christians had wandered far away from the simplicity of the Gospel: nor was it easy for them to discern the clue, and tread back the mazes of the labyrinth. The worship of images was inseparably blended, at least to a pious fancy, with the Cross, the Virgin, the saints and their relics; the holy ground was involved in a cloud of miracles and visions; and the nerves of the mind, curiosity and scepticism, were benumbed by the habits of obedience and belief. Constantine himself is accused of indulging a royal licence to doubt, or deny, or deride the mysteries of the Catholics, but they were deeply inscribed in the public creed of his bishops; and the boldest Iconoclast might assault with a secret horror the monuments of popular devotion, which were consecrated to the honour of his celestial patrons. In the reformation of the sixteenth century freedom and knowledge had expanded all the faculties of man: the thirst of innovation superseded the reverence of antiquity; and the vigour of Europe could disdain those phantoms which terrified the sickly and servile weakness of the Greeks.

The scandal of an abstract heresy can be only proclaimed

to the people by the blast of the ecclesiastical trumpet; but the most ignorant can perceive, the most torpid must feel, the profanation and downfall of their visible deities. The first hostilities of Leo were directed against a lofty Christ on the vestibule, and above the gate, of the palace. A ladder had been planted for the assault, but it was furiously shaken by a crowd of zealots and women: they beheld, with pious transports, the ministers of sacrilege tumbling from on high and dashed against the pavement; and the honours of the ancient martyrs were prostituted to these criminals, who justly suffered for murder and rebellion. The execution of the Imperial edicts was resisted by frequent tumults in Constantinople and the provinces: the person of Leo was endangered, his officers were massacred, and the popular enthusiasm was quelled by the strongest efforts of the civil and military power. Of the Archipelago, or Holy Sea, the numerous islands were filled with images and monks: their votaries abjured, without scruple, the enemy of Christ, his mother, and the saints; they armed a fleet of boats and galleys, displayed their consecrated banners, and boldly steered for the harbour of Constantinople, to place on the throne a new favourite of God and the people. They depended on the succour of a miracle: but their miracles were inefficient against the *Greek fire;* and, after the defeat and conflagration of their fleet, the naked islands were abandoned to the clemency or justice of the conqueror. The son of Leo, in the first year of his reign, had undertaken an expedition against the Saracens: during his absence the capital, the palace, and the purple were occupied by his kinsman Artavasdes, the ambitious champion of the orthodox faith. The worship of images was triumphantly restored: the patriarch renounced his dissimulation, or dissembled his sentiments; and the righteous claim of the usurper was acknowledged, both in the new and in ancient Rome. Constantine flew for refuge to his paternal mountains; but he descended at the head of the bold and affectionate Isaurians; and his final victory confounded the arms and predictions of the fanatics. His long reign was distracted with clamour, sedition, conspiracy, and mutual hatred and sanguinary revenge: the persecution of images was the motive or pretence of his adversaries; and, if they missed a temporal diadem, they were rewarded by the Greeks with the crown of martyrdom. In every act of open and clandestine treason the emperor felt the unforgiving enmity of the monks, the faithful slaves of the superstition to which they owed their riches and influence. They prayed, they preached, they absolved, they inflamed, they conspired; the solitude of Palestine poured forth a torrent of invective; and the pen of St. John Damascenus,[1] the last of the Greek fathers, devoted the tyrant's head, both in this world and the next. I am not at leisure to examine how far the monks provoked, nor how much they have exaggerated, their real and pretended sufferings, nor how many lost their lives or limbs, their eyes or their beards, by the cruelty of the emperor. From the chastisement of individuals he proceeded to the abolition of the order; and, as it was wealthy and useless, his resentment might be stimulated by avarice, and justified by patriotism. The formidable name and mission of the *Dragon,* his visitor-general, excited the terror and abhorrence of the *black* nation: the religious communities were dissolved, the buildings were converted into magazines or barracks; the lands, moveables, and cattle were confiscated; and our modern precedents will support the charge, that much wanton or malicious havoc was exercised against the relics, and even the books, of the monasteries. With the habit and profession of monks, the public and private worship of images was rigorously proscribed; and it should seem that a solemn abjuration of idolatry was exacted from the subjects, or at least from the clergy, of the Eastern empire.

REVOLT OF ITALY

The patient East abjured with reluctance her sacred images; they were fondly cherished, and vigorously defended, by the independent zeal of the Italians. In ecclesiastical rank and jurisdiction the patriarch of Constantinople and the pope of Rome were nearly equal. But the Greek prelate was a domestic slave under the eye of his master, at whose nod he alternately passed from the convent to the throne, and from the throne

---

[1] John, or Mansur, was a noble Christian of Damascus, who held a considerable office in the service of the caliph. His zeal in the cause of images exposed him to the resentment and treachery of the Greek emperor; and, on the suspicion of a treasonable correspondence, he was deprived of his right hand, which was miraculously restored by the Virgin. After this deliverance he resigned his office, distributed his wealth, and buried himself in the monastery of St. Sabas, between Jerusalem and the Dead Sea. The legend is famous; but his learned editor, Father Lequien, has unluckily proved that St. John Damascenus was already a monk before the Iconoclast dispute.

to the convent. A distant and dangerous station, amidst the barbarians of the West, excited the spirit and freedom of the Latin bishops. Their popular election endeared them to the Romans: the public and private indigence was relieved by their ample revenue; and the weakness of neglect of the emperors compelled them to consult, both in peace and war, the temporal safety of the city. In the school of adversity the priest insensibly imbibed the virtues and the ambition of a prince; the same character was assumed, the same policy was adopted, by the Italian, the Greek, or the Syrian, who ascended the chair of St. Peter; and, after the loss of her legions and provinces, the genius and fortune of the popes again restored the supremacy of Rome. It is agreed that in the eighth century their dominion was founded on rebellion, and that the rebellion was produced, and justified, by the heresy of the Iconoclasts; but the conduct of the second and third Gregory, in this memorable contest, is variously interpreted by the wishes of their friends and enemies. The Byzantine writers unanimously declare that, after a fruitless admonition, they pronounced the separation of the East and West, and deprived the sacrilegious tyrant of the revenue and sovereignty of Italy. Their excommunication is still more clearly expressed by the Greeks, who beheld the accomplishment of the papal triumphs; and as they are more strongly attached to their religion than to their country, they praise, instead of blaming, the zeal and orthodoxy of these apostolic men. The modern champions of Rome are eager to accept the praise and the precedent: this great and glorious example of the deposition of royal heretics is celebrated by the cardinals Baronius and Bellarmine; and if they are asked why the same thunders were not hurled against the Neros and Julians of antiquity? they reply, that the weakness of the primitive church was the sole cause of her patient loyalty. On this occasion the effects of love and hatred are the same; and the zealous Protestants, who seek to kindle the indignation and to alarm the fears of princes and magistrates, expatiate on the insolence and treason of the two Gregories against their lawful sovereign. They are defended only by the moderate Catholics, for the most part of the Gallican church, who respect the saint without approving the sin. These common advocates of the crown and the mitre circumscribe the truth of facts by the rule of equity, Scripture, and tradition, and appeal to the evidence of the Latins, and the lives and epistles of the popes themselves.

Two original epistles, from Gregory the Second to the emperor Leo, are still extant; and if they cannot be praised as the most perfect models of eloquence and logic, they exhibit the portrait, or at least the mask, of the founder of the papal monarchy. "During ten pure and fortunate years," says Gregory to the emperor, "we have tasted the annual comfort of your royal letters, subscribed in purple ink with your own hand, the sacred pledges of your attachment to the orthodox creed of our fathers. How deplorable is the change! how tremendous the scandal! You now accuse the Catholics of idolatry; and, by the accusation, you betray your own impiety and ignorance. To this ignorance we are compelled to adapt the grossness of our style and arguments: the first elements of holy letters are sufficient for your confusion; and were you to enter a grammar-school, and avow yourself the enemy of our worship, the simple and pious children would be provoked to cast their horn-books at your head." After this decent salutation the pope attempts the usual distinction between the idols of antiquity and the Christian images. The former were the fanciful representations of phantoms or dæmons, at a time when the true God had not manifested his person in any visible likeness. The latter are the genuine forms of Christ, his mother, and his saints, who had approved, by a crowd of miracles, the innocence and merit of this relative worship. He must indeed have trusted to the ignorance of Leo, since he could assert the perpetual use of images from the apostolic age, and their venerable presence in the six synods of the Catholic church. A more specious argument is drawn from the present possession and recent practice: the harmony of the Christian world supersedes the demand of a general council; and Gregory confesses that such assemblies can only be useful under the reign of an orthodox prince. To the impudent and inhuman Leo, more guilty than a heretic, he recommends peace, silence, and implicit obedience to his spiritual guides of Constantinople and Rome. The limits of civil and ecclesiastical powers are defined by the pontiff. To the former he appropriates the body; to the latter the soul: the sword of justice is in the hands of the magistrate: the more formidable weapon of excommunication is intrusted to the clergy; and in the exercise of their divine commission a zealous son will not spare his offending father: the successor of St. Peter may lawfully chastise the kings of the earth. "You assault us, O tyrant! with a carnal and military hand: unarmed and naked we can only implore the Christ, the prince of the heavenly host, that he will send unto you a devil for the destruction of your body and the salvation of your soul. You declare, with foolish arrogance, I will despatch my orders to Rome: I will break in pieces the image of St. Peter; and Gregory, like his predecessor Martin, shall be transported in chains and in exile to the foot of the imperial throne. Would to God that I might be permitted to tread in the footsteps of the holy Martin! but may the fate of Constans serve as a warning to the persecutors of the church! After his just condemnation by the bishops of Sicily, the tyrant was cut off in the fulness of his sins, by a domestic servant: the saint is still adored by the nations of Scythia, among whom he ended his banishment and his life. But it is our duty to live for the edification and support of the faithful people; nor are we reduced to risk our safety on the event of a combat. Incapable as you are of defending Roman subjects, the maritime situation of the city may perhaps expose it to your depredation; but we can remove to the distance of four-and-twenty *stadia,* to the first fortress of the Lombards, and then—you may pursue the winds. Are you ignorant that the popes are the bond of union, the mediators of peace between the East and West? The eyes of the nations are fixed on our humility; and they revere, as a God upon earth, the apostle St. Peter, whose image you threaten to destroy. The remote and interior kingdoms of the West present their homage to Christ and his vicegerent; and we now prepare to visit one of their most powerful monarchs who desires to receive from our hands the sacrament of baptism. The barbarians have submitted to the yoke of the Gospel, while you alone are deaf to the voice of the shepherd. These pious barbarians are kindled into rage: they thirst to avenge the persecution of the East. Abandon your rash and fatal enterprise; reflect, tremble, and repent. If you persist, we are innocent of the blood that will be spilt in the contest; may it fall on your own head!"

The first assault of Leo against the images of Constantinople had been witnessed by a crowd of strangers from Italy and the West, who related with grief and indignation the

sacrilege of the emperor. But on the reception of his proscriptive edict they trembled for their domestic deities; the
images of Christ and the Virgin, of the angels, martyrs, and
saints, were abolished in all the churches of Italy; and a
strong alternative was proposed to the Roman pontiff, the
royal favour as the price of his compliance, degradation and
exile as the penalty of his disobedience. Neither zeal nor
policy allowed him to hesitate; and the haughty strain in
which Gregory addressed the emperor displays his confidence
in the truth of his doctrine or the powers of resistance. Without depending on prayers or miracles, he boldly armed against
the public enemy, and his pastoral letters admonished the
Italians of their danger and their duty. At this signal,
Ravenna, Venice, and the cities of the Exarchate and Pentapolis adhered to the cause of religion; their military force by
sea and land consisted, for the most part, of the natives; and
the spirit of patriotism and zeal was transfused into the
mercenary strangers. The Italians swore to live and die in
the defence of the pope and the holy images; the Roman
people was devoted to their father, and even the Lombards
were ambitious to share the merit and advantage of his holy
war. The most treasonable act, but the most obvious revenge,
was the destruction of the statues of Leo himself: the most
effectual and pleasing measure of rebellion was the with-
holding the tribute of Italy, and depriving him of a power
which he had recently abused by the imposition of a new
capitation. A form of administration was preserved by the
election of magistrates and governors; and so high was the
public indignation, that the Italians were prepared to create
an orthodox emperor, and to conduct him with a fleet and
army to the palace of Constantinople. In that palace the
Roman bishops, the second and third Gregory, were condemned as the authors of the revolt, and every attempt was
made, either by fraud or force, to seize their persons and to
strike at their lives. The city was repeatedly visited or assaulted by captains of the guards, and dukes and exarchs of
high dignity or secret trust; they landed with foreign troops,
they obtained some domestic aid, and the superstition of
Naples may blush that her fathers were attached to the cause
of heresy. But these clandestine or open attacks were repelled
by the courage and vigilance of the Romans; the Greeks were
overthrown and massacred, their leaders suffered an ignomin-

ious death, and the popes, however inclined to mercy, refused to intercede for these guilty victims. At Ravenna, the several quarters of the city had long exercised a bloody and hereditary feud; in religious controversy they found a new aliment of faction: but the votaries of images were superior in numbers or spirit, and the exarch, who attempted to stem the torrent, lost his life in a popular sedition. To punish this flagitious deed, and restore his dominion in Italy, the emperor sent a fleet and army into the Adriatic gulf. After suffering from the winds and waves much loss and delay, the Greeks made their descent in the neighbourhood of Ravenna: they threatened to depopulate the guilty capital, and to imitate, perhaps to surpass, the example of Justinian the Second, who had chastised a former rebellion by the choice and execution of fifty of the principal inhabitants. The women and clergy, in sackcloth and ashes, lay prostrate in prayer; the men were in arms for the defence of their country; the common danger had united the factions, and the event of a battle was preferred to the slow miseries of a siege. In a hard-fought day, as the two armies alternately yielded and advanced, a phantom was seen, a voice was heard, and Ravenna was victorious by the assurance of victory. The strangers retreated to their ships, but the populous sea-coast poured forth a multitude of boats; the waters of the Po were so deeply infected with blood, that during six years the public prejudice abstained from the fish of the river; and the institution of an annual feast perpetuated the worship of images and the abhorrence of the Greek tyrant. Amidst the triumph of the Catholic arms, the Roman pontiff convened a synod of ninety-three bishops against the heresy of the Iconoclasts. With their consent, he pronounced a general excommunication against all who by word or deed should attack the tradition of the fathers and the images of the saints: in this sentence the emperor was tacitly involved, but the vote of a last and hopeless remonstrance may seem to imply that the anathema was yet suspended over his guilty head. No sooner had they confirmed their own safety, the worship of images, and the freedom of Rome and Italy, than the popes appear to have relaxed of their severity, and to have spared the relics of the Byzantine dominion. Their moderate counsels delayed and prevented the election of a new emperor, and they exhorted the Italians not to separate from the body of the Roman monarchy. The exarch was permitted to reside within the walls of Ravenna, a captive rather than a master; and till the Imperial coronation of Charlemagne, the government of Rome and Italy was exercised in the name of the successors of Constantine.

The liberty of Rome, which had been oppressed by the arms and arts of Augustus, was rescued, after seven hundred and fifty years of servitude, from the persecution of Leo the Isaurian. By the Cæsars the triumphs of the consuls had been annihilated: in the decline and fall of the empire, the god Terminus, the sacred boundary, had insensibly receded from the ocean, the Rhine, the Danube, and the Euphrates; and Rome was reduced to her ancient territory from Viterbo to Terracina, and from Narni to the mouth of the Tiber. When the kings were banished, the republic reposed on the firm basis which had been founded by their wisdom and virtue. Their perpetual jurisdiction was divided between two annual magistrates: the senate continued to exercise the powers of administration and counsel; and the legislative authority was distributed in the assemblies of the people by a well-proportioned scale of property and service. Ignorant of the arts of luxury, the primitive Romans had improved the science of government and war: the will of the community was absolute: the rights of individuals were sacred: one hundred and thirty thousand citizens were armed for defence of conquest; and a band of robbers and outlaws was moulded into a nation, deserving of freedom and ambitious of glory. When the sovereignty of the Greek emperors was extinguished, the ruins of Rome presented the sad image of depopulation and decay: her slavery was a habit, her liberty an accident; the effect of superstition, and the object of her own amazement and terror. The last vestige of the substance, or even the forms, of the constitution, was obliterated from the practice and memory of the Romans; and they were devoid of knowledge, or virtue, again to build the fabric of a commonwealth. Their scanty remnant, the offspring of slaves and strangers, was despicable in the eyes of the victorious barbarians. As often as the Franks or Lombards expressed their most bitter contempt of a foe, they called him a Roman; "and in this name," says the bishop Liutprand, "we include whatever is base, whatever is cowardly, whatever is perfidious, the extremes of avarice and luxury, and every vice that can prostitute the dignity of human nature." By the necessity of their situation, the inhabitants of Rome were cast into the rough model of a republican government: they were compelled to elect some judges in peace and some leaders in war: the nobles assembled to deliberate, and their resolves could not be executed without the union and consent of the multitude. The style of the Roman senate and people was revived, but the spirit was fled; and their new independence was disgraced by the tumultuous conflict of licentiousness and oppression. The want of laws could only be supplied by the influence of religion, and their foreign and domestic counsels were moderated by the authority of the bishop. His alms, his sermons, his correspondence with the kings and prelates of the West, his recent services, their gratitude and oath, accustomed the Romans to consider him as the first magistrate or prince of the city. The Christian humility of the popes was not offended by the name of *Dominus*, or Lord; and their face and inscription are still apparent on the most ancient coins. Their temporal dominion is now confirmed by the reverence of a thousand years; and their noblest title is the free choice of a people whom they had redeemed from slavery.

The Lombards subdued Ravenna, putting an end to the exarchate, and attacked Rome. Rome was delivered by Pepin, king of the Franks, and the Lombards finally surrendered to his son, Charlemagne, in 774.

RELATIONS OF PEPIN AND CHARLEMAGNE WITH THE POPES

The mutual obligations of the popes and the Carlovingian family form the important link of ancient and modern, of civil and ecclesiastical, history. In the conquest of Italy, the champions of the Roman church obtained a favourable occasion, a specious title, the wishes of the people, the prayers and intrigues of the clergy. But the most essential gifts of the popes to the Carlovingian race were the dignities of king of France and of patrician of Rome. I. Under the sacerdotal monarchy of St. Peter the nations began to resume the practice of seeking, on the banks of the Tiber, their kings, their laws, and the oracles of their fate. The Franks were perplexed between the name and substance of their government. All the powers of royalty were exercised by Pepin, mayor of the palace; and nothing, except the regal title, was wanting to his ambition. His enemies were crushed by his valour; his friends were multiplied by his liberality; his father had been the saviour of Christendom; and the claims of personal merit were repeated and ennobled in a descent of four generations. The name and image of royalty was still preserved in the last descendant of Clovis, the feeble Childeric; but his obsolete right could only be used as an instrument of sedition: the nation was desirous of restoring the simplicity of the constitution; and Pepin, a subject and a prince, was ambitious to ascertain his own rank and the fortune of his family. The mayor and the nobles were bound, by an oath of fidelity, to the royal phantom: the blood of Clovis was pure and sacred in their eyes; and their common ambassadors addressed the Roman pontiff to dispel their scruples or to absolve their promise. The interest of Pope Zachary, the successor of the two Gregories, prompted him to decide in their favour: he pronounced that the nation might lawfully unite, in the same person, the title and authority of king; and that the unfortunate Childeric, a victim of the public safety, should be degraded, shaved, and confined in a monastery for the remainder of his days. An answer so agreeable to their wishes was accepted by the Franks, as the opinion of a casuist, the sentence of a judge, or the oracle of a prophet: the Merovingian race disappeared from the earth; and Pepin was exalted on a buckler by the suffrage of a free people, accustomed to obey his laws and to march under his standard. His coronation was twice performed, with the sanction of the popes, by their most faithful servant St. Boniface, the apostle of Germany, and by the grateful hands of Stephen the Third, who, in the monastery of St. Denys, placed the diadem on the head of his benefactor. The royal unction of the kings of Israel was dexterously applied: the successor of St. Peter assumed the character of a divine ambassador: a German chieftain was transformed into the Lord's anointed; and this Jewish rite has been diffused and maintained by the superstition and vanity of modern Europe. The Franks were absolved from their ancient oath; but a dire anathema was thundered against them and their posterity, if they should dare to renew the same freedom of choice, or to elect a king, except in the holy and meritorious race of the Carlovingian princes. Without apprehending the future danger, these princes gloried in their present security: the secretary of Charlemagne affirms that the French sceptre was transferred by the authority of the popes; and, in their boldest enterprises, they insist, with confidence, on this signal and successful act of temporal jurisdiction.

II. In the change of manners and language the patricians of Rome were far removed from the senate of Romulus, or the palace of Constantine—from the free nobles of the republic, or the fictitious parents of the emperor. After the recovery of Italy and Africa by the arms of Justinian, the importance and danger of those remote provinces required the presence of a supreme magistrate; he was indifferently styled the exarch or the patrician; and these governors of Ravenna, who fill their place in the chronology of princes, extended their jurisdiction over the Roman city. Since the revolt of Italy and the loss of the Exarchate, the distress of the Romans had exacted some sacrifice of their independence. Yet, even in this act, they exercised the right of disposing of themselves; and the decrees of the senate and people successively invested Charles Martel and his posterity with the honours of patrician of Rome. The leaders of a powerful nation would have disdained a servile title and subordinate office; but the reign of the Greek emperors was suspended; and, in the vacancy of the empire, they derived a more glorious commission from the pope and the republic. The Roman ambassadors presented these patricians with the keys of the shrine of St. Peter, as a pledge and symbol of sovereignty; with a holy banner which it was their right and duty to unfurl in the defence of the church and city. In the time of Charles Martel and of Pepin, the interposition of the Lombard kingdom covered the freedom, while it threatened the safety, of Rome; and the *patriciate* represented only the title, the service, the alliance, of these distant protectors. The power and policy of Charlemagne annihilated an enemy and imposed a master. In his first visit to the capital he was received with all the honours which had formerly been paid to the exarch, the representative of the emperor; and these honours obtained some new decorations from the joy and gratitude of Pope Adrian the First. No sooner was he informed of the sudden approach of the monarch, than he despatched the magistrates and nobles of Rome to meet him, with the banner, about thirty miles from the city. At the distance of one mile the Flaminian Way was lined with the *schools*, or national communities, of Greeks, Lombards, Saxons, etc.: the Roman youth was under arms; and the children of a more tender age, with palms and olive-branches in their hands, chanted the praises of their great deliverer. At the aspect of the holy crosses, and ensigns of the saints, he dismounted from his horse, led the procession of his nobles to the Vatican, and, as he ascended the stairs, devoutly kissed each step of the threshold of the apostles. In the portico, Adrian expected him at the head of his clergy: they embraced, as friends and equals; but in their march to the altar, the king or patrician assumed the right hand of the pope. Nor was the Frank content with these vain and empty demonstrations of respect. In the twenty-six years that elapsed between the conquest of Lombardy and his Imperial coronation, Rome, which had been delivered by the sword, was subject, as his own, to the sceptre of Charlemagne. The people swore allegiance to his person and family: in his name money was coined and justice was administered; and the election of the popes was examined and confirmed by his authority. Except an original and self-inherent claim of sovereignty, there was not any prerogative remaining which the title of emperor could add to the patrician of Rome.

The gratitude of the Carlovingians was adequate to these obligations, and their names are consecrated as the saviours and benefactors of the Roman church. Her ancient patrimony of farms and houses was transformed by their bounty into the temporal dominion of cities and provinces; and the donation of the Exarchate was the first-fruits of the conquests of Pepin. Astolphus with a sigh relinquished his prey; the keys and the hostages of the principal cities were delivered to the French ambassador; and, in his master's name, he presented them before the tomb of St. Peter. The ample measure of the Exarchate might comprise all the provinces of Italy which had obeyed the emperor and his vicegerent; but its strict and proper limits were included in the territories of Ravenna, Bologna, and Ferrara: its inseparable dependency was the Pentapolis, which stretched along the Adriatic from Rimini to Ancona, and advanced into the midland country as far as the ridges of the Apennine. In this transaction the ambition and avarice of the popes had been severely condemned. Perhaps the humility of a Christian priest should

have rejected an earthly kingdom, which it was not easy for
him to govern without renouncing the virtues of his profession. Perhaps a faithful subject, or even a generous enemy,
would have been less impatient to divide the spoils of the
barbarian; and if the emperor had intrusted Stephen to solicit
in his name the restitution of the Exarchate, I will not absolve
the pope from the reproach of treachery and falsehood.
But in the rigid interpretation of the laws, every one may
accept, without injury, whatever his benefactor can bestow
without injustice. The Greek emperor had abdicated or forfeited his right to the Exarchate; and the sword of Astolphus
was broken by the stronger sword of the Carlovingian. It was
not in the cause of the Iconoclast that Pepin had exposed his
person and army in a double expedition beyond the Alps: he
possessed, and might lawfully alienate, his conquests: and
to the importunities of the Greeks he piously replied that
no human consideration should tempt him to resume the
gift which he had conferred on the Roman pontiff for the
remission of his sins and the salvation of his soul. The
splendid donation was granted in supreme and absolute dominion, and the world beheld for the first time a Christian bishop
invested with the prerogatives of a temporal prince—the
choice of magistrates, the exercise of justice, the imposition
of taxes, and the wealth of the palace of Ravenna. In the dissolution of the Lombard kingdom the inhabitants of the duchy
of Spoleto sought a refuge from the storm, shaved their heads
after the Roman fashion, declared themselves the servants and
subjects of St. Peter, and completed, by this voluntary surrender, the present circle of the ecclesiastical state. That
mysterious circle was enlarged to an indefinite extent by the
verbal or written donation of Charlemagne, who, in the
first transports of his victory, despoiled himself and the
Greek emperor of the cities and islands which had formerly
been annexed to the Exarchate. But in the cooler moments
of absence and reflection he viewed with an eye of jealousy
and envy the recent greatness of his ecclesiastical ally. The
execution of his own and his father's promises was respectfully
eluded: the king of the Franks and Lombards asserted the
inalienable rights of the empire; and, in his life and death,
Ravenna, as well as Rome, was numbered in the list of his
metropolitan cities. The sovereignty of the Exarchate melted
away in the hands of the popes; they found in the archbishops

of Ravenna a dangerous and domestic rival: the nobles and
people disdained the yoke of a priest; and in the disorders
of the time they could only retain the memory of an ancient
claim, which, in a more prosperous age, they have revived
and realised.

Fraud is the resource of weakness and cunning; and the
strong, though ignorant, barbarian was often entangled in the
net of sacerdotal policy. The Vatican and Lateran were an
arsenal and manufacture which, according to the occasion,
have produced or concealed a various collection of false or
genuine, of corrupt or suspicious acts, as they tended to promote the interest of the Roman church. Before the end of
the eighth century some apostolical scribe, perhaps the
notorious Isidore, composed the decretals and the donation of
Constantine, the two magic pillars of the spiritual and temporal monarchy of the popes. This memorable donation was
introduced to the world by an epistle of Adrian the First, who
exhorts Charlemagne to imitate the liberality and revive the
name of the great Constantine. According to the legend, the
first of the Christian emperors was healed of the leprosy, and
purified in the waters of baptism, by St. Silvester, the Roman
bishop; and never was physician more gloriously recompensed.
His royal proselyte withdrew from the seat and patrimony of
St. Peter; declared his resolution of founding a new capital
in the East; and resigned to the popes the free and perpetual
sovereignty of Rome, Italy, and the provinces of the West.
This fiction was productive of the most beneficial effects. The
Greek princes were convicted of the guilt of usurpation; and
the revolt of Gregory was the claim of his lawful inheritance.
The popes were delivered from their debt of gratitude; and
the nominal gifts of the Carlovingians were no more than the
just and irrevocable restitution of a scanty portion of the ecclesiastical state. The sovereignty of Rome no longer depended
on the choice of a fickle people; and the successors of St.
Peter and Constantine were invested with the purple and
prerogatives of the Cæsars. So deep was the ignorance and
credulity of the times that the most absurd of fables was
received with equal reverence in Greece and in France, and
is still enrolled among the decrees of the canon law. The
emperors and the Romans were incapable of discerning a
forgery that subverted their rights and freedom; and the only
opposition proceeded from a Sabine monastery, which in the

beginning of the twelfth century disputed the truth and validity of the donation of Constantine. In the revival of letters and liberty this fictitious deed was transpierced by the pen of Laurentius Valla, the pen of an eloquent critic and a Roman patriot. His contemporaries of the fifteenth century were astonished at his sacrilegious boldness; yet such is the silent and irresistible progress of reason, that before the end of the next age the fable was rejected by the contempt of historians and poets, and the tacit or modest censure of the advocates of the Roman church. The popes themselves have indulged a smile at the credulity of the vulgar; but a false and obsolete title still sanctifies their reign; and by the same fortune which has attended the decretals and the Sibylline oracles, the edifice has subsisted after the foundations have been undermined.

RESTORATION OF IMAGES IN THE EAST

While the popes established in Italy their freedom and dominion, the images, the first cause of their revolt, were restored in the Eastern empire. Under the reign of Constantine the Fifth, the union of civil and ecclesiastical power had overthrown the tree, without extirpating the root, of superstition. The idols, for such they were now held, were secretly cherished by the order and the sex most prone to devotion; and the fond alliance of the monks and females obtained a final victory over the reason and authority of man. Leo the Fourth maintained with less rigour the religion of his father and grandfather; but his wife, the fair and ambitious Irene, had imbibed the zeal of the Athenians, the heirs of the idolatry, rather than the philosophy, of their ancestors. During the life of her husband these sentiments were inflamed by danger and dissimulation, and she could only labour to protect and promote some favourite monks whom she drew from their caverns and seated on the metropolitan thrones of the East. But as soon as she reigned in her own name and that of her son, Irene more seriously undertook the ruin of the Iconoclasts; and the first step of her future persecution was a general edict for liberty of conscience. In the restoration of the monks a thousand images were exposed to the public veneration; a thousand legends were invented of their sufferings and miracles. By the opportunities of death or removal the episcopal seats were judiciously filled; the most eager competitors for earthly or celestial favour anticipated and flattered the judgment of their sovereign; and the promotion of her secretary Tarasius gave Irene the patriarch of Constantinople, and the command of the Oriental church. But the decrees of a general council could only be repealed by a similar assembly: the Iconoclasts whom she convened were bold in possession, and averse to debate; and the feeble voice of the bishops was re-echoed by the more formidable clamour of the soldiers and people of Constantinople. The delay and intrigues of a year, the separation of the disaffected troops, and the choice of Nice for a second orthodox synod, removed these obstacles; and the episcopal conscience was again, after the Greek fashion, in the hands of the prince. No more than eighteen days were allowed for the consummation of this important work: the Iconoclasts appeared, not as judges, but as criminals or penitents: the scene was decorated by the legates of Pope Adrian and the Eastern patriarchs; the decrees were framed by the president Tarasius, and ratified by the acclamations and subscriptions of three hundred and fifty bishops. They unanimously pronounced that the worship of images is agreeable to Scripture and reason, to the fathers and councils of the church: but they hesitate whether that worship be relative or direct; whether the Godhead and the figure of Christ be entitled to the same mode of adoration. Of this second Nicene council the acts are still extant; a curious monument of superstition and ignorance, of falsehood and folly. I shall only notice the judgment of the bishops, on the comparative merit of image-worship and morality. A monk had concluded a truce with the dæmon of fornication, on condition of interrupting his daily prayers to a picture that hung in his cell. His scruples prompted him to consult the abbot. "Rather than abstain from adoring Christ and his Mother in their holy images, it would be better for you," replied the casuist, "to enter every brothel, and visit every prostitute, in the city." For the honour of orthodoxy, at least the orthodoxy of the Roman church, it is somewhat unfortunate that the two princes who convened the two councils of Nice are both stained with the blood of their sons. The second of these assemblies was approved and rigorously executed by the despotism of Irene, and she refused her adversaries the toleration which at first she had granted to her friends. During the five succeeding reigns, a period of thirty-eight years, the contest was maintained with unabated rage and various success between the worshippers and the breakers of the images; but I am not inclined to pursue with minute diligence the repetition of the same events. Nicephorus allowed a general liberty of speech and practice; and the only virtue of his reign is accused by the monks as the cause of his temporal and eternal perdition. Superstition and weakness formed the character of Michael the First, but the saints and images were incapable of supporting their votary on the throne. In the purple, Leo the Fifth asserted the name and religion of an Armenian; and the idols, with their seditious adherents, were condemned to a second exile. Their applause would have sanctified the murder of an impious tyrant, but his assassin and successor, the second Michael, was tainted from his birth with the Phrygian heresies: he attempted to mediate between the contending parties; and the intractable spirit of the Catholics insensibly cast him into the opposite scale. His moderation was guarded by timidity; but his son Theophilus, alike ignorant of fear and pity, was the last and most cruel of the Iconoclasts. The enthusiasm of the times ran strongly against them; and the emperors, who stemmed the torrent, were exasperated and punished by the public hatred. After the death of Theophilus the final victory of the images was achieved by a second female, his widow Theodora, whom he left the guardian of the empire. Her measures were bold and decisive. The fiction of a tardy repentance absolved the fame and the soul of her deceased husband; the sentence of the Iconoclast patriarch was commuted from the loss of his eyes to a whipping of two hundred lashes: the bishops trembled, the monks shouted, and the festival of orthodoxy preserves the annual memory of the triumph of the images. A single question yet remained, whether they are endowed with any proper and inherent sanctity; it was agitated by the Greeks of the eleventh century; and as this opinion has the strongest recommendation of absurdity, I am surprised that it was not more explicitly decided in the affirmative. In the West, Pope Adrian the First accepted and announced the decrees of the Nicene assembly, which is now revered by the Catholics as the seventh in rank of the general councils. Rome and Italy were docile to the voice of their father; but the greatest part of the Latin Christians were far behind in the race of superstition. The churches of France, Germany, England, and Spain steered a middle course between the adoration and the destruction of images, which they admitted into their temples, not as objects of worship, but as lively and useful memorials of faith and history. An angry book of controversy was composed and published in the name of Charlemagne: under his authority a synod of three hundred bishops was assembled at Frankfort: they blamed the fury of the Iconoclasts, but they pronounced a more severe censure against the superstition of the Greeks, and the decrees of their pretended council, which was long despised by the barbarians of the West. Among them the worship of images advanced with a silent and insensible progress; but a large atonement is made for their hesitation and delay by the gross idolatry of the ages which precede the reformation, and of the countries, both in Europe and America, which are still immersed in the gloom of superstition.

THE FINAL SEPARATION OF THE POPES FROM THE EASTERN EMPIRE

It was after the Nicene synod, and under the reign of the pious Irene, that the popes consummated the separation of Rome and Italy, by the translation of the empire to the less orthodox Charlemagne. They were compelled to choose between the rival nations: religion was not the sole motive of their choice; and while they dissembled the failings of their friends, they beheld, with reluctance and suspicion, the Catholic virtues of their foes. The difference of language and manners had perpetuated the enmity of the two capitals; and they were alienated from each other by the hostile opposition of seventy years. In that schism the Romans had tasted of freedom, and the popes of sovereignty: their submission would have exposed them to the revenge of a jealous tyrant; and the revolution of Italy had betrayed the impotence, as well as the tyranny of the Byzantine court. The Greek emperors had restored the images, but they had not restored the Calabrian estates and the Illyrian diocese, which the Iconoclasts had torn away from the successors of St. Peter; and Pope Adrian threatens them with a sentence of excommunication unless they speedily abjure this practical heresy. The Greeks were now orthodox; but their religion might be tainted by the breath of the reigning monarch: the Franks were now contumacious; but a discerning eye might discern their approaching conversion, from the use, to the adoration, of images. The name of Charlemagne was stained by the polemic acrimony of his scribes; but the conqueror himself conformed, with the temper of a statesman, to the various practice of France and Italy. In his four pilgrimages or visits to the Vatican he embraced the popes in the communion of friendship and piety; knelt before the tomb, and consequently before the image, of the apostle; and joined, without scruple, in all the prayers and processions of the Roman liturgy. Would prudence or gratitude allow the pontiffs to renounce their benefactor? Had they a right to alienate his gift of the Exarchate? Had they power to abolish his government of Rome? The title of patrician was below the merit and greatness of Charlemagne; and it was only by reviving the Western empire that they could pay their obligations or secure their establishment. By this decisive measure they would finally eradicate the claims of the Greeks: from the debasement of a provincial town, the majesty of Rome would be restored; the Latin Christians would be united, under a supreme head, in their ancient metropolis; and the conquerors of the West would receive their crown from the successors of St. Peter. The Roman church would acquire a zealous and respectable advocate; and, under the shadow of the Carlovingian power, the bishop might exercise, with honour and safety, the government of the city.

Before the ruin of Paganism in Rome the competition for a wealthy bishopric had often been productive of tumult and bloodshed. The people was less numerous, but the times were more savage, the prize more important, and the chair of St. Peter was fiercely disputed by the leading ecclesiastics who aspired to the rank of sovereign. The reign of Adrian the First surpasses the measure of past or succeeding ages; the walls of Rome, the sacred patrimony, the ruin of the Lombards, and the friendship of Charlemagne, were the trophies of his fame: he secretly edified the throne of his successors, and displayed in a narrow space the virtues of a great prince. His memory was revered; but in the next election, a priest of the Lateran, Leo the Third, was preferred to the nephew and the favourite of Adrian, whom he had promoted to the first dignities of the church. Their acquiescence or repentance disguised, above four years, the blackest intention of revenge, till the day of a procession, when a furious band of conspirators dispersed the unarmed multitude, and assaulted with blows and wounds the sacred person of the pope. But their enterprise on his life or liberty was disappointed, perhaps by their own confusion and remorse. Leo was left for dead on the ground: on his revival from the swoon, the effect of his loss of blood, he recovered his speech and sight; and this natural event was improved to the miraculous restoration of his eyes and tongue, of which he had been deprived, twice deprived, by the knife of the assassins. From his prison he escaped to the Vatican: the duke of Spoleto hastened to his rescue, Charlemagne sympathised in his injury, and in his camp of Paderborn in Westphalia accepted, or solicited, a visit from the Roman pontiff. Leo repassed the Alps with a commission of counts and bishops, the guards of his safety and the judges of his innocence; and it was not without reluctance that the conqueror of the Saxons delayed till the ensuing year the personal discharge of this pious office. In his fourth and last pilgrimage he was received at Rome with the due honours of king and patrician: Leo was permitted to purge himself by oath of the crimes imputed to his charge: his enemies were silenced, and the sacrilegious attempt against his life was punished by the mild and insufficient penalty of exile. On the festival of Christmas, the last year of the eighth century, Charlemagne appeared in the church of St. Peter; and to gratify the vanity of Rome, he had exchanged the simple dress of his country for the habit of a patrician. After the celebration of the holy mysteries, Leo suddenly placed a precious crown on his head, and the dome resounded with the acclamations of the people, "Long life and victory to Charles, the most pious Augustus, crowned by God the great and pacific emperor of the Romans!" The head and body of Charlemagne were consecrated by the royal unction: after the example of the Cæsars, he was saluted or adored by the pontiff: his coronation oath represents a promise to maintain the faith and privileges of the church; and the first-fruits were paid in his rich offerings to the shrine of the apostle. In his familiar conversation the emperor protested his ignorance of the intentions of Leo, which he would have disappointed by his absence on that memorable day. But the preparations of the ceremony must have disclosed the secret;

and the journey of Charlemagne reveals his knowledge and expectation: he had acknowledged that the Imperial title was the object of his ambition, and a Roman synod had pronounced that it was the only adequate reward of his merit and services.

THE REIGN AND CHARACTER OF CHARLEMAGNE

The appellation of *great* has been often bestowed, and sometimes deserved, but CHARLEMAGNE is the only prince in whose favour the title has been indissolubly blended with the name. That name, with the addition of *saint*, is inserted in the Roman calendar; and the saint, by a rare felicity, is crowned with the praises of the historians and philosophers of an enlightened age. His *real* merit is doubtless enhanced by the barbarism of the nation and the times from which he emerged: but the *apparent* magnitude of an object is likewise enlarged by an unequal comparison; and the ruins of Palmyra derive a casual splendour from the nakedness of the surrounding desert. Without injustice to his fame, I may discern some blemishes in the sanctity and greatness of the restorer of the Western empire. Of his moral virtues, chastity is not the most conspicuous:[1] but the public happiness could not be materially injured by his nine wives or concubines, the various indulgence of meaner or more transient amours, the multitude of his bastards whom he bestowed on the church, and the long celibacy and licentious manners of his daughters,[2] whom the father was suspected of loving with too fond a passion. I shall be scarcely permitted to accuse the ambition of a conqueror; but in a day of equal retribution, the sons of his brother Carloman, the Merovingian princes of Aquitain, and the four thousand five hundred Saxons who were beheaded on the same spot, would have something to allege against the justice and humanity of Charlemagne. His treatment of the vanquished Saxons was an abuse of the right of conquest; his laws were not less sanguinary than his arms, and, in the

---

[1] The vision of Weltin, composed by a monk eleven years after the death of Charlemagne, shows him in purgatory, with a vulture, who is perpetually gnawing the guilty member, while the rest of his body, the emblem of his virtues, is sound and perfect.

[2] The marriage of Eginhard with Imma, daughter of Charlemagne, is, in my opinion, sufficiently refuted by the *probrum* and *suspicio* that sullied these fair damsels, without excepting his own wife. The husband must have been too strong for the historian.

discussion of his motives, whatever is subtracted from bigotry must be imputed to temper. The sedentary reader is amazed by his incessant activity of mind and body; and his subjects and enemies were not less astonished at his sudden presence at the moment when they believed him at the most distant extremity of the empire; neither peace nor war, nor summer nor winter, were a season of repose; and our fancy cannot easily reconcile the annals of his reign with the geography of his expeditions. But this activity was a national, rather than a personal virtue: the vagrant life of a Frank was spent in the chase, in pilgrimage, in military adventures; and the journeys of Charlemagne were distinguished only by a more numerous train and a more important purpose. His military renown must be tried by the scrutiny of his troops, his enemies, and his actions. Alexander conquered with the arms of Philip, but the *two* heroes who preceded Charlemagne bequeathed him their name, their examples, and the companions of their victories. At the head of his veteran and superior armies he oppressed the savage or degenerate nations, who were incapable of confederating for their common safety; nor did he ever encounter an equal antagonist in numbers, in discipline, or in arms. The science of war has been lost and revived with the arts of peace; but his campaigns are not illustrated by any siege or battle of singular difficulty and success; and he might behold with envy the Saracen trophies of his grandfather. After his Spanish expedition his rearguard was defeated in the Pyrenæan mountains; and the soldiers, whose situation was irretrievable, and whose valour was useless, might accuse, with their last breath, the want of skill or caution of their general. I touch with reverence the laws of Charlemagne, so highly applauded by a respectable judge. They compose not a system, but a series, of occasional and minute edicts, for the correction of abuses, the reformation of manners, the economy of his farms, the care of his poultry, and even the sale of his eggs. He wished to improve the laws and the character of the Franks; and his attempts, however feeble and imperfect, are deserving of praise: the inveterate evils of the times were suspended or mollified by his government; but in his institutions I can seldom discover the general views and the immortal spirit of a legislator, who survives himself for the benefit of posterity. The union and stability of his empire depended on the life of a single man:

he imitated the dangerous practice of dividing his kingdoms among his sons; and, after his numerous diets, the whole constitution was left to fluctuate between the disorders of anarchy and despotism. His esteem for the piety and knowledge of the clergy tempted him to intrust that aspiring order with temporal dominion and civil jurisdiction; and his son Lewis, when he was stripped and degraded by the bishops, might accuse, in some measure, the imprudence of his father. His laws enforced the imposition of tithes, because the dæmons had proclaimed in the air that the default of payment had been the cause of the last scarcity. The literary merits of Charlemagne are attested by the foundation of schools, the introduction of arts, the works which were published in his name, and his familiar connection with the subjects and strangers whom he invited to his court to educate both the prince and people. His own studies were tardy, laborious, and imperfect; if he spoke Latin, and understood Greek, he derived the rudiments of knowledge from conversation, rather than from books; and, in his mature age, the emperor strove to acquire the practice of writing, which every peasant now learns in his infancy. The grammar and logic, the music and astronomy, of the times were only cultivated as the handmaids of superstition; but the curiosity of the human mind must ultimately tend to its improvement, and the encouragement of learning reflects the purest and most pleasing lustre on the character of Charlemagne. The dignity of his person, the length of his reign, the prosperity of his arms, the vigour of his government, and the reverence of distant nations, distinguish from the royal crowd; and Europe dates a new era from his restoration of the Western empire.

In 962 Otho, king of Germany, subdued Italy and appropriated the Western empire. The Imperial Crown was now vested in the name and nation of Germany.

THE EMPEROR CHARLES IV

It is in the fourteenth century that we may view in the strongest light the state and contrast of the Roman empire of Germany, which no longer held, except on the borders of the Rhine and Danube, a single province of Trajan or Constantine. Their unworthy successors were the counts of Hapsburg, of

Nassau, of Luxembourg, and of Schwartzenburg: the emperor
Henry the Seventh procured for his son the crown of Bohemia,
and his grandson Charles the Fourth was born among a
people strange and barbarous in the estimation of the Germans themselves. After the excommunication of Lewis of
Bavaria, he received the gift or promise of the vacant empire
from the Roman pontiffs, who, in the exile and captivity of
Avignon, affected the dominion of the earth. The death of
his competitors united the electoral college, and Charles
was unanimously saluted king of the Romans, and future emperor; a title which in the same age was prostituted to the
Cæsars of Germany and Greece. The German emperor was
no more than the elective and impotent magistrate of an
aristocracy of princes, who had not left him a village that he
might call his own. His best prerogative was the right of
presiding and proposing in the national senate, which was
convened at his summons; and his native kingdom of Bohemia,
less opulent than the adjacent city of Nuremberg, was the
firmest seat of his power and the richest source of his revenue.
The army with which he passed the Alps consisted of three
hundred horse. In the cathedral of St. Ambrose, Charles was
crowned with the *iron* crown, which tradition ascribed to
the Lombard monarchy; but he was admitted only with a
peaceful train; the gates of the city were shut upon him;
and the king of Italy was held a captive by the arms of the
Visconti, whom he confirmed in the sovereignty of Milan. In
the Vatican he was again crowned with the *golden* crown of
the empire; but, in obedience to a secret treaty, the Roman
emperor immediately withdrew, without reposing a single
night within the walls of Rome. The eloquent Petrarch,
whose fancy revived the visionary glories of the Capitol, deplores and upbraids the ignominious flight of the Bohemian;
and even his contemporaries could observe that the sole
exercise of his authority was in the lucrative sale of privileges
and titles. The gold of Italy secured the election of his son;
but such was the shameful poverty of the Roman emperor, that
his person was arrested by a butcher in the streets of Worms,
and was detained in the public inn as a pledge or hostage for
the payment of his expenses.

From this humiliating scene let us turn to the apparent
majesty of the same Charles in the diets of the empire. The
golden bull, which fixes the Germanic constitution, is pro-

mulgated in the style of a sovereign and legislator. An hundred princes bowed before his throne, and exalted their own dignity by the voluntary honours which they yielded to their chief or minister. At the royal banquet the hereditary great officers, the seven electors, who in rank and title were equal to kings, performed their solemn and domestic service of the palace. The seals of the triple kingdom were borne in state by the archbishops of Maintz, Cologne, and Treves, the perpetual arch-chancellors of Germany, Italy, and Arles. The great marshal, on horseback, exercised his function with a silver measure of oats, which he emptied on the ground, and immediately dismounted to regulate the order of the guests. The great steward, the count palatine of the Rhine, placed the dishes on the table. The great chamberlain, the margrave of Brandenburg, presented, after the repast, the golden ewer and basin, to wash. The king of Bohemia, as great cupbearer, was represented by the emperor's brother, the duke of Luxembourg and Brabant; and the procession was closed by the great huntsmen, who introduced a boar and a stag, with a loud chorus of horns and hounds. Nor was the supremacy of the emperor confined to Germany alone: the hereditary monarchs of Europe confessed the pre-eminence of his rank and dignity: he was the first of the Christian princes, the temporal head of the great republic of the West: to his person the title of majesty was long appropriated; and he disputed with the pope the sublime prerogative of creating kings and assembling councils. The oracle of the civil law, the learned Bartolus, was a pensioner of Charles the Fourth; and his school resounded with the doctrine that the Roman emperor was the rightful sovereign of the earth, from the rising to the setting sun. The contrary opinion was condemned, not as an error, but as an heresy, since even the Gospel had pronounced, "And there went forth a decree from Cæsar Augustus, that *all the world* should be taxed."

COMPARISON OF CHARLES IV AND AUGUSTUS

If we annihilate the interval of time and space between Augustus and Charles, strong and striking will be the contrast between the two Cæsars: the Bohemian, who concealed his weakness under the mask of ostentation, and the Roman, who disguised his strength under the semblance of modesty.

At the head of his victorious legions, in his reign over the sea and land, from the Nile and Euphrates to the Atlantic Ocean, Augustus professed himself the servant of the state and the equal of his fellow-citizens. The conqueror of Rome and her provinces assumed the popular and legal form of a censor, a consul, and a tribune. His will was the law of mankind, but in the declaration of his laws he borrowed the voice of the senate and people; and, from their decrees, their master accepted and renewed his temporary commission to administer the republic. In his dress, his domestics, his titles, in all the offices of social life, Augustus maintained the character of a private Roman; and his most artful flatterers respected the secret of his absolute and perpetual monarchy.

INDEX

INDEX